![BIOZONE] **BIOZONE** *Biology Modular* ... *es*

Environmental Science

Second Edition

The Biozone Writing Team

Kent Pryor

Tracey Greenwood (Editor)

Lissa Bainbridge-Smith

Richard Allan

Editorial Consultant: Benjy Wood, BioGuild Consulting LLC
College Board Consultant
AP Exam Reader, Environmental Science

Published by:
BIOZONE International Ltd
109 Cambridge Road, Hamilton 3216, New Zealand

Printed by REPLIKA PRESS PVT LTD using paper
produced from renewable and waste materials

Distribution Offices:

United Kingdom & Europe — **Biozone Learning Media (UK) Ltd, UK**
Telephone: +44 1283-553-257
Fax: +44 1283-553-258
Email: sales@biozone.co.uk
Website: www.biozone.co.uk

USA, Canada, South America, Africa — **Biozone International Ltd**, New Zealand
Telephone: +64 7-856-8104
Freefax: 1-800717-8751 (USA-Canada only)
Fax: +64 7-856-9243
Email: sales@biozone.co.nz
Website: www.thebiozone.com

Asia & Australia — **Biozone Learning Media Australia**, Australia
Telephone: +61 7-5535-4896
Fax: +61 7-5508-2432
Email: sales@biozone.com.au
Website: www.biozone.com.au

© 2011 **BIOZONE International Ltd**
ISBN: 978-1-877462-76-4

First edition: 2007
Second edition: 2011

Front cover photographs:
City in smog. Image courtesy of CDC ©2006

Polar bears. Image ©2011 istockphotos (www.istockphoto.com)

NOTICE TO TEACHERS

Biology Modular Workbook Series

The BIOZONE *Biology Modular Workbook Series* has been developed to meet the demands of customers with the requirement for a flexible modular resource. Each workbook provides a collection of visually interesting and accessible activities, catering for students with a wide range of abilities and background. The workbooks are divided into a series of chapters, each comprising an introductory section with detailed learning objectives and useful resources, and a series of write-on activities ranging from paper practicals and data handling exercises, to questions requiring short essay style answers. Page tabs identifying "**Related activities**" and "**Weblinks**" help students to find related material within the workbook and locate weblinks and activities that will enhance their understanding of the topic. During the development of this series, we have taken the opportunity to develop new content, while retaining the basic philosophy of a student-friendly resource, which spans the gulf between textbook and study guide. Its highly visual presentation engages students, increasing their motivation and empowering them to take control of their learning.

Environmental Science

This much revised second edition of *Environmental Science* is the ideal companion for students of environmental biology, encompassing the basic principles of earth sciences and ecology. This workbook comprises nine chapters each focusing on one particular area within this broad topic. These areas are explained through a series of activities, each of which explores a specific concept (e.g. energy conservation or globalization). Model answers (on CD-ROM) accompany each **school order** free of charge, when ordered directly from the publisher. *Environmental Science* is a student-centered resource and is part of a larger package, which includes the ***Environmental Science Presentation Media***. Students completing the activities, in concert with their classroom and practical work, will consolidate existing knowledge and develop and practise skills that they will use throughout their course. This workbook may be used in the classroom or at home as a supplement to a standard textbook. Biozone has a commitment to produce a cost-effective, high quality resource, which acts as a student's companion throughout their study. Please do not photocopy from this workbook; we cannot afford to provide single copies to schools and continue to develop, update, and improve the material they contain.

Acknowledgements & Photo Credits

Royalty free images, purchased by Biozone International Ltd, are used throughout this workbook and have been obtained from the following sources: istockphotos (www.istockphoto.com) • Corel Corporation from various titles in their Professional Photos CD-ROM collection; ©Hemera Technologies Inc, 1997-2001; © 2005 JupiterImages Corporation; **CA** www.clipart.com; PhotoDisc®, Inc. USA, www.photodisc.com; ©Digital Vision; 3D models created using Poser IV, Curious Labs, 3D landscapes, Bryce 5.5. Biozone's authors also acknowledge the generosity of those who have kindly provided photographs for this edition: The three-spined stickleback image, which was originally prepared by Ellen Edmonson as part of the 1927-1940 New York Biological Survey. Permission for use granted by the New York State Department of Environmental Conservation. • Sandia National Laboratory • USAID Bangladesh • Campus Photography at the University of Waikato for photographs monitoring instruments • Kurchatov Institute for the photographs of Chernobyl • Exxon Valdez Oil Spill Trustee Council for their photograph of dead seabirds • Stephen Moore for his photos of aquatic invertebrates • PASCO for their photographs of probeware • **EPA**: US Environmental Protection Agency • Jane Ussher for her photograph of the Albatross • Sam Banks for the Wombat scat photo • Dr John Dale Defenders Ltd • United States Navy • K Pryor Coded credits are: **BH**: Brendan Hicks (Uni. of Waikato), • **BLM**: United States Bureau of Land Management, • **COD**: Colin O'Donnell, **DEQ**: Dept. of Environment QL, **DoC**: Dept. of Conservation (NZ), **DRNI**: Dept. of Natural Resources, Illinois, **EII**: Education Interactive Imaging, **EW**: Environment Waikato, **IF**: I. Flux (DoC), **JB-BU**: Jason Biggerstaff, Brandeis University, **JDG**: John Green (University of Waikato), **NASA**: National Aeronautics and Space Administration, **NASA-GSFC**: National Aeronautics and Administration- Goddard Space Flight Centre, **NOAA**: National Oceanic & Atmospheric Administration, www.photolib.noaa.gov, **RA**: Richard Allan, **RCN**: Ralph Cocklin, **TG**: Tracey Greenwood, • **USDA**: United States Department of Agriculture, • **USCG**: United States Coast Guard. • **USGS**: United States Geological Survey. • **USDE**: United States Department of Energy **USAF**: United States Airforce • **WBS**: Warwick Sylvester • **NIWA**: National Institute Water and Atmosphere • **NYSDEC**: New York State Dept of Environmental Conservation • **CDC** Centre for Disease Control

Photographers who have made their photographs available through Wikimedia commons: Wawny • Nick Carson • Reykholt • Bob Metcalf • Wiki05 • Wojsyl • Mark Jobling • Maungatautari Ecological Island Trust • KVDP • Ocean Flow Energy Ltd • Scott Ehardt • Diego Gruz • David Monniaux • Wikimedia Commons under Creative Common Licences 2.0, 2.5 or 3.0: Houi, Sam Beebe, Komencanto, BS Thurner Hof, Afloresm, Bertil Videt, Steffen Hillebrand, Beyond My Ken, Julien Harneis, Steve Cadman, Luca Galuzzi, Luca Ferdiani.

Also in this series:

Skills in Biology

Ecology

Microbiology & Biotechnology

Anatomy & Physiology

For other titles in this series go to:
www.thebiozone.com/modular.html

Contents

CODES: △ **Significant changes** in this edition   ☆ **New** this edition   **Activity** is marked: ☐ to be done; ☑ when completed

Contents (continued)

Explanation of Terms

Questions come in a variety of forms. Whether you are studying for an exam or writing an essay, it is important to understand exactly what the question is asking. A question has two parts to it: one part of the question will provide you with information, the second part of the question will provide you with instructions as to how to answer the question. Following these instructions is most important. Often students in examinations know the material but fail to follow instructions and do not answer the question appropriately. Examiners often use certain key words to introduce questions. Look out for them and be clear as to what they mean. Below is a description of terms commonly used when asking questions in biology.

Commonly Used Questioning Terms

The following terms are frequently used when asking questions in examinations and assessments. Students should have a clear understanding of each of the following terms and use this understanding to answer questions appropriately.

Account for: Provide a satisfactory explanation or reason for an observation.

Analyze: Interpret data to reach stated conclusions.

Annotate: Add **brief** notes to a diagram, drawing or graph.

Apply: Use an idea, equation, principle, theory, or law in a new situation.

Appreciate: To understand the meaning or relevance of a particular situation.

Calculate: Find an answer using mathematical methods. Show the working unless instructed not to.

Compare: Give an account of similarities and differences between two or more items, referring to both (or all) of them throughout. Comparisons can be given using a table. Comparisons generally ask for similarities more than differences (see contrast).

Construct: Represent or develop in graphical form.

Contrast: Show differences. Set in opposition.

Deduce: Reach a conclusion from information given.

Define: Give the precise meaning of a word or phrase as concisely as possible.

Derive: Manipulate a mathematical equation to give a new equation or result.

Describe: Give an account, including all the relevant information.

Design: Produce a plan, object, simulation or model.

Determine: Find the only possible answer.

Discuss: Give an account including, where possible, a range of arguments, assessments of the relative importance of various factors, or comparison of alternative hypotheses.

Distinguish: Give the difference(s) between two or more different items.

Draw: Represent by means of pencil lines. Add labels unless told not to do so.

Estimate: Find an approximate value for an unknown quantity, based on the information provided and application of scientific knowledge.

Evaluate: Assess the implications and limitations.

Explain: Give a clear account including causes, reasons, or mechanisms.

Identify: Find an answer from a number of possibilities.

Illustrate: Give concrete examples. Explain clearly by using comparisons or examples.

Interpret: Comment upon, give examples, describe relationships. Describe, then evaluate.

List: Give a sequence of names or other brief answers with no elaboration. Each one should be clearly distinguishable from the others.

Measure: Find a value for a quantity.

Outline: Give a brief account or summary. Include essential information only.

Predict: Give an expected result.

Solve: Obtain an answer using algebraic and/or numerical methods.

State: Give a specific name, value, or other answer. No supporting argument or calculation is necessary.

Suggest: Propose a hypothesis or other possible explanation.

Summarize: Give a brief, condensed account. Include conclusions and avoid unnecessary details.

In Conclusion

Students should familiarize themselves with this list of terms and, where necessary throughout the course, they should refer back to them when answering questions. The list of terms mentioned above is not exhaustive and students should compare this list with past examination papers / essays etc. and add any new terms (and their meaning) to the list above. The aim is to become familiar with interpreting the question and answering it appropriately.

Getting The Most From This Resource

This workbook is designed as a resource to increase your understanding of and engagement with environmental science. An understanding of geological and ecological theory is central to this topic. It is a subject of high interest, with many opportunities to combine theory and practical work in the field. This workbook is suitable for all environmental science students, and will reinforce and extend the ideas developed by teachers. It is not a textbook; its aim is to complement the text you are using for your course. The chapters in *Environmental Science* follow a standardized format, which enables you to identify and focus on important concepts. You should refer back to the introductory pages as you work through each set of worksheets.

Features of the Concept Map

A summary of the emphasis in each major section of the workbook. Each major part of the workbook deals with one or more aspects of Environmental Science: Earth's Systems, The Living World, Global Resources, and Global Change.

Chapter panels identify and summarize the material covered within each chapter.

A summary of why this material is important and where it fits into your understanding of the wider framework of this subject.

Features of the Chapter Topic Page

The section of the course to which this chapter applies.
For **course guides** and topic allignments go to www.thebiozone.com/weblink/EnvSci-2764.html

The important key ideas in this chapter. You should have a thorough understanding of the concepts summarized here.

The objectives provide a point by point summary of what you should have achieved by the end of the chapter.
They can also be used to derive **essential questions** for this chapter.

A list of important key terms used throughout the chapter. These will help you focus on important ideas.

The page numbers for the activities covering the material in this subsection of objectives.

Periodicals of interest are identified by title on a tab on the activity page to which they are relevant. The full citation appears in the Appendix in the page indicated.

You can use the check boxes to mark objectives to be completed (a dot to be done; a tick when completed).

The Weblinks citations on many of the activities can be accessed through the web links page at: www.thebiozone.com/weblink/EnvSci-2764.html
See page 3 for more details.

The Environmental Science Presentation Media covers this material under the listed heading.

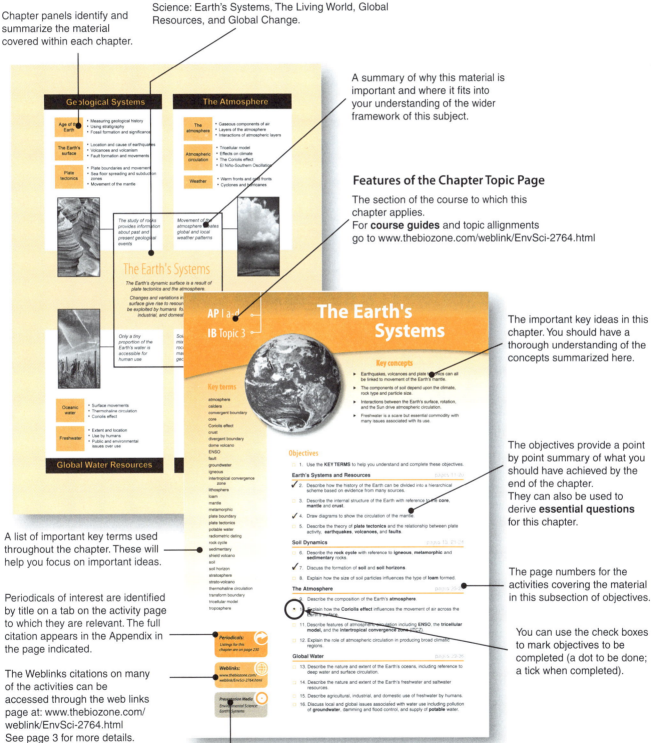

Activity Pages

The activities make up most of the content of this workbook. Your teacher may use the activity pages to introduce a topic for the first time, or you may use them to revise ideas already covered by other means. They are excellent for use in the classroom, as homework exercises, revision, and as self directed study and personal reference. As a self-check, model answers for each activity are provided on CD-ROM with each order of workbooks.

Encouraging Key Competencies

Thinking - bringing ideas together

Relating to others - communicating

Using language, symbols, and text

Managing self - independence

Participating and contributing

Introductory paragraph:
The introductory paragraph sets the 'scene' for the focus of the page and provides important background information. Note any words appearing in bold; these are 'key words' which could be included in a glossary of biological terms for the topic.

Easy to understand diagrams:
The main ideas of the topic are represented and explained by clear, informative diagrams.

Tear-out pages:
Each page of the book has a perforation that allows easy removal. Your teacher may ask you to remove activity pages for marking, or so that they can be placed in a ringbinder with other work on the topic.

Write-on format:
You can test your understanding of the main ideas of the topic by answering the questions in the spaces provided. Your answers should be concise. Questions requiring explanation or discussion are spaced accordingly. Answer the questions appropriately according to the specific questioning term used.

Periodicals:
Articles related to the activity are listed here. The appendix lists the full citation.

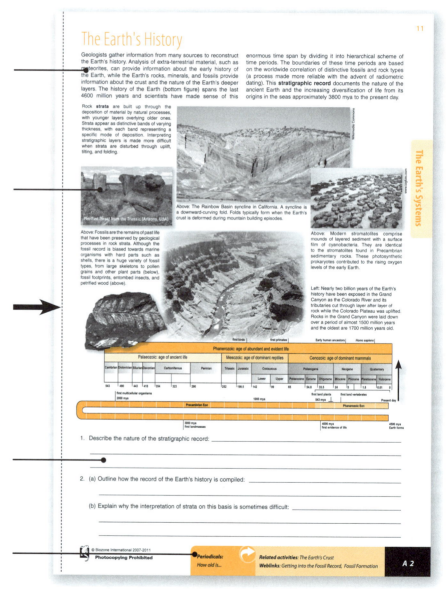

Page Tabs

Some teachers will already be familiar with the one concept-one activity format of Biozone's workbooks. Features of each activity include an introductory paragraph which provides some brief explanatory background to the activity. Clearly drawn and annotated diagrams and photographs are a major part of almost all activities and the student's understanding of the information is tested through a series of (describe, explain, discuss, predict, summarize) questions. Students must interact with the information on the page in order to answer the questions; it is this interaction that provides the valuable learning experience. The new tab system at the base of each activity page is a relatively new feature with which many teachers and students may not yet be familiar. With it, we have aimed to tag valuable resources to the activity to which they apply. Use this guide to help your students use the tab system to best effect.

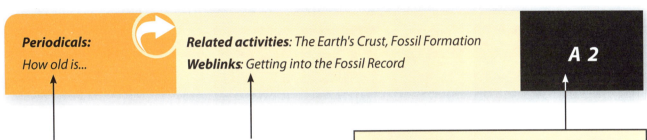

Periodicals:

How old is...

Related activities: *The Earth's Crust, Fossil Formation*

Weblinks: *Getting into the Fossil Record*

A 2

Students (and teachers) who would like to know more about this topic area are encouraged to locate the periodical cited on the periodicals tabs. Recent articles of interest directly relevant to the topic content are cited. The full citation appears in the appendix as indicated at the beginning of the topic chapter.

Related activities

Other activities in the workbook cover related topics or may help your student with answering the questions on the page. In most cases, extra information for activities that are coded R can be found on the pages indicated here.

Weblinks

This citation indicates a valuable video clip or animation that can be accessed from the Weblinks page specifically for this workbook (below).

INTERPRETING THE ACTIVITY CODING SYSTEM

Type of Activity

D = includes some data handling or interpretation

P = includes a paper practical

R = *may* require extra reading (e.g. text or other activity)

A = includes application of knowledge to solve a problem

E = extension to the specified curriculum content.

Level of Activity

1 = generally simpler, including mostly describe questions

2 = more challenging, including explain questions

3 = challenging content and/or questions, including discuss

www.thebiozone.com/weblink/EnvSci-2764.html

This Weblinks page provides links to **external web sites** with supporting information for the activities. These sites are separate to those provided in the BIOLINKS area of Biozone's web site. Almost exclusively, they are narrowly focussed animations and video clips directly relevant to the activity on which they are cited. They provide great support to aid student understanding of basic concepts. The Weblinks page also includes a small number of color coded links to downloadable **Acrobat (PDF) files** which provide supplementary activities (usually as extension).

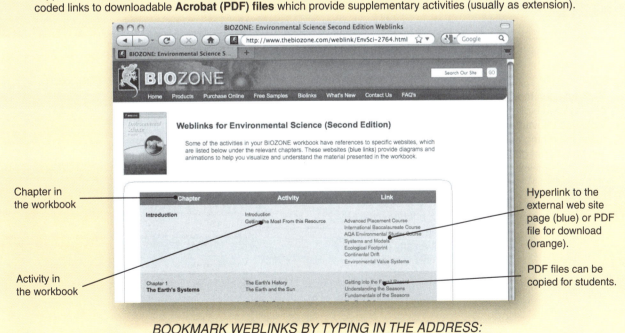

Chapter in the workbook

Activity in the workbook

Hyperlink to the external web site page (blue) or PDF file for download (orange).

PDF files can be copied for students.

BOOKMARK WEBLINKS BY TYPING IN THE ADDRESS:
IT IS NOT ACCESSIBLE DIRECTLY FROM BIOZONE'S WEBSITE

Using BIOZONE's Website

BIOZONE's web site should be the first stop for students of environmental science. As well as providing all our product information (including shipping dates) and updates, *www.thebiozone.com* provides quick access to the latest RSS newsfeeds and podcasts from around the world. The Resource hub also provides quick links to access the websites of publishers of references cited in the workbooks. Perhaps of greatest value to students and teachers is the BIOLINKS area of Biozone's website. The BIOLINKS pages are distinct from *Weblinks* (which are specific to each workbook edition) and provide a database of well organized hyperlinks pertaining to topics of interest in biology. The database is updated regularly, so that outdated, not operational, or no longer relevant sites are removed and new sites are added as they appear.

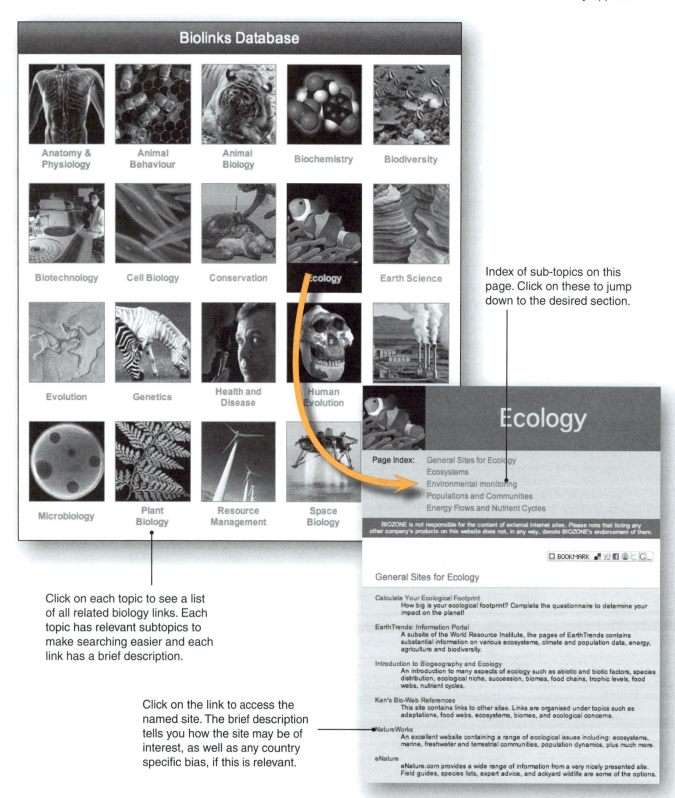

Index of sub-topics on this page. Click on these to jump down to the desired section.

Click on each topic to see a list of all related biology links. Each topic has relevant subtopics to make searching easier and each link has a brief description.

Click on the link to access the named site. The brief description tells you how the site may be of interest, as well as any country specific bias, if this is relevant.

Meeting Key Competencies

We want today's biology students to be self-motivated, lifelong learners, to develop a sound grasp or biological knowledge, to plan and evaluate their work, and to think critically and independently. We have identified five key competencies, which we identify using the acronym TRUMP. Biozone's workbooks and associated products provide a varied and interesting suite of resources which, if used effectively, can help your students achieve key competencies in all areas of biology. Implicit in achieving these aims is the requirement for a flexible resource; one that can be used in a variety of ways, alongside the many other resources that are now be available to teachers in various topic areas. Biozone's workbooks provide this flexibility, with activities that can be used in a variety of ways.

Key Competencies

Thinking
Relating to others
Using symbols, language, and texts
Managing self
Participating and contributing

USAGE OPTIONS	DESCRIPTION
Classroom activities	Use activities in class to introduce a topic, or to consolidate student understanding and summarize the material covered by other methods. Using activities in class provides valuable opportunities for peer-to-peer learning.
Homework activities	Use simpler activities to cover basic material before practicals, or before attempting more difficult work in class. Use review activities to revise and consolidate.
Self directed study and differential instruction	Biozone's workbooks provide more opportunities for differential instruction. Students requiring extension can work quickly through the core material and move on to more challenging activities. Students needing longer can review or finish their activities at home.
Topic review	Use the activities to review a topic prior to formal assessment. Or use the activities themselves for assessment. Collect the papers in for marking (tear-out pages) or mark in class.
Achievement of scientific literacy	"Mix and match" style key terms lists at the end of each chapter provide a non-threatening way in which students can practise their understanding of key terms.
A reference source	Students can refer quickly to the information on each page. Each spread is concept-based, making the information easier to locate and access.
A planning document	Students can use the concept maps, chapter objectives, and key terms to plan their way through course, drawing on their classroom and practical work, and other supplementary resources as required. Using the workbooks in this way helps students to become more resourceful, empowered, and better prepared, and it helps them to identify their areas of strength and weakness.

Choosing Activities for Homework

Many of the workbook activities are ideal for homework or as vehicles for a quick synoptic assessment. Review activities are ideal as homework. They provide a way in which to review a topic that has recently been completed, while at the same time extending the learning and consolidation process by presenting the material in a slightly different way. The information for review activities can be found in other material within the chapter, although stronger students may not need to refer back to source material to complete the set work. Generally, choose level 1 and 2 activities for homework.

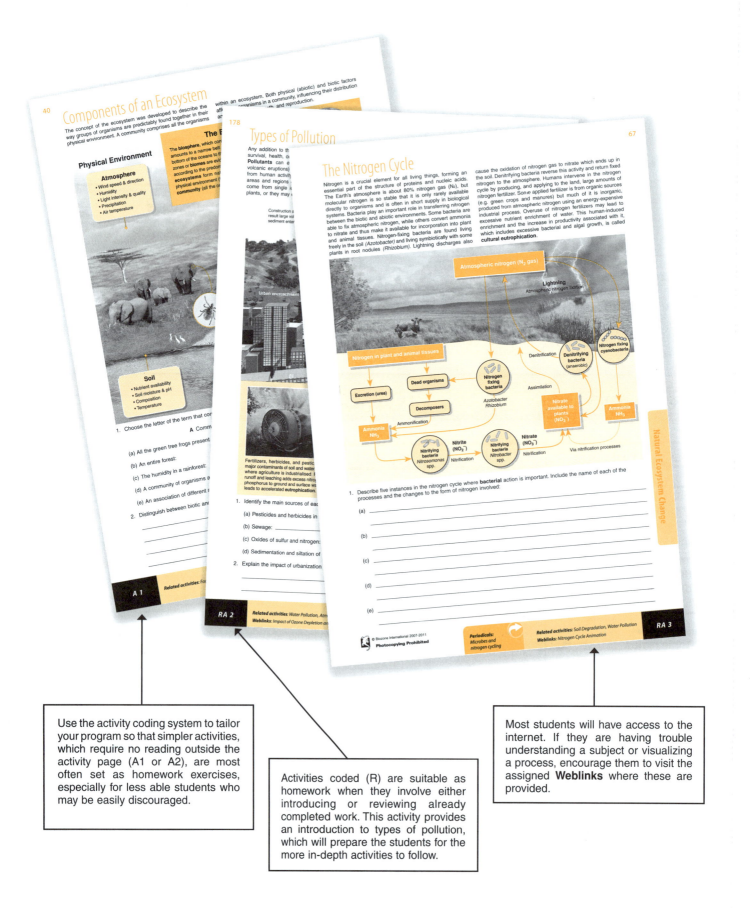

Use the activity coding system to tailor your program so that simpler activities, which require no reading outside the activity page (A1 or A2), are most often set as homework exercises, especially for less able students who may be easily discouraged.

Activities coded (R) are suitable as homework when they involve either introducing or reviewing already completed work. This activity provides an introduction to types of pollution, which will prepare the students for the more in-depth activities to follow.

Most students will have access to the internet. If they are having trouble understanding a subject or visualizing a process, encourage them to visit the assigned **Weblinks** where these are provided.

Concept Map for Environmental Science

The Earth's Systems

Geological systems
- Age of the Earth
- The Earth's surface
- Plate tectonics

The atmosphere
- The atmosphere
- Atmospheric circulation
- Weather and climate

Global water resources
- Oceanic water
- Fresh water

Soil
- Rocks and minerals
- Soil dynamics

Living World

Biomes and ecosystems
- Biome and ecosystem structure
- Energy flow
- Species interactions

Natural ecosystem change
- Biogeochemical cycles
- Ecosystem stability

Populations
- Features of populations
- Population dynamics

Field studies
- Sampling populations
- Abiotic factors

The resources used by humans are a result of constantly changing global systems

Complex systems arise as a result of the interactions between organisms and their environment

Environmental Science

All of the Earth's systems are connected. Changes in one system may cause changes in other systems.

Environmental science is an interdisciplinary field of study involving both natural and social sciences.

Resources must be carefully managed to ensure they are available to future generations

Understanding environmental systems is critical to understanding the environmental effects of human activities

Global Resources

Land
- Agriculture
- Land management

Water
- Fisheries
- Irrigation

Energy for human use
- Energy concepts
- Non-renewable energy
- Renewable energy

Energy conservation
- Energy efficiency
- Economic and ecological considerations

Global Change

Types of pollution
- Air pollution
- Water pollution

Pollution issues
- Treating pollution
- Impacts of pollution

Climate change
- Ozone
- Global warming

Conserving biodiversity
- Loss of biodiversity
- Maintaining biodiversity

Resources Information

Your set textbook should always be a starting point for information, but there are also many other resources available. A list of readily available resources is provided below. Access to the publishers of these resources can be made directly from Biozone's website through the Biolinks database: **www.thebiozone.com/links.html** and select *Link to Other Publishers*. Please note that our listing of any product in this workbook does not denote Biozone's endorsement of it.

Supplementary Texts

Brower, J.E, J.H. Zar, & C.N. von Ende, 1997.
Field and Laboratory Methods for General Ecology, 288 pp. (spiral bound)
Publisher: McGraw-Hill
ISBN: 0697243583
An introductory manual for ecology, focusing on the collection, recording, and analysis of data. Provides balanced coverage of plants and animals, and physical elements.

Christopherson, R.W, 2009. (6 edn).
Elemental Geosystems, 640 pp.
ISBN: 978-0321595218
Although written as a geography textbook, much of the material in this book is relevant to environmental sciences courses. Relevant material includes chapters on the atmosphere, weather, climate, and landscape and biogeographical systems.

Miller, G.T. 2008. (16 edn).
Living in the Environment: Principles, Connections and Solutions, 832 pp.
ISBN: 978-0495556718
A comprehensive textbook covering aspects of ecology, biodiversity, natural resources, human impact on the environment, and sustainability issues. A large number of appendices expand the scope of the material further.

Raven, P.H, Berg, L.R, & Hassenzahi, D.M. 2009. (7 edn).
Environment, 656pp
ISBN: 978-0470525982
A comprehensive textbook providing an overview of ecosystems, populations, the world's resources, and the impact of human activity on the environment.

Smith, R.L. and T.M. Smith, R. 2001 (6 edn).
Ecology and Field Biology, 720 pp.
ISBN: 0321042905
A comprehensive overview of all aspects of ecology, including evolution, ecosystems theory, practical application, biogeochemical cycles, and global change. A field package, comprising a student "Ecology Action Guide" and a subscription to the web based "The Ecology Place" are also available.

Withgott, J.H. and Brennan,S.R. 2010 (4 edn).
Environment: The Science Behind the Stories, 792 pp.
ISBN: 978-0321715340
Integrated central case studies provide real life stories to help learn and understand the science behind environmental issues.

Biology Dictionaries

Access to a good biology dictionary is useful when dealing with biological terms. Some of the titles available are listed below. Link to the relevant publisher via Biozone's biolinks database or by typing: **www.thebiozone.com/resources/Dictionary.html**

Hale, W.G., J.P. Margham, & V.A. Saunders.
Collins: Dictionary of Biology 3 ed. 2003, 672 pp. HarperCollins. **ISBN**: 0-00-714709-0.
Updated to take in the latest developments in biology from the Human Genome Project to advancements in cloning (new edition pending).

E. Lawrence (ed). **Henderson's Dictionary of Biology** 14 ed., 2008, 776 pp. Benjamin Cummings. **ISBN**: 0321505794.
This 14th edition has updated many existing definitions. An essential reference and the dictionary of choice for many.

McGraw-Hill (ed). **McGraw-Hill Dictionary of Bioscience**, 2 ed., 2003, 662 pp. McGraw-Hill. **ISBN**: 0-07-141043-0
22 000 entries encompassing more than 20 areas of the life sciences. It includes synonyms, acronyms, abbreviations, and pronunciations for all terms.

Periodicals, Magazines, & Journals

Biological Sciences Review: *An informative quarterly publication for biology students.* Enquiries: **UK**: Philip Allan Publishers **Tel**: 01869 338652 **Fax**: 01869 338803 **E-mail**: sales@philipallan.co.uk **Australasia**: **Tel**: 08 8278 5916, **E-mail**: rjmorton@adelaide.on.net

New Scientist: *Widely available weekly magazine with research summaries and features.* Enquiries: Reed Business Information Ltd, 51 Wardour St. London WIV 4BN **Tel**: (UK and intl):+44 (0) 1444 475636 **E-mail**: ns.subs@qss-uk.com *or subscribe from their web site.*

Scientific American: *A monthly magazine containing specialist features. Articles range in level of reading difficulty and assumed knowledge.* Subscription enquiries: 415 Madison Ave. New York. NY10017-1111 **Tel**: (outside North America): 515-247-7631 **Tel**: (US& Canada): 800-333-1199

National Geographic: *A monthly magazine containing a wide variety of articles accompanied by high quality photography.* Subscription enquiries: ngmservice.com. **Tel**: (outside North America): 1-813-979-6845 **Tel**: (US & Canada): 1-800-647-5463.

Time Magazine: *Issued weekly. In depth articles on global political, economic and environmental issues.* Time & Life Building, Rockefeller Center, New York, NY 10020-1391, U.S. Website: www.time.com/time/ Customer services: www.time.com/customer services **Tel**: 1-800-843-8463

Geological Systems

Age of the Earth
- Measuring geological history
- Using stratigraphy
- Fossil formation and significance

The Earth's surface
- Location and cause of earthquakes
- Volcanoes and volcanism
- Fault formation and movements

Plate tectonics
- Plate boundaries and movement
- Sea floor spreading and subduction zones
- Movement of the mantle

The study of rocks provides information about past and present geological events

The Atmosphere

The atmosphere
- Gaseous components of air
- Layers of the atmosphere
- Interactions of atmospheric layers

Atmospheric circulation
- Tricellular model
- Effects on climate
- The Coriolis effect
- El Niño-Southern Oscillation

Weather
- Warm fronts and cold fronts
- Cyclones and hurricanes

Movement of the atmosphere creates global and local weather patterns

The Earth's Systems

The Earth's dynamic surface is a result of plate tectonics and the atmosphere.

Changes and variations in the Earth's surface give rise to resources that can be exploited by humans for agricultural, industrial, and domestic uses.

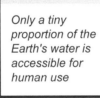

Only a tiny proportion of the Earth's water is accessible for human use

Soils are a complex mix of weathered rock and organic matter determined by geology and climate

Oceanic water
- Surface movements
- Thermohaline circulation
- Coriolis effect

Freshwater
- Extent and location
- Use by humans
- Public and environmental issues over use

Global Water Resources

Rocks and minerals
- The rock cycle
- Rock types and significance
- Weathering and erosion

Soil dynamics
- Features of a loam
- Formation and features of horizons
- Climatic influences on soil formation

Rocks and Soil

The Earth's Systems

Key concepts

► Earthquakes, volcanoes and plate tectonics can all be linked to movement of the Earth's mantle.

► The components of soil depend upon the climate, rock type and particle size.

► Interactions between the Earth's surface, rotation, and the Sun drive atmospheric circulation.

► Freshwater is a scarce but essential commodity with many issues associated with its use.

Key terms

atmosphere
caldera
convergent boundary
core
Coriolis effect
crust
divergent boundary
dome volcano
ENSO
fault
groundwater
igneous
intertropical convergence zone
lithosphere
loam
mantle
metamorphic
plate boundary
plate tectonics
potable water
radiometric dating
rock cycle
sedimentary
shield volcano
soil
soil horizon
stratosphere
strato-volcano
thermohaline circulation
transform boundary
tricellular model
troposphere

Objectives

☐ 1. Use the **KEY TERMS** to help you understand and complete these objectives.

Earth's Systems and Resources
pages 11-20

☐ 2. Describe how the history of the Earth can be divided into a hierarchical scheme based on evidence from many sources.

☐ 3. Describe the internal structure of the Earth with reference to the **core**, **mantle** and **crust**.

☐ 4. Draw diagrams to show the circulation of the mantle.

☐ 5. Describe the theory of **plate tectonics** and the relationship between plate activity, **earthquakes**, **volcanoes,** and **faults**.

Soil Dynamics
pages 15, 21-24

☐ 6. Describe the **rock cycle** with reference to **igneous**, **metamorphic** and **sedimentary** rocks.

☐ 7. Discuss the formation of **soil** and **soil horizons**.

☐ 8. Explain how the size of soil particles influences the type of **loam** formed.

The Atmosphere
pages 25-28

☐ 9. Describe the composition of the Earth's **atmosphere**.

☐ 10. Explain how the **Coriolis effect** influences the movement of air across the Earth's surface.

☐ 11. Describe features of atmospheric circulation including **ENSO**, the **tricellular model,** and the **intertropical convergence zone** (ITCZ).

☐ 12. Explain the role of atmospheric circulation in producing broad climatic regions.

Global Water
pages 29-36

☐ 13. Describe the nature and extent of the Earth's oceans, including reference to deep water and surface circulation.

☐ 14. Describe the nature and extent of the Earth's freshwater and saltwater resources.

☐ 15. Describe agricultural, industrial, and domestic use of freshwater by humans.

☐ 16. Discuss local and global issues associated with water use including pollution of **groundwater**, damming and flood control, and supply of **potable** water.

Periodicals:
Listings for this chapter are on page 230

Weblinks:
www.thebiozone.com/
weblink/EnvSci-2764.html

Presentation Media
Environmental Science: Earth's Systems

The Earth's History

Geologists gather information from many sources to reconstruct the Earth's history. Analysis of extra-terrestrial material, such as meteorites, can provide information about the early history of the Earth, while the Earth's rocks, minerals, and fossils provide information about the crust and the nature of the Earth's deeper layers. The history of the Earth (bottom figure) spans the last 4600 million years and scientists have made sense of this enormous time span by dividing it into hierarchical scheme of time periods. The boundaries of these time periods are based on the worldwide correlation of distinctive fossils and rock types (a process made more reliable with the advent of radiometric dating). This **stratigraphic record** documents the nature of the ancient Earth and the increasing diversification of life from its origins in the seas approximately 3800 mya to the present day.

Rock **strata** are built up through the deposition of material by natural processes, with younger layers overlying older ones. Strata appear as distinctive bands of varying thickness, with each band representing a specific mode of deposition. Interpreting stratigraphic layers is made more difficult when strata are disturbed through uplift, tilting, and folding.

Wikimedia Commons

Petrified forest from the Triassic (Arizona, USA)

Above: The Rainbow Basin syncline in California. A syncline is a downward-curving fold. Folds typically form when the Earth's crust is deformed during mountain building episodes.

www.bigfoto.com

Above: Fossils are the remains of past life that have been preserved by geological processes in rock strata. Although the fossil record is biased towards marine organisms with hard parts such as shells, there is a huge variety of fossil types, from large skeletons to pollen grains and other plant parts (below), fossil footprints, entombed insects, and petrified wood (above).

Above: Modern stromatolites comprise mounds of layered sediment with a surface film of cyanobacteria. They are identical to the stromatolites found in Precambrian sedimentary rocks. These photosynthetic prokaryotes contributed to the rising oxygen levels of the early Earth.

Left: Nearly two billion years of the Earth's history have been exposed in the Grand Canyon as the Colorado River and its tributaries cut through layer after layer of rock while the Colorado Plateau was uplifted. Rocks in the Grand Canyon were laid down over a period of almost 1500 million years and the oldest are 1700 million years old.

The Earth's Systems

	first birds		first primates			Early human ancestors		Homo sapiens	

Phanerozoic: age of abundant and evident life																
Palaeozoic: age of ancient life							Mesozoic: age of dominant reptiles				Cenozoic: age of dominant mammals					
Cambrian	Ordovician	Silurian	Devonian	Carboniferous		Permian	Triassic	Jurassic	Cretaceous		Palaeogene			Neogene		Quaternary	
									Lower	Upper	Palaeocene	Eocene	Oligocene	Miocene	Pliocene	Pleistocene	Holocene
543	490	443	418	354	323	290	252	199.5	142	99	65	54.8	33.5	24	5	1.8	0.01	0

first multicellular organisms
2000 mya

1000 mya

first land plants
543 mya

first land vertebrates

Present day

Precambrian Eon

Phanerozoic Eon

3000 mya
first landmasses

4000 mya
first evidence of life

4500 mya
Earth forms

1. Describe the nature of the stratigraphic record: _____

   _____

   _____

2. (a) Outline how the record of the Earth's history is compiled: _____

   _____

   (b) Explain why the interpretation of strata on this basis is sometimes difficult: _____

   _____

   _____

© Biozone International 2007-2011
Photocopying Prohibited

Periodicals:
How old is...

Related activities: The Earth's Crust, Fossil Formation
Weblinks: Getting into the Fossil Record

A 2

Sedimentary Rock Profile

This diagram represents a cutting through layers of sedimentary rock in which fossils are exposed. Fossils are the remains or impressions of plants or animals that become trapped in the sediments after death. Layers of sedimentary rock are arranged in the order that they were deposited, with the most recent layers near the surface (unless they have been disturbed).

Ground surface

Youngest sediments

Oldest sediments

Recent fossils are found in more recent sediments
The more recent the layer of rock, the more resemblance there is between the fossils found in it and living forms.

Numerous extinct species
The number of extinct species is enormously greater than the number living today.

Fossil types differ in each sedimentary rock layer
Fossils found in a given layer of sedimentary rock generally differ in significant respects from those in other layers.

Only primitive fossils are found in older sediments
Phyla are represented by more generalized forms in the older layers, and not by specialized forms (such as those alive today).

New fossil types mark changes in environment
In the rocks marking the end of one geological period, it is common to find new fossils that become dominant in the next. Each geological time period had an environment very different from those before and after. The boundaries of these coincided with considerable environmental change and the creation of new niches. These produced new selection pressures and resulted in diversification of surviving genera.

A Case Study in the Fossil Record

The history of modern day species can be traced
The evolution of many modern species can be well reconstructed. For instance, the evolutionary history of modern elephants is well documented for the last 40 million years. and the modern horse has a well understood fossil record spanning 50 million years.

Fossil species are similar to but different from today's species
Most fossil animals and plants belong to the same major taxonomic groups as organisms living today. However, they do differ from the living species in many features.

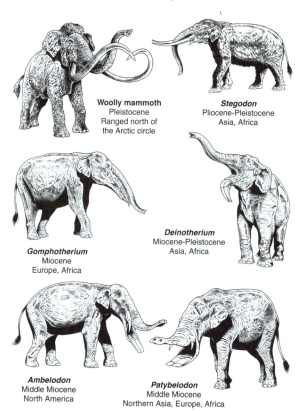

Woolly mammoth
Pleistocene
Ranged north of the Arctic circle

Stegodon
Pliocene-Pleistocene
Asia, Africa

Gomphotherium
Miocene
Europe, Africa

Deinotherium
Miocene-Pleistocene
Asia, Africa

Ambelodon
Middle Miocene
North America

Patybelodon
Middle Miocene
Northern Asia, Europe, Africa

African and Indian elephants have descended from a diverse group of **proboscideans** (named for their long trunks). The first pig-sized, trunkless members of this group lived in Africa 40 million years ago. From Africa, their descendants invaded all continents except Antarctica and Australia. As the group evolved in response to predation, they became larger. Examples of extinct members of this group are illustrated above.

3. Explain how radiometric dating has made the construction and interpretation of the stratigraphic record more reliable:

_____

_____

4. Describe an animal or plant taxon (e.g. class, family, or genus) that has:

   (a) A good fossil record of evolutionary development: _____

   (b) Shown little evolutionary change despite a long fossil history (stasis): _____

5. Discuss the use of fossils as indicators of environmental change: _____

_____

_____

_____

_____

_____

Fossil Formation

Fossils are the remains of organisms that have escaped decay and have become preserved in rock strata. A fossil may be the preserved remains of the organism itself, a mould or cast, or the marks made by it during its lifetime (trace fossils). Fossilization requires the normal processes of decay to be permanently arrested. This can occur if the remains are buried rapidly and isolated from air, water, or decomposing microbes. Fossils provide a record of the appearance and extinction of organisms. Once this record is calibrated against a time scale, it is possible to build up an evolutionary history of life on Earth.

The Earth's Systems

Some Fossil Types and Modes of Preservation

Brachiopod (lamp shell), Jurassic (New Zealand)

Mould: An organism-shaped impression left after the original remains were dissolved or otherwise destroyed.

Shell and chambers replaced by iron pyrite

Ammonite cast, late Cretaceous (Charmouth, England).

Cast: The original materials of the organism have been replaced by new unrelated ones, in this case, iron pyrite.

Fossil fern frond Carboniferous (USA).

This **compression fossil** of a fern frond shows traces of carbon and wax from the original plant. Compression fossils are preserved in sedimentary rock that has been compressed.

Ants in amber about 25 mya (Madagascar).

Polished amber

Fossilized resin (or amber) produced by some ancient conifers trapped organisms, such as these ants, before it hardened.

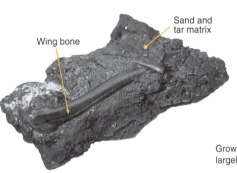

Sand and tar matrix

Wing bone

Fossilized bones of a bird that lived about 5 mya and became stuck in the **tar pits** at la Brea, Los Angeles, USA.

Growth rings largely destroyed

Bark

Permineralization: In some fossils, the organic material is replaced by minerals, as in this **petrified wood** from Madagascar.

Rock phosphate matrix

Teeth and bones (being hard) are often well preserved. This shark tooth is from Eocene phosphate beds in Morocco.

Ammonite, Jurassic (Madagascar).

The fossil record is biased toward organisms with hard parts. This ammonite still has a layer of the original shell covering the stone interior.

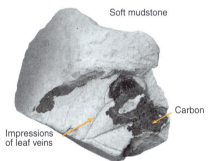

Soft mudstone

Carbon

Impressions of leaf veins

In a **sub-fossil**, the fossilization process is incomplete. In this leaf impression in soft mudstone, some of the leaf remains are still intact (a few thousand years old, New Zealand).

1. Describe the natural process that must be arrested in order for fossilization to take place: _____

2. Explain why the fossil record is biased towards marine organisms with hard parts: _____

_____

3. Fossils tell us much about the organisms that lived in the past. Suggest what other information they might provide:

_____

The Earth and the Sun

Of all celestial bodies, the Sun has the greatest influence on the Earth, affecting its movements, determining the day-night and seasonal cycles, driving climatic systems and longer term climate cycles, and providing the energy for most life on the planet. The Sun also lays a part in tidal movement on Earth, modifying the effect of the Moon to produce monthly variations in the tidal range. The Sun emits various types of radiation, but most is absorbed high in the Earth's atmosphere. Only visible light, some infra-red radiation, and some ultraviolet light reach the surface in significant amounts. Visible light is pivotal to the producer base of Earth's biological systems, but infra-red is also important because it heats the atmosphere, oceans, and land. The intensity of solar radiation is not uniform around the Earth and this uneven heating effect, together with the Earth's rotation, produce the global patterns of wind and ocean circulation that profoundly influence the Earth's climate.

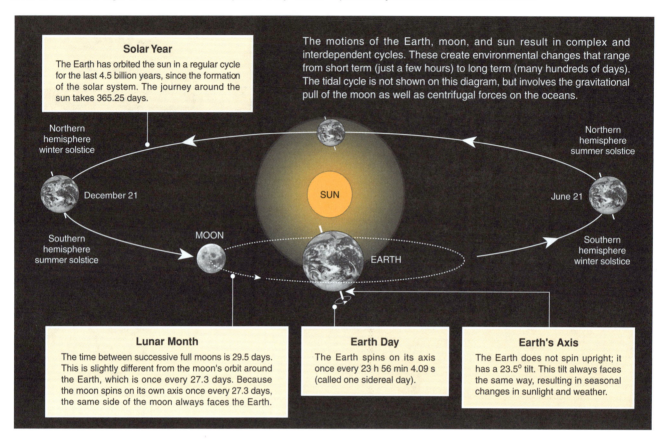

Solar Year

The Earth has orbited the sun in a regular cycle for the last 4.5 billion years, since the formation of the solar system. The journey around the sun takes 365.25 days.

The motions of the Earth, moon, and sun result in complex and interdependent cycles. These create environmental changes that range from short term (just a few hours) to long term (many hundreds of days). The tidal cycle is not shown on this diagram, but involves the gravitational pull of the moon as well as centrifugal forces on the oceans.

Northern hemisphere winter solstice

Northern hemisphere summer solstice

December 21

SUN

June 21

Southern hemisphere summer solstice

MOON

EARTH

Southern hemisphere winter solstice

Lunar Month

The time between successive full moons is 29.5 days. This is slightly different from the moon's orbit around the Earth, which is once every 27.3 days. Because the moon spins on its own axis once every 27.3 days, the same side of the moon always faces the Earth.

Earth Day

The Earth spins on its axis once every 23 h 56 min 4.09 s (called one sidereal day).

Earth's Axis

The Earth does not spin upright; it has a 23.5° tilt. This tilt always faces the same way, resulting in seasonal changes in sunlight and weather.

For questions 1 to 4, circle the letter with the correct answer:

1. The solar year is based on:
   A. The number of rotations of the Earth
   B. The time for the Earth to complete one orbit of the Sun
   C. The number of orbits of the Moon
   D. The time taken for four seasons to pass

2. The seasons experienced on Earth are caused by:
   A. A change in distance from the Earth to the Sun
   B. A reduction in sunshine hours due to cloud formation
   C. The angle of the Earth relative to the Sun
   D. A reduction in solar output

3. The time for the Earth to complete one rotation on its axis is:
   A. 24 hours, 0 minutes, and 0 seconds
   B. 23 hours, 56 minutes, and 4.09 seconds
   C. The time taken for the Sun to reach its zenith
   D. One day

4. The movement of the Earth's atmosphere is due to:
   A. The rotation of the Earth
   B. The unequal intensity of solar radiation over the globe
   C. Air rising at the equator and descending at the poles
   D. A, B, and C

5. (a) Explain why tropical regions receive a greater input of solar radiation than the poles: _____

_____

_____

(b) Describe the consequences of this to the Earth's climate: _____

_____

_____

_____

Related activities: Atmosphere and Weather
Weblinks: Understanding the Seasons, Fundamentals of the Seasons

The Earth's Crust

The Earth has a layered structure comprising a solid inner core, a liquid outer core, a highly viscous mantle, and an outer silicate solid crust. The Earth's crust is thin compared to the bulk of the Earth, averaging just 25-70 km thick below the continents and about 10 km thick below the oceans. Overall, the crust is less dense than the mantle, being relatively rich in lighter minerals such as silicon, calcium, and aluminum. The crust is a dynamic structure, subject to constant change as a result of ocean formation, mountain building, and volcanism. It supports the **biosphere**, the hydrosphere, and the atmosphere.

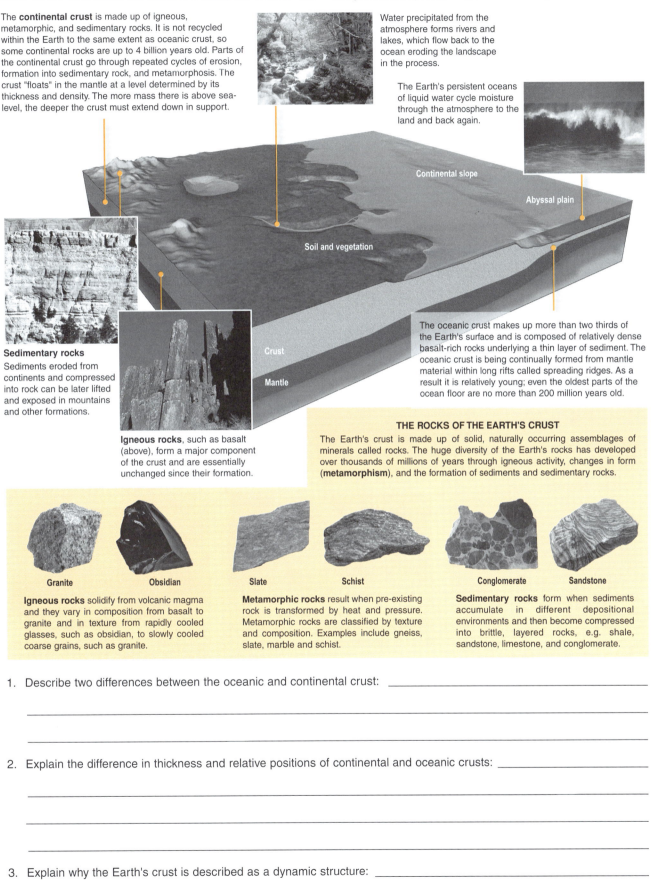

The **continental crust** is made up of igneous, metamorphic, and sedimentary rocks. It is not recycled within the Earth to the same extent as oceanic crust, so some continental rocks are up to 4 billion years old. Parts of the continental crust go through repeated cycles of erosion, formation into sedimentary rock, and metamorphosis. The crust "floats" in the mantle at a level determined by its thickness and density. The more mass there is above sea-level, the deeper the crust must extend down in support.

Water precipitated from the atmosphere forms rivers and lakes, which flow back to the ocean eroding the landscape in the process.

The Earth's persistent oceans of liquid water cycle moisture through the atmosphere to the land and back again.

Continental slope

Abyssal plain

Soil and vegetation

Crust

Mantle

Sedimentary rocks
Sediments eroded from continents and compressed into rock can be later lifted and exposed in mountains and other formations.

Igneous rocks, such as basalt (above), form a major component of the crust and are essentially unchanged since their formation.

The oceanic crust makes up more than two thirds of the Earth's surface and is composed of relatively dense basalt-rich rocks underlying a thin layer of sediment. The oceanic crust is being continually formed from mantle material within long rifts called spreading ridges. As a result it is relatively young; even the oldest parts of the ocean floor are no more than 200 million years old.

THE ROCKS OF THE EARTH'S CRUST
The Earth's crust is made up of solid, naturally occurring assemblages of minerals called rocks. The huge diversity of the Earth's rocks has developed over thousands of millions of years through igneous activity, changes in form (**metamorphism**), and the formation of sediments and sedimentary rocks.

| Granite | Obsidian | Slate | Schist | Conglomerate | Sandstone |

Igneous rocks solidify from volcanic magma and they vary in composition from basalt to granite and in texture from rapidly cooled glasses, such as obsidian, to slowly cooled coarse grains, such as granite.

Metamorphic rocks result when pre-existing rock is transformed by heat and pressure. Metamorphic rocks are classified by texture and composition. Examples include gneiss, slate, marble and schist.

Sedimentary rocks form when sediments accumulate in different depositional environments and then become compressed into brittle, layered rocks, e.g. shale, sandstone, limestone, and conglomerate.

1. Describe two differences between the oceanic and continental crust: _____

_____

_____

2. Explain the difference in thickness and relative positions of continental and oceanic crusts: _____

_____

_____

_____

3. Explain why the Earth's crust is described as a dynamic structure: _____

_____

© Biozone International 2007-2011
Photocopying Prohibited

Periodicals:
Earth, fire and fury

Related activities: The Rock Cycle
Weblinks: The Rock Gallery, Types of Rock

A 2

Plate Boundaries

The outer rock layer of the Earth, comprising the crust and upper mantle, is called the **lithosphere** and it is broken up into seven large, continent-sized **tectonic plates** and about a dozen smaller plates. Throughout geological time, these plates have moved about the Earth's surface, shuffling continents, opening and closing oceans, and building mountains. The evidence for past plate movements has come from several sources: mapping of plate boundaries, the discovery of sea floor spreading, measurement of the direction and rate of plate movement, and geological evidence such as the distribution of ancient mountain chains, unusual deposits, and fossils. The size of the lithospheric plates is constantly changing, with some expanding and some getting smaller. These changes occur along **plate boundaries**, which are marked by well-defined zones of seismic and volcanic activity. Plate growth occurs at **divergent boundaries** along **sea floor spreading ridges** (e.g. the Mid-Atlantic Ridge and the Red Sea) whereas plate attrition occurs at **convergent boundaries** marked by deep ocean trenches and subduction zones. Divergent and convergent zones make up approximately 80% of plate boundaries. The remaining 20% are called **transform boundaries**, where two plates slide past one another with no significant change in the size of either plate.

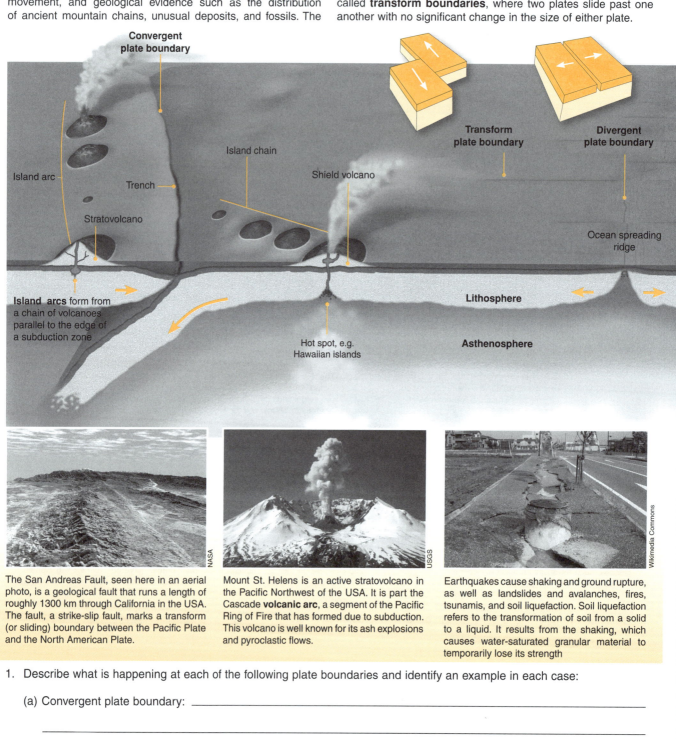

The San Andreas Fault, seen here in an aerial photo, is a geological fault that runs a length of roughly 1300 km through California in the USA. The fault, a strike-slip fault, marks a transform (or sliding) boundary between the Pacific Plate and the North American Plate.

Mount St. Helens is an active stratovolcano in the Pacific Northwest of the USA. It is part the Cascade **volcanic arc**, a segment of the Pacific Ring of Fire that has formed due to subduction. This volcano is well known for its ash explosions and pyroclastic flows.

Earthquakes cause shaking and ground rupture, as well as landslides and avalanches, fires, tsunamis, and soil liquefaction. Soil liquefaction refers to the transformation of soil from a solid to a liquid. It results from the shaking, which causes water-saturated granular material to temporarily lose its strength

1. Describe what is happening at each of the following plate boundaries and identify an example in each case:

    (a) Convergent plate boundary: _____

    _____

    (b) Divergent plate boundary: _____

    _____

    (c) Transform plate boundary: _____

    _____

Related activities: The Earth's Crust
Weblinks: Plate Tectonics, Savage Earth Animations

Periodicals:
Climate and evolution
of mountains

The Mechanism of Plate Movement

The relatively cool **lithosphere** overlies the hotter, plastic and more fluid **asthenosphere**. Heat from the mantle drives two kinds of asthenospheric movement: **convection** and **mantle plumes**. Plate motion is partly driven by the weight of cold, dense plates sinking into the mantle at trenches. This heavier, cooler material sinking under the influence of gravity displaces heated material that rises as mantle plumes.

The movements of the tectonic plates puts the brittle rock of the crust under strain creating **faults** where rocks fracture and slip past each other. Earthquakes are caused by energy release during rapid slippage along faults. Consequently, the Earth's major earthquake (and volcanic) zones occur along plate boundaries.

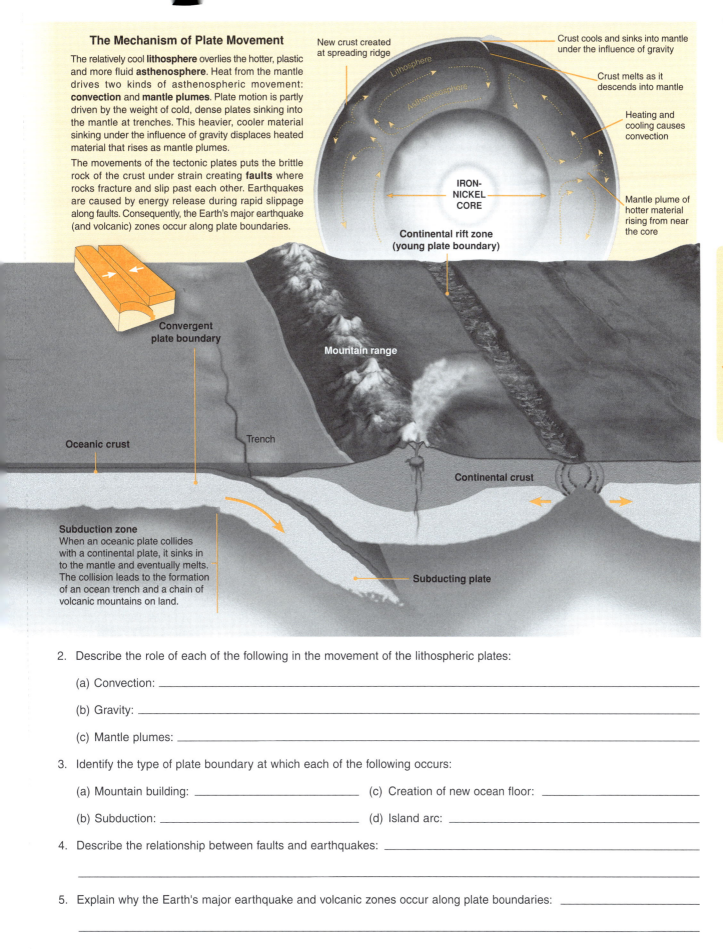

New crust created at spreading ridge

Crust cools and sinks into mantle under the influence of gravity

Crust melts as it descends into mantle

Heating and cooling causes convection

Mantle plume of hotter material rising from near the core

Lithosphere

Asthenosphere

IRON-NICKEL CORE

Continental rift zone (young plate boundary)

Convergent plate boundary

Mountain range

Oceanic crust

Trench

Continental crust

Subduction zone
When an oceanic plate collides with a continental plate, it sinks in to the mantle and eventually melts. The collision leads to the formation of an ocean trench and a chain of volcanic mountains on land.

Subducting plate

2. Describe the role of each of the following in the movement of the lithospheric plates:

   (a) Convection: _____

   (b) Gravity: _____

   (c) Mantle plumes: _____

3. Identify the type of plate boundary at which each of the following occurs:

   (a) Mountain building: _____ (c) Creation of new ocean floor: _____

   (b) Subduction: _____ (d) Island arc: _____

4. Describe the relationship between faults and earthquakes: _____

   _____

5. Explain why the Earth's major earthquake and volcanic zones occur along plate boundaries: _____

   _____

   _____

6. Explain why soil liquefaction is a major contributor to damage to dams and buildings during an earthquake:

   _____

   _____

Lithosphere and Asthenosphere

The **lithosphere** (*lithos* = "stone") comprises the crust and the uppermost part of the mantle. It is both rigid and solid, and broken up into **tectonic plates**. The lithosphere can be divided into continental lithosphere, which contains relatively light minerals, and oceanic lithosphere, which contains much denser minerals. The lithosphere ranges from 400 km thick over the continents to 70 km thick in the oceans. The **asthenosphere** (*asthenes* = "weak") lies below the lithosphere. This layer of rock is viscous and plastic (semi-fluid) in its behavior. It changes through plastic deformation, slowly moving about and so allowing for plate tectonic movement. The asthenosphere is relatively thin at around 100 kilometers thick. The boundary between the lithosphere and asthenosphere is thermal; the lithosphere conducts heat out to the surface while the asthenosphere retains its heat. The crust and the mantle are chemically distinct, forming a compositional boundary.

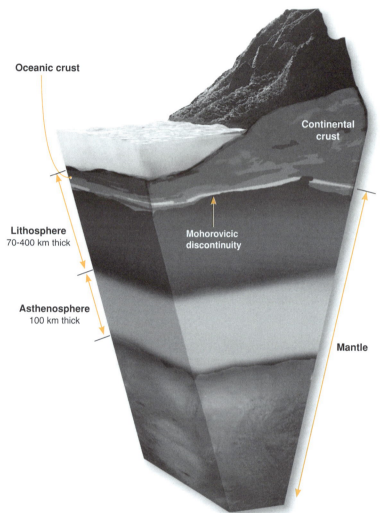

Oceanic crust

Continental crust

Lithosphere
70-400 km thick

Mohorovicic discontinuity

Asthenosphere
100 km thick

Mantle

Locating the Layers

The **Mohorovicic discontinuity** marks the boundary between the **crust** and the **mantle**. Seismic waves from earthquakes increase in velocity when travelling below this boundary.

Travel time of S wave

Increased velocity

Mohorovicic discontinuity

Increasing distance from epicentre

A number of techniques can be used to approximate the boundary between the **lithosphere** and the **asthenosphere** (LAB).

Depth →

LAB →

Temperature

Temperature increases rapidly with depth in the lithosphere but only slowly in the asthenosphere.

Seismic waves also move more slowly through the asthenosphere, providing evidence of a weak, semi-molten zone.

1. (a) Describe the structure of the lithosphere _____

_____

_____

(b) Describe the structure of the asthenosphere: _____

_____

2. Describe how the lithosphere-asthenosphere boundary can be detected: _____

_____

_____

3. The continental lithosphere is much older than the oceanic lithosphere. Explain why this is the case: _____

_____

_____

_____

Related activities: Plate Boundaries

Volcanoes and Volcanism

Volcanoes generally form along the edge of the tectonic plate overriding a **subduction** zone. Cracks in the crust caused by the buckling of the overriding plate allow **magma** to move towards the surface and form a magma chamber. Further cracks in the crust allow the magma to be ejected from the chamber and form a volcano. Magma reaching the surface is termed **lava**, and its chemical properties depend upon the composition of both the original magma and the crust through which it passes. Lava can be placed into three general groups: **basaltic**, **andesitic** and **rhyolitc**. Basaltic lava contains 48%-58% silica, is basic and is very fluid, with a temperature of around 1160°C. Rhyolitic lava contains 65% silica and above and is acidic and viscous with a temperature around 900°C. Andesite is intermediate between these lava types. Volcanoes formed from these lavas have very different and quite distinct properties ranging from relatively flat and unexplosive to extremely steep and violently explosive.

Shield volcano

Shield volcanoes are formed from fluid basalt lava. The lava ejected from the vent contains low levels of silica and runs freely down the sides of the volcano, causing its base to spread out without increasing its height. These volcanoes tend to have an extremely large basal radius. Examples include Mt Kilauea (Hawaii), Skjaldbreiður (Iceland) (right), from which the term shield-volcano is derived, and Olympus Mons (Mars).

Reykholt

Caldera

Calderas are the remains of large volcanic craters formed by the collapse of a volcano. The magma chamber empties causing the land above to collapse along a characteristic ring fault. The crater may eventually fill with water, forming a lake. Examples include Santorini caldera (Greece) (right), Yellowstone caldera (US), and Lake Taupo (New Zealand) which formed after a giant eruption around 180 AD and may have been recorded by Roman and Chinese scholars.

NASA

Strato-volcano

Strato-volcanoes tend to have steep upper slopes and a shallower gradient on the lower slopes. The lava ejected is commonly andesitic and relatively viscous, containing moderate levels of silica. This causes the lava to build up on the upper slopes before rolling (or being blasted) down to the lower slopes and so forming the characteristic shape. Examples include Mt Fuji (Japan) (right), Mt Taranaki (New Zealand, and Mt St Helens (US).

Dome volcano

Dome volcanoes form from viscous silica-rich rhyolitic magma that slowly oozes from the vent or may build up slowly underground. This magma traps a large amount of gas. The pressure caused by the build up of gases is not easily released because the magma is so viscous, and so eruptions are often extremely violent. Examples include Mt Tarawera (New Zealand) and Chaitén (Chile) (right).

Sam Beebe

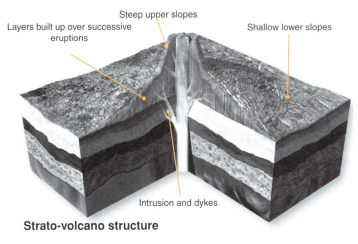

Layers built up over successive eruptions
Steep upper slopes
Shallow lower slopes
Intrusion and dykes

Strato-volcano structure

Mount Pinatubo began eruptions on June 3 1991, after almost 500 years of virtual inactivity. On June 15, after many large explosions, it entered its final eruptive phase, blasting ash 34 km into the atmosphere. The Earth's climate was severely affected by Pinatubo's eruption. Over the course of the eruption some 17 million tonnes of SO_2 was released into the atmosphere. The ash released into the atmosphere caused an almost 10% reduction in sunlight reaching the Earth's surface over the following year, and global temperatures dropped by 0.4°C. Ozone levels, especially in the Southern Hemisphere, reached some of their lowest recorded levels. In addition, the eruption brought large amounts of heavy metals to the surface and left hundreds of square kilometers of arable land infertile.

Mount Pinatubo eruption 1991 Image : USGS

Periodicals:
Hotstops unplugged

Related activities: Lithosphere and Asthenosphere, Plate Boundaries
Weblinks: Animated Guide: Volcanoes

Tectonic plate boundaries

Pacific plate

Nazca plate

Pacific Ring of Fire

Subduction zones around the Pacific rim

Volcanoes around the Pacific rim

Hawaiian Islands
(Hot spot)

Much of the northern and western edges of the Pacific plate form subduction zones. This produces an area that is seismically and volcanically extremely active. Along with parts of the Nazca plate it forms the Pacific Ring of Fire. Around three quarters of the world's active and dormant volcanoes are found around the edge of the ring and nearly 90% of all earthquake activity is located there.

1. Match the following lava types to the appropriate volcano below: basaltic, andesitic, rhyolitic.

   (a) Strato-volcano: _andestic_   (b) Dome: _basaltc v rhyolitc_ (c) Shield: _Basaltic, rhyolitc_

For questions 2 to 3, circle the letter with the correct answer:

2. Volcanoes are most commonly located:
   A. Along plate boundaries
   B. In Eastern Asia
   C. Above subduction zones
   D. Near continents

3. The Hawaiian islands:
   A. Are located near a subduction zone
   B. Are an island chain formed above a hotspot
   C. Are all strato-volcanoes
   D. Are slowly moving in a south-west direction

4. Describe the formation of shield and strato volcanoes, explaining how each develops its distinctive shape:

   _____

   _____

   _____

   _____

5. Explain how the Hawaiian islands were formed: _____

   _____

   _____

6. Explain the relationship between the Pacific Ring of Fire, volcanism, and subduction zones: _____

   _____

   _____

7. Describe how volcanoes can affect global climate patterns: _____

   _____

   _____

   _____

The Rock Cycle

The Earth's many rock types are grouped together according to the way they formed as **igneous**, **metamorphic**, and **sedimentary rocks** (as well as meteorites). These rocks form in a continuous cycle. Volcanism creates rocks at the Earth's surface. Erosion of these and other surface rocks produces sediments, which burial transforms into sedimentary rocks. Heat and pressure within the Earth can then transform pre-existing rocks to form metamorphic rocks such as slate and schist. When rocks are exposed at the surface, they are then subjected to the physical, chemical, and biological processes collectively known as **weathering**. This cycle of rock formation, exposure, weathering, erosion, and deposition is known as the **rock cycle**.

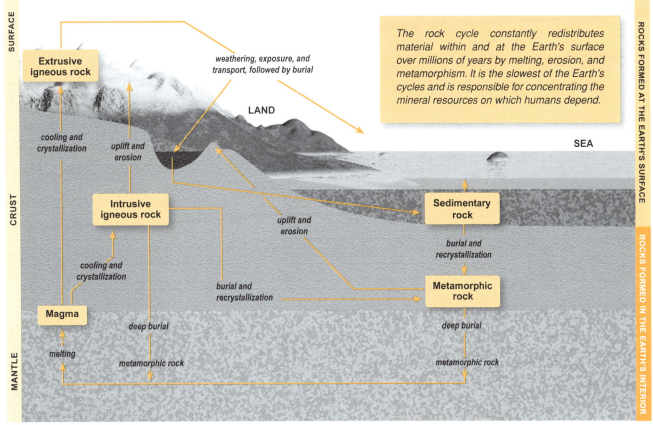

The rock cycle constantly redistributes material within and at the Earth's surface over millions of years by melting, erosion, and metamorphism. It is the slowest of the Earth's cycles and is responsible for concentrating the mineral resources on which humans depend.

ROCKS FORMED AT THE EARTH'S SURFACE

ROCKS FORMED IN THE EARTH'S INTERIOR

The Earth's Systems

These formations, known as hoodoos, are composed of soft sedimentary rock topped by a piece of harder, less easily-eroded rock that protects the column from the elements. Hoodoo shapes are affected by the erosional patterns of alternating hard and softer rock layers, while different minerals produce color.

Water and ice are powerful agents of erosion. Water lifts and transports rock fragments, and the freezing and thawing splits rocks apart. The flow of seawater millions of years ago, together with ice wedging and collapse along joints in the rock have resulted in the formation of this spectacular arch in Utah, USA.

Salt weathering of rock produces a distinctive honeycombing effect. Seawater penetrates the rock and then evaporates to leave behind salt crystals, which expand to produce holes in the rock surface. Softer parts of the rock are eroded at a greater rate than harder parts.

1. Using appropriate examples, distinguish between **igneous**, **sedimentary**, and **metamorphic** rocks:

_____

_____

2. Distinguish between **weathering** and **erosion** and describe the role of these processes in the rock cycle:

_____

_____

3. The Earth's mineral resources are produced by recycling processes, but are essentially non-renewable. Explain:

_____

_____

Related activities: The Earth's Crust
Weblinks: Interactive Rock Cycle

A 2

Soil Textures

Soil texture depends on the amount of sand, silt, and clay present. A **loam** contains a 40/40/20 mix of sand, silt, and clay and is considered the ideal soil for cultivating crops. Soils with too much clay hold water, become heavy, and are difficult to work, whereas soils with too much sand allow water to drain away too quickly. A loam contains enough clay to bind the water and hold it in place, but also enough sand to create spaces between the particles, allowing air to penetrate and water to drain. Because of these features a loam is able to retain nutrients and humus better than other soil types.

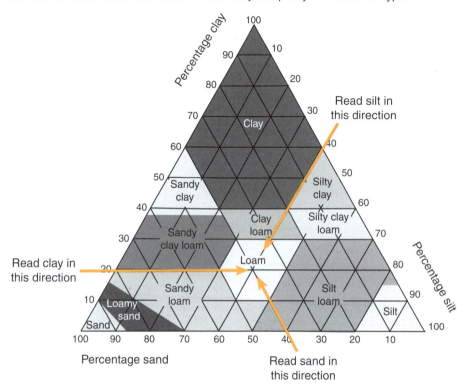

Soil sample 1

Soil sample 2

The percentage of sand, silt, and clay and therefore the type of soil can easily be measured by mixing a sample with water and letting it settle.

A loam consists of around 20% clay, 40% sand, and 40% silt. Around this point, various other loams exist which are named after their primary components. For example a sandy loam consists of around 65% sand, 35% silt, and 10% clay.

	Clay	Silt	Sand	Loam
Nutrient holding capacity	++	+	0	+
Water infiltration capacity	0	+	++	+
Water holding capacity	++	+	0	+
Aeration	0	+	++	+
Workability	0	+	++	+

0 = low + =medium ++= high

Loams are easily worked...   ...while silts and clays can be very muddy

The capacity of soil to be worked and produce viable crops depends on the mixture of particles within it. Silt provides an moderate capacity in all areas due to its intermediate particle size. By itself it, does not provide good soil as it too easily turns to mud when wet and is blown away by winds when dry. Loam consists of a variety of particle sizes and so remains more consistent in texture when both wet and dry.

1. Explain the term loam and how it applies to soil: _____

    _____

    _____

    _____

2. Using the scale on soil samples 1 and 2 above, calculate the percentage of sand, silt and clay in each sample and then use the soil triangle to identify the type of soil:

    Soil sample 1: % sand: _____ % silt: _____ % clay: _____ Soil type: _____

    Soil sample 2: % sand: _____ % silt: _____ % clay: _____ Soil type: _____

3. Explain why loamy soils are more easily worked and produce better crops than other soil types: _____

    _____

    _____

Related activities: Soil and Soil Dynamics, Soil Degradation

Soil and Soil Dynamics

Soils are a complex mixture of unconsolidated weathered rock and organic material. Soils are essential to terrestrial life. Plants require soil and the microbial populations, responsible for recycling organic wastes, live in the soil and contribute to its fertility. Soils are named and classified on the basis of physical and chemical properties in their **horizons** (layers). Soils have three basic horizons (A,B,C). The A horizon is the **topsoil**, which is rich in organic matter. The B horizon is a **subsoil** containing clay and soluble minerals.

The C horizon is made up of weathered **parent material** and rock fragments. Soils and their horizons differ widely, and are grouped according to their characteristics, which are determined by the underlying parent rock, the age of the soil, and the conditions under which the soil developed. A few soils weather directly from the underlying rocks and these **residual soils** have the same general chemistry as the original rocks. More commonly, soils form in materials that have moved in from elsewhere.

Disintegrating parent rock

① Bedrock

The parent rock is broken down by weathering to form a **regolith** which overlies the solid bedrock. The soil that forms is part of the regolith.

Layer of organic matter or O horizon

Weathered parent rock (C horizon)

② Bedrock

Plants establish and organic material builds up on the surface. The organic material aids the disintegration of the parent material.

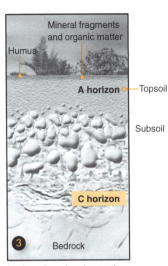

Mineral fragments and organic matter

Humus

A horizon — Topsoil

C horizon

③ Bedrock

As the mineral and organic content mix, horizons begin to form, with humus-rich layers at the surface and mineral-rich layers at the base.

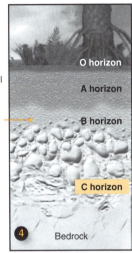

O horizon

A horizon

Subsoil — **B horizon**

C horizon

④ Bedrock

Horizons are well developed in mature soils. The final characteristics of the soil are determined by the regional conditions and the rock type.

The Earth's Systems

Influences on Soil Development

The character and composition of the parent material is important in determining the properties of a soil. Parent materials include volcanic deposits, and sediments deposited by wind, water or glaciers.

The occurrence of freeze-thaw and wet-dry cycles, as well as average temperature and moisture levels are important in soil development. Climate also affects vegetation, which in turn influences soil development.

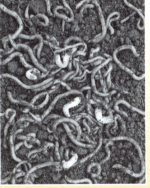

Plants, animals, fungi, and bacteria help to create a soil both through their activities and by adding to the soil's organic matter when they die. Moist soils with a high organic content tend to be higher in biological activity.

The topography (hilliness) of the land influences soil development by affecting soil moisture and tendency towards erosion. Soils in steep regions are more prone to loss of the topsoil and erosion of the subsoil.

1. Explain the role of weathering in soil formation: _____

_____

_____

2. Discuss the influence of climate, rock type, and topography on the characteristics of a mature soil: _____

_____

_____

_____

Related activities: The Earth's Crust, The Rock Cycle, Soil Degradation
Weblinks: Soil Classification and Formation

A 2

Soils In Different Climates

Soils are formed by the break down of rock and the mixing of inorganic and organic material. The soil profile is a series of horizontal layers that differ in composition and physical properties. Each recognizable layer is called a horizon. Soils have three basic horizons (A,B,C). The A horizon is the **topsoil**, which is rich in organic matter. If there is also a layer of litter (undecomposed or partly decomposed organic matter), this is called the O horizon, but it is often absent. The B horizon is a **subsoil** containing clay and soluble minerals. The C horizon is made up of weathered **parent material** and rock fragments. These horizons may be variously developed depending on whether or not the soil is mature. Mature soils have had enough time to develop distinct horizons. Immature soils have horizons that are lacking.

Dry, reddish A horizon

Deep B horizon of clay

ARID REGIONS
Desert soils are alkaline mineral soils with variable amounts of clay, low levels of organic matter, and poorly developed vertical profiles.

Shallow, acidic A horizon

Deep B horizon of clay

HUMID TROPICS
Tropical soils: Leaching and chemical weathering make these soils acidic. Aluminum and iron oxides accumulate in the deep B horizon.

Dark, humus-rich A horizon

B horizon with clay and calcium compounds

MID-LATITUDES
Grassland soils: Mature, alkaline, deep, well drained soils. They are typically nutrient-rich and productive with a high organic content.

Soil Texture

Soil texture depends on the amount of each size of mineral particle in the soil (sand, silt, and clay sized particles). Coarse textured soils are dominated by sand, medium textures by silt, and fine textured soils by clay.

SAND
...feels gritty

SILT
...feels silky

CLAY
...feels sticky

decreasing particle size →

Accumulated organic matter

Permafrost

POLAR REGIONS
Very low temperatures slow the decomposition of organic matter and maintain the permafrost layer in these frozen soils.

Deep A horizon

Clay

TEMPERATE
Weathered forest soils: Well developed soils with a deep organic layer and accumulated clay at lower levels.

Cracked B horizon

Clay-rich parent rock

SEASONALLY WET
Swelling soils: Marked seasonal rainfall results in deep cracks as the soil alternately swells and shrinks.

3. Describe the role of soil organisms in soil structure and development: _____

_____

For questions 4 to 5, circle the letter with the correct answer:

4. The A soil horizon:
   A. Is located below the O horizon
   B. Is rich in organic matter
   C. Can vary in thickness
   D. All of A,B and C.

5. Silt particles:
   A. Are smaller than sand particles
   B. Feel gritty when moistened
   C. Form from organic material
   D. Form fine textured soils.

6. Identify which feature of a soil would most influence its:

   (a) Fertility: _____ (b) Water-holding capacity: _____

7. Explain how the characteristics described below arise in each of the following soil types:

   (a) Accumulation of organic matter in the frozen soils of the Arctic: _____

   _____

   (b) Shallow A horizon and poorly developed vertical profile of a desert soil: _____

   _____

The Atmosphere and Climate

The Earth's atmosphere is a layer of gases surrounding the globe and retained by gravity. It contains roughly 78% nitrogen, 20.95% oxygen, 0.93% argon, 0.038% carbon dioxide, trace amounts of other gases, and a variable amount (average around 1%) of water vapor. This mixture of gases, known as **air**, protects life on Earth by absorbing ultraviolet radiation and reducing temperature extremes between day and night. The atmosphere consists of layers around the Earth, each one defined by the way temperature changes within its limits. The outermost troposphere thins slowly, fading into space with no boundary. The air of the atmosphere moves in response to heating from the sun and,

globally, the **atmospheric circulation** transports warmth from equatorial areas to high latitudes and returning cooler air to the tropics. It is the interaction of the atmosphere and the oceans that creates the Earth's the longer term pattern of atmospheric conditions we call **climate** (as opposed to shorter-term weather). The world's climates are not static; they have been both warmer and cooler in the past. At present, the average global temperature is increasing, but this rise is not evenly spread around the globe. The present climate warming is most likely to be due, at least in part, to an enhanced **greenhouse effect**, caused by higher concentrations of greenhouse gases in the atmosphere.

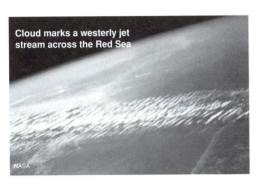

Cloud marks a westerly jet stream across the Red Sea

NASA

Jet streams are narrow, winding ribbons of strong wind in the upper troposphere. They mark the boundary between air masses at different temperatures. Cloud forms in the air that is lifted as it is driven into the core of the jet stream.

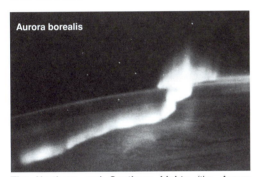

Aurora borealis

The Northern and Southern Lights (the Aurora Borealis and the Aurora Australis respectively), appear in the thermosphere. Typically, auroras appear either as a diffuse glow or as "curtains" that extend in an approximately east to west direction.

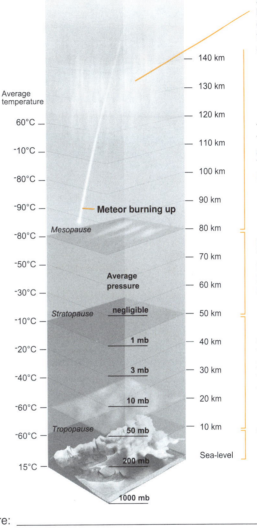

Aurora caused by collisions between protons and electrons from the Sun and the nitrogen and oxygen atoms in the atmosphere.

Thermosphere
This layer extends as high as 1000 km. Temperature increases rapidly after about 88 km.

Meteor burning up

Mesosphere
Temperature is constant in the lower mesosphere, but decreases steadily with height above 56 km.

Stratosphere
Temperature is stable to 20 km, then increases due to absorption of UV by the thin layer of ozone.

Troposphere
Air mixes vertically and horizontally. All weather occurs in this layer.

Average temperature: 60°C, -10°C, -80°C, -90°C, -80°C, -50°C, -30°C, -10°C, -20°C, -40°C, -60°C, -60°C, 15°C

140 km, 130 km, 120 km, 110 km, 100 km, 90 km, 80 km, 70 km, 60 km, 50 km, 40 km, 30 km, 20 km, 10 km, Sea-level

Mesopause, Stratopause, Tropopause

Average pressure: negligible, 1 mb, 3 mb, 10 mb, 50 mb, 200 mb, 1000 mb

1. Describe two important roles of the atmosphere: _____

_____

_____

2. Explain what drives the atmospheric circulation: _____

_____

_____

3. Describe a characteristic feature and environmental issue for each of the following layers of the atmosphere:

(a) Troposphere: _____

_____

(b) Stratosphere: _____

_____

Periodicals:
Climate and evolution of mountains

Related activities: Ocean Circulation and Currents, Global Warming
Weblinks: Consequences of Rotation for Weather, Jetstream

The Tricellular Model of Atmospheric Circulation

High temperatures over the equator and low temperatures over the poles, combined with the rotation of the Earth, produce a series of cells in the atmosphere. This model of atmospheric circulation, with three cells in each hemisphere, is known as the **tricellular model**.

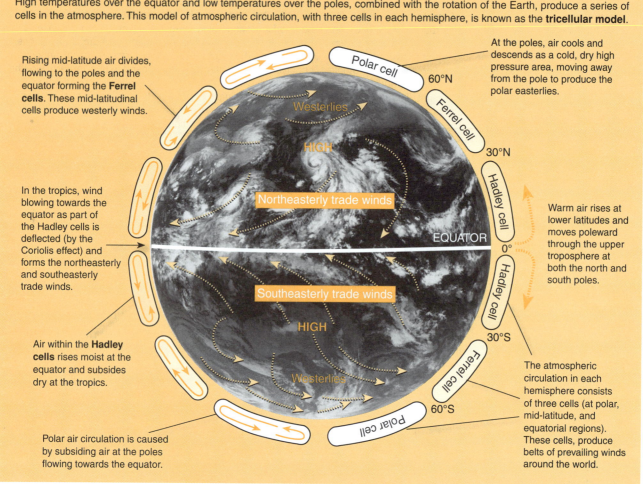

Rising mid-latitude air divides, flowing to the poles and the equator forming the **Ferrel cells**. These mid-latitudinal cells produce westerly winds.

At the poles, air cools and descends as a cold, dry high pressure area, moving away from the pole to produce the polar easterlies.

In the tropics, wind blowing towards the equator as part of the Hadley cells is deflected (by the Coriolis effect) and forms the northeasterly and southeasterly trade winds.

Warm air rises at lower latitudes and moves poleward through the upper troposphere at both the north and south poles.

Air within the **Hadley cells** rises moist at the equator and subsides dry at the tropics.

The atmospheric circulation in each hemisphere consists of three cells (at polar, mid-latitude, and equatorial regions). These cells, produce belts of prevailing winds around the world.

Polar air circulation is caused by subsiding air at the poles flowing towards the equator.

Polar cell · 60°N · Ferrel cell · 30°N · Hadley cell · 0° · Hadley cell · 30°S · Ferrel cell · 60°S · Polar cell

Westerlies · HIGH · Northeasterly trade winds · EQUATOR · Southeasterly trade winds · HIGH · Westerlies

In sandy deserts and polar regions, prevailing winds form dunes and drifts with characteristic shapes. Sand or snow grains are blown up the slope and fall down the far side to create sinuous crests extending for great distances.

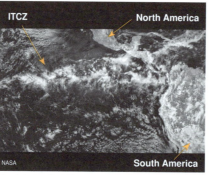

ITCZ · North America · South America · NASA

The Intertropical Convergence zone (ITCZ) marks the meeting of trade winds at the equator. It is characterized by varying, often calm winds, as well as violent thunderstorms. The position of the ITCZ can drastically affect the rainfall in equatorial nations.

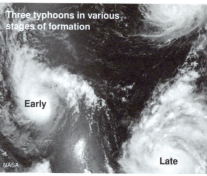

Three typhoons in various stages of formation · Early · Late · NASA

Tropical cyclones (also called typhoons or hurricanes), are low pressure systems that develop mainly over warm seas where winds start the air spiralling, producing low surface pressure into which air accelerates.

4. (a) Explain what is meant by a **prevailing wind**: _____

_____

(b) Describe some of the physical and biological effects of prevailing winds: _____

_____

_____

_____

5. The ITCZ was also called *the doldrums* by early sailors. Suggest why it was given this name: _____

_____

_____

Variation and Oscillation

Energy from the Sun is distributed through a global system of atmospheric and ocean circulation that creates the Earth's **climate**. Heated air moving towards the poles from the equator does not flow in a single uniform convection current. Friction, drag, and momentum cause air close to the Earth's surface to be pulled in the direction of the Earth's rotation. This deflection is called the **Coriolis effect** and it is responsible for the direction of movement of large-scale weather systems in both hemispheres. The interactions of atmospheric systems are so complex that climatic conditions are never exactly the same from one year to the next. However, it is possible to find periodic patterns or **oscillations** in climate. The **El-Niño-Southern Oscillation**, which has a periodicity of three to seven years, is one such climate cycle. El-Niño years cause a reversal of the ordinary climate regime and are connected to such economically disastrous events as the collapse of fisheries stocks (e.g the Peruvian anchovy stock), severe flooding in the Mississippi Valley, drought-induced crop failures and forest fires in Australia and Indonesia.

The Earth's Systems

The Coriolis Effect

Air flowing towards, or away from, the equator follows a curved path that swings it to the right in the northern hemisphere and to the left in the southern hemisphere (right). This phenomenon, known as the **Coriolis effect**, is caused by the anticlockwise rotation of the Earth about its axis, so as air moves across the Earth's surface, the surface itself is moving but at a different speed. The magnitude of the Coriolis effect depends on the latitude and the speed of the moving air. It is greatest at the poles and is responsible for the direction of the rotation of large hurricanes.

Air flows from high pressure to low pressure (see inset). In the northern hemisphere, the Coriolis effect deflects this moving air to the right, causing cyclonic (low pressure) systems to rotate counter-clockwise as seen here in a low pressure system over Iceland. Cyclonic weather is usually dull, with grey cloud and persistent rain.

In the southern hemisphere, cyclonic systems spiral in a clockwise direction, seen in this photograph of cyclone Catarina, a rare South Atlantic tropical cyclone which hit Brazil in March 2004. As air rushes into the low pressure area, it is defected to the left, causing a clockwise spiral.

Frontal Weather

A **weather front** marks the boundary between two air-masses at different densities. A front is about 100-200 km wide and slopes where warm and cool air masses collide. A front appears on a weather map as a line with triangles (cold front) or semicircles (warm front) attached.

In a **cold front**, cold air undercuts warm air, forcing it steeply upwards along the line of the front and triggering the formation of towering cumulus clouds and rain. Cold fronts are often associated with low-pressure systems and unsettled weather conditions. As the front passes the cold air mass behind it can cause a rapid drop in temperature.

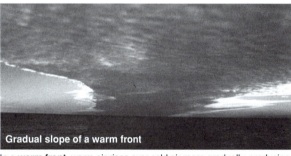

Gradual slope of a warm front

In a **warm front**, warm air rises over cold air more gradually, producing flattened, stratus-type clouds. Warm fronts produce low intensity rainfall that may last for some time and preceed warm weather. Because it moves more quickly, a cold front will eventually overtake a warm front, creating an occlusion.

---

1. Explain the role of the Coriolis effect in creating the prevailing winds in different regions of the globe:

   _____

   _____

   _____

2. In the spaces provided below, draw schematic diagrams to show:

   (a) The movement of a cold front into an area of warm air:

   (b) The movement of air in a Southern Hemisphere cyclone and a Northern Hemisphere hurricane:

   (a)

   (b)

© Biozone International 2007-2011
Photocopying Prohibited

Periodicals:
El niño, La niña

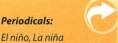

Related activities: The Atmosphere and Climate

RA 3

Variation and Oscillation

Interactions between the atmosphere and the oceans are at the core of most global climate patterns. These climate patterns are referred to as **oscillations** because they fluctuate on time scales ranging from days to decades. The **El-Niño-Southern Oscillation cycle** (ENSO) is the most prominent of these global oscillations, causing weather patterns involving increased rain in specific places but not in others. It is one of the many causes of drought.

In non-El-Niño conditions, a low pressure system over Australia draws the southeast trade winds across the eastern Pacific from a high pressure system over South America. These winds drive the warm South Equatorial Current towards Australia's coast. Off the coast of South America, upwelling of cold water brings nutrients to the surface.

In an El Niño event, the pressure systems that normally develop over Australia and South America are weakened or reversed, beginning with a rise in air pressure over the Indian Ocean, Indonesia, and Australia. Warm water extends deeper and flows eastwards, blocking the nutrient upwelling along the west coast of the Americas. This has a devastating effect on fish stocks. El Niño brings drought to Indonesia and northeastern South America, while heavy rain over Peru and Chile causes the deserts to bloom.

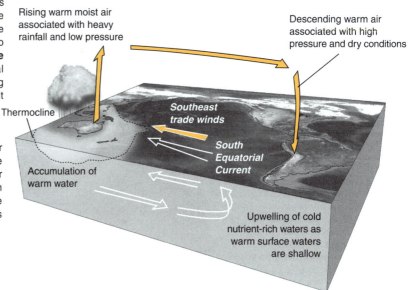

Normal climatic conditions

Rising warm moist air associated with heavy rainfall and low pressure

Descending warm air associated with high pressure and dry conditions

Thermocline

Southeast trade winds

South Equatorial Current

Accumulation of warm water

Upwelling of cold nutrient-rich waters as warm surface waters are shallow

El Niño Effect

Descending air and high pressure brings warm dry weather

Southeast trade winds reversed or weakened

Low pressure and rising air associated with rainfall

Warm water flows eastwards

Thermocline

Upwelling blocked by warm water which accumulates off South America

3. Describe the events that cause El Niño conditions and its effects on ocean circulation:

_____

_____

_____

_____

_____

4. Describe the effect of an El Niño year on:

(a) The climate of the western coast of South America: _____

_____

_____

(b) The climate of Indonesia and Australia: _____

_____

_____

_____

Ocean Circulation and Currents

Throughout the oceans, there is a constant circulation of water, both across the surface and at depth. Surface circulation, much of which is in the form of circular **gyres**, is driven by winds. In contrast, the deep-water ocean currents (the **thermohaline circulation**) is driven by the cooling and sinking of water masses in polar and subpolar regions. Cold water circulates through the Atlantic, penetrating the Indian and Pacific oceans, before returning as warm upper ocean currents to the South Atlantic.

Deep water currents move slowly and once a body of water sinks it may spend hundreds of years away from the surface. The polar oceans comprise the Arctic Ocean in the northern hemisphere and the Southern Ocean in the south. They differ from other oceans in having vast amounts of ice, in various forms, floating in them. This ice coverage has an important stabilizing effect on global climate, insulating large areas of the oceans from solar radiation in summer and preventing heat loss in winter.

The Earth's Systems

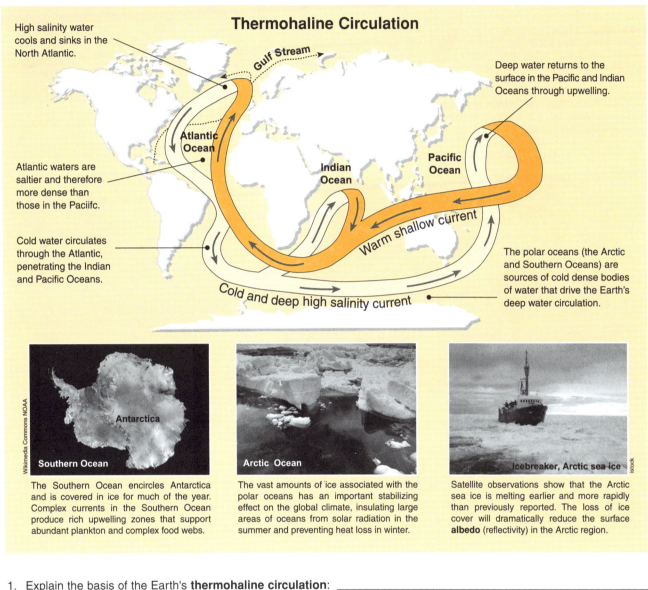

Thermohaline Circulation

High salinity water cools and sinks in the North Atlantic.

Gulf Stream

Deep water returns to the surface in the Pacific and Indian Oceans through upwelling.

Atlantic Ocean

Atlantic waters are saltier and therefore more dense than those in the Paciifc.

Indian Ocean

Pacific Ocean

Cold water circulates through the Atlantic, penetrating the Indian and Pacific Oceans.

Warm shallow current

The polar oceans (the Arctic and Southern Oceans) are sources of cold dense bodies of water that drive the Earth's deep water circulation.

Cold and deep high salinity current

Antarctica

Southern Ocean

The Southern Ocean encircles Antarctica and is covered in ice for much of the year. Complex currents in the Southern Ocean produce rich upwelling zones that support abundant plankton and complex food webs.

Arctic Ocean

The vast amounts of ice associated with the polar oceans has an important stabilizing effect on the global climate, insulating large areas of oceans from solar radiation in summer and preventing heat loss in winter.

Icebreaker, Arctic sea ice

Satellite observations show that the Arctic sea ice is melting earlier and more rapidly than previously reported. The loss of ice cover will dramatically reduce the surface **albedo** (reflectivity) in the Arctic region.

1. Explain the basis of the Earth's **thermohaline circulation**: _____

_____

_____

2. Explain how thermohaline circulation could influence global climate: _____

_____

_____

_____

3. Describe a possible consequence if the melting of sea ice significantly reduces the surface albedo of the Arctic region:

_____

_____

_____

Surface Circulation in the Oceans

The surface circulation of the oceans is driven by winds, but modified by the **Coriolis effect**. In the northern hemisphere, the Coriolis effect deflects the wind-driven water movements slightly to the right and in the southern hemisphere to the left. Drag accentuates the Coriolis effect so that the average water motion in the top few hundred metres of the ocean surface is almost at right angle to the wind direction. The overall effect is a pattern of large scale circular movements of water, or **gyres**, which rotate clockwise in the northern hemisphere and anticlockwise in the southern (below and right). These currents carry warm water away from the equator and colder water towards it.

The **Great Pacific Garbage Patch** is an accumulation of plastic and other debris in an area in the center of the North Pacific gyre that spans approximately 1.2 million km².

Overall Pattern of Surface Currents

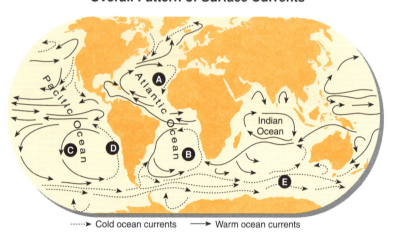

-----> Cold ocean currents   ——→ Warm ocean currents

Local Currents and Upwelling

Local currents and vertical transport of water (upwelling and downwelling) are important phenomena around coastal regions. Upwelling in particular has important biological effects because it returns nutrients to surface waters, which promotes the growth of plankton.

Local currents are the result of interactions between tidal forces and coastlines. The whirlpools (vortices), seen above at Saltstraumen in Norway, are created by exceptionally strong tidal movements as water forces its way through a long narrow strait.

Plankton blooms, seen here as bright spots around the coast of England and Ireland, often occur in **upwelling zones**, as nutrients are brought to the surface. Upwelling occurs to replace the seawater that is moved offshore by surface circulation.

4. Contrast the mechanisms operating to drive deep water and surface water circulation: _____

_____

_____

5. Match each description below with its appropriate letter on the above diagram "*Overall Pattern of Surface Currents*":

   (a) Antarctic circumpolar current: _____   (d) North Atlantic gyre: _____

   (b) Peru current: _____   (e) South Atlantic gyre: _____

   (c) South Pacific gyre: _____

6. Describe a similarity between **atmospheric circulation** and **surface ocean circulation** patterns: _____

_____

7. (a) Describe the biological importance of upwelling in coastal regions: _____

_____

   (b) Explain how normal patterns of upwelling are affected during an El Niño year: _____

_____

_____

_____

_____

Global Water Resources

The Earth is an **aqueous planet**; 71% of its surface is covered by water. The majority of the Earth's water (a little over 97%) is stored within the oceans, and less than 3% of the total water supply is freshwater. A small amount (0.0071%) of the world's water exists as usable freshwater at the Earth's surface (in lakes, rivers, and wetlands). The remaining freshwater is contained within ice caps or glaciers, groundwater, or atmospheric moisture. The total amount of water on Earth is fairly constant at any one time, cycling constantly between liquid, vapor, and ice. This cyclic process is termed the water or **hydrological cycle**.

The Earth's Systems

The **Ogallala aquifer** is a vast water-table aquifer located beneath the Great Plains in the US. It covers portions of eight states and is extensively used for irrigation. At current usage rates it may be depleted by 2020, and is essentially non-renewable as it will take thousands of years to recharge.

The **Volga River** and its many tributaries form an extensive river system, which drains an area of about 1.35 million km^2 in the most heavily populated part of Russia. High levels of chemical pollution currently give cause for environmental concern.

From glacial origins, the **Yangtze River** flows 6300 km eastwards into the East China Sea. The Yangtze is subject to extensive flooding, which is only partly controlled by the massive Three Gorges Dam, and it is heavily polluted.

Arctic Ocean

Pacific Ocean

The North American **Great Lakes** are the largest group of freshwater lakes on Earth, containing 22% of the world's fresh surface water.

Atlantic Ocean

Indian Ocean

The **Mississippi River** drains most of the area between the Rocky Mountains and the Appalachians. A series of locks and dams provide for barge traffic.

The **Congo River** is the largest river in Western Central Africa with the second-largest flow in the world (after the Amazon). Like the Amazon, it drains an extensive area of rainforest.

The fertile Ganges Basin is central to the agricultural economies of India and Bangladesh. The **Ganges** and its tributaries currently provide irrigation to a large and populous region, although a recent UN climate report indicates that the glaciers feeding the Ganges may disappear by 2030, leaving it as a seasonal system fed by the **monsoon** rains.

Southern Ocean

The **Amazon River** accounts for 20% of the world's total river flow and drains 40% of South America. The Amazon is the largest rainforest in the world and has the world's highest biodiversity

The **Murray-Darling Basin** drains one-seventh of the Australian land mass and over 70% of Australia's irrigation resources are concentrated there.

Amazon River

North American Great Lakes

Big Spring Missouri: 1 million m^3 flow per day

Rivers form when rain and meltwater are channelled downhill along surface irregularities. They typically end in either a lake or at the sea. Rivers are used for transportation, recreation and irrigation, and supply food and hydroelectric power. They shape the landscape through erosion and deposition.

Lakes form naturally in surface depressions or a result of damming and, when large enough, can have a profound effect on regional weather. The Great Lakes moderate seasonal temperatures somewhat, by absorbing heat and cooling the air in summer, then slowly radiating that heat in autumn.

Aquifers are typically saturated regions of the subsurface that produce an economically feasible quantity of water to a well or spring. Aquifers can occur at various depths but those closer to the surface are more likely to be exploited for water supply and irrigation.

Iceberg, Antarctica

Meltwater is the water released by the melting of snow or ice, including glacial ice. Meltwater can destabilize glacial lakes and snowpack causing floods and avalanches. Meltwater also acts as a lubricant in the basal sliding of glaciers.

Polar icecaps and glaciers store the majority of the world's freshwater. While the Antarctic ice-sheet is growing, Arctic ice is thinning. Because snow and ice form a protective, cooling layer over the Arctic, this thinning accelerates temperature rise.

Consecutive years of poor rainfall are behind the **East African** drought. Readily available water reserves have been used up in many areas, leaving insufficient water for irrigation and stock. Fires and desertification are also consequences of drought.

Related activities: The Hydrological Cycle, Water and People, Water and Industry
Weblinks: The Earth In Our Hands: Groundwater, World Water Hotspots

A 2

The World's Oceans

Desalination plant

The major minerals in seawater (sodium and chloride) make it too salty for drinking or irrigation unless it is desalinated. Large-scale desalination typically requires large amounts of energy, making it costly compared to the use of fresh water from rivers or groundwater. The large energy reserves of many Middle Eastern countries, along with their relative scarcity of water, have led to extensive construction of desalination plants in this region.

Fish harvest

The ocean supplies humans with a vast range of resources and opportunities, including fisheries (above) and aquaculture, transportation, tourism and recreation, offshore extraction (of oil and gas, gravel, sand, and minerals), energy production (tidal, wave, thermal, salinity, and wind), marine biotechnology (pharmaceuticals), conservation of biodiversity (through protected areas and marine reserves), waste disposal.

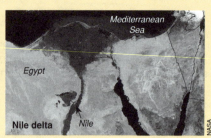

Nile delta *Nile* *Egypt* *Mediterranean Sea*

Oceans receive the outflow from the world's major river systems. A delta is formed when a river enters an ocean or sea and sediments are deposited in a fan-shaped pattern. Deltas are among the most fertile regions on Earth and are heavily populated. Since construction of the Aswan High Dam, the Nile Delta (above) no longer receives an annual supply of nutrients and sediments from upstream. Its floodplain soils are now poorer as a result.

1. Distinguish between surface water and groundwater: _____

_____

2. (a) Explain why some deep but extensive aquifers, such as the Ogallala, are considered non-renewable:

_____

   (b) Describe the factors that might influence the long term viability of an aquifer: _____

_____

3. Only a small proportion of the Earth's water exists as usable freshwater at the Earth's surface. Describe some ways in which supplies of freshwater could be increased in a particular area:

   (a) _____

   (b) _____

   (c) _____

4. Much of the Earth's freshwater is locked up in ice. Describe the critical role of this unavailable water: _____

_____

5. (a) Explain why delta regions are among the most fertile in the world: _____

_____

   (b) Describe the effect of water diversion schemes on the fertility of a delta region: _____

_____

6. Discuss the association between the location of the world's major water resources, areas of high biodiversity, and human population density. You may need to consult other resources to bring together your lines of evidence.

_____

_____

_____

_____

_____

_____

_____

_____

Water and People

Water is the most important substance on the planet. Life could not exist without it. There are approximately 1.4 billion trillion liters of water on Earth and Earth is the only planet in the solar system where large volumes of water are found on the surface in liquid form. However, water is not evenly distributed throughout the globe; deserts receive very little rainfall whereas other places experience large volumes of seasonal or daily rainfall. Despite the enormous amount of water on this planet, wasteful usage and poor management of treatment and supply has reduced the amount of fresh water that is available to much of humanity.

Water's unique properties make it an unusual substance. It has no taste or odor, it is less dense in its solid form than in its liquid form (allowing ice to float), and has an extremely high boiling point compared to other similar molecules (such as H_2S). It is polar and so able to dissolve ionic solids and conduct electricity. It also has an extremely high surface tension caused by forming strong bonds between water molecules.

The human body is nearly 70% water and to keep it healthy and functioning correctly health authorities recommend drinking between 1.8 and 2 liters of water per day. In some countries, access even to this small amount is difficult. In some areas people may use just 15 liters of water per day for all of their domestic uses including drinking water (compared to over 570 liters per person per day in the United States).

Nearly half of the water supplied by municipal water systems in the US is used to flush toilets and water lawns, and another 20-35% is lost through leakages. Treatment of waste water places major demands on cities yet there are few incentives to reduce water use and recycle. Providing a reliable clean water remains a major public health issue in many poorer regions of the world.

Photo: Bob Metcalf

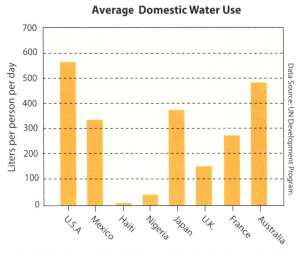

Average Domestic Water Use

Data Source: UN Development Program.

Potable water (water suitable to drink) is a rare commodity in large parts of the world. Access to potable water is limited by the availability of suitable water resources (e.g. rivers), its ease of distribution, and level of water treatment (water borne diseases and dissolved toxins need to be removed). Once it is treated, the distribution and storage of water becomes important. In many countries, distribution of water is difficult and storage of large amounts is almost impossible.

Industrialized countries tend to use the most amount of water, with the United States being one of the largest domestic users. The amount of water used by people in domestic situations depends upon the efficiency of the water use, its cost to the user (higher supply prices usually mean lower use), and the amount of water available for use.

1. (a) Describe some of the properties of water: _____

    _____

    (b) Explain why water is so important in living organisms: _____

    _____

    _____

2   Describe the factors that limit water supply to some countries: _____

    _____

    _____

    _____

Periodicals:
Water, water everywhere,
Water: Our thirsty world

Related activities: Global Water Resources, Water and Industry
Weblinks: Interactive House, Water Sense

Water Conflict

Water is a strategic community resource. Its scarcity has led to disputes throughout the world and throughout history. Conflicts over water can occur both within and between countries. Water conflicts between countries often occur when a water course flows through or is bounded by more than one country. Water polluted in one country may affect the next or water removed for irrigation in one country will reduce supply to another. Water conflicts within countries often occur because of the differing demands and interests of industrial, agricultural, domestic, and recreational users. Government policies need to ensure fair water access for all parties.

The Colorado River and the Rio Grande River are sources of water conflict between the USA and Mexico. A treaty signed in 1944 requires Mexico to deliver 431.7 million m^3 of water from the Rio Grande per year. The USA must deliver 1.85 billion m^3 of water from the Colorado to Mexico per year. In 2004, 17 irrigation districts, the North Alamo Water Supply Corporation, and 29 farmers threatened to take legal action against Mexico over its failure to supply the agreed volume. According to the claim, Mexico owed the group more than 1.2 billion m^3 of water.

Colorado River

Since 2003, the Rio Grande has often run dry

Scott Ehardt

The Rio Grande Compact was signed between Colorado, Texas, and New Mexico in 1938 to share the waters of the Rio Grande fairly. However the agreement failed to ensure the supply of water. By 1966, Colorado owed New Mexico 1.2 billion m^3 of water while New Mexico owed Texas 600 million m^3 of water. New Mexico and Texas sued Colorado and, while Colorado cleared its debt to New Mexico, New Mexico must still pay water debts to Texas.

Colorado River

Colorado

New Mexico

Rio Grande River

Texas

Mexico

Rio Grande forms the border between Mexico and Texas

3. Describe one way in which to improve efficiency of water use in each of the domestic situations:

(a) Irrigation: _____

_____

(b) Drinking supply: _____

_____

(c) Sanitation: _____

_____

(d) Cooking: _____

_____

4. Explain why water is a common source of conflict: _____

_____

_____

For questions 5 to 6, circle the letter with the correct answer:

5. Identify which of the following considerations below are important in effective water management:

I. Mismanagement of water can lead to large volumes being wasted either at the source or en-route to the user.
II. Water is mostly used near its source.
III. Removal of too much water from a body of water can severely disrupt its natural systems.

A. I and II
B. II and III
C. I and III
D. I, II, and III

6. The water on Earth is:
A. Evenly distributed about the globe
B. Effectively finite in volume
C. Mostly freshwater
D. Easily accessible to all people

Water and Industry

Water is an essential commodity in communities. Not only is it essential for domestic supply but it is also important in industry and agriculture. Water is most often used by industry as a solvent, a coolant and for cleaning purposes. The majority of water in agriculture is used for irrigation of crops, although it is also drunk by stock and used as a solvent for sprays. Every year millions of cubic meters of water are diverted or pumped out of rivers and aquifers to meet the demands for industry or agriculture.

Agricultural use of water

Intensive agriculture uses large volumes of water. Crop irrigation accounts for 65% of the world's water use yet it is largely inefficient, with only 40% of the water reaching the crops and the rest being lost through evaporation, seepage, and runoff. Improved irrigation practices, such as drip irrigation, could double the amount of water delivered to crops and free large amounts of water for other uses.

Industrial use of water

Industrial related water usage increases as the human population increases. The processing of food, and the manufacture of metal, wood and paper products, gasoline and oils all consume large amounts of water. High consumer demand and low levels of recycling exacerbate the problem, but there are large savings to be made by using recycled water and improving the efficiency of water use.

From Bull to Beef

(over three years):

Pasture, feed and hay:	3 060 129	L
Drinking water:	23 848	L
Cleaning equipment:	7 192	L
	= 3 091 169	L

If each animal is 500 kg when alive, it will produce 220 kg of beef once cut and boned by a butcher.

$$\frac{3\ 091\ 169}{220} = \textbf{14 050.8 L}\text{ of water per kg of beef.}$$

The Earth's Systems

Using the World's Freshwater

Global rates of water withdrawal from surface and groundwater sources are projected to more than double in the next two decades as population growth and economic development increase. This will exceed available surface runoff in a number of regions.

Manufacturing and production processes are usually water intensive. Some everyday items (right) use surprisingly large amounts of water in their production. This is termed **virtual water**, as the water is in the manufacturing process, not in the end product. Efficiency of water use will be increasingly important as urbanization and industrialization of common processes continue to grow.

The cotton in a pair of jeans: 6,800 liters

An automobile: 380,000 liters

One can of soda: 38 liters

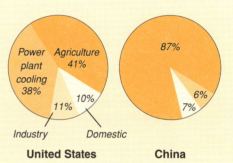

Power plant cooling 38%   Agriculture 41%   Industry 11%   Domestic 10%

United States

87%   6%   7%

China

Uses of withdrawn water vary both regionally and between countries. The USA, for example, uses more water for power generation and industry than China, where agricultural uses account for most of the withdrawals.

1. Account for the differences between China and the USA in terms of how water use is apportioned: _____

_____

_____

_____

2. Explain why water availability is considered to be one of the critical global resource issues in the 21st Century:

_____

_____

3. Describe ways in which the efficiency of water use could be improved in the following areas:

(a) Crop irrigation: _____

_____

_____

_____

Periodicals:
Water pressure

Related activities: Global Water Resources, Humans and Resources

RA 3

Damming the Nile

Two dams straddle the Nile River at Aswan, Egypt. The newer (and by far larger) of the two, the **Aswan High Dam**, was completed in 1970 and formed Lake Nasser, a 550 km long reservoir capable of holding two years of the Nile's annual water flow.

The main objectives of the project were energy generation, flood control, and the provision of water for agriculture. These goals have have been achieved, but construction of the Aswan Dams has also had a number of detrimental effects. Before impoundment, the Nile flooded annually, bringing minerals and nutrient-rich sediments to the floodplain and flushing out accumulated salts. Without flooding, fertilizers must be applied to the land and salts build up in the soils, causing crops to fail. Moreover, without annual deposition of river sediments, the land is eroding, allowing the sea to encroach up the river delta. If global warming causes a rise in sea levels, 60% of Egypt's habitable land may be flooded. Damming has also caused 64% of commercially fished species in the Nile to disappear. Time will tell if better management will help to reverse the problems currently being experienced in the Nile Delta region.

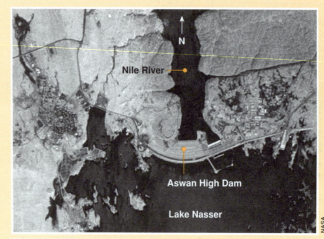

Satellite image (above) and panoramic view (below) of the Aswan High Dam

(b) Industrial water use: _____

_____

_____

_____

4. Using a local or international example, discuss the environmental and economic problems generally associated with damming a large river:

5. Investigate water use in your community, identifying major surface and groundwater sources, how water usage is apportioned, and projected water problems. Summarize your findings below. Attach extra pages if required:

KEY TERMS: Mix and Match

INSTRUCTIONS: Test your vocabulary by matching each term to its definition, as identified by its preceding letter code.

ATMOSPHERE

CALDERA

CONVERGENT BOUNDARY

CORE

CORIOLIS EFFECT

CRUST

DIVERGENT BOUNDARY

DOME VOLCANO

ENSO

FAULT

GROUNDWATER

IGNEOUS

INTERTROPICAL CONVERGENCE ZONE

LITHOSPHERE

LOAM

MANTLE

METAMORPHIC

PLATE BOUNDARY

PLATE TECTONICS

RADIOMETRIC DATING

ROCK CYCLE

SEDIMENTARY

SHIELD VOLCANO

SOIL

SOIL HORIZON

STRATOSPHERE

THERMOHALINE CIRCULATION

TRANSFORM BOUNDARY

TRICELLULAR MODEL

TROPOSPHERE

A Rock type made up of sediments that have been compressed over time.

B Model that describes the circulation of air cells in the atmosphere.

C Type of soil that is commonly identified as having the most desirable structure and texture with 40% sand, 40% silt, and 20% clay.

D Material that forms from the breakdown of organic matter and minerals and which usually overlies bedrock.

E Type of volcano that forms from fluid basaltic lava, having shallow slopes and a large radius.

F The layer of rock that forms the outer surface of the Earth.

G The central layer of the Earth thought to consist of molten iron and nickle.

H A volcanic structure that forms when viscous, usually rhyolitic magma rises to the surface.

I Water found underground that does not flow in a particular water course but as a large body.

J A fracture line in the Earth's crust associated with a plate boundary.

K Boundary formed when two adjacent tectonic plates move in opposite directions.

L Dating method that uses isotopes or measurement of radioactivity to produce an absolute time since the formation of a substance, +/- a specific error.

M Process by which rocks are formed, changed and reformed from sedimentary, metamorphic, and igneous rocks.

N Layer of the Earth that combines the crust and the upper, more solid part of the mantle.

O A collective term for the processes of plate movement, building and degradation caused by the motions of the mantle.

P The molten layer of the Earth upon which the crust rides.

Q Type of rock formed by a change in its original structure due to high heat and pressure.

R The junction of two or more tectonic plates.

S Type of rock formed by volcanic activity.

T Layer of the atmosphere above the troposphere in which the ozone layer is found.

U Circulation of the oceans driven by thermal and salinity gradients.

V A layer in the soil profile that possesses specific characteristics that distinguish it from the layer above or below.

W Area of the atmosphere near the equator where air flows from the Northern and Southern Hemispheres meet.

X Boundary of tectonic plates at which the plates are sliding past each other parallel to the line of contact.

Y Atmospheric layer closest to the Earth in which all weather occurs.

Z Phenomenon in which weather patterns rotate in opposite directions in the Northern and Southern Hemispheres due to the Earth's rotation.

AA Volcanic structure that forms when an empty magma chamber collapses after an eruption.

BB Large scale weather phenomenon that is caused by reversal of trade winds between South America and Australia and warmer waters off South America. One of the major causes of drought.

CC Boundary formed when two tectonic plates collide.

DD The layers of gases that surround the Earth.

Ecosystems

Biomes & ecosystems
- Distribution and features of biomes
- Habitat and niche
- Environmental gradients
- Photosynthesis and respiration

Energy flow
- Food webs and food chains
- Trophic structure
- Ecological pyramids
- Measuring productivity

Natural Ecosystem Change

Bio-geochemical cycles
- Importance of biogeochemical cycles
- Carbon, nitrogen, phosphorus and sulfur cycling
- Hydrological cycle
- Bacteria and biogeochemical cycles

Ecosystem stability
- Time scales of change
- Primary and secondary succession
- Key species and their importance
- Environmental change

Both biotic and abiotic factors interact to form the environment in which we live

Large and small natural changes occur on both long and short time scales

Ecology

Ecological principles can be applied at any scale and to any environment.

Studying the various aspects of ecology develops an overall understanding of the interactions between and within the biotic and abiotic worlds, and our place in them.

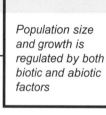

Population size and growth is regulated by both biotic and abiotic factors

Sampling populations helps to analyze current trends and predict future ones

Features of populations
- Population density
- Population distribution
- Age structure and its effects

Population growth
- Population regulation
- Natality, mortality, and migration
- Limiting factors
- Survivorship curves
- Humans and demography

Species interactions
- Interspecific competition
- Intraspecific competition

Sampling populations
- Sampling and collecting equipment
- Quantitative sampling methods
- Qualitative sampling methods
- Recording data
- Diversity indices

Abiotic factors
- Monitoring equipment
- Measuring environmental change

Classification
- Plant and animal keys

Populations

Investigating Ecosystems

Ecosystems

Key concepts

▶ Both biotic and abiotic factors contribute to the characteristics of an ecosystem.

▶ An organism's range is limited by its ability to exploit its habitat and compete with others for resources.

▶ Trophic levels and food chains describe how energy moves through an ecosystem.

▶ Only a fraction of the energy in one trophic level is transferred to the next level.

Key terms

abiotic factors
biome
biosphere
biotic factors
community
consumer
decomposer
detritivore
ecological niche
ecology
ecosystem
environment
environmental gradient
food chain
food web
fundamental niche
habitat
interspecific
intraspecific
microclimate
microhabitat
photosynthesis
population
producer
realized niche
respiration
saprotrophic
species
trophic level

Objectives

☐ 1. Use the **KEY TERMS** to help you understand and complete these objectives.

Ecosystems, Habitats and Adaptation   pages 40-50

☐ 2. Define the terms **ecology**, **ecosystem**, **population**, **species,** and **environment.** Describe the relationship of each of these to the biosphere.

☐ 3. Recognize the Earth's major **biomes** and explain how they classified according to vegetation type. Describe the effect of latitude and local climate in determining the distribution of biomes.

☐ 4. Explain how gradients within the **abiotic** environment can occur over relatively short distances, e.g. on a rocky shore, or in a forest, desert or lake. Explain the role of these **environmental gradients** on species distribution.

☐ 5. Describe components of an organism's **ecological niche**, distinguishing between the **fundamental** and the **realized niche**.

☐ 6. Describe examples of physiological, behavioral, and structural adaptations in a organism and explain how they enhance survival.

☐ 7. Describe the significance of Gause's competitive exclusion principle with respect to niche overlap between species.

Energy in Ecosystems   pages 51-62

☐ 8. Explain how **photosynthesis** provides the main route by which energy enters an ecosystem and how **respiration** uses this energy.

☐ 9. Explain the importance of photosynthesis and respiration in carbon cycling.

☐ 10. Explain how **trophic levels** are used to describe energy flow in an **ecosystem**. Explain how energy is transferred between these levels.

☐ 11. Construct diagrams, including **food chains** and **food webs,** to explain the flow of energy through an **ecosystem**.

☐ 12. Distinguish between **producers**, primary and secondary **consumers**, **detritivores,** and **saprotrophs**.

Periodicals:
Listings for this chapter are on page 230

Weblinks:
www.thebiozone.com/
weblink/EnvSci-2764.html

Presentation Media
Environmental Science:
Ecosystems

Components of an Ecosystem

The concept of the ecosystem was developed to describe the way groups of organisms are predictably found together in their physical environment. A community comprises all the organisms within an ecosystem. Both physical (abiotic) and biotic factors affect the organisms in a community, influencing their distribution and their survival, growth, and reproduction.

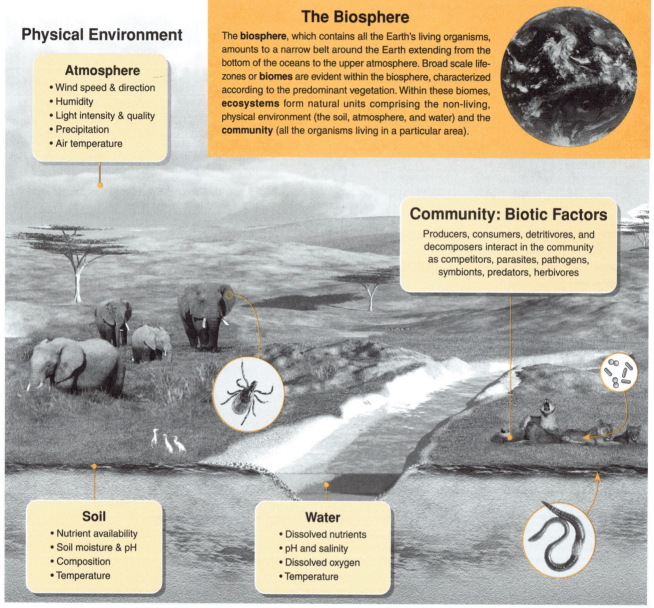

Physical Environment

Atmosphere
- Wind speed & direction
- Humidity
- Light intensity & quality
- Precipitation
- Air temperature

The Biosphere

The **biosphere**, which contains all the Earth's living organisms, amounts to a narrow belt around the Earth extending from the bottom of the oceans to the upper atmosphere. Broad scale life-zones or **biomes** are evident within the biosphere, characterized according to the predominant vegetation. Within these biomes, **ecosystems** form natural units comprising the non-living, physical environment (the soil, atmosphere, and water) and the **community** (all the organisms living in a particular area).

Community: Biotic Factors

Producers, consumers, detritivores, and decomposers interact in the community as competitors, parasites, pathogens, symbionts, predators, herbivores

Soil
- Nutrient availability
- Soil moisture & pH
- Composition
- Temperature

Water
- Dissolved nutrients
- pH and salinity
- Dissolved oxygen
- Temperature

1. Choose the letter of the term that corresponds to each of the statements below:

   A Community   **B** Population   **C** Ecosystem   **D** Physical factor

   (a) All the green tree frogs present in a rainforest: _C_

   (b) An entire forest: _C_

   (c) The humidity in a rainforest: _D_

   (d) A community of organisms and their environment: _A_

   (e) An association of different species interacting together: _B_

2. Distinguish between biotic and abiotic factors: _Biotic factors are living organisms etc, however abiotic are chemical and physicals factors of environment (not living)_

Related activities: Factors Affecting Biome Distribution

Periodicals: Ecosystems

Factors Affecting Biome Distribution

Biomes represent large areas with the same or similar climate and vegetation characteristics. These biomes exist in part because of the regular arrangement of weather conditions around the planet. The Earth is circled in the Northern and Southern hemispheres by three air cells. The interaction of these cells plays a major in the formation of biomes. The cells form areas of rising or descending air, affecting the amount of rainfall. Surface features, such as oceans and mountain ranges, affect the final positions and size of these biomes but four general areas in each hemisphere can be identified.

Earth's Climate and Biomes

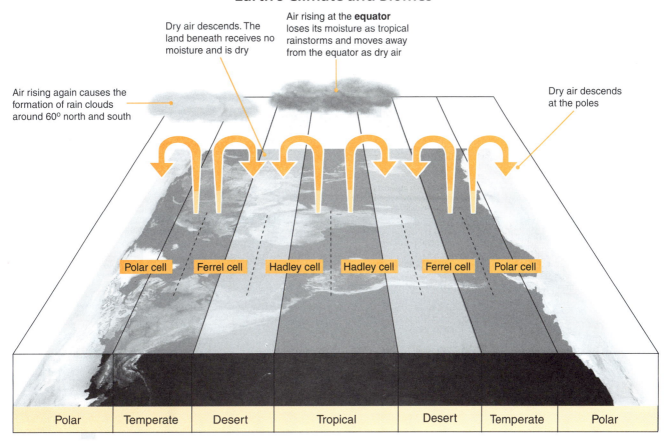

Dry air descends. The land beneath receives no moisture and is dry

Air rising at the **equator** loses its moisture as tropical rainstorms and moves away from the equator as dry air

Air rising again causes the formation of rain clouds around 60° north and south

Dry air descends at the poles

Polar cell   Ferrel cell   Hadley cell   Hadley cell   Ferrel cell   Polar cell

| Polar | Temperate | Desert | Tropical | Desert | Temperate | Polar |

Ecosystems

Biomes and Landscapes

Climate is heavily modified by the landscape. Where there are large mountain ranges, wind is deflected upwards causing rain on the windward side and a **rain shadow** on the leeward side. The biome that results from this is considerably different from the one that may have appeared with no wind deflection. Large expanses of ocean and flat land also change the climate by modifying air temperatures and the amount of rainfall.

Leeward plains

Windward slopes

The Rain Shadow Effect

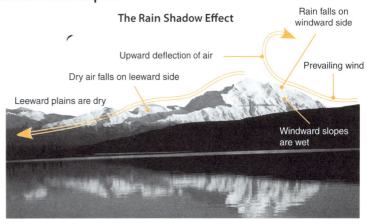

Rain falls on windward side

Upward deflection of air

Prevailing wind

Dry air falls on leeward side

Leeward plains are dry

Windward slopes are wet

1. Explain why the tropics tend to be both hot and wet: _____

_____

_____

2. Explain why the distribution of biomes in the Northern Hemisphere is similar, but not identical to, the distribution of biomes in the Southern Hemisphere:

_____

_____

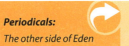

Periodicals:
The other side of Eden

Related activities: Atmosphere and Climate, Physical Factors and Gradients **Weblinks**: The World's Biomes

World Distribution of Biomes

Global patterns of vegetation distribution are closely related to climate. Although they are complex, major vegetation **biomes** can be recognized. These are large areas where the vegetation type shares a particular suite of physical requirements. Biomes have characteristic features, but the boundaries between them are not distinct. The same biome may occur in widely separated regions of the world wherever the climatic and soil conditions are similar.

Tropical rainforest

Tropical seasonal forest

Savanna

Temperate forest

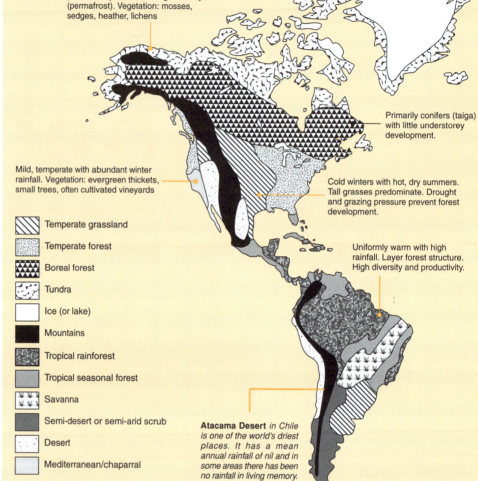

Low temperatures, short growing season, permanently frozen lower ground layer (permafrost). Vegetation: mosses, sedges, heather, lichens

Primarily conifers (taiga) with little understorey development.

Mild, temperate with abundant winter rainfall. Vegetation: evergreen thickets, small trees, often cultivated vineyards

Cold winters with hot, dry summers. Tall grasses predominate. Drought and grazing pressure prevent forest development.

Uniformly warm with high rainfall. Layer forest structure. High diversity and productivity.

Temperate grassland
Temperate forest
Boreal forest
Tundra
Ice (or lake)
Mountains
Tropical rainforest
Tropical seasonal forest
Savanna
Semi-desert or semi-arid scrub
Desert
Mediterranean/chaparral

Atacama Desert in Chile is one of the world's driest places. It has a mean annual rainfall of nil and in some areas there has been no rainfall in living memory.

Boreal forest

Temperate grassland

Ice

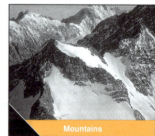
Mountains

1. Suggest a reason for the distribution of deserts and semi-desert areas in northern parts of Asia and in the west of North and South America (away from equatorial regions):

_____

2. Compared with its natural extent (on the map), little unaltered temperate forest now exists. Explain why this is the case:

_____

_____

_____

_____

Related activities: Factors Affecting Biome Distribution

Vegetation patterns are determined largely by climate but can be modified markedly by human activity. Semi-arid areas that are overgrazed will revert to desert and have little ability to recover. Similarly, many chaparral regions no longer support their original vegetation, but are managed for vineyards and olive groves. Wherever they occur, mountainous regions are associated with their own altitude adapted vegetation. The rainshadow effect of mountains governs the distribution of deserts in some areas too, as in Chile and the Gobi desert in Asia. The classification of biomes may vary slightly; some sources distinguish hot deserts (such as the Sahara) from cold deserts and semi-deserts (such as the Gobi). However, most classifications recognize desert, tundra, grassland and forest types and differentiate them on the basis of latitude.

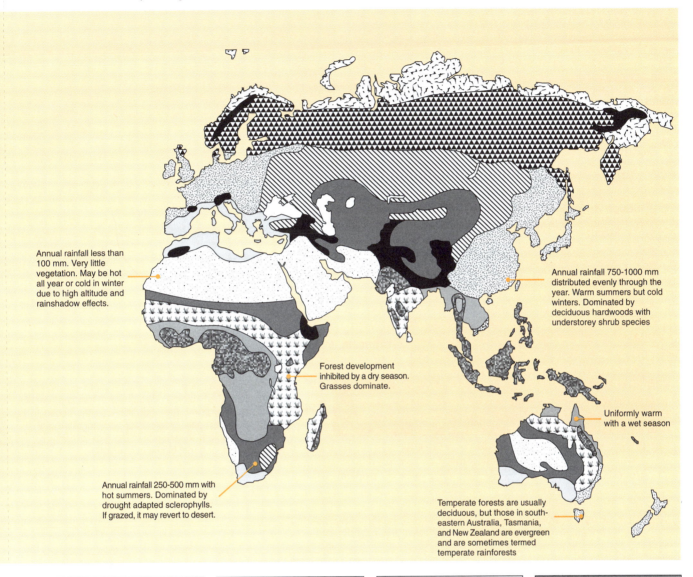

Annual rainfall less than 100 mm. Very little vegetation. May be hot all year or cold in winter due to high altitude and rainshadow effects.

Annual rainfall 750-1000 mm distributed evenly through the year. Warm summers but cold winters. Dominated by deciduous hardwoods with understorey shrub species

Forest development inhibited by a dry season. Grasses dominate.

Uniformly warm with a wet season

Annual rainfall 250-500 mm with hot summers. Dominated by drought adapted sclerophylls. If grazed, it may revert to desert.

Temperate forests are usually deciduous, but those in south-eastern Australia, Tasmania, and New Zealand are evergreen and are sometimes termed temperate rainforests

Ecosystems

Tundra

Semi-arid scrub

Mediterranean/chaparral

Desert

3. Suggest what abiotic factor(s) limit the northern extent of boreal forest: _____

_____

_____

_____

_____

_____

_____

The Effect of Temperature on Biomes

Latitude directly affects solar input and temperature. As the Earth curves towards the poles, solar energy is spread out over an ever increasing area. This energy must also travel through a greater amount of the atmosphere, expending more energy than at low latitudes.

Within a single latitudinal region, the level of precipitation (rainfall) governs the type of plant community found. Note that the effect of altitude is similar to that of latitude (ice will occur at high altitudes even at low-latitudes).

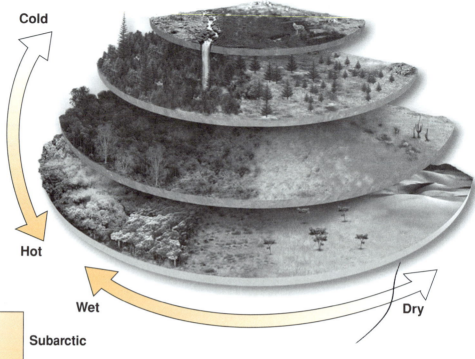

Cold

Hot

Wet

Dry

Latitudinal region: Polar → Equatorial

Snow & ice				**Arctic**
Tundra				
Boreal forest (taiga)				**Subarctic**
Chaparral		Temperate forests		**Temperate**
Desert	Grassland			
Desert	Semi-desert	Savanna	Tropical forest	**Tropical**

0   250   1000   4000

Annual precipitation (mm)

Desert ⟶ Tropical

Temperature and precipitation are excellent predictors of biome distribution. Temperature decreases from the equator to the poles. Temperature and precipitation act together as limiting factors to determine the type of desert, grassland, or forest biome in a region.

1. Explain how temperature and rainfall affect the distribution of biomes: _____

_____

_____

_____

2. Explain why biomes are not evenly distributed about the globe: _____

_____

_____

3. Explain how the landscape can modify climate: _____

_____

_____

_____

4. Explain why higher latitudes receive less solar energy than lower latitudes: _____

_____

_____

_____

Related activities: Factors Affecting Biome Distribution

Physical Factors and Gradients

Gradients in abiotic factors are found in almost every environment; they influence habitats and microclimates, and determine patterns of species distribution. This activity, covering the next four pages, examines the physical gradients and microclimates that might typically be found in four, very different environments. Note that **dataloggers** (pictured right), are being increasingly used to gather such data. The principles of their use are covered in the topic *Investigating Ecosystems*.

A Desert Environment

Desert environments experience extremes in temperature and humidity, but they are not uniform with respect to these factors. This diagram illustrates hypothetical values for temperature and humidity for some of the microclimates found in a desert environment at midday.

300 m altitude

Burrow
25°C
95% Hum

Under rock
28°C
60% Hum

Surface
45°C
<20% Hum

Crevice
27°C
95% Hum

High air
27°C
20% Hum

Low air
33°C
20% Hum

1 m above the ground

1 m underground

2 m underground

Ecosystems

1. Distinguish between **climate** and **microclimate**: _____

_____

_____

2. Study the diagram above and describe the general conditions where high humidity is found: _____

_____

_____

3. Identify the three microclimates that a land animal might exploit to avoid the extreme high temperatures of midday:

_____

_____

4. Describe the likely consequences for an animal that was unable to find a suitable microclimate to escape midday sun:

_____

_____

5. Describe the advantage of high humidity to the survival of most land animals: _____

_____

_____

6. Describe the likely changes to the temperature and relative humidity that occur during the night: _____

_____

_____

Related activities: Monitoring Physical Factors
Weblinks: Tide Pool Ecology

DA 2

Physical Factors at Low Tide on a Rock Platform

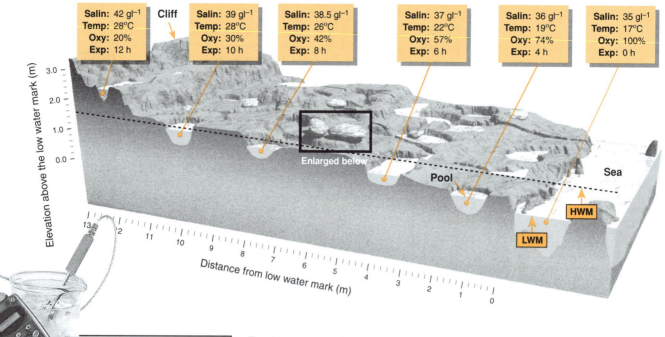

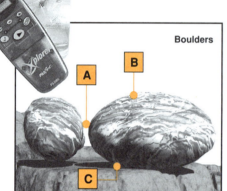

The diagram above shows a profile of a rock platform at low tide. The **high water mark** (HWM) shown here is the average height the spring tide rises to. In reality, the high tide level will vary with the phases of the moon (i.e. spring tides and neap tides). The **low water mark** (LWM) is an average level subject to the same variations due to the lunar cycle. The rock pools vary in size, depth, and position on the platform. They are isolated at different elevations, trapping water from the ocean for time periods that may be brief or up to 10 – 12 hours duration. Pools near the HWM are exposed for longer periods of time than those near the LWM. The difference in exposure times results in some of the physical factors exhibiting a **gradient**; the factor's value gradually changes over distance. Physical factors sampled in the pools include salinity, or the amount of dissolved salts (g) per liter (**Salin**), temperature (**Temp**), dissolved oxygen compared to that of open ocean water (**Oxy**), and exposure, or the amount of time isolated from the ocean water (**Exp**).

7. Describe the environmental gradient (general trend) from the low water mark (LWM) to the high water mark (HWM) for:

   (a) Salinity: _____

   (b) Temperature: _____

   (c) Dissolved oxygen: _____

   (d) Exposure: _____

8. Rock pools above the normal high water mark (HWM), such as the uppermost pool in the diagram above, can have wide extremes of salinity. Explain the conditions under which these pools might have either:

   (a) Very low salinity: _____

   _____

   (b) Very high salinity: _____

   _____

9. (a) The inset diagram (above, left) is an enlarged view of two boulders on the rock platform. Describe how the physical factors listed below might differ at each of the labelled points **A**, **B**, and **C**:

   Mechanical force of wave action: _____

   _____

   Surface temperature when exposed: _____

   _____

   (b) State the term given to these localized variations in physical conditions: _____

Physical Factors in a Tropical Rainforest

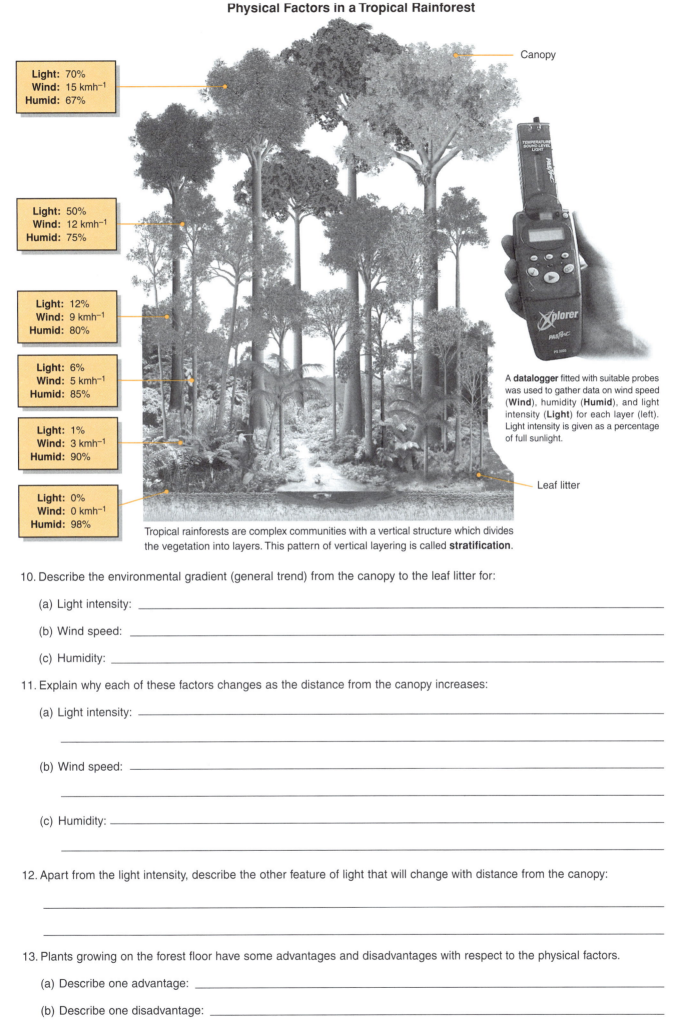

Canopy

Light: 70%
Wind: 15 kmh⁻¹
Humid: 67%

Light: 50%
Wind: 12 kmh⁻¹
Humid: 75%

Light: 12%
Wind: 9 kmh⁻¹
Humid: 80%

Light: 6%
Wind: 5 kmh⁻¹
Humid: 85%

Light: 1%
Wind: 3 kmh⁻¹
Humid: 90%

Light: 0%
Wind: 0 kmh⁻¹
Humid: 98%

A **datalogger** fitted with suitable probes was used to gather data on wind speed (**Wind**), humidity (**Humid**), and light intensity (**Light**) for each layer (left). Light intensity is given as a percentage of full sunlight.

Leaf litter

Tropical rainforests are complex communities with a vertical structure which divides the vegetation into layers. This pattern of vertical layering is called **stratification**.

Ecosystems

10. Describe the environmental gradient (general trend) from the canopy to the leaf litter for:

(a) Light intensity: _____

(b) Wind speed: _____

(c) Humidity: _____

11. Explain why each of these factors changes as the distance from the canopy increases:

(a) Light intensity: _____

_____

(b) Wind speed: _____

_____

(c) Humidity: _____

_____

12. Apart from the light intensity, describe the other feature of light that will change with distance from the canopy:

_____

_____

13. Plants growing on the forest floor have some advantages and disadvantages with respect to the physical factors.

(a) Describe one advantage: _____

(b) Describe one disadvantage: _____

Physical Factors in an Oxbow Lake in Summer

Oxbow lakes are formed from old river meanders which have been cut off and become isolated from the main channel following a change of the river's course. They are shallow (about 2-9 m deep) but often deep enough to develop temporary, but relatively stable, temperature gradients from top to bottom (below). Oxbows are commonly very productive and this can influence values for abiotic factors such as dissolved oxygen and light penetration, which can vary widely both with depth and proximity to the shore. Typical values for water temperature (**Temp**), dissolved oxygen (**Oxygen**), and light penetration as a percentage of the light striking the surface (**Light**) are indicated below.

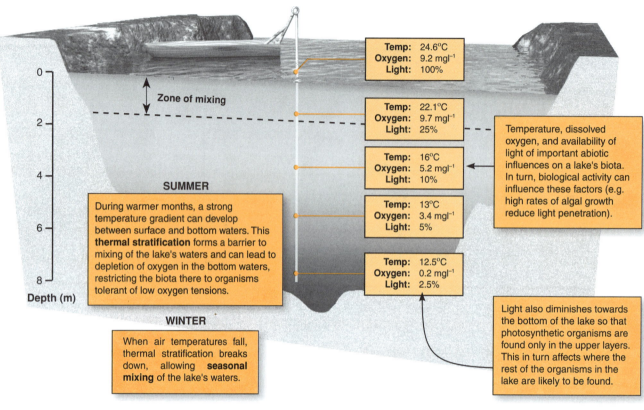

Temp: 24.6°C
Oxygen: 9.2 mgl⁻¹
Light: 100%

Temp: 22.1°C
Oxygen: 9.7 mgl⁻¹
Light: 25%

Temp: 16°C
Oxygen: 5.2 mgl⁻¹
Light: 10%

Temp: 13°C
Oxygen: 3.4 mgl⁻¹
Light: 5%

Temp: 12.5°C
Oxygen: 0.2 mgl⁻¹
Light: 2.5%

Zone of mixing

SUMMER

During warmer months, a strong temperature gradient can develop between surface and bottom waters. This **thermal stratification** forms a barrier to mixing of the lake's waters and can lead to depletion of oxygen in the bottom waters, restricting the biota there to organisms tolerant of low oxygen tensions.

WINTER

When air temperatures fall, thermal stratification breaks down, allowing **seasonal mixing** of the lake's waters.

Temperature, dissolved oxygen, and availability of light of important abiotic influences on a lake's biota. In turn, biological activity can influence these factors (e.g. high rates of algal growth reduce light penetration).

Light also diminishes towards the bottom of the lake so that photosynthetic organisms are found only in the upper layers. This in turn affects where the rest of the organisms in the lake are likely to be found.

Depth (m)

14. With respect to the diagram above, describe the environmental gradient (general trend) from surface to lake bottom for:

(a) Water temperature: _____

(b) Dissolved oxygen: _____

(c) Light penetration: _____

15. During the summer months, the warm surface waters are mixed by gentle wind action. Deeper cool waters are isolated from this surface water. This sudden change in the temperature profile is called a **thermocline** which itself is a further barrier to the mixing of shallow and deeper water.

(a) Explain the effect of the thermocline on the dissolved oxygen at the bottom of the lake: _____

_____

_____

(b) Explain what causes the oxygen level to drop to the low level: _____

_____

16. Many of these shallow lakes can undergo great changes in their salinity (sodium, magnesium, and calcium chlorides):

(a) Name an event that could suddenly reduce the salinity of a small lake: _____

(b) Name a process that can gradually increase the salinity of a small lake: _____

17. Describe the general effect of physical gradients on the distribution of organisms in habitats: _____

_____

_____

_____

Habitat

The environment in which a species population (or a individual organism) lives (including all the physical and biotic factors) is termed its **habitat**. Within a prescribed habitat, each species population has a range of tolerance to variations in its physical and chemical environment. Within the population, individuals will have slightly different tolerance ranges based on small differences in genetic make-up, age, and health. The wider an organism's tolerance range for a given abiotic factor (e.g. temperature or salinity), the more likely it is that the organism will be able to survive variations in that factor. Species **dispersal** is also strongly influenced by **tolerance range**. The wider the tolerance range of a species, the more widely dispersed the organism is likely to be. As well as a tolerance range, organisms have a narrower **optimum range** within which they function best. This may vary from one stage of an organism's development to another or from one season to another. Every species has its own optimum range. Organisms will usually be most abundant where the abiotic factors are closest to the optimum range.

Habitat Occupation and Tolerance Range

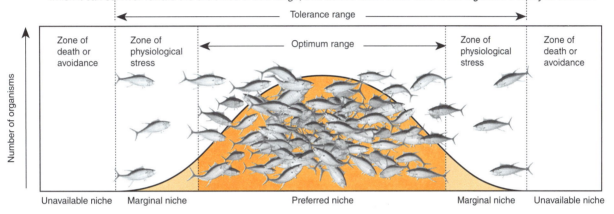

Examples of abiotic factors influencing niche size:

Too acidic — pH — Too alkaline

Too cold — Temperature — Too hot

The law of tolerances states that *for each abiotic factor, a species population (or organism) has a tolerance range within which it can survive. Toward the extremes of this range, that abiotic factor tends to limit the organism s ability to survive .*

Tolerance range

Zone of death or avoidance | Zone of physiological stress | Optimum range | Zone of physiological stress | Zone of death or avoidance

Number of organisms

Unavailable niche | Marginal niche | Preferred niche | Marginal niche | Unavailable niche

The Scale of Available Habitats

A habitat may be vast and relatively homogeneous, as is the open ocean. Barracuda (above) occur around reefs and in the open ocean where they are aggressive predators.

For non-mobile organisms, such as the fungus above, a suitable habitat may be defined by the particular environment in a relatively tiny area, such as on this decaying log.

For microbial organisms, such as the bacteria and protozoans of the ruminant gut, the habitat is defined by the chemical environment within the rumen (R) of the host animal, in this case, a cow.

1. Explain how an organism's habitat occupation relates to its tolerance range: _____

_____

_____

2. (a) Identify the range in the diagram above in which most of the species population is found. Explain why this is the case:

_____

_____

(b) Describe the greatest constraints on an organism's growth and reproduction within this range: _____

_____

3. Describe some probable stresses on an organism forced into a marginal niche: _____

_____

_____

Related activities: Ecological Niche

DA 2

Ecosystems

Ecological Niche

The **ecological niche** describes the functional position of a species in its ecosystem; how it responds to the distribution of resources and how it, in turn, alters those resources for other species. The full range of environmental conditions (biological and physical) under which an organism can exist describes its **fundamental niche**. As a result of direct and indirect interactions with other organisms, species are usually forced to occupy a niche that is narrower than this and to which they are best adapted. This is termed the **realized niche**. From the concept of the niche arose the idea that two species with the same niche requirements could not coexist, because they would compete for the same resources, and one would exclude the other. This is known as **Gause's competitive exclusion principle**. If two species compete for some of the same resources (e.g. food items of a particular size), their resource use curves will overlap (below, right). Within the zone of overlap, competition will be intense.

The Ecological Niche

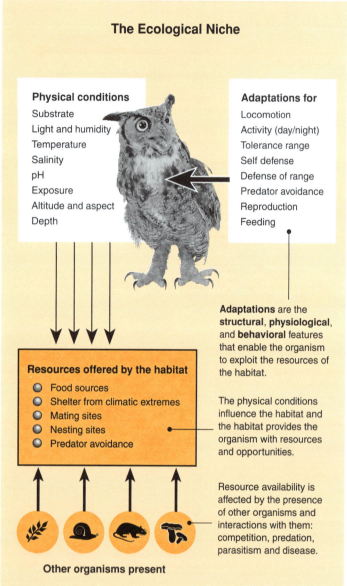

Physical conditions
Substrate
Light and humidity
Temperature
Salinity
pH
Exposure
Altitude and aspect
Depth

Adaptations for
Locomotion
Activity (day/night)
Tolerance range
Self defense
Defense of range
Predator avoidance
Reproduction
Feeding

Adaptations are the **structural**, **physiological**, and **behavioral** features that enable the organism to exploit the resources of the habitat.

Resources offered by the habitat
- Food sources
- Shelter from climatic extremes
- Mating sites
- Nesting sites
- Predator avoidance

The physical conditions influence the habitat and the habitat provides the organism with resources and opportunities.

Resource availability is affected by the presence of other organisms and interactions with them: competition, predation, parasitism and disease.

Other organisms present

Competition and Niche Size

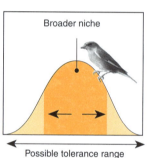

Realized niche of species A

Possible tolerance range

The realized niche
The tolerance range represents the potential (**fundamental**) niche a species could exploit. The actual or **realized** niche of a species is narrower than this because of competition with other species.

Broader niche

Possible tolerance range

Intraspecific competition
Competition is strongest between individuals of the same species, because their resource needs exactly overlap. When intraspecific competition is intense, individuals are forced to exploit resources in the extremes of their tolerance range. This leads to expansion of the realized niche.

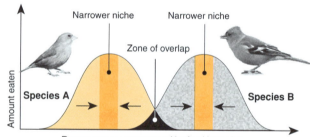

Narrower niche   Narrower niche

Zone of overlap

Amount eaten

Species A   Species B

Resource use as measured by food item size

Interspecific competition
If two (or more) species compete for some of the same resources, their resource use curves will overlap. Within the zone of overlap, resource competition will be intense and selection will favor niche specialization so that one or both species occupy a narrower niche.

1. (a) Explain in what way the realized niche could be regarded as flexible: _____

_____

_____

(b) Describe factors that might constrain the extent of the realized niche: _____

_____

2. Explain the contrasting effects of interspecific competition and intraspecific competition on niche breadth:

_____

_____

_____

Related activities: Interspecific Competition, Intraspecific Competition

Periodicals: The ecological niche

© Biozone International 2007-2011
Photocopying Prohibited

Energy Inputs and Outputs

Within ecosystems, organisms are assigned to **trophic** levels based on the way in which they obtain their energy. **Producers** or **autotrophs** manufacture their own food from simple inorganic substances. Most producers utilize sunlight as their energy source for this, but some use simple chemicals. The **consumers** or **heterotrophs** (herbivores, carnivores, omnivores, decomposers, and detritivores), obtain their energy from other organisms. Energy flows through trophic levels rather inefficiently, with only 5-20% of usable energy being transferred to the subsequent level. Energy not used for metabolic processes is lost as heat.

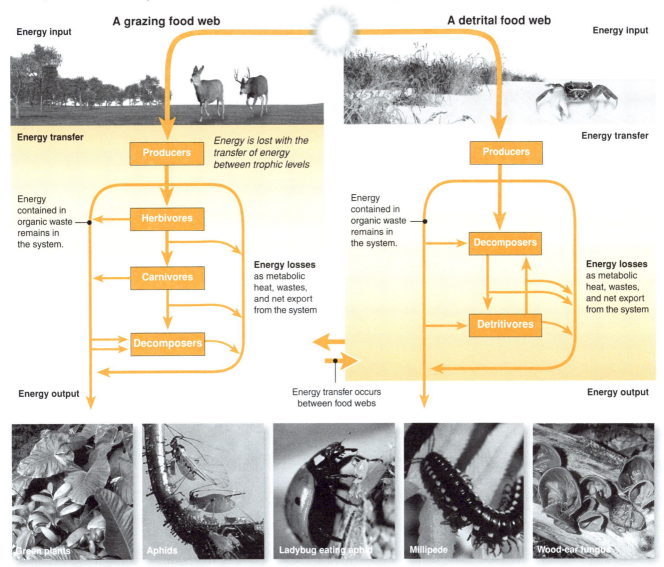

A grazing food web

Energy input

Energy transfer

Energy is lost with the transfer of energy between trophic levels

Producers

Energy contained in organic waste remains in the system.

Herbivores

Carnivores

Energy losses as metabolic heat, wastes, and net export from the system

Decomposers

Energy output

A detrital food web

Energy input

Energy transfer

Producers

Energy contained in organic waste remains in the system.

Decomposers

Detritivores

Energy losses as metabolic heat, wastes, and net export from the system

Energy transfer occurs between food webs

Energy output

Green plants · Aphids · Ladybug eating aphid · Millipede · Wood-ear fungus

Ecosystems

Producers (green plants, algae, and some bacteria) make their own food from simple inorganic carbon sources (e.g. CO_2). Sunlight is the most common energy source for this process.

Consumers: Consumer organisms (animals, non-photosynthetic protists, and some bacteria) rely on other living organisms or organic particulate matter for both their energy and their source of carbon. **First order consumers**, such as aphids (left), feed directly on producers. **Second** (and higher) **order consumers**, such as ladybugs (center) feed on other consumers. **Detritivores** consume (ingest and digest) detritus (decomposing organic material) from every trophic level. In doing so, they contribute to decomposition and the recycling of nutrients. Common detritivores includes millipedes (right), woodlice, and many terrestrial worms.

Decomposers (fungi and some bacteria) obtain their energy and carbon from the extracellular breakdown of (usually dead) organic matter (DOM). Decomposers play a central role in nutrient cycling.

1. Describe the differences between **producers** and **consumers** with respect to their role in energy transfers:

_____

_____

2. With respect to energy flow, describe a major difference between a detrital and a grazing food web: _____

_____

_____

3. Distinguish between detritivores and decomposers with respect to how their contributions to nutrient cycling:

_____

_____

Related activities: *Energy Flow in an Ecosystem, Food Chains, Food Webs, Ecological Pyramids*

RA 1

Photosynthesis

Photosynthesis is of fundamental importance to living things because it transforms sunlight energy into chemical energy stored in molecules, releases free oxygen gas, and absorbs carbon dioxide (a waste product of cellular metabolism). Photosynthetic organisms use special pigments, called **chlorophylls**, to capture light energy by absorbing light of specific wavelengths. Visible light is a small fraction of the electromagnetic radiation reaching Earth from the Sun. Of this only wavelengths corresponding to red and blue are absorbed for photosynthesis. Other wavelengths, particularly green, are reflected or transmitted. Photosynthesis plays an important role in the cycling of carbon and oxygen, producing the oxygen used and removing the carbon dioxide produced during respiration of living organisms. It also helps fix carbon that may be buried and removed temporarily from the cycle.

Summary of Photosynthesis in a C₃ Plant

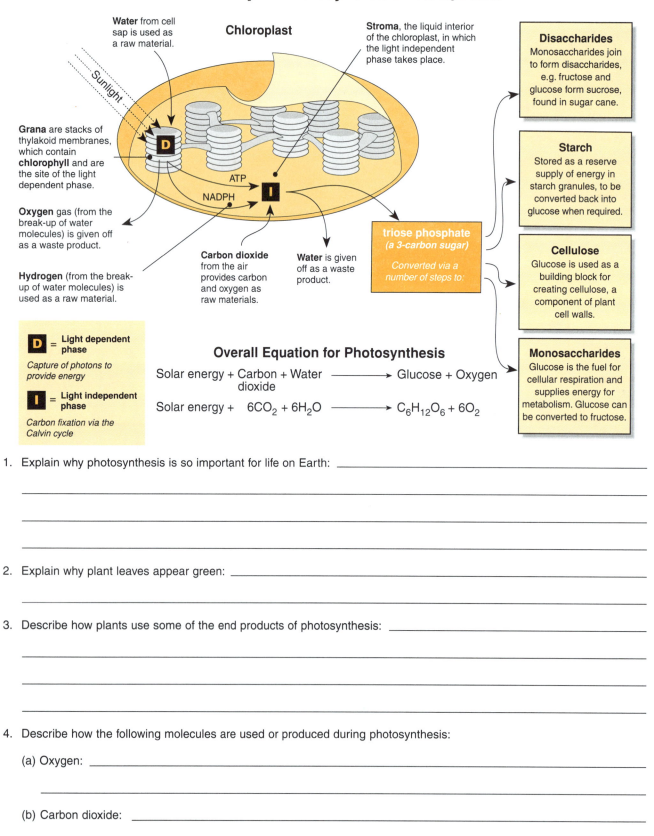

Water from cell sap is used as a raw material.

Chloroplast

Stroma, the liquid interior of the chloroplast, in which the light independent phase takes place.

Disaccharides
Monosaccharides join to form disaccharides, e.g. fructose and glucose form sucrose, found in sugar cane.

Sunlight

Grana are stacks of thylakoid membranes, which contain **chlorophyll** and are the site of the light dependent phase.

Oxygen gas (from the break-up of water molecules) is given off as a waste product.

Hydrogen (from the break-up of water molecules) is used as a raw material.

Carbon dioxide from the air provides carbon and oxygen as raw materials.

Water is given off as a waste product.

ATP

NADPH

triose phosphate
(a 3-carbon sugar)
Converted via a number of steps to:

Starch
Stored as a reserve supply of energy in starch granules, to be converted back into glucose when required.

Cellulose
Glucose is used as a building block for creating cellulose, a component of plant cell walls.

D = **Light dependent phase**
Capture of photons to provide energy

I = **Light independent phase**
Carbon fixation via the Calvin cycle

Overall Equation for Photosynthesis

Solar energy + Carbon dioxide + Water $\longrightarrow$ Glucose + Oxygen

Solar energy + $6CO_2 + 6H_2O \longrightarrow C_6H_{12}O_6 + 6O_2$

Monosaccharides
Glucose is the fuel for cellular respiration and supplies energy for metabolism. Glucose can be converted to fructose.

1. Explain why photosynthesis is so important for life on Earth: _____

_____

_____

_____

2. Explain why plant leaves appear green: _____

_____

3. Describe how plants use some of the end products of photosynthesis: _____

_____

_____

_____

4. Describe how the following molecules are used or produced during photosynthesis:

(a) Oxygen: _____

_____

(b) Carbon dioxide: _____

_____

Related activities: Primary Productivity

Periodicals: Photosynthesis: most hated topic?

Cellular Respiration

Cellular respiration is the process by which organisms break down energy rich molecules (e.g. glucose) to release the energy in a usable form (ATP). All living cells respire in order to exist, although the substrates they use may vary. **Aerobic respiration** requires oxygen. Forms of cellular respiration that do not require oxygen are said to be **anaerobic**. Some plants and animals can generate ATP anaerobically for short periods of time. Other organisms use only anaerobic respiration and live in oxygen-free environments. For these organisms, there is some other final electron acceptor other than oxygen (e.g. nitrate or Fe^{2+}). Respiration plays a part in the cycling of carbon by adding it to oxygen and releasing it to the atmosphere as carbon dioxide.

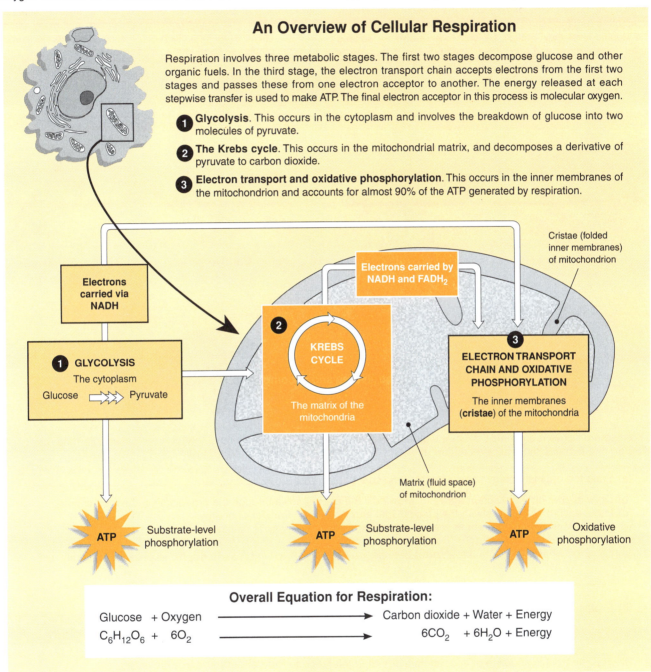

An Overview of Cellular Respiration

Respiration involves three metabolic stages. The first two stages decompose glucose and other organic fuels. In the third stage, the electron transport chain accepts electrons from the first two stages and passes these from one electron acceptor to another. The energy released at each stepwise transfer is used to make ATP. The final electron acceptor in this process is molecular oxygen.

1 **Glycolysis**. This occurs in the cytoplasm and involves the breakdown of glucose into two molecules of pyruvate.

2 **The Krebs cycle**. This occurs in the mitochondrial matrix, and decomposes a derivative of pyruvate to carbon dioxide.

3 **Electron transport and oxidative phosphorylation**. This occurs in the inner membranes of the mitochondrion and accounts for almost 90% of the ATP generated by respiration.

Electrons carried via NADH

Cristae (folded inner membranes) of mitochondrion

Electrons carried by NADH and $FADH_2$

1 GLYCOLYSIS
The cytoplasm
Glucose ⟹ Pyruvate

2 KREBS CYCLE
The matrix of the mitochondria

3 ELECTRON TRANSPORT CHAIN AND OXIDATIVE PHOSPHORYLATION
The inner membranes (**cristae**) of the mitochondria

Matrix (fluid space) of mitochondrion

ATP Substrate-level phosphorylation

ATP Substrate-level phosphorylation

ATP Oxidative phosphorylation

Overall Equation for Respiration:

Glucose + Oxygen ⟶ Carbon dioxide + Water + Energy

$$C_6H_{12}O_6 + 6O_2 \longrightarrow 6CO_2 + 6H_2O + Energy$$

1. Describe precisely in which part of the cell the following take place:

   (a) Glycolysis: _____

   (b) Krebs cycle reactions: _____

   (c) Electron transport chain: _____

2. (a) Name the usable end product of cellular respiration: _____

   (b) Explain the importance of this molecule: _____

   _____

   _____

Periodicals:
Fuelled for Life

Related activities: Food Chains

A 2

Ecosystems

Food Chains

Every ecosystem has a **trophic structure**: a hierarchy of feeding relationships that determines the pathways for energy flow and nutrient cycling. Organisms are assigned to **trophic levels** based on the way in which they obtain their energy. **Producers (autotrophs)** manufacture their own food from simple inorganic substances. This producer level ultimately supports all other levels. The **consumers** or **heterotrophs**, obtain their energy from other organisms. Consumers are ranked according to the trophic level they occupy, i.e. first order (primary), second order (secondary), and third order (tertiary). The sequence of organisms, each of which is a source of food for the next, is called a **food chain**. Energy flows through trophic levels rather inefficiently, with only 5-20% of usable energy being transferred to the subsequent level. For this reason, food chains seldom have more than six links. Those organisms whose food is obtained through the same number of links belong to the same trophic level. Note that some consumers may feed at several different trophic levels, and many primary consumers eat many plant species. The different food chains in an ecosystem therefore tend to form complex webs of interactions (**food webs**).

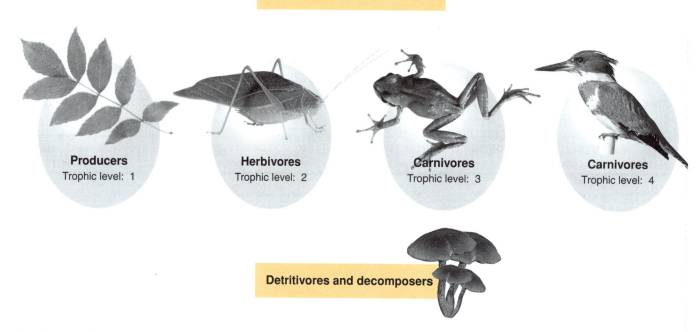

The diagram above represents the basic elements of a food chain. In the questions below, you are asked to add to the diagram the features that indicate the flow of energy through the community of organisms.

1. (a) State the original energy source for this food chain: _____

    (b) Draw arrows on the diagram above to show how the energy flows through the organisms in the food chain.
    (c) Label each of the arrows with the process that carries out this transfer of energy.
    (d) Draw arrows on the diagram to show how the energy is lost by way of respiration.

2. (a) Describe what happens to the **amount** of energy available to each successive trophic level in a food chain:

    _____

    (b) Explain why this is the case: _____

    _____

3. Discuss the trophic structure of ecosystems, including reference to **food chains** and **trophic** levels:

    _____

    _____

    _____

    _____

    _____

    _____

4. Explain what you could infer about the tropic level(s) of the kingfisher, if it was found to eat both katydids and frogs:

    _____

Food Webs

The organisms that inhabit lakes will vary from one location to the next. The organisms illustrated below are typical of those found in lakes. For the sake of simplicity, only fourteen organisms are represented here. Real lake communities may have hundreds of different species interacting together. Your task is to assemble the organisms below into a food web, in a way that illustrates their position in trophic levels and their relative positions in food chains. One part of the food web that is not

represented below is the **detritus**. Detritus is the accumulated debris of dead organisms from within the lake and washed in from the surrounding lake margins and streams. It contains the remains of land plants (such as leaves), algae, zooplankton, and larger animals that are in various stages of decay. The detritus forms a layer at the bottom of the lake that provides a rich food source for any animal that can exploit it.

Feeding Requirements of Lake Organisms

Daphnia
Small freshwater crustacean that forms part of the zooplankton. It feeds on planktonic algae by filtering them from the water with its limbs.

Autotrophic protists
e.g. Chlamydomonas, Euglena (pictured) Two of genera that form the phytoplankton (commonly called **algae** or "plant plankton").

Asplanchna (planktonic rotifer)
A large, carnivorous rotifer that feeds on protozoa and young zooplankton (e.g. *Daphnia*). Note that most rotifers are small herbivores.

Leech (*Glossiphonia*)
Leeches are fluid feeding predators of smaller invertebrates, including rotifers, small pond snails and worms.

Macrophytes (various species)
A variety of flowering aquatic plants are adapted for being submerged, free-floating, or growing at the lake margin.

Three-spined stickleback (*Gasterosteus*)
A common fish of freshwater ponds and lakes. It feeds mainly on small invertebrates such as *Daphnia* and insect larvae.

Diving beetle (*Dytiscus*)
Diving beetles feed on aquatic insect larvae and adult insects blown into the lake community. The will also eat organic detritus collected from the bottom mud.

Carp (*Cyprinus*)
A heavy bodied freshwater fish that feeds mainly on bottom living insect larvae and snails, but will also take some plant material (not algae).

Dragonfly larva
Large aquatic insect larvae that are voracious predators of small invertebrates including *Hydra*, *Daphnia*, other insect larvae, and leeches.

Great pond snail (*Limnaea*)
Omnivorous pond snail, eating both plant and animal material, living or dead, although the main diet is aquatic macrophytes.

Herbivorous water beetles (*e.g. Hydrophilus*)
Feed on water plants, although the young beetle larvae are carnivorous, feeding primarily on small pond snails.

Protozan (*e.g. Paramecium*)
Ciliated protozoa such as *Paramecium* feed primarily on bacteria and microscopic green algae such as *Chlamydomonas*.

Pike (*Esox lucius*)
A top ambush predator of all smaller fish and amphibians, although they are also opportunistic predators of rodents and small birds.

Mosquito larva
(*Culex* spp.)
The larvae of most mosquito species, e.g. *Culex*, feed on planktonic algae before passing through a pupal stage and undergoing metamorphosis into adult mosquitoes.

Hydra
A small carnivorous cnidarian that captures small prey items such as small *Daphnia* and insect larvae using its stinging cells on the tentacles.

1. From the information provided for the lake food web components on the previous page, construct **ten** different **food chains** (using their names only) to show the feeding relationships between the organisms. Some food chains may be shorter than others and most species will appear in more than one food chain. An example has been completed for you.

Example 1:

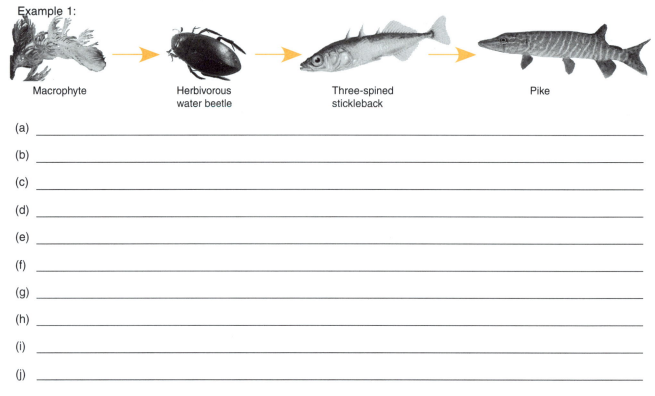

Macrophyte → Herbivorous water beetle → Three-spined stickleback → Pike

(a) _____

(b) _____

(c) _____

(d) _____

(e) _____

(f) _____

(g) _____

(h) _____

(i) _____

(j) _____

2. (a) Use the food chains that you have created above to help you to draw up a complete **food web** for this community. Use only the supplied information to draw arrows showing the flow of **energy** between species. (NOTE: Only energy **from** (not to) the detritus is required)

   (b) Label each species with the following codes to indicate its trophic level and status: Indicate:
   • Diet type: **P** = Producer, **H** = Herbivore, **C** = Carnivore, **O** = Omnivore (Note: based on the information given).
   • Position in the food chain as a consumer (1st, 2nd, 3rd, 4th order consumer): **1–4** (does not include producers).

   Example: Mosquito larva is **C2**

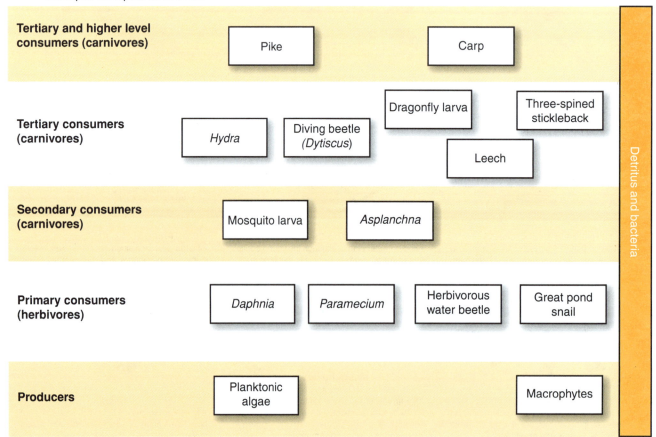

Energy Flow in an Ecosystem

The flow of energy through an ecosystem can be measured and analyzed. It provides some idea as to the energy trapped and passed on at each trophic level. Each trophic level in a food chain or web contains a certain amount of biomass: the dry weight of all organic matter contained in its organisms. Energy stored in biomass is transferred from one trophic level to another (by eating, defecation etc.), with some being lost as low-grade heat energy to the environment in each transfer. Three definitions are useful:

- **Gross primary production**: The total of organic material produced by plants (including that lost to respiration).
- **Net primary production**: The amount of biomass that is available to consumers at subsequent trophic levels.

- **Secondary production**: The amount of biomass at higher trophic levels (consumer production). Production figures are sometimes expressed as rates (productivity).

The percentage of energy transferred from one trophic level to the next varies between 5% and 20% and is called the **ecological efficiency** (efficiency of energy transfer). An average figure of 10% is often used. The path of energy flow in an ecosystem depends on its characteristics. In a tropical forest ecosystem, most of the primary production enters the detrital and decomposer food chains. However, in an ocean ecosystem or an intensively grazed pasture more than half the primary production may enter the grazing food chain.

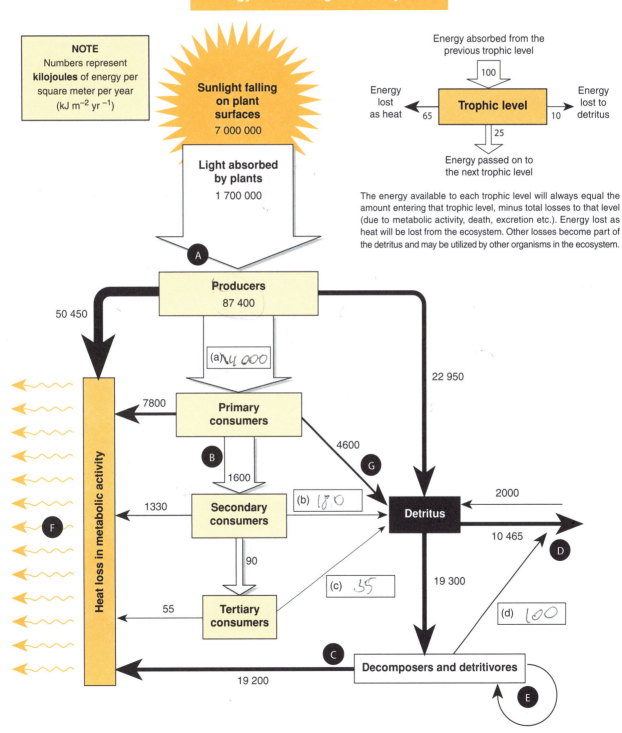

Energy Flow Through an Ecosystem

NOTE
Numbers represent **kilojoules** of energy per square meter per year
$(kJ\ m^{-2}\ yr^{-1})$

Sunlight falling on plant surfaces
7 000 000

Light absorbed by plants
1 700 000

A

Energy absorbed from the previous trophic level
100

Energy lost as heat 65 — **Trophic level** — 10 Energy lost to detritus

25

Energy passed on to the next trophic level

The energy available to each trophic level will always equal the amount entering that trophic level, minus total losses to that level (due to metabolic activity, death, excretion etc.). Energy lost as heat will be lost from the ecosystem. Other losses become part of the detritus and may be utilized by other organisms in the ecosystem.

Ecosystems

Producers
87 400

50 450

(a) 14 000

22 950

7800

Primary consumers

B

1600

4600

G

Heat loss in metabolic activity

F

1330

Secondary consumers

(b) 18.0

Detritus

2000

10 465

D

90

(c) 55

19 300

(d) 100

55

Tertiary consumers

C

19 200

Decomposers and detritivores

E

58

1. Study the diagram on the previous page illustrating energy flow through a hypothetical ecosystem. Use the example at the top of the page as a guide to calculate the missing values (a)–(d) in the diagram. Note that the sum of the energy inputs always equals the sum of the energy outputs. Place your answers in the spaces provided on the diagram.

2. Describe the original source of energy that powers this ecosystem: _sunlight_

3. Identify the processes that are occurring at the points labelled **A – G** on the diagram:

   A. _Photosynthesis_   E. _Top carnivores_

   B. _Herbivores_   F. _Heat (lose)_

   C. _Decomposers_   G. _cellular respiration_

   D. _Energy export_

4. (a) Calculate the percentage of light energy falling on the plants that is absorbed at point **A**:

   Light absorbed by plants ÷ sunlight falling on plant surfaces x 100 = _246_

   (b) Describe what happens to the light energy that is not absorbed: _It just loses_
   via the heat

5. (a) Calculate the percentage of light energy absorbed that is actually converted (fixed) into producer energy:

   Producers ÷ light absorbed by plants x 100 = _5%_

   (b) State the **amount** of light energy absorbed that is **not** fixed: _1612600_

   (c) Account for the difference between the amount of energy absorbed and the amount actually fixed by producers:

   _1612600_

6. Of the total amount of energy **fixed** by producers in this ecosystem (at point **A**) calculate:

   (a) The total amount that ended up as metabolic waste heat (in kJ): _____

   (b) The percentage of the energy fixed that ended up as waste heat: _____

7. (a) State the groups for which detritus is an energy source: _____

   (b) Describe by what means detritus could be removed or added to an ecosystem: _____

8. In certain conditions, detritus will build up in an environment where few (or no) decomposers can exist.

   (a) Describe the consequences of this lack of decomposer activity to the energy flow:

   _____

   (b) Add an additional arrow to the diagram on the previous page to illustrate your answer.

   (c) Describe three examples of materials that have resulted from a lack of decomposer activity on detrital material:

   _____

9. The **ten percent law** states that the total energy content of a trophic level in an ecosystem is only about one-tenth (or 10%) that of the preceding level. For each of the trophic levels in the diagram on the preceding page, determine the amount of energy passed on to the next trophic level as a percentage:

   (a) Producer to primary consumer: _____

   (b) Primary consumer to secondary consumer: _____

   (c) Secondary consumer to tertiary consumer: _____

Ecological Pyramids

The trophic levels of any ecosystem can be arranged in pyramid of increasing trophic level. The first trophic level is placed at the bottom and subsequent trophic levels are stacked on top in their 'feeding sequence'. Ecological pyramids can illustrate changes in the numbers, biomass (weight), or energy content of organisms at each level. Each of these three kinds of pyramids tells us something different about the flow of energy and movement of materials between one trophic level and the next. The type of pyramid you choose in order to express information about an ecosystem will depend on what particular features of the ecosystem you are interested in and, of course, the type of data you have collected.

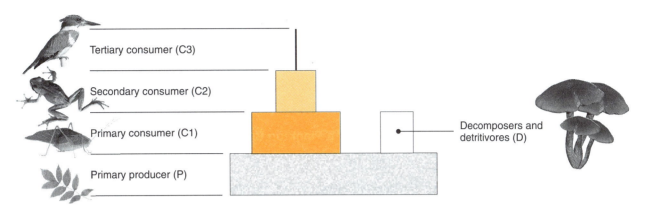

Tertiary consumer (C3)
Secondary consumer (C2)
Primary consumer (C1)
Primary producer (P)
Decomposers and detritivores (D)

The generalized ecological pyramid pictured above shows a conventional pyramid shape, with a large number (or biomass) of producers forming the base for an increasingly small number (or biomass) of consumers. Decomposers are placed at the level of the primary consumers and off to the side. They may obtain energy from many different trophic levels and so do not fit into the conventional pyramid structure. For any particular ecosystem at any one time (e.g. the forest ecosystem below), the shape of this typical pyramid can vary greatly depending on whether the trophic relationships are expressed as numbers, biomass or energy.

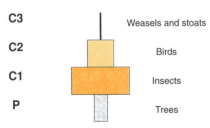

C3 — Weasels and stoats
C2 — Birds
C1 — Insects
P — Trees

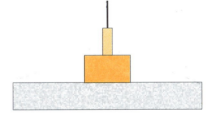

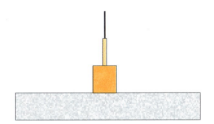

Numbers in a forest community

Pyramids of numbers display the number of individual organisms at each trophic level. The pyramid above has few producers, but they may be of a very large size (e.g. trees). This gives an 'inverted pyramid' although not all pyramids of numbers are like this.

Biomass in a forest community

Biomass pyramids measure the 'weight' of biological material at each trophic level. Water content of organisms varies, so 'dry weight' is often used. Organism size is taken into account, so meaningful comparisons of different trophic levels are possible.

Energy in a forest community

Pyramids of energy are often very similar to biomass pyramids. The energy content at each trophic level is generally comparable to the biomass (i.e. similar amounts of dry biomass tend to have about the same energy content).

1. Describe what the three types of ecological pyramids measure:

   (a) Number pyramid: _____

   (b) Biomass pyramid: _____

   (c) Energy pyramid: _____

2. Explain the advantage of using a biomass or energy pyramid rather than a pyramid of numbers to express the relationship between different trophic levels:

   _____

   _____

   _____

3. Explain why it is possible for the forest community (on the next page) to have very few producers supporting a large number of consumers:

   _____

   _____

Ecosystems

Related activities: Food Chains, Food Webs, Energy Flow in an Ecosystem

DA 2

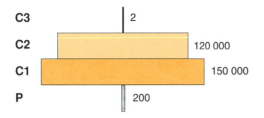

Pyramid of numbers: forest community

In a forest community a few producers may support a large number of consumers. This is due to the large size of the producers; large trees can support many individual consumer organisms. The example above shows the numbers at each trophic level for an oak forest in England, in an area of 10 m².

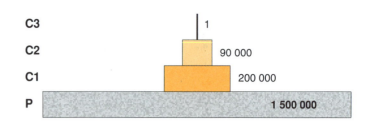

Pyramid of numbers: grassland community

In a grassland community a large number of producers are required to support a much smaller number of consumers. This is due to the small size of the producers. Grass plants can support only a few individual consumer organisms and take time to recover from grazing pressure. The example above shows the numbers at each trophic level for a derelict grassland area (10 m²) in Michigan, United States.

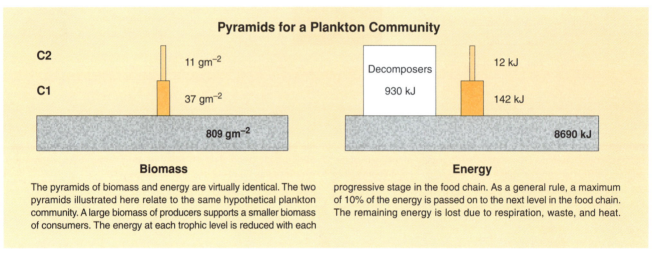

Pyramids for a Plankton Community

Biomass

Energy

The pyramids of biomass and energy are virtually identical. The two pyramids illustrated here relate to the same hypothetical plankton community. A large biomass of producers supports a smaller biomass of consumers. The energy at each trophic level is reduced with each progressive stage in the food chain. As a general rule, a maximum of 10% of the energy is passed on to the next level in the food chain. The remaining energy is lost due to respiration, waste, and heat.

4. Determine the **energy transfer** between trophic levels in the plankton community example in the above diagram:

   (a) Between producers and the primary consumers: _____

   (b) Between the primary consumers and the secondary consumers: _____

   (c) Explain why the energy passed on from the producer to primary consumers is considerably less than the normally expected 10% occurring in most other communities (describe where the rest of the energy was lost to):

   _____

   _____

   (d) After the producers, which trophic group has the greatest energy content: _____

   (e) Give a likely explanation why this is the case: _____

   _____

   _____

An unusual biomass pyramid

The biomass pyramids of some ecosystems appear rather unusual with an inverted shape. The first trophic level has a lower biomass than the second level. What this pyramid does not show is the rate at which the producers (algae) are reproducing in order to support the larger biomass of consumers.

| Zooplankton and bottom fauna | 21 gm⁻² |
| Algae | 4 gm⁻² |

Biomass

5. Give a possible explanation of how a small biomass of producers (algae) can support a larger biomass of consumers (zooplankton):

_____

_____

_____

Primary Productivity

The energy entering ecosystems is fixed by producers in photosynthesis. The rate of photosynthesis is dependent on factors such as temperature and the amount of light, water, and nutrients. The total energy fixed by a plant through photosynthesis is referred to as the **gross primary production** (GPP) and is usually expressed as Jm^{-2} (or kJm^{-2}), or as gm^{-2}. However, a portion of this energy is required by the plant for respiration. Subtracting respiration from GPP gives the **net primary production** (NPP). The **rate** of biomass production, or **net primary productivity**, is the biomass produced per area per unit time.

Measuring Productivity

Primary productivity of an ecosystem depends on a number of interrelated factors (light intensity, nutrients, temperature, water, and mineral supplies), making its calculation extremely difficult. Globally, the least productive ecosystems are those that are limited by heat energy and water. The most productive ecosystems are systems with high temperatures, plenty of water, and non-limiting supplies of soil nitrogen. The primary productivity of oceans is lower than that of terrestrial ecosystems because the water reflects (or absorbs) much of the light energy before it reaches and is utilized by producers. The table below compares the difference in the net primary productivity of various ecosystems.

Ecosystem Type	Net Primary Productivity	
	kcal m^{-2} y^{-1}	kJ m^{-2} y^{-1}
Tropical rainforest	15 000	63 000
Swamps and marshes	12 000	50 400
Estuaries	9000	37 800
Savanna	3000	12 600
Temperate forest	6000	25 200
Boreal forest	3500	14 700
Temperate grassland	2000	8400
Tundra/cold desert	500	2100
Coastal marine	2500	10 500
Open ocean	800	3360
Desert	< 200	< 840

* Data compiled from a variety of sources.

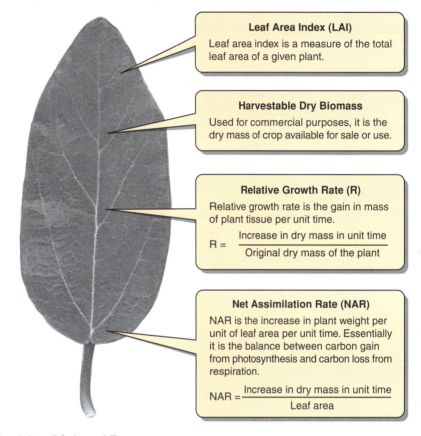

Leaf Area Index (LAI)
Leaf area index is a measure of the total leaf area of a given plant.

Harvestable Dry Biomass
Used for commercial purposes, it is the dry mass of crop available for sale or use.

Relative Growth Rate (R)
Relative growth rate is the gain in mass of plant tissue per unit time.

$$R = \frac{\text{Increase in dry mass in unit time}}{\text{Original dry mass of the plant}}$$

Net Assimilation Rate (NAR)
NAR is the increase in plant weight per unit of leaf area per unit time. Essentially it is the balance between carbon gain from photosynthesis and carbon loss from respiration.

$$NAR = \frac{\text{Increase in dry mass in unit time}}{\text{Leaf area}}$$

Net Primary Productivity of Selected Ecosystems (figures are in kJ m^{-2} y^{-1})

< 2500	< 12 500 – 42 000	< 42 000 – 105 000	2500 – 42 000
Arid desert	Temperate forest	Tropical rain forest	Continental shelf waters
Polar tundra and ice desert	Grassland agriculture	Intensive horticulture	Open ocean

1. Briefly describe three factors that may affect the primary productivity of an ecosystem:

    (a) _____

    (b) _____

    (c) _____

2. Explain the difference between **productivity** and **production** in relation to plants: _____

    _____

    _____

3. Suggest how the LAI might influence the rate of primary production: _____

_____

4. Using the data table on the previous page, choose a suitable graph format and plot the differences in the net primary productivity of various ecosystems (use either of the data columns provided, but not both). Use the grid provided, right. Include a title and axes.

5. With reference to the graph:

   (a) Suggest why tropical rainforests are among the most productive terrestrial ecosystems, while tundra and desert ecosystems are among the least productive:

   _____

   _____

   _____

   _____

   _____

   _____

   (b) Suggest why, amongst aquatic ecosystems, the NPP of the open ocean is low relative to that of coastal systems:

   _____

   _____

   _____

6. Estimating the NPP is relatively simple: all the plant material (including root material) from a measured area (e.g. 1 m^2) is collected and dried (at 105°C) until it reaches a constant mass. This mass, called the **standing crop**, is recorded (in kg m^{-2}). The procedure is repeated after some set time period (e.g. 1 month). The difference between the two calculated masses represents the *estimated* NPP:

   (a) Explain why the plant material was dried before weighing: _____

   _____

   (b) Define the term **standing crop**: _____

   (c) Suggest why this procedure only provides an estimate of NPP: _____

   _____

   (d) State what extra information would be required in order to express the standing crop value in kJ m^{-2}: _____

   _____

   (e) Suggest what information would be required in order to calculate the GPP: _____

   _____

7. Intensive horticultural systems achieve very high rates of production (about 10X those of subsistence systems).

   (a) Outline the means by which these high rates are achieved: _____

   _____

   (b) Comment on the sustainability of these high rates (summary of a group discussion if you wish): _____

   _____

   _____

   _____

KEY TERMS: Mix and Match

INSTRUCTIONS: Test your vocabulary by matching each term to its definition, as identified by its preceding letter code.

ABIOTIC FACTORS

BIOME

BIOSPHERE

BIOTIC FACTORS

COMMUNITY

CONSUMER

DETRITIVORE

ECOLOGICAL NICHE

ECOLOGY

ECOSYSTEM

ENVIRONMENT

FOOD CHAIN

FOOD WEB

HABITAT

INTERSPECIFIC

INTRASPECIFIC

MICROHABITAT

PHOTOSYNTHESIS

POPULATION

PRODUCER

REALIZED NICHE

RESPIRATION

SAPROTROPH

SPECIES

TROPHIC LEVEL

A The niche size that is actually occupied by an organism or species and is usually, as a result of competition, narrower than it could potentially occupy.

B A complex series of interactions showing the feeding relationships between organisms in an ecosystem.

C A naturally occurring association of different species living within the same environment and interacting together.

D Factors that include all living things within an environment. E.g. consumers, producers.

E The area surrounding the Earth in which life is able to exist.

F The study of the distribution, abundance and interrelationships of organisms and their interactions with the environment.

G An organism that obtains its carbon and energy from other organisms.

H The total number of individuals of a species within a set habitat or area.

I A major regional ecological community.

J The functional role of an organism or a species in the ecosystem, including its relationships with other species.

K Interactions occurring between different species.

L A group of related individuals able to breed together to produce viable offspring.

M A sequence of steps describing how an organism derives energy from the ones before it.

N The part of the environment which an organism occupies, e.g. stream or grassland.

O Interactions occurring between members of the same species.

P An organism that obtains energy from dead material by extracellular digestion.

Q The surroundings in which an organism lives, including biotic and abiotic factors.

R A subdivision of a habitat that possesses its own specific features.

S A community of interacting organisms and the environment (both biotic and abiotic) in which they both live and interact.

T An autotrophic organism, usually a photosynthetic plant. Synthesizes organic matter from inorganic matter.

U Any non-living (chemical or physical) part of the environment, e.g. wind, rain, temperature.

V An organism the feeds on decaying matter (detritus).

W Process by which gases (O_2 and CO_2) are exchanged between an organism and its surroundings.

X The biochemical process that uses light energy to convert carbon dioxide and water into glucose molecules and oxygen.

Y Any of the feeding levels that energy passes through as it proceeds through the ecosystem.

Ecosystems

Natural Ecosystem Change

Key concepts

▶ Nutrients and elements constantly cycle through the ecosystem in a complex series of reactions and interactions.

▶ Microbial activity plays fundamental roles in biogeochemical cycling.

▶ Ecological succession is a natural process by which an ecosystem changes over time.

▶ Ecological change can involve both small and large scales and occur over short or long time spans.

Key terms

biogeochemical cycling
carbon cycle
climax community
cultural eutrophication
denitrifying bacteria
decomposer
eutrophication
hydrological cycle
keystone species
nitrifying bacteria
nitrogen cycle
nitrogen-fixing bacteria
nutrient cycling
phosphorus cycle
pioneer species
primary succession
resilience
secondary succession
sere
stability
sulfur cycle

Objectives

☐ 1. Use the **KEY TERMS** to help you understand and complete these objectives.

Biogeochemical Cycles   pages 65-73

☐ 2. Describe the **carbon cycle**, using arrows to show the direction of nutrient flow and labels to identify the processes involved. Describe how human activity may intervene in various aspects of the carbon cycle.

☐ 3. Describe the **nitrogen cycle**, using arrows to show the direction of nutrient flow. Describe the processes involved and the role of microorgansims in the cycle. Describe how human activity may intervene in the nitrogen cycle.

☐ 4. Identify and explain the role of **nitrifying bacteria**, **nitrogen-fixing bacteria** and **denitrifying bacteria** in the nitrogen cycle.

☐ 5. Describe the processes involved in nitrogen pollution and the environmental effects of nitrogen, including **eutrophication**.

☐ 6. Explain how **cultural eutrophication** is the acceleration of a natural process caused by human activities such as fertilizer use and effluent discharge.

☐ 7. Describe the **phosphorus cycle**, using arrows to show the direction of nutrient flow. Describe the processes involved and the role of microorganisms in the cycle. Contrast the phosphorus cycle with other biogeochemical cycles.

☐ 8. Describe the **sulfur cycle**. Identify the forms of sulfur at various stages. Use arrows to show the direction of nutrient flow and labels to identify the processes involved.

☐ 9. Describe the **hydrological** (water) **cycle**. Understand the way in which water is cycled between various reservoirs and describe the major processes involved including evaporation, condensation, precipitation and run-off.

Ecosystem Stability   pages 74-79

☐ 10. Explain how an **ecosystem**'s stability is related to its diversity, including reference to **keystone species**.

☐ 11. Use examples to help describe the process of **primary succession**, including the role of **pioneer species** (colonizing) and the characteristics of a **climax community**.

☐ 12. Use examples to help describe the process of **secondary succession** and characteristics that distinguish it from primary succession.

Periodicals:
Listings for this chapter are on page 230

Weblinks:
www.thebiozone.com/
weblink/EnvSci-2764.html

Presentation Media
Environmental Science: Ecosystems

The Carbon Cycle

Carbon is an essential element in living systems, providing the chemical framework to form the molecules that make up living organisms (e.g. proteins, carbohydrates, fats, and nucleic acids). Carbon also makes up approximately 0.03% of the atmosphere as the gas carbon dioxide (CO_2), and it is present in the ocean as carbonate and bicarbonate, and in rocks such as limestone. Carbon cycles between the living (biotic) and non-living (abiotic) environment: it is fixed in the process of photosynthesis and returned to the atmosphere in respiration. Carbon may remain locked up in biotic or abiotic systems for long periods of time as, for example, in the wood of trees or in fossil fuels such as coal or oil. Human activity has disturbed the balance of the carbon cycle (the global carbon budget) through activities such as combustion (e.g. the burning of wood and **fossil fuels**) and deforestation.

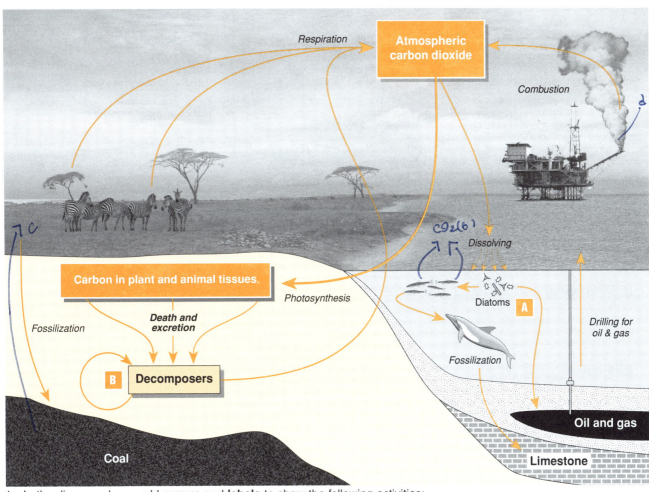

1. In the diagram above, add **arrows** and **labels** to show the following activities:

   (a) Dissolving of limestone by acid rain   (c) Mining and burning of coal
   (b) Release of carbon from the marine food chain   (d) Burning of plant material.

2. Describe the **biological origin** of the following geological deposits:

   (a) Coal: _Swamp forest fell into stagnant water, didn't decay, compressed._

   (b) Oil: _oxygen and organic materials falls, then covered by sediment pressure temperature = oil_

   (c) Limestone: _billions tiny shells compressed together._

3. Describe the two processes that release carbon into the atmosphere: _1) with Carbon Dioxide by respiration. 2) Through the decay of animal and plant matter._

4. Name the four geological reservoirs (sinks), in the diagram above, that can act as a source of carbon:

   (a) _Limestone_   (c) _Coal_

   (b) _Atmospheric carbon dioxide_   (d) _Oil_

5. (a) Identify the process carried out by diatoms at point [**A**]: _Photosynthesis_

   (b) Identify the process carried out by decomposers at [**B**]: _Respiration_

Periodicals:
The carbon cycle

Related activities: Oil, Coal, Global Warming

A 2

Natural Ecosystem Change

Termite mound in rainforest

Dung beetle on cow pat

Bracket fungus on tree trunk

Termites: These insects play an important role in nutrient recycling. With the aid of symbiotic protozoans and bacteria in their guts, they can digest the tough cellulose of woody tissues in trees. Termites fulfill a vital function in breaking down the endless rain of debris in tropical rainforests.

Dung beetles: Beetles play a major role in the decomposition of animal dung. Some beetles merely eat the dung, but true dung beetles, such as the scarabs and *Geotrupes*, bury the dung and lay their eggs in it to provide food for the beetle grubs during their development.

Fungi: Together with decomposing bacteria, fungi perform an important role in breaking down dead plant matter in the leaf litter of forests. Some mycorrhizal fungi have been found to link up to the root systems of trees where an exchange of nutrients occurs (a mutualistic relationship).

6. Predict the consequences to carbon cycling if there were no decomposers present in an ecosystem:

There won't be any materials. Would probably really mess up the carbon cycle Because there's no way to get carbon back

7. Explain how each of the three organisms listed below has a role to play in the carbon cycle:

(a) Dung beetles: They eat materials and then lay their eggs, which provides food for beetle.

(b) Termites: digging cellars in plants letting carbon get back into ecosystem

(c) Fungi: Break down died organisms, letting carbon go out

8. Using specific examples, explain the role of insects in carbon cycling: When insects respirate or die, they release carbon dioxide

9. In natural circumstances, accumulated reserves of carbon such as peat, coal and oil represent a **sink** or natural diversion from the cycle. Eventually the carbon in these sinks returns to the cycle through the action of geological processes which return deposits to the surface for oxidation.

(a) Describe the effects human activity on the amount of carbon stored in sinks:

Break balance of CO_2 balance

(b) Describe two **global effects** of this activity: Human activity releases too much CO_2, also events such as volcano explosions can change CO_2 into atmosphere

(c) Suggest what could be done to prevent or alleviate these effects: Decrease usage of oil and gas, decrease fabrical production

The Nitrogen Cycle

Nitrogen is a crucial element for all living things, forming an essential part of the structure of proteins and nucleic acids. The Earth's atmosphere is about 80% nitrogen gas (N_2), but molecular nitrogen is so stable that it is only rarely available directly to organisms and is often in short supply in biological systems. Bacteria play an important role in transferring nitrogen between the biotic and abiotic environments. Some bacteria are able to fix atmospheric nitrogen, while others convert ammonia to nitrate and thus make it available for incorporation into plant and animal tissues. Nitrogen-fixing bacteria are found living freely in the soil (Azotobacter) and living symbiotically with some plants in root nodules (Rhizobium). Lightning discharges also cause the oxidation of nitrogen gas to nitrate which ends up in the soil. Denitrifying bacteria reverse this activity and return fixed nitrogen to the atmosphere. Humans intervene in the nitrogen cycle by producing, and applying to the land, large amounts of nitrogen fertilizer. Some applied fertilizer is from organic sources (e.g. green crops and manures) but much of it is inorganic, produced from atmospheric nitrogen using an energy-expensive industrial process. Overuse of nitrogen fertilizers may lead to excessive nutrient enrichment of water. This human-induced enrichment and the increase in productivity associated with it, which includes excessive bacterial and algal growth, is called **cultural eutrophication**.

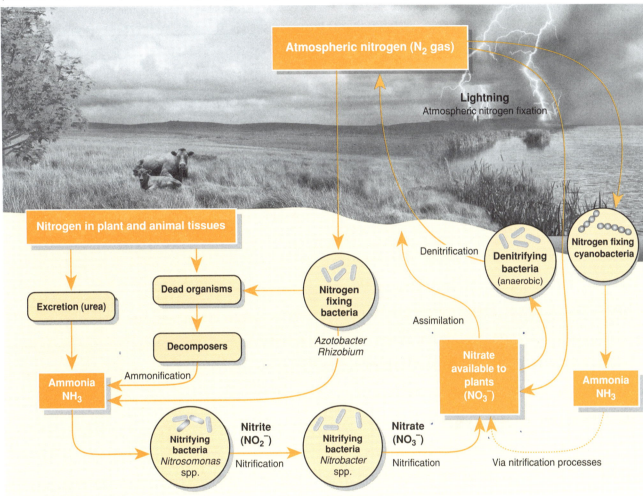

1. Describe five instances in the nitrogen cycle where **bacterial** action is important. Include the name of each of the processes and the changes to the form of nitrogen involved:

(a) ___1) Intrefying bacteria.___

(b) ___Nitrogen process___

(c) ___Azotospher___

(d) ___Nautrification (NO₂)___

(e) ___Nautrification (NO₃)___

Periodicals: Microbes and nitrogen cycling

Related activities: Soil Degradation, Water Pollution
Weblinks: Nitrogen Cycle Animation

RA 3

Natural Ecosystem Change

Nitrogen Fixation in Root Nodules

Root nodules are a root **symbiosis** between a higher plant and a bacterium. The bacteria fix atmospheric nitrogen and are extremely important to the nutrition of many plants, including the economically important legume family. Root nodules are extensions of the root tissue caused by entry of a bacterium. In legumes, this bacterium is *Rhizobium*. Other bacterial genera are involved in the root nodule symbioses in non-legume species.

The bacteria in these symbioses live in the nodule where they fix atmospheric nitrogen and provide the plant with most, or all, of its nitrogen requirements. In return, they have access to a rich supply of carbohydrate. The fixation of atmospheric nitrogen to ammonia occurs within the nodule, using the enzyme **nitrogenase**. Nitrogenase is inhibited by oxygen and the nodule provides a low O_2 environment in which fixation can occur.

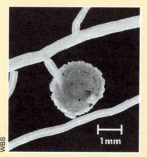 

1 mm

WBS

Two examples of legume nodules caused by *Rhizobium*. The photographs above show the size of a single nodule (left), and the nodules forming clusters around the roots of *Acacia* (right).

Human Intervention in the Nitrogen Cycle

Until about sixty years ago, microbial nitrogen fixation (left) was the only mechanism by which nitrogen could be made available to plants. However, during WW II, Fritz Haber developed the **Haber process** whereby nitrogen and hydrogen gas are combined to form gaseous ammonia. The ammonia is converted into ammonium salts and sold as inorganic fertilizer. Its application has revolutionized agriculture by increasing crop yields.

As well as adding nitrogen fertilizers to the land, humans use anaerobic bacteria to break down livestock wastes and release NH_3 into the soil. They also intervene in the nitrogen cycle by discharging **effluent** into waterways. Nitrogen is removed from the land through burning, which releases nitrogen oxides into the atmosphere. It is also lost by mining, harvesting crops, and irrigation, which leaches nitrate ions from the soil.

Two examples of human intervention in the nitrogen cycle. The photographs above show the aerial application of a commercial fertilizer (left), and the harvesting of an agricultural crop (right).

2. Identify three processes that **fix** atmospheric nitrogen:

(a) _Haber_   (b) _dicarBoration_   (c) _lighting_

3. Identify the process that releases nitrogen gas into the atmosphere: _Neutralisation_

4. Identify the main geological reservoir that provides a source of nitrogen: _Atmospher_

5. Identify the form in which nitrogen is available to most plants: _Nitrate_

6. Identify a vital organic compound that plants need nitrogen containing ions for: _Amonia_

7. Describe how animals acquire the nitrogen they need: _Harvesting agreculture._

8. Explain why farmers may plow a crop of legumes into the ground rather than harvest it: ___
Restoring soil to improve it structure

9. Describe five ways in which humans may intervene in the nitrogen cycle and the effects of these interventions:

(a) _To produce great deal of nitrogen fertilizers to the soil._

(b) _To break down wastes using anaethatic bacteria_

(c) _____

(d) _____

(e) _____

Nitrogen Pollution

The effect of excess nitrogen compounds on the environment is varied. Depending on the compound formed, nitrogen can cause smog in cities or algal blooms in lakes and seas. Nitrogen gas makes up almost 80% of the atmosphere but is unreactive at normal pressure and temperature. At the high pressures and temperatures reached in factories and combustion engines nitrogen gas forms nitric oxide along with other nitrogen oxides, most of which contribute to atmospheric pollution. Nitrates in fertilizers are washed into ground water by rain and slowly make their way to lakes and rivers and eventually out to sea. This process can take time to become noticeable as ground water can take many decades to reach a waterway. In many places where nitrate effects are only just becoming apparent, the immediate cessation of their use could take a long time to have any effect as it might take many years before the last of the ground water carrying the nitrates reaches a waterway.

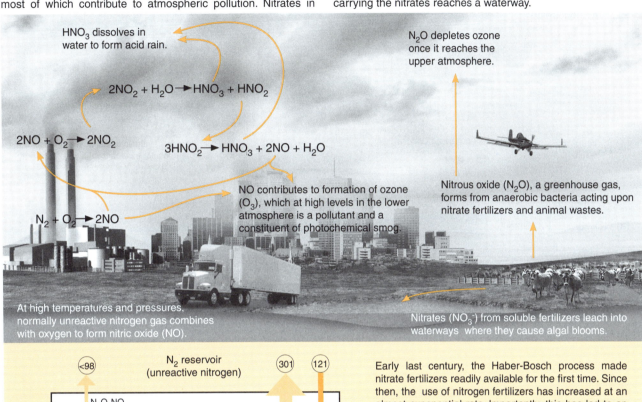

HNO$_3$ dissolves in water to form acid rain.

N$_2$O depletes ozone once it reaches the upper atmosphere.

$$2NO_2 + H_2O \rightarrow HNO_3 + HNO_2$$

$$2NO + O_2 \rightarrow 2NO_2$$

$$3HNO_2 \rightarrow HNO_3 + 2NO + H_2O$$

$$N_2 + O_2 \rightarrow 2NO$$

NO contributes to formation of ozone (O$_3$), which at high levels in the lower atmosphere is a pollutant and a constituent of photochemical smog.

Nitrous oxide (N$_2$O), a greenhouse gas, forms from anaerobic bacteria acting upon nitrate fertilizers and animal wastes.

At high temperatures and pressures, normally unreactive nitrogen gas combines with oxygen to form nitric oxide (NO).

Nitrates (NO$_3^-$) from soluble fertilizers leach into waterways where they cause algal blooms.

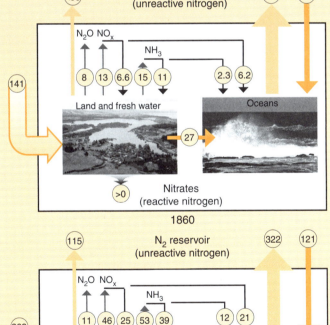

1860

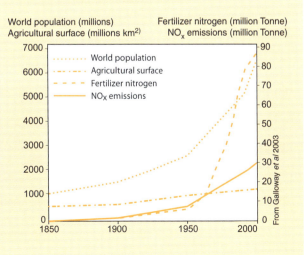

Changes in nitrogen inputs and outputs between 1860 and 1995 in millions of tonnes (modified from Galloway *et al* 2004)

Early last century, the Haber-Bosch process made nitrate fertilizers readily available for the first time. Since then, the use of nitrogen fertilizers has increased at an almost exponential rate. Importantly, this has led to an increase in the levels of nitrogen in land and water by up to 60 times those of 100 years ago. This extra nitrogen load is one of the causes of human-induced accelerated enrichment (**cultural eutrophication**) of lakes and coastal waters. An increase in algal production also results in higher decomposer activity and, consequently, oxygen depletion, fish deaths, and depletion of aquatic biodiversity. Many aquatic microorganisms also produce toxins, which may accumulate in the water, fish, and shellfish. The diagrams (left) show the increase in nitrates in water sources from 1860 to 1995. The rate at which nitrates are added has increased faster than the rate at which nitrates are returned to the atmosphere as unreactive N$_2$ gas. This has led to the widespread accumulation of nitrogen.

Natural Ecosystem Change

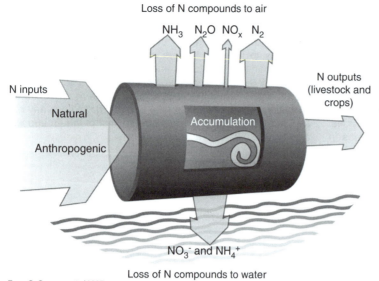

Loss of N compounds to air

NH_3 N_2O NO_x N_2

N inputs

Natural

Anthropogenic

Accumulation

N outputs (livestock and crops)

NO_3^- and NH_4^+

Loss of N compounds to water

From O. Oenema *et al* 2007

The "hole in the pipe" model (left) demonstrates inefficiencies in nitrogen fertilizer use. Nitrogen that is added to the soil and not immediately taken up by plants is washed into waterways or released into the air by bacterial action. These losses can be minimized to an extent by using slow release fertilizers during periods of wet weather and by careful irrigation practices.

Algal blooms

Satellite photo of algal blooms around Florida. Excessive nitrogen contributes to algal blooms in both coastal and inlands waters. *Image: NASA*

1. Describe the effect each of the following nitrogen compounds have on air and water quality:

   (a) NO: _Formation of the Ozon, which is high lavls in the lowe-atmosphere apollutant_

   (b) N_2O: _Animal wastes are Fretelizers_

   (c) NO_2: _Formation of photochemical smog_

   (d) NO_3^-: _Cases deal to the water habitat_

2. Explain why the formation of NO can cause large scale and long term environmental problems: _It can cause acid rain, which will Bring damage to the envirmomental._

3. Explain why an immediate halt in the use of nitrogen fertilizers will not cause an immediate stop in their effects: _Because parts of it still countinue excisting in the sal._

4. (a) Calculate the increase in nitrogen deposition in the oceans from 1860 to 1995 and compare this to the increase in release of nitrogen from the oceans:

   _____

   (b) Describe the effect these increases are having on the oceans: _Cultural ._

   _____

5. (a) Explain why nitrogen inputs tend to be so much more than outputs in livestock and crops: _____

   _____

   (b) Suggest how the nitrogen losses could be minimized: _____

   _____

   _____

The Hydrological Cycle

The hydrological cycle (water cycle), collects, purifies, and distributes the Earth's fixed supply of water. The main processes in this water recycling are described below. Besides replenishing inland water supplies, rainwater causes erosion and is a major medium for transporting dissolved nutrients within and among ecosystems. On a global scale, evaporation (conversion of water to gaseous water vapor) exceeds precipitation (rain, snow etc.) over the oceans. This results in a net movement of water vapor (carried by winds) over the land. On land, precipitation exceeds evaporation. Some of this precipitation becomes locked up in snow and ice, for varying lengths of time. Most forms surface and groundwater systems that flow back to the sea, completing the major part of the cycle. Living organisms, particularly plants, participate to varying degrees in the hydrological cycle. Over the sea, most of the water vapor is due to evaporation alone. However on land, about 90% of the vapor results from plant transpiration. Animals (particularly humans) intervene in the cycle by utilizing the resource for their own needs.

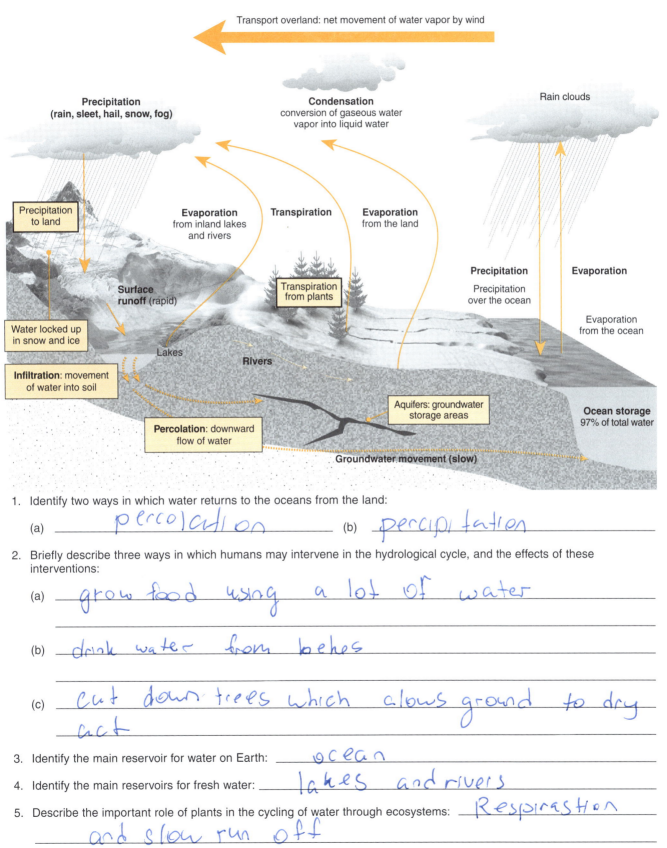

Transport overland: net movement of water vapor by wind

1. Identify two ways in which water returns to the oceans from the land:

    (a) _percolation_

    (b) _percipitation_

2. Briefly describe three ways in which humans may intervene in the hydrological cycle, and the effects of these interventions:

    (a) _grow food using a lot of water_

    (b) _drink water from lakes_

    (c) _cut down trees which alows ground to dry act_

3. Identify the main reservoir for water on Earth: _ocean_

4. Identify the main reservoirs for fresh water: _lakes and rivers_

5. Describe the important role of plants in the cycling of water through ecosystems: _Respirastion and slow run off_

Related activities: Global Water Resources, Water and People, Water and Industry, Water Pollution

Natural Ecosystem Change

A 2

The Phosphorus Cycle

Phosphorus is an essential component of nucleic acids and ATP. Unlike carbon, phosphorus has no atmospheric component; cycling of phosphorus is very slow and tends to be local. Small losses from terrestrial systems by leaching are generally balanced by gains from weathering. In aquatic and terrestrial ecosystems, phosphorus is cycled through food webs. Bacterial decomposition breaks down the remains of dead organisms and excreted products. Phosphatizing bacteria further break down these products and return phosphates to the soil. Phosphorus is lost from ecosystems through run-off, precipitation, and sedimentation. Sedimentation may lock phosphorus away but, in the much longer term, it can become available again through processes such as geological uplift. Some phosphorus returns to the land as **guano**; phosphate-rich manure (typically of fish eating birds). This return is small though compared with the phosphate transferred to the oceans each year by natural processes and human activity. Excess phosphorus entering water bodies through runoff is a major contributor to **eutrophication** and excessive algal and weed growth, primarily because phosphorus is often limiting in aquatic systems.

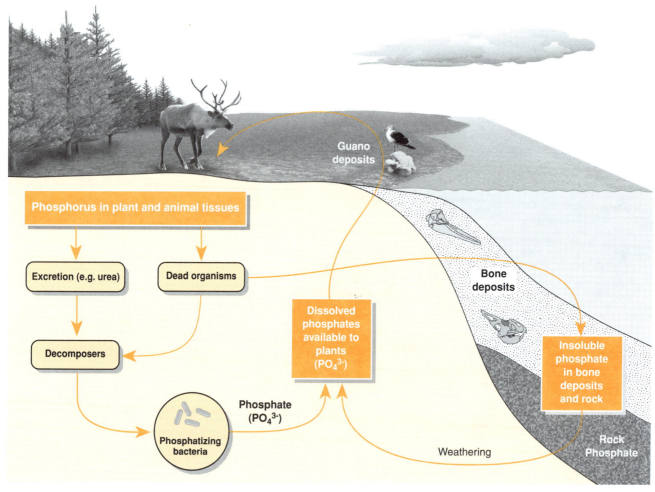

1. In the diagram, add an arrow and label to show where one human activity might intervene in the phosphorus cycle.

2. Identify and describe:

    (a) Two instances in the phosphorus cycle where bacterial action is important: _photosynthesis_
    bacteria breakdown

    (b) Two types of molecules found in living organisms which include phosphorus as a part of their structure:
    DNA

    (c) The origin of three forms of inorganic phosphate making up the geological reservoir: _Photohorus_
    and animal tissues

3. Describe the processes that must occur in order to make rock phosphate available to plants again: _____
    geological uplift

4. Describe one major difference between the phosphorus and carbon cycles: _____
    philosphures n gas state

Related activities: *Water Pollution*

Periodicals:
Phosphorus: a looming crisis

© Biozone International 2007-2011
Photocopying Prohibited

The Sulfur Cycle

Although much of the Earth's sulfur is tied up underground in rock and mineral deposits and ocean sediments, it plays a central role in the biosphere. Sulfur is an essential component of proteins and sulfur compounds are important in determining the acidity of precipitation, surface water, and soil. Sulfur circulates through the biosphere in the sulfur cycle, which is complicated because of the many oxidation states of sulfur, including hydrogen sulfide (H_2S), sulfur dioxide (SO_2) sulfate (SO_4^{-2}), and elemental sulfur. Both inorganic processes and living organisms (especially bacteria) are responsible for these transformations.

Human activity also releases large quantities of sulfur, primarily through combustion of sulfur-containing coal and oil, but also as a result of refining petroleum, smelting, and other industrial processes. Although SO_2 and sulfate aerosols contribute to air pollution, they also absorb UV radiation and create cloud cover that increases the Earth's albedo (reflectivity) and may offset the effects of rising greenhouse gases. Sulfate aerosols are also produced as a result of the biogenic activity of marine plankton (which release dimethylsulfide or DMS into the atmosphere) and thus may play a natural role in global climate regulation.

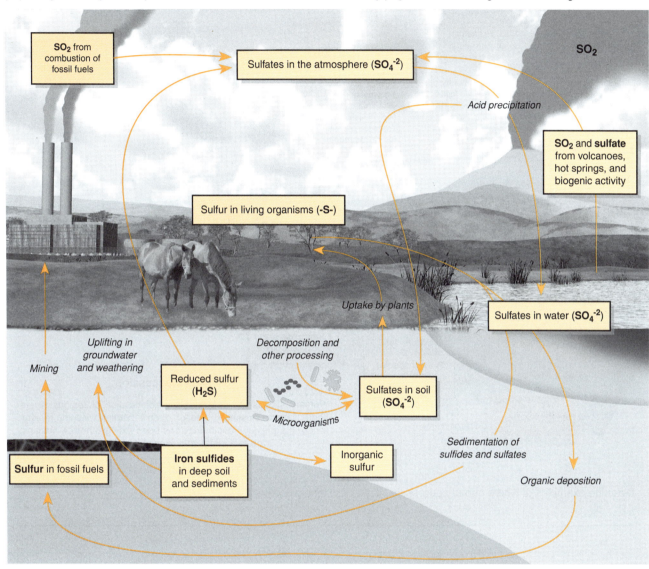

1. Describe two ways in which sulfur can enter the atmosphere from natural sources:

   (a) _uptake by plant_

   (b) _Volcanos_

2. Describe two ways in which sulfur can enter the atmosphere from as a result of human activity:

   (a) _mining_

   (b) _combustion_

3. Describe three processes that make sulfur available for uptake by plants:

   (a) _Preoposition_

   (b) _micro organisms_

   (c) _acid preceptation_

4. Describe two major roles of sulfur in the biosphere:

   (a) _acidity of ppt_

   (b) _acidify of surfa water._

Related activities: Atmospheric Pollution, Acid Rain

A 2

Natural Ecosystem Change

Primary Succession

Ecological succession is the process by which communities in a particular area change over time. Succession takes place as a result of the complex interactions between biotic and abiotic factors. Early communities modify the physical environment causing it to change. This in turn alters the biotic community, which further alters the physical environment and so on. Each successive community makes the environment more favorable for the establishment of new species. An "idealized" succession (or **sere**) proceeds in seral stages, until the formation of a climax (old growth) community, which is generally stable until further disturbance. Early successional communities are characterized by a low species diversity, a simple structure, and broad niches. In contrast, climax communities are complex, with a large number of species interactions, narrow niches, and high species diversity.

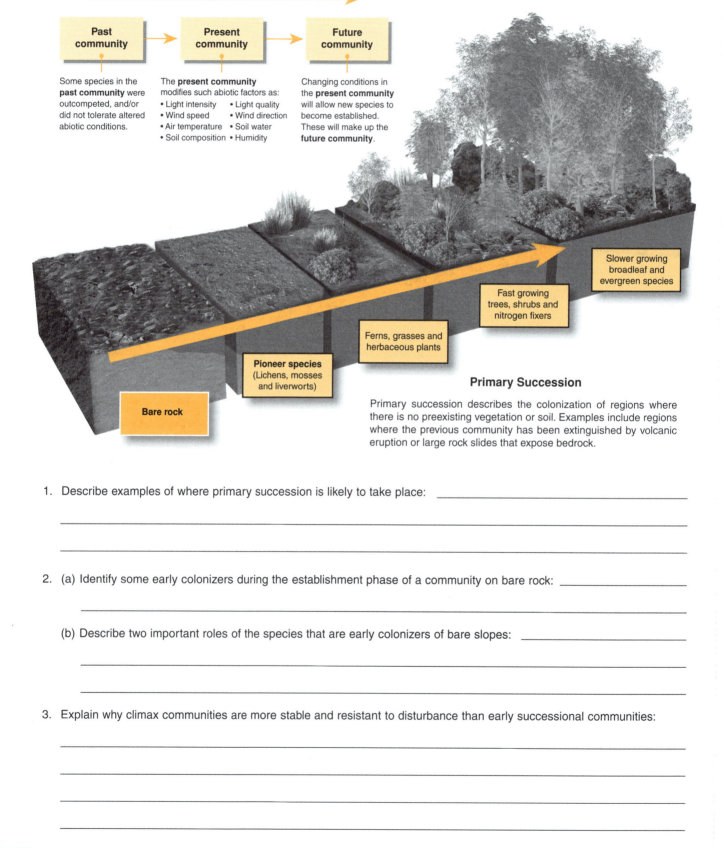

Composition of the community changes with time

| Past community | Present community | Future community |

Some species in the **past community** were outcompeted, and/or did not tolerate altered abiotic conditions.

The **present community** modifies such abiotic factors as:
- Light intensity
- Light quality
- Wind speed
- Wind direction
- Air temperature
- Soil water
- Soil composition
- Humidity

Changing conditions in the **present community** will allow new species to become established. These will make up the **future community**.

Bare rock

Pioneer species (Lichens, mosses and liverworts)

Ferns, grasses and herbaceous plants

Fast growing trees, shrubs and nitrogen fixers

Slower growing broadleaf and evergreen species

Primary Succession

Primary succession describes the colonization of regions where there is no preexisting vegetation or soil. Examples include regions where the previous community has been extinguished by volcanic eruption or large rock slides that expose bedrock.

1. Describe examples of where primary succession is likely to take place: _____

_____

_____

2. (a) Identify some early colonizers during the establishment phase of a community on bare rock: _____

_____

(b) Describe two important roles of the species that are early colonizers of bare slopes: _____

_____

_____

3. Explain why climax communities are more stable and resistant to disturbance than early successional communities:

_____

_____

_____

_____

Related activities: Secondary Succession
Weblinks: Mount St. Helens

Periodicals: Plant Succession

© Biozone International 2007-2011
Photocopying Prohibited

Secondary Succession

A **secondary succession** takes place after a land clearance (e.g. following a fire or a landslide). Such events do not involve the loss of the soil and seed and root stocks are often undamaged. As a result secondary succession tends to be more rapid than primary succession, although the time scale depends on the species involved and the climate and edaphic (soil) factors. Secondary succession events may occur over a wide area (such as after a forest fire), or in smaller areas where single trees have fallen.

Secondary Succession in Cleared Land

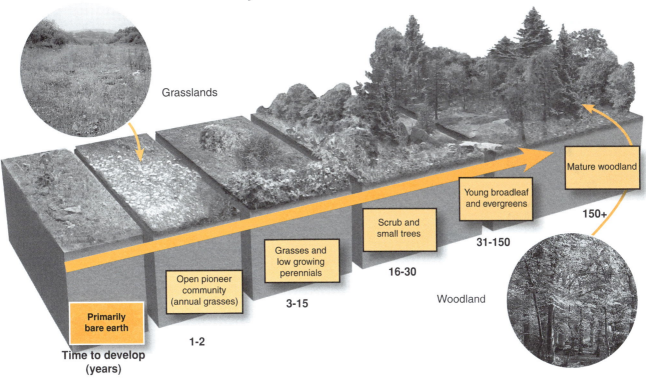

Grasslands

Mature woodland

Young broadleaf and evergreens

150+

Scrub and small trees

31-150

Grasses and low growing perennials

16-30

Open pioneer community (annual grasses)

Woodland

3-15

Primarily bare earth

1-2

Time to develop (years)

Secondary Succession: Gap Regeneration

Large canopy trees have a profound effect on the make-up of a forest community, reducing light penetration and impeding the growth of saplings. When a large tree falls, it opens a hole in the gap allowing far more light through to the forest floor than normal. This stimulates young trees below to start growing towards the light.

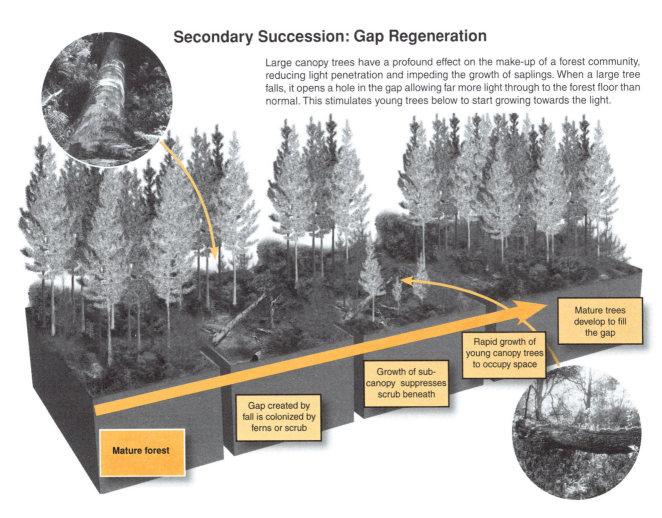

Mature trees develop to fill the gap

Rapid growth of young canopy trees to occupy space

Growth of sub-canopy suppresses scrub beneath

Gap created by fall is colonized by ferns or scrub

Mature forest

Natural Ecosystem Change

Periodicals:
Plant Succession

Related activities: *Primary Succession*

A 2

Deflected Succession

Humans (and sometimes nature) may deflect the natural course of succession (e.g. by mowing or fire) and the climax community that results will differ from the community that would occur if there had been no disturbance.

Mature or developing forest land

Forest is felled. Low scrub and grasses begin to regenerate.

Livestock eat saplings and scrub, so grasses are not over-topped.

Grasses spread and become the dominant vegetation.

A climax community arising from deflected succession is called a **plagioclimax**.

1. Distinguish between **primary** succession and **secondary** succession: _____

   _____

   _____

2. Explain why secondary succession is more rapid than primary succession: _____

   _____

   _____

   _____

3. Describe an event resulting in a secondary succession in a temperate ecosystem: _____

   _____

   _____

   _____

4. (a) Describe the effect of selective logging on the composition of a forest community: _____

   _____

   _____

   (b) Suggest why selective logging could be considered preferable (for forest conservation) to clear felling of trees:

   _____

   _____

5. (a) Explain what is meant by a **deflected succession**: _____

   _____

   (b) Discuss the role that deflected successions might have in maintaining managed habitats: _____

   _____

   _____

   _____

Ecosystem Stability

Ecological theory suggests that all species in an ecosystem contribute in some way to ecosystem function. Therefore, species loss past a certain point is likely to have a detrimental effect on the functioning of the ecosystem and on its ability to resist change (its **stability**). Although many species still await discovery, we do know that the rate of species extinction is increasing. Scientists estimate that human destruction of natural habitat is driving up to 100 000 species to extinction every year. This substantial loss of biodiversity has serious implications for the long term stability of many ecosystems.

The Concept of Ecosystem Stability

Ecosystem stability has various components, including **inertia** (the ability to resist disturbance) and **resilience** (ability to recover from external disturbances). Ecosystem stability is closely linked to the biodiversity of the system, although it is difficult to predict which factors will stress an ecosystem beyond its range of tolerance. It was once thought that the most stable ecosystems were those with the most species, because they had the greatest number of biotic interactions operating to buffer them against change. This assumption is supported by experimental evidence but there is uncertainty over what level of biodiversity provides an insurance against catastrophe.

Monoculture

Natural grassland

Rainforest

Deforestation

©Digital Image 2000. T. Worden

Single species crops (monocultures), such as the soy bean crop (above, left), represent low diversity systems that can be vulnerable to disease, pests, and disturbance. In contrast, natural grasslands (above, right) may appear homogeneous, but contain many species which vary in their predominance seasonally. Although they may be easily disturbed (e.g. by burning) they are very resilient and usually recover quickly.

Tropical rainforests (above, left) represent the highest diversity systems on Earth. Whilst these ecosystems are generally resistant to disturbance, once degraded, (above, right) they have little ability to recover. The biodiversity of ecosystems at low latitudes is generally higher than that at high latitudes, where climates are harsher, niches are broader, and systems may be dependent on a small number of key species.

Community Response to Environmental Change

Environmental change or community response (y-axis)

Time or space (x-axis)

Legend:
— Environmental variation
········· Response of a low diversity community
- - - - Response of a high diversity community

Modified from Biol. Sci. Rev., March 1999 (p. 22)

In models of ecosystem function, higher species diversity increases the stability of ecosystem functions such as productivity and nutrient cycling. In the graph above, note how the low diversity system varies more consistently with the environmental variation, whereas the high diversity system is buffered against major fluctuations. In any one ecosystem, some species may be more influential than others in the stability of the system. Such **keystone (key) species** have a disproportionate effect on ecosystem function due to their pivotal role in some ecosystem function such as nutrient recycling or production of plant biomass.

Elephants can change the entire vegetation structure of areas into which they migrate. Their pattern of grazing on taller plant species promotes a predominance of lower growing grasses with small leaves.

Termites are amongst the few larger soil organisms able to break down plant cellulose. They shift large quantities of soil and plant matter and have a profound effect on the rates of nutrient processing in tropical environments.

The starfish *Pisaster* is found along the coasts of North America where it feeds on mussels. If it is removed, the mussels dominate, crowding out most algae and leading to a decrease in the number of herbivore species.

Natural Ecosystem Change

Periodicals: Biodiversity and ecosystems

Related activities: Monitoring Change in an Ecosystem, Loss of Biodiversity

A 2

Keystone Species in North America

Gray wolf

Beaver, *Castor canadensis*

Sea otter, *Enhydra lutris*

Quaking aspen

Gray or **timber wolves** (*Canis lupus*) are a keystone predator and were once widespread in North American ecosystems. Historically, wolves were eliminated from Yellowstone National Park because of their perceived threat to humans and livestock. As a result, elk populations increased to the point that they adversely affected other flora and fauna. Wolves have since been reintroduced to the park and balance is returning to the ecosystem.

Two smaller mammals are also important keystone species in North America. **Beavers** (top) play a crucial role in biodiversity and many species, including 43% of North America's endangered species, depend partly or entirely on beaver ponds. **Sea otters** are also critical to ecosystem function. When their numbers were decimated by the fur trade, sea urchin populations exploded and the kelp forests, on which many species depend, were destroyed.

Quaking aspen (*Populus tremuloides*) is one of the most widely distributed tree species in North America, and aspen communities are among the most biologically diverse in the region, with a rich understorey flora supporting an abundance of wildlife. Moose, elk, deer, black bear, and snowshoe hare browse its bark, and aspen groves support up to 34 species of birds, including ruffed grouse, which depends heavily on aspen for its winter survival.

For question 1 circle the letter with the correct answer:

1. Identify which of the following statements are correct:
   As the conditions in an ecosystem change:
   I. A high diversity community has little response
   II. A low diversity community has little response
   III. A high diversity community has a large response
   IV. A low diversity has a large response

   A. I and II
   B. II and III
   C. I and IV
   D. II and IV

2. Explain why **keystone species** are so important to ecosystem function: _____
   _____
   _____

3. For each of the following species, discuss features of their biology that contribute to their position as keystone species:

   (a) Sea otter: _____
   _____

   (b) Beaver: _____
   _____

   (c) Gray wolf: _____
   _____

   (d) Quaking aspen: _____
   _____

4. Giving examples, explain how the actions of humans to remove a keystone species might result in ecosystem change:
   _____
   _____

Environmental Change

Environmental changes come from three sources: the **biosphere** itself, **geological forces** (crustal movements and plate tectonics), and **cosmic forces** (the movement of the moon around the Earth, and the Earth and planets around the sun). All three forces can cause cycles, steady states, and trends (directional changes) in the environment. Environmental trends (such as climate cooling) cause long term changes in communities. Some short term cycles may also influence patterns of behavior and growth in many species, regulating endogenous cyclical behavior patterns, called **biological rhythms**.

Climatic change during the last 2-3 million years has involved cycles of glacial and interglacial conditions. These cycles are largely the result of an interplay between astronomical cycles and atmospheric CO_2 concentrations.

Volcanic eruptions may have a large effect on local biological communities. They may also cause prolonged changes to regional and global weather (e.g. Mount Pinatubo eruption, 1989).

Some weather patterns are responsible for subtle changes to ecosystems, such as the gradual onset of a drought. They may also provide large scale and forceful changes, such as those caused by hurricanes or cyclones.

Time scale and geographic extent of environmental change

(Time scale: horizontal axis / geographic extent: vertical axis)

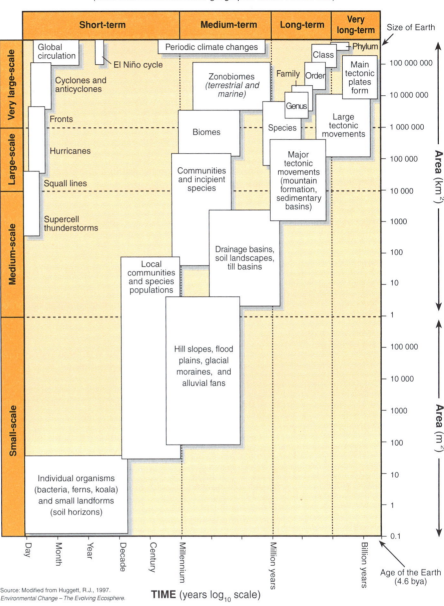

Source: Modified from Huggett, R.J., 1997.
Environmental Change – The Evolving Ecosphere.

1. Periodic long term changes in the Earth's orbit, a change in the sun's heat output, and continental drift may have been the cause of cycles of climate change in the distant past. These climate changes involved a cooling of the Earth:

   (a) Identify the term referring to these periods of global cooling: _____

   (b) Describe two changes to the landscape that occurred during this period: _____

2. On the diagram above, color-code each of the rectangles to indicate the four themes of environmental change:

   Climatic: _____   Ecological: _____   Tectonic: _____   Evolutionary: _____

3. Explain to what extent these four types of environmental change are interlinked: _____

   _____

   _____

   _____

Related activities: Ecosystem Stability, Primary Succession, Secondary Succession

Natural Ecosystem Change

A 3

KEY TERMS: Mix and Match

INSTRUCTIONS: Test your vocabulary by matching each term to its definition, as identified by its preceding letter code.

BIOGEOCHEMICAL CYCLING

CARBON CYCLE

CLIMAX COMMUNITY

CULTURAL EUTROPHICATION

DECOMPOSER

EUTROPHICATION

HYDROLOGICAL CYCLE

KEYSTONE SPECIES

NUTRIENT CYCLING

NITRIFYING BACTERIA

NITROGEN CYCLE

NITROGEN FIXING BACTERIA

PHOSPHORUS CYCLE

PIONEER SPECIES

PIONEER COMMUNITY

PRIMARY SUCCESSION

RESILIENCE

SECONDARY SUCCESSION

SERE

SULFUR CYCLE

STABILITY

A A succession sequence that occurs on land that has not had plants or soil in the past or has been cleared of its vegetation by volcanic eruption etc.

B A species that is influential in aspect of ecosystem function and has a disproportionate effect due to its pivotal role.

C A succession sequence that takes place after a land clearance event (e.g. forest fire or landslide). It does not involve the loss of seeds and root stock.

D An organism that breaks down dead or decaying matter.

E Cycle in which inorganic nutrients move from the abiotic to the biotic environment and back.

F The cycling of nutrients within and between ecosystems, involving exchanges between the atmosphere, the Earth's crust, water and living organisms.

G The biogeochemical cycle in which carbon is exchanged among the biosphere and the inorganic reservoirs on Earth.

H Ability of an ecosystem to resist change. I.e remain unchanged over time.

I The process that speeds up natural eutrophication due to human activities such as agriculture or effluent discharges.

J Accelerated primary production in an ecosystem (usually a water body) as a result of an increase in the concentration of nutrients.

K The cycling of water (in its various states) through the environment.

L Group of bacteria which consume inorganic nitrogen compounds (e.g. ammonia) and produce nitrates.

M An alternative name for succession in a community.

N Bacteria which reduce nitrogen gas and incorporate it into nitrogen compounds.

O The cycling of phosphorus in its various chemical forms from the environment to living organisms and back.

P A species that is the first to colonize areas of bare ground or soil. They usually provide shelter for seedlings of other plants that become established later.

Q The earliest community that becomes established on a bare site.

R The ability of an ecosystem to recover from external disturbances.

S The processes by which nitrogen circulates between the atmosphere and the biosphere. Ammonification, denitrification and nitrification are all part of this cycle.

T The cycling of sulfur in its various chemical forms form the environment to living organisms and back.

U A community that has reached an equilibrium with the environment and no longer appears to be changing in composition.

Populations

Key concepts

► Populations are dynamic collections of interbreeding individuals.

► Populations exhibit attributes not shown by the individuals themselves, including natality, mortality, survivorship, and age structure.

► Population growth is regulated by density dependent and density independent factors.

► Intraspecific and interspecific interactions can be beneficial, neutral, or harmful to an individual.

Key terms

allelopathy
amensalism
carrying capacity
commensalism
community
competition
demographics
density
distribution
emigration
environmental resistance
exploitation
exponential growth
immigration
interspecific
intraspecific
K-selection
life tables
limiting factors
logistic growth
mortality
mutualism
natality
parasitism
population size
predation
r-selection
sigmoidal growth
survivorship curve
urbanization

Objectives

☐ 1. Use the **KEY TERMS** to help you understand and complete these objectives.

Features of Populations — pages 82-84

☐ 2. Recall the difference between a **population** and a **community**.

☐ 3. Distinguish between **population density** and **population size**.

☐ 4. Use the terms **uniform**, **random**, and **clumped** to describe the **distribution** of individuals in a population. Describe factors governing these distributions.

☐ 5. Use the terms **density**, **distribution**, **natality** (birth rate), **mortality** (death rate), **age structure**, **survivorship**, and fecundity to describe a population.

Population Growth and Size — pages 85-86

☐ 6. Explain how births, deaths, **emigration** and **immigration** affect population size.

☐ 7. Explain how **survivorship curves** are used to analyze populations. Use examples to describe features of type I, II and, III survivorship curves.

☐ 8. Describe features of *r* and K selection and give examples of organisms with each strategy. Recognize *r* and K strategies as extremes of a continuum.

☐ 9. Explain the terms **carrying capacity** and **environmental resistance**.

☐ 10. Describe how carrying capacity, environmental resistance, and **limiting factors** affect population size. Distinguish between **density dependent factors** and **density independent factors** in population regulation.

☐ 11. Describe the characteristics of **exponential** and **sigmoidal** growth curves. Identify phases of growth in populations with sigmoidal growth and describe factors regulating growth at each stage.

☐ 12. Describe aspects of human population dynamics, including the:
  • effect of **urbanization** on **demographics**
  • environmental and economic impacts of an increasing human population.

Species Interactions — pages 87-100

☐ 13. Explain the nature of **interspecific** and **intraspecific** interactions within communities.

☐ 14. Describe examples of interspecific relationships including: **competition**, **mutualism**, **commensalism**, **exploitation**, **amensalism**, and **allelopathy**.

Periodicals:
Listings for this chapter are on page 230

Weblinks:
www.thebiozone.com/
weblink/EnvSci-2764.html

Presentation Media
Environmental Science: Populations

Features of Populations

Populations have a number of attributes that may be of interest. Usually, biologists wish to determine **population size** (the total number of organisms in the population). It is also useful to know the **population density** (the number of organisms per unit area). The density of a population is often a reflection of the **carrying capacity** of the environment, i.e. how many organisms an environment can support. Populations also have structure; particular ratios of different ages and sexes. These data enable us to determine whether the population is declining or increasing in size. We can also look at the **distribution** of organisms within

their environment and so determine what particular aspects of the habitat are favored over others. One way to retrieve information from populations is to **sample** them. Sampling involves collecting data about features of the population from samples of that population (since populations are usually too large to examine in total). Sampling can be carried out directly (by sampling the population itself using appropriate equipment) or indirectly (e.g. by monitoring calls or looking for droppings or other signs). Some of the population attributes that we can measure or calculate are illustrated on the diagram below.

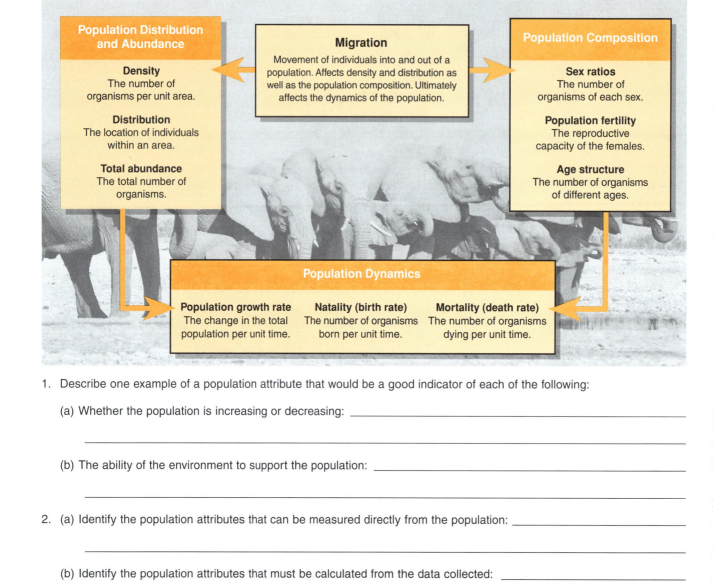

Population Distribution and Abundance

Density
The number of organisms per unit area.

Distribution
The location of individuals within an area.

Total abundance
The total number of organisms.

Migration
Movement of individuals into and out of a population. Affects density and distribution as well as the population composition. Ultimately affects the dynamics of the population.

Population Composition

Sex ratios
The number of organisms of each sex.

Population fertility
The reproductive capacity of the females.

Age structure
The number of organisms of different ages.

Population Dynamics

Population growth rate
The change in the total population per unit time.

Natality (birth rate)
The number of organisms born per unit time.

Mortality (death rate)
The number of organisms dying per unit time.

1. Describe one example of a population attribute that would be a good indicator of each of the following:

(a) Whether the population is increasing or decreasing: _____

_____

(b) The ability of the environment to support the population: _____

_____

2. (a) Identify the population attributes that can be measured directly from the population: _____

_____

(b) Identify the population attributes that must be calculated from the data collected: _____

_____

3. Describe the value of population sampling for each of the following situations:

(a) Conservation of a population of an endangered species: _____

_____

_____

(b) Management of a fisheries resource: _____

_____

_____

_____

Density and Distribution

Distribution and density are two interrelated properties of populations. Population density is the number of individuals per unit area (for land organisms) or volume (for aquatic organisms). Careful observation and precise mapping can determine the distribution patterns for a species. The three basic distribution patterns are: random, clumped and uniform. In the diagram below, the circles represent individuals of the same species. It can also represent populations of different species.

Low Density

In low density populations, individuals are spaced well apart. There are only a few individuals per unit area or volume (e.g. highly territorial, solitary mammal species).

High Density

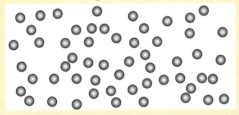

In high density populations, individuals are crowded together. There are many individuals per unit area or volume (e.g. colonial organisms, such as many corals).

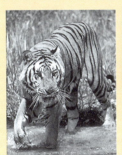

Tigers are solitary animals, found at low densities.

Termites form well organized, high density colonies.

Random Distribution

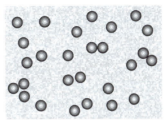

Random distributions occur when the spacing between individuals is irregular. The presence of one individual does not directly affect the location of any other individual. Random distributions are uncommon in animals but are often seen in plants.

Clumped Distribution

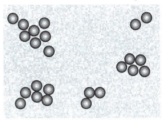

Clumped distributions occur when individuals are grouped in patches (sometimes around a resource). The presence of one individual increases the probability of finding another close by. Such distributions occur in herding and highly social species.

Uniform Distribution

Regular distribution patterns occur when individuals are evenly spaced within the area. The presence of one individual decreases the probability of finding another individual very close by. The penguins illustrated above are also at a high density.

1. Describe why some organisms may exhibit a clumped distribution pattern because of:

   (a) Resources in the environment: _____

   _____

   (b) A group social behavior: _____

   _____

2. Describe a social behavior found in some animals that may encourage a uniform distribution:

   _____

3. Describe the type of environment that would encourage uniform distribution:

   _____

4. Describe an example of each of the following types of distribution pattern:

   (a) Clumped: _____

   (b) Random (more or less): _____

   (c) Uniform (more or less): _____

Related activities: Features of Populations

A 1

Population Regulation

Very few species show continued exponential growth. Population size is regulated by factors that limit population growth. The diagram below illustrates how population size can be regulated by environmental factors. **Density independent factors** may affect all individuals in a population equally. Some, however, may be better able to adjust to them. **Density dependent factors** have a greater affect when the population density is higher. They become less important when the population density is low.

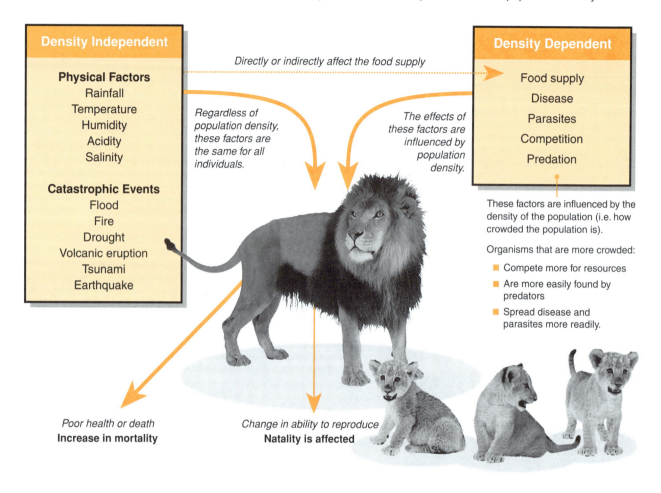

Density Independent

Physical Factors
Rainfall
Temperature
Humidity
Acidity
Salinity

Catastrophic Events
Flood
Fire
Drought
Volcanic eruption
Tsunami
Earthquake

Directly or indirectly affect the food supply

Regardless of population density, these factors are the same for all individuals.

The effects of these factors are influenced by population density.

Density Dependent

Food supply
Disease
Parasites
Competition
Predation

These factors are influenced by the density of the population (i.e. how crowded the population is).

Organisms that are more crowded:

■ Compete more for resources
■ Are more easily found by predators
■ Spread disease and parasites more readily.

Poor health or death
Increase in mortality

Change in ability to reproduce
Natality is affected

1. Discuss the role of **density dependent factors** and **density independent factors** in population regulation. In your discussion, make it clear that you understand the meaning of each of these terms:

_____

_____

_____

_____

_____

_____

2. Explain how an increase in population density allows disease to have a greater influence in regulating population size:

_____

_____

_____

3. In cooler climates, aphids go through a huge population increase during the summer months. In autumn, population numbers decline steeply. Describe a density dependent and a density independent factor regulating the population:

(a) Density dependent: _____

(b) Density independent: _____

Related activities: Density and Distribution
Weblinks: Checks on Population Growth

© Biozone International 2007-2011
Photocopying Prohibited

Population Growth

Organisms do not generally live alone. A **population** is a group of organisms of the same species living together in one geographical area. This area may be difficult to define as populations may comprise widely dispersed individuals that come together only infrequently (e.g. for mating). The number of individuals comprising a population may also fluctuate considerably over time. These changes make populations dynamic: populations gain individuals through births or immigration, and lose individuals through deaths and emigration. For a population in **equilibrium**, these factors balance out and there is no net change in the population abundance. When losses exceed gains, the population declines.

Births, deaths, immigrations (movements into the population) and emigrations (movements out of the population) are events that determine the numbers of individuals in a population. Population growth depends on the number of individuals added to the population from births and immigration, minus the number lost through deaths and emigration. This is expressed as:

Population growth =

Births – Deaths + Immigration – Emigration
(B)   (D)   (I)   (E)

The difference between immigration and emigration gives net migration. Ecologists usually measure the **rate** of these events. These rates are influenced by environmental factors (see below) and by the characteristics of the organisms themselves. Rates in population studies are commonly expressed in one of two ways:

- Numbers per unit time, e.g. 20,150 live births per year.
- Per capita rate (number per head of population), e.g. 122 live births per 1000 individuals per year (12.2%).

Limiting Factors

Population size is also affected by limiting factors; factors or resources that control a process such as organism growth, or population growth or distribution. Examples include availability of food, predation pressure, or available habitat.

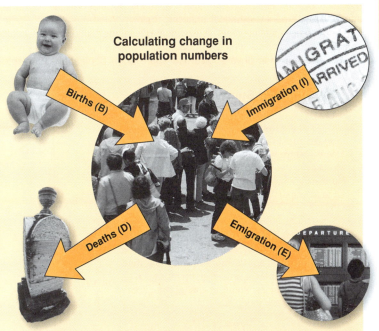

Calculating change in population numbers

Births (B)

Immigration (I)

Deaths (D)

Emigration (E)

Human populations often appear exempt from limiting factors as technology and efficiency solve many food and shelter problems. However as the last arable land is used and agriculture reaches its limits of efficiency, it is estimated that the human population will peak at around 9 billion by 2050.

1. Define the following terms used to describe changes in population numbers:

   (a) Death rate (mortality): _____

   (b) Birth rate (natality): _____

   (e) Net migration rate: _____

2. Using the terms, B, D, I, and E (above), construct equations to express the following (the first is completed for you):

   (a) A population in equilibrium: _____ $B + I = D + E$ _____

   (b) A declining population: _____

   (c) An increasing population: _____

3. The rate of population change can be expressed as the interaction of all these factors:

   Rate of population change = Birth rate – Death rate + Net migration rate (positive or negative)

   Using the formula above, determine the annual rate of population change for Mexico and the United States in 1972:

	USA	Mexico
Birth rate	1.73%	4.3%
Death rate	0.93%	1.0%
Net migration rate	+0.20%	0.0%

   Rate of population change for USA   = _____

   Rate of population change for Mexico = _____

4. A population started with a total number of 100 individuals. Over the following year, population data were collected. Calculate birth rates, death rates, net migration rate, and rate of population change for the data below (as percentages):

   (a) Births = 14: Birth rate = _____ (b) Net migration = +2: Net migration rate = _____

   (c) Deaths = 20: Death rate = _____ (d) Rate of population change = _____

   (e) State whether the population is increasing or declining: _____

© Biozone International 2007-2011
Photocopying Prohibited

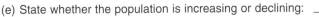

Related activities: Features of Populations
Weblinks: Modeling Population Growth 1, Modeling Population Growth 2

DA 1

Survivorship Curves

The survivorship curve depicts age-specific mortality. It is obtained by plotting the number of individuals of a particular cohort against time. Survivorship curves are standardized to start at 1000 and, as the population ages, the number of survivors progressively declines. The shape of a survivorship curve thus shows graphically at which life stages the highest mortality occurs. Survivorship curves in many populations fall into one of three hypothetical patterns (below). Wherever the curve becomes steep, there is an increase in mortality. The convex Type I curve is typical of populations whose individuals tend to live out their physiological life span. Such populations usually produce fewer young and show some degree of parental care. Organisms that suffer high losses of the early life stages (a Type III curve) compensate by producing vast numbers of offspring. These curves are conceptual models only, against which real life curves can be compared. Many species exhibit a mix of two of the three basic types. Some birds have a high chick mortality (Type III) but adult mortality is fairly constant (Type II). Some invertebrates (e.g. crabs) have high mortality only when moulting and show a stepped curve. Typically, **K-selection** predominates in organisms with Type I survivorship and *r*-selection predominates in organisms with Type III survivorship.

Hypothetical Survivorship Curves

Type I
Late loss survivorship curve
Mortality (death rate) is very low in the infant and juvenile years, and throughout most of adult life. Mortality increases rapidly in old age. **Examples**: Humans (in developed countries) and many other large mammals (e.g. big cats, elephants).

Type II
Constant loss survivorship curve
Mortality is relatively constant through all life stages (no one age is more susceptible than another). **Examples**: Some invertebrates such as *Hydra*, some birds, some annual plants, some lizards, and many rodents.

Type III
Early loss survivorship curve
Mortality is very high during early life stages, followed by a very low death rate for the few individuals reaching adulthood. **Examples**: Many fish (not mouth brooders) and most marine invertebrates (e.g. oysters, barnacles).

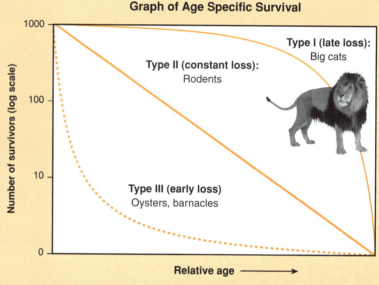

Graph of Age Specific Survival

Type I (late loss): Big cats
Type II (constant loss): Rodents
Type III (early loss) Oysters, barnacles

Number of survivors (log scale)

Relative age →

Three basic types of survivorship curves and representative organisms for each type. The vertical axis may be scaled arithmetically or logarithmically.

Elephants have a close matriarchal society and a long period of parental care. Elephants are long-lived and females usually produce just one calf.

Rodents are well known for their large litters and prolific breeding capacity. Individuals are lost from the population at a more or less constant rate.

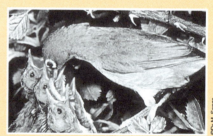

Despite vigilant parental care, many birds suffer high juvenile losses (Type III). For those surviving to adulthood, deaths occur at a constant rate.

©Dr M. Soper

1. Match the following terms to the statements below: **A** Type I **B** Type II **C** Type III **D** Human **E** Oyster

   (a) Curve followed by organisms with high mortality rates early in life: _____

   (b) Human populations in developed countries follow this type of curve: _____

   (c) Organism which compensates for high juvenile mortality by producing large numbers of young: _____

2. Describe the features of a species with type I survivorship that aid in high juvenile survival: _____

   _____

3. Discuss the following statement: "There is no standard survivorship curve for a given species; the curve depicts the nature of a population at a particular time and place and under certain environmental conditions.":

   _____

   _____

   _____

Related activities: Life Expectancy and Survivorship, r and K Selection
Weblinks: Modeling Population Growth 1, Modeling Population Growth 2

Population Growth Curves

Populations becoming established in a new area for the first time are often termed **colonizing populations** (below, left). They may undergo a rapid **exponential** (logarithmic) increase in numbers as there are plenty of resources to allow a high birth rate, while the death rate is often low. Exponential growth produces a J-shaped growth curve that rises steeply as more and more individuals contribute to the population increase. If the resources of the new habitat were endless (inexhaustible) then the population would continue to increase at an **exponential** rate. However, this rarely happens in natural populations. Initially, growth may be exponential (or nearly so), but as the population grows, its increase will slow and it will stabilize at a level that can be supported by the environment (called the carrying capacity or K). This type of growth is called **sigmoidal** and produces the **logistic growth curve** (below, right). **Established populations** will fluctuate about K, often in a regular way (shaded area on the graph below, right). Some species will have populations that vary little from this stable condition, while others may oscillate wildly.

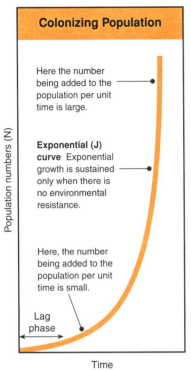

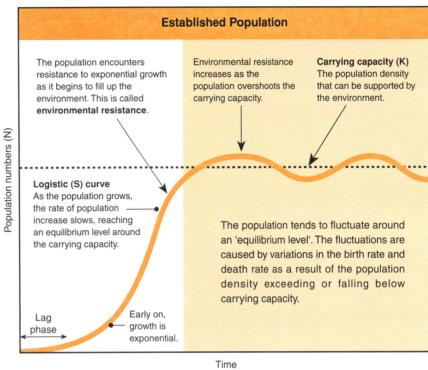

1. Explain why populations tend not to continue to increase exponentially in an environment: _____

2. Explain what is meant by environmental resistance: _____

3. (a) Explain what is meant by carrying capacity: _____

(b) Explain the importance of **carrying capacity** to the growth and maintenance of population numbers: _____

4. Species that expand into a new area, such as rabbits did in areas of Australia, typically show a period of rapid population growth followed by a slowing of population growth as density dependent factors become more important and the population settles around a level that can be supported by the carrying capacity of the environment.

(a) Explain why a newly introduced consumer (e.g. rabbit) would initially exhibit a period of exponential population growth: _____

(b) Describe a likely outcome for a rabbit population after the initial rapid increase had slowed: _____

5. Describe the effect that introduced grazing species might have on the carrying capacity of the environment: _____

r and K Selection

Two parameters govern the logistic growth of populations: the intrinsic rate of natural increase or biotic potential (this is the maximum reproductive potential of an organism, symbolized by an italicised *r*), and the carrying capacity (saturation density) of the environment (represented by the letter **K**). Species can be characterized by the relative importance of *r* and K in their life cycles. Species with a high intrinsic capacity for population increase are called **r-selected species**, and include algae, bacteria, rodents, many insects, and most annual plants. These species show life history features associated with rapid growth in disturbed environments. To survive, they must continually

invade new areas to compensate for being replaced by more competitive species. In contrast, **K-selected** species, which include most large mammals, birds of prey, and large, long-lived plants, exist near the carrying capacity of their environments and are pushed in competitive environments to use resources more efficiently. These species have fewer offspring and longer lives, and put their energy into nuturing their young to reproductive age. Most organisms have reproductive patterns between these two extremes. Both *r*-selected species (crops) and K-selected species (livestock) are found in agriculture.

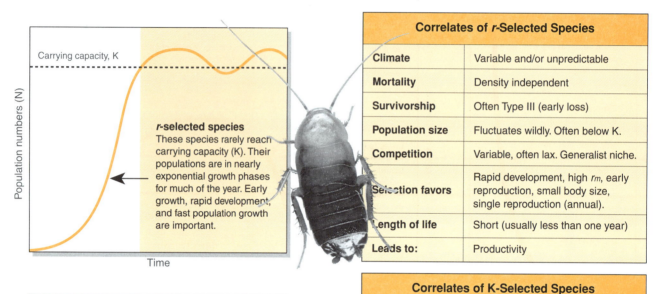

r-selected species
These species rarely reach carrying capacity (K). Their populations are in nearly exponential growth phases for much of the year. Early growth, rapid development, and fast population growth are important.

Correlates of *r*-Selected Species

Climate	Variable and/or unpredictable
Mortality	Density independent
Survivorship	Often Type III (early loss)
Population size	Fluctuates wildly. Often below K.
Competition	Variable, often lax. Generalist niche.
Selection favors	Rapid development, high r_m, early reproduction, small body size, single reproduction (annual).
Length of life	Short (usually less than one year)
Leads to:	Productivity

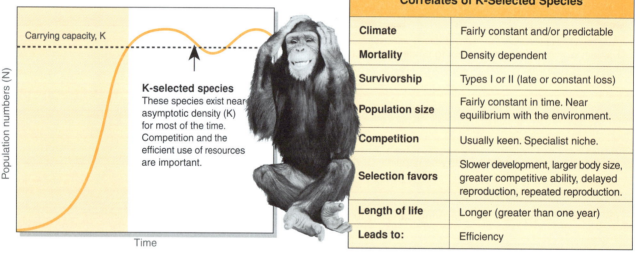

K-selected species
These species exist near asymptotic density (K) for most of the time. Competition and the efficient use of resources are important.

Correlates of K-Selected Species

Climate	Fairly constant and/or predictable
Mortality	Density dependent
Survivorship	Types I or II (late or constant loss)
Population size	Fairly constant in time. Near equilibrium with the environment.
Competition	Usually keen. Specialist niche.
Selection favors	Slower development, larger body size, greater competitive ability, delayed reproduction, repeated reproduction.
Length of life	Longer (greater than one year)
Leads to:	Efficiency

1. Explain the significance of the *r* and the K notation when referring to *r* and **K selection**: _____

_____

2. Giving an example, explain why *r*-selected species tend to be **opportunists**: _____

_____

_____

3. Describe some benefits of being a K selected species: _____

_____

_____

4. Suggest why many K-selected species are often vulnerable to extinction: _____

_____

Related activities: Survivorship Curves, Population Growth Curves

Population Age Structure

The **age structure** of a population refers to the relative proportion of individuals in each age group in the population. The age structure of populations can be categorized according to specific age categories (such as years or months), but also by other measures such as life stage (egg, larvae, pupae, instars), of size class (height or diameter in plants). Population growth is strongly influenced by age structure; a population with a high proportion of reproductive and prereproductive aged individuals has a much greater potential for population growth than one that is dominated by older individuals. The ratio of young to adults in a relatively stable population of most mammals and birds is approximately 2:1 (below, left). Growing populations in general are characterized by a large and increasing number of young, whereas a population in decline typically has a decreasing number of young. Population age structures are commonly represented as pyramids, in which the proportions of individuals in each age/size class are plotted with the youngest individuals at the pyramid's base. The number of individuals moving from one age class to the next influences the age structure of the population from year to year. The loss of an age class (e.g. through overharvesting) can profoundly influence a population's viability and can even lead to population collapse.

Age Structures in Animal Populations

These theoretical age pyramids, which are especially applicable to birds and mammals, show how growing populations are characterized by a high ratio of young (white bar) to adult age classes (shaded bars). Aging populations with poor production are typically dominated by older individuals.

4	76 young : 24 adults
8	Rapidly growing population
12	
76	

Virginia opposum: growing population

4	64:36
8	Normal
24	
64	

White tailed deer: normal growth

4	48:52
8	Poor production (aging)
12	
24	
48	

Serval: locally at risk

4	24:76
6	Very poor production
12	
16	
16	
20	
24	

Kakapo: endangered

Age Structures in Human Populations

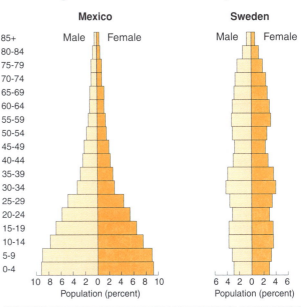

Extended family: Samoa

Most of the growth in human populations in recent years has occurred in the developing countries in Africa, Asia, and Central and South America. This is reflected in their age structure; a large proportion of the population comprises individuals younger than 15 years (age pyramid above, left). Even if each has fewer children, the population will continue to increase for many years. The stable age structure of Sweden is shown for comparison.

1. For the theoretical age pyramids above left:

   (a) State the approximate ratio of young to adults in a rapidly increasing population: _____

   (b) Suggest why changes in population age structure alone are not necessarily a reliable predictor of population trends:

   _____

   _____

2. Explain why the population of Mexico is likely to continue to increase rapidly even if the rate of population growth slows:

   _____

   _____

Periodicals:
Human population grows up

Related activities: *Features of Populations, Fisheries Management*

RDA 2

Analysis of the age structure of a population can assist in its management because it can indicate where most of the mortality occurs and whether or not reproductive individuals are being replaced. The age structure of both plant and animal populations can be examined; a common method is through an analysis of size which is often related to age in a predictable way.

Managed Fisheries

The graphs below illustrate the age structure of a hypothetical fish population under different fishing pressures. The age structure of the population is determined by analyzing the fish catch to determine the frequency of fish in each size (age) class.

Thatch Palm Populations on Lord Howe Island

Lord Howe Island is a narrow sliver of land approximately 770 km northeast of Sydney. The age structure of populations of the thatch palm *Howea forsteriana* was determined at three locations on the island: the golf course, Gray Face and Far Flats. The height of the stem was used as an indication of age. The differences in age structure between the three sites are mainly due to the extent of grazing at each site.

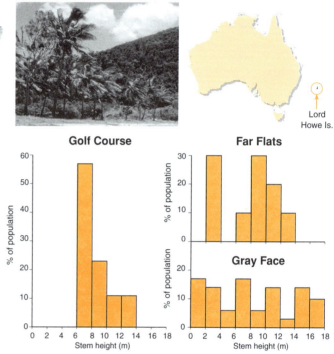

Lord Howe Is.

Golf Course

Far Flats

Gray Face

3. For the managed fish population above left:

    (a) Name the general factor that changes the age structure of this fish population: _____

    (b) Describe how the age structure changes when the fishing pressure increases from light to heavy levels:

    _____

4. State the most common age class for each of the above fish populations with different fishing pressures:

    (a) Heavy: _____   (b) Moderate: _____   (c) Light: _____

5. Determine which of the three sites sampled on Lord Howe Island (above, right), best reflects the age structure of:

    (a) An ungrazed population: _____

    Reason for your answer: _____

    (b) A heavily grazed and mown population: _____

    Reason for your answer: _____

6. Describe the likely long term prospects for the population at the golf course: _____

    _____

7. Describe a potential problem with using size to estimate age: _____

    _____

8. Explain why a knowledge of age structure could be important in managing a resource: _____

    _____

World Population Growth

For most of human history, humans have not been very numerous compared to other species. It took all of human history to reach a population of 1 billion in 1804, but little more than 150 years to reach 3 billion in 1960. The world's population, now at 6.8 billion, is growing at the rate of about 80 million per year. This growth is slower than predicted but the world's population is still expected to increase substantially before stabilizing (see Figure 1). World population increase carries important environmental consequences, particularly when it is associated with increasing **urbanization**. Although the world as a whole still has an average fertility rate of 2.8, growth rates are now lower than at any time since World War II. Continued declines may give human populations time to address some to the major problems posed by the increasing the scope and intensity of human activities.

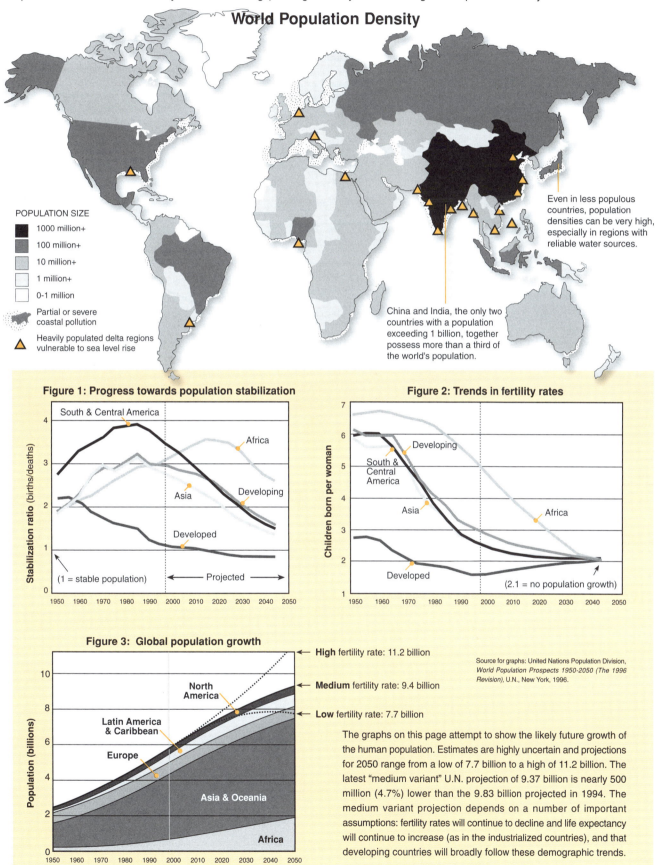

World Population Density

POPULATION SIZE

- 1000 million+
- 100 million+
- 10 million+
- 1 million+
- 0-1 million

Partial or severe coastal pollution

Heavily populated delta regions vulnerable to sea level rise

Even in less populous countries, population densities can be very high, especially in regions with reliable water sources.

China and India, the only two countries with a population exceeding 1 billion, together possess more than a third of the world's population.

Figure 1: Progress towards population stabilization

Stabilization ratio (births/deaths)

South & Central America
Africa
Asia
Developing
Developed

(1 = stable population) ← Projected →

1950 1960 1970 1980 1990 2000 2010 2020 2030 2040 2050

Figure 2: Trends in fertility rates

Children born per woman

Developing
South & Central America
Asia
Africa
Developed

(2.1 = no population growth)

1950 1960 1970 1980 1990 2000 2010 2020 2030 2040 2050

Figure 3: Global population growth

Population (billions)

North America
Latin America & Caribbean
Europe
Asia & Oceania
Africa

← **High** fertility rate: 11.2 billion
← **Medium** fertility rate: 9.4 billion
← **Low** fertility rate: 7.7 billion

Source for graphs: United Nations Population Division, *World Population Prospects 1950-2050 (The 1996 Revision)*, U.N., New York, 1996.

1950 1960 1970 1980 1990 2000 2010 2020 2030 2040 2050

The graphs on this page attempt to show the likely future growth of the human population. Estimates are highly uncertain and projections for 2050 range from a low of 7.7 billion to a high of 11.2 billion. The latest "medium variant" U.N. projection of 9.37 billion is nearly 500 million (4.7%) lower than the 9.83 billion projected in 1994. The medium variant projection depends on a number of important assumptions: fertility rates will continue to decline and life expectancy will continue to increase (as in the industrialized countries), and that developing countries will broadly follow these demographic trends.

Periodicals:
Population bombshell

Related activities: Population Growth, Population Age Structure
Weblinks: Human Impact: Overpopulation

The Shift to Urban Living

The traditional villages characteristic of the rural populations of less economically developed countries have a close association with the land. The households depend directly on agriculture or harvesting natural resources for their livelihood and are linked through family ties, culture, and economics.

Cities are differentiated communities, where the majority of the population does not depend directly on natural resource-based occupations. While cities are centers of commerce, education, and communication, they are also centers of crowding, pollution, and disease.

Cities, especially those that are growing rapidly, face a range of problems associated with providing residents with adequate water, food, sanitation, housing, jobs, and basic services, such as health care. Slums or squatter settlements are found in most large cities in developing countries as more poor people migrate from rural to urban areas.

The redistribution of people from rural to urban environments, or **urbanization**, has been an important characteristic of human societies. Almost half of the people in the world already live in urban areas and by the end of the 21st century, this figure is predicted to increase to 80-90%. Urban populations can grow through natural increase (i.e. more births than deaths) or by **immigration**. Immigration is driven both by **push factors** that encourage people to leave their rural environment and **pull factors** that draw them to the cities.

Immigration push factors

- Rural overpopulation
- Lack of work or food
- Changing agricultural practices
- Desire for better education
- Racial or religious conflict
- Political instability

Immigration pull factors

- Opportunity for better jobs
- Chance of better housing
- More reliable food supply
- Opportunity for greater wealth
- Freedom from village traditions
- Government policy

Rural and Urban Populations in the USA

— % of US population in urban areas
····· % of US population in rural areas

Total urban population
Total rural population

The United States underwent a dramatic rural to urban shift in the 19th and early 20th centuries. Many developing countries are now experiencing similar shifts. Graph compiled from UN data

1. Fertility rates of populations for all geographic regions are predicted to decline over the next 50 years.

   (a) State which continent is predicted to have the highest fertility rate at the beginning of next century: _____

   (b) Suggest why the population of this region is slower to achieve a low fertility rate than other regions: _____

   _____

   _____

2. Describe the kinds of changes in agricultural practices that could contribute to urbanization: _____

   _____

   _____

3. (a) Describe some of the positive effects of urbanization: _____

   _____

   _____

   (b) Describe some negative effects of urbanization: _____

   _____

Human Demography

Human populations through time have undergone demographic shifts related to societal changes and economic development. The demographic transition model (DTM) was developed in 1929 to explain the transformation of countries from high birth rates and high death rates to low birth rates and low death rates as part of their economic development from a pre-industrial to an industrialized economy. The transition involves four stages, or possibly five (with some nations, including England, being recognized as moving beyond stage four). Each stage of the transition reflects the changes in birth and death rates observed in human societies over the last 200 years. Most developed countries are beyond stage three of the model; the majority of developing countries are in stage two or stage three. The model was based on the changes seen in Europe, so these countries follow the DTM relatively well. Many developing countries have moved into stage three. The exceptions include some poor countries, mainly in sub-Saharan Africa and some Middle Eastern countries, which are poor or affected by government policy or civil strife.

Stage one: Birth and death rates balanced but high as a result of starvation and disease.

Stage two: Improvement in food supplies and public health result in reduced death rates.

Stage three moves the population towards stability through a decline in the birth rate.

Stage four: Birth and death rates are both low and the total population is high and stable.

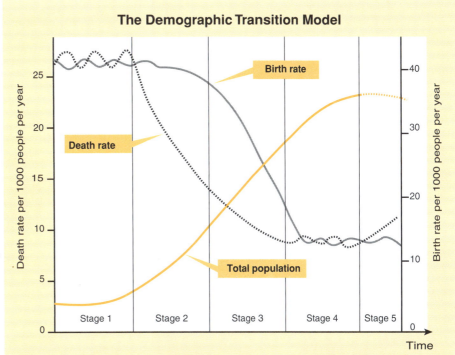

The Demographic Transition Model

Death rate per 1000 people per year — *Birth rate per 1000 people per year* — *Time*

Birth rate / Death rate / Total population

Stage 1 | Stage 2 | Stage 3 | Stage 4 | Stage 5

USAID Bangladesh

Wiki: Komencanto

Stage one (pre-modern): A balance between birth and death rates as was true of all populations until the late 18th Century. Children are important contributors to the household economy. Losses as a result of starvation and disease are high. Stage 1 is sometimes called the "High Stationary Stage" of population growth (high birth and death rates and stationary total population numbers).

Stage two (early expanding): Rapid population expansion as a result of a decline in death rates. The changes leading to this stage in Europe were initiated in the Agricultural Revolution of the 18th century but have been more rapid in developing countries since then. Stage two is associated with more reliable food supplies and improvements in public health.

Stage three (late expanding): The population moves towards stability through a decline in the birth rate. This stage is associated with increasing urbanization and a decreased reliance on children as a source of family wealth. Family planning in nations such as Malaysia (photo left) has been instrumental in their move to stage three.

Stage four (post-industrial): Birth and death rates are both low and the total population is high and stable. The population ages and in some cases the fertility rate falls below replacement.

Stage five (declining): Proposed by some theorists as representing countries that have undergone the economic transition from manufacturing based industries into service and information based industries and the population reproduces well below replacement levels. Countries in stage five include the United Kingdom (the earliest nation recognized as reaching Stage Five) and Germany.

1. Each of the first four stages of the DTM is associated with a particular age structure. Identify which of the diagrams (right) corresponds to stage one of the DTM and explain your choice:

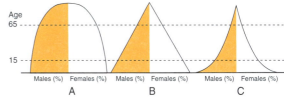

Age 65 ---- 15 ----
Males (%) Females (%) | Males (%) Females (%) | Males (%) Females (%)
A | B | C

_____

_____

2. Suggest why it might become less important to have a large number of children in more economically developed nations:

_____

_____

Related activities: World Population Growth, Population Growth Curves

DA 2

Life Expectancy and Survivorship

Life expectancy is the average number of years of life remaining when at any given age, and therefore changes as an individual ages. For example in the US, at birth a human has a life expectancy of around 78 years. However a 66 year old has a life expectancy of around 16 years meaning they should live to the age of 82. In human societies, life expectancy is heavily dependent on aspects of the socio-economic structure such as public health facilities, presence and treatment of endemic disease, and level of poverty. These factors are not static. Countries where war, famine or disease are common invariably have low life expectancies. Life expectancy is also affected by gender; international life expectancy for males is 64 compared with 68 for females.

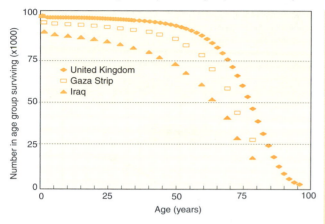

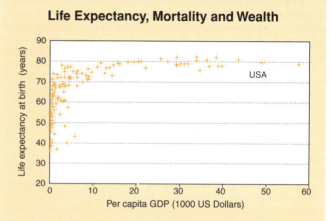

Life Expectancy, Mortality and Wealth

Human populations typically follow a type I survivorship curve. However, the average life expectancy can vary greatly between developed and developing nations. The average life expectancy can be estimated from the survivorship curves above as being the age at which 50% of the people in the sample are still alive.

Life expectancy is linked to many factors but in human society there is a close correlation between life expectancy and a country's per capita gross domestic product (GDP). Those countries with high GDP can be expected to have citizens with long life expectancies.

Photo: Bertil Videt

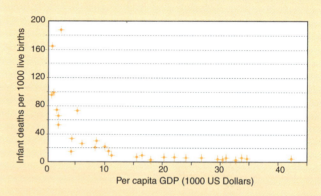

War, civil instability, poor infrastructure and social services, and poverty can greatly reduce life expectancy. Life expectancy in stable, industrialized nations, e.g. Japan, can be around 80 at birth, while war-torn, poor, or developing nations may have life expectancies as low as 39 at birth e.g. Swaziland.

In developed nations, the **infant mortality rate** (IMR) is low because of better standards of living and advanced medical technology. People in developing countries often lack access to quality medical care and the IMR can be high, especially where there are high rates of endemic disease. However, populations in developing countries often have high birth rates so that population growth rates remain high despite a high IMR.

Life expectancy and survivorship of a population are closely linked to the wealth of the country they live in:

1. (a) Describe the relationship between a country's per capita GDP and life expectancy of its citizens: _____

    _____

    (b) Explain why IMR might be linked to a nation's wealth: _____

    _____

    (c) Identify some factors that lower life expectancy and survivorship of a country: _____

    _____

2. Explain why life expectancy changes as one ages: _____

    _____

3. Estimate average life expectancy for: (a) United Kingdom: _____   (b) Gaza Strip: _____   (c) Iraq: _____

Related activities: Survivorship Curves

Human Sustainability

The human population has increased from fewer than 3 billion people to nearly 7 billion in the past 50 years. Since the 1950s, improvements in medicine and access to more food have allowed the world's population to grow at rate of almost 2% each year. Many scientists believe growth of this magnitude is not sustainable and that the human population has already surpassed the planet's carrying capacity. They predict the inevitable collapse of food supplies and populations in the near future. In many countries, initiatives have been taken to lower birth rates in an attempt to relieve pressure on resources.

A major reason for high growth rates in some countries is a societal belief that a large family is needed to help with work. In countries where there is no government support for those unable to work, children often contribute to the family income. Child mortality is high so parents produce a large number of children to ensure some can support the family.

High population growth rates can quickly cause the depletion of a country's resources and increase problems with supply of goods and sanitation, especially if the infrastructure is poor. Often the cost of addressing these issues is beyond the means of the people and the country, leading to permanent poverty and a decline in the population health and wellbeing.

Most developed countries have low population growth rates. These are through easy access to education, contraception, and family planning, gender equality, and a social focus on individual success and self support. Having a large family can cause financial burden and so restrict access to education and commodities and this acts as a disincentive for high birth rates.

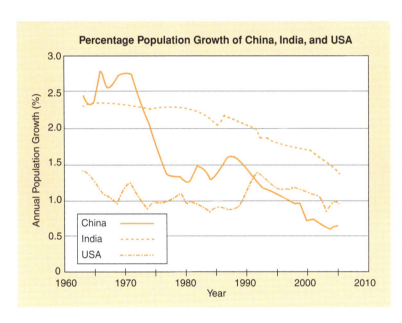

Percentage Population Growth of China, India, and USA

China is the world's most populous nation. During the 1960s, officials realized that the country's growth rate could not be sustained and implemented strict regulations for family planning. Couples were encouraged to marry late and have only one child. Contraception and sterilization were made free and those that followed the guidelines were given access to better jobs, food, education for their child, housing, pensions, medical care, and salary bonuses.

India began the world's first national family planning campaign in 1952, when the population was 400 million. Fertility rates have dropped from 5.3 to 3.5 children for women but, unlike the program in China, the campaign suffered from slow uptake by families, poor planning, bureaucratic delays, and a lack of financial support or incentives. As a result, India's population is now more than 1 billion people and India will overtake China as the most populous nation around 2050.

The birth rates in most Westernized nations (e.g. the USA) began to decline during industrialization and dropped even further with the introduction of the contraceptive pill. Developing countries are only now beginning to show a reduction in their population growth rates as they move from industrialized to post-industrialized status.

1. Explain why mainly developing countries have high population growth rates: _____

_____

_____

2. Explain the reasons for the differences in the success of China's and India's family planning campaigns: _____

_____

_____

_____

3. (a) Describe some benefits of reducing population sizes: _____

_____

   (b) Discuss some negative aspects of a rapidly declining population: _____

_____

_____

Related activities: Population Growth, Population Age Structure

A 2

Humans and Resources

The expanding human population puts increasing strain on the world's resources, creates problems of pollution and waste disposal, and often places other species at risk. Even when resources are potentially sufficient to meet demands, problems with distribution and supply create inequalities between regions. This page outlines some of the problems associated with the availability and use of resources. Although the world's situation might seem bleak, progress is being made towards a more sustainable future. Houses and cities are now being designed with greater energy efficiency in mind, steps are being taken to reduce greenhouse gas emissions and other forms of pollution, and sustainable agricultural practices are being increasingly encouraged. Advancements in technology combined with a political commitment to sustainability will add to these gains.

Air pollution contributes to global warming, ozone depletion, and acid rain, and is set to increase markedly in the next 30 years.

Global water consumption is rising rapidly. The availability of water is likely to become one of the most pressing resource issues of the 21st century.

Combustion engine emissions are increasing rapidly in Asia as their economies develop and their populations become more affluent.

A dwindling supply of fossil fuels provides about 85% of the world's commercial energy. Most of this is consumed by the richest countries.

Global climate change as a result of the greenhouse effect will cause a rise in sea levels and threaten coastal populations such as those in Bangladesh (above).

In industrialized societies, one person consumes many tonnes of raw materials each year, which must be extracted, processed, and then disposed of as waste.

Aquatic environments, such as coral reefs and freshwater habitats in lakes, rivers, and wetlands are at risk from population pressure (58% of the worlds reefs and 34% of all fish species).

Threats to biodiversity from all sources are rapidly reaching a critical level. Current extinction rates have increased 100 to 1000 times due to human impact on natural environments.

Consumption of natural resources, including fuels, water, and minerals, by modern industrial economies remains very high (in the range of 45 to 85 tonnes per person annually).

Forest fires and logging continue to cause shrinkage of the world's tropical and temperate forests. Deforestation in the Amazon doubled from 1994 to 1995 before declining in 1996.

The unsustainable fishing of the world's fish stocks has occurred in many fishing grounds (e.g. cod fishing in the North Atlantic). Many of these fish populations are unlikely to recover.

Although the world's food production is theoretically adequate to meet human needs there are problems with distribution. Some 800 million people remain undernourished.

1. Describe some of the predicted impacts of shortages of fossil fuel and freshwater on world agriculture:

_____

_____

_____

_____

2. Chose two of the following resources and describe its use and the subsequent impact on the environment:

Water   Coal   Timber   Fish

(a) Resource 1: _____

_____

_____

(b) Resource 2: _____

_____

_____

Related activities: *World Population Growth*

Weblinks: *Dimensions of Need*

Periodicals:

Time to rethink everything

© Biozone International 2007-2011

Species Interactions

No organism exists in isolation. Each takes part in many interactions, both with other organisms and with the non-living components of the environment. Species interactions may involve only occasional or indirect contact (predation or competition) or they may involve close association or **symbiosis**. Symbiosis is a term that encompasses a variety of interactions involving close species contact. There are three types of symbiosis: **parasitism** (a form of exploitation), **mutualism**, and **commensalism**. Species interactions affect population densities and are important in determining community structure and composition. Some interactions, such as allelopathy, may even determine species presence or absence in an area.

Examples of Species Interactions

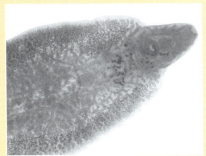 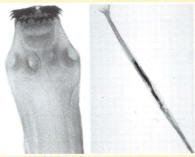

Parasitism is a common exploitative relationship in plants and animals. A parasite exploits the resources of its host (e.g. for food, shelter, warmth) to its own benefit. The host is harmed, but usually not killed. **Endoparasites**, such as liver flukes (left), tapeworms (center) and nematodes (right), are highly specialized to live inside their hosts, attached by hooks or suckers to the host's tissues.

Ectoparasites, such as ticks (above), mites, and fleas, live attached to the outside of the host, where they suck body fluids, cause irritation, and may act as vectors for disease causing microorganisms.

Mutualism involves an intimate association between two species that offers advantage to both. **Lichens** (above) are the result of a mutualism between a fungus and an alga (or cyanobacterium).

Termites have a mutualistic relationship with the cellulose digesting bacteria in their guts. A similar mutualistic relationship exists between ruminants and their gut microflora of bacteria and ciliates.

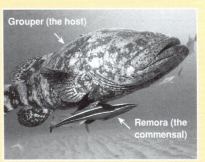

In **commensal** relationships, such as between this large grouper and a remora, two species form an association where one organism, the commensal, benefits and the other is neither harmed or helped.

Many species of decapod crustaceans, such as this anemone shrimp, are commensal with sea anemones. The shrimp gains by being protected from predators by the anemone's tentacles.

Interactions involving **competition** for the same food resources are dominated by the largest, most aggressive species. Here, hyaenas compete for a carcass with vultures and maribou storks.

Predation is an easily identified relationship, as one species kills and eats another (above). Herbivory is similar type of exploitation, except that the plant is usually not killed by the herbivore.

1. Discuss each of the following interspecific relationships, including reference to the species involved, their role in the interaction, and the specific characteristics of the relationship:

   (a) **Mutualism** between ruminant herbivores and their gut microflora: _____

   _____

   _____

   _____

   _____

© Biozone International 2007-2011
Photocopying Prohibited

Periodicals:
Inside story

Related activities: Interspecific Competition, Intraspecific Competition
Weblinks: Ecological Interactions from EcoLibrary, Nearctica Ecology

RA 2

(b) **Commensalism** between a shark and a remora: _____

_____

_____

_____

(c) **Parasitism** between a tapeworm and its human host: _____

_____

_____

_____

(d) **Parasitism** between a cat flea and its host: _____

_____

_____

_____

2. Summarize your knowledge of species interactions by completing the following, entering a (+), (−), or (0) for species B, and writing a brief description of each term. Codes: (+): species benefits, (−): species is harmed, (0): species is unaffected.

Interaction	Species A	Species B	Description of relationship
(a) Mutualism	+		
(b) Commensalism	+		
(c) Parasitism	−		
(d) Amensalism	0		
(e) Predation	−		
(f) Competition	−		
(g) Herbivory	+		
(h) Antibiosis	+ / 0		

3. For each of the interactions between two species described below, choose the correct term to describe the interaction and assign a +, − or 0 for each species involved in the space supplied. Use the completed table above to help you:

Description	Term	Species A	Species B
(a) A tiny cleaner fish picking decaying food from the teeth of a much larger fish (e.g. grouper).	Mutualism	Cleaner fish +	Grouper +
(b) Ringworm fungus growing on the skin of a young child.		Ringworm	Child
(c) Human effluent containing poisonous substances killing fish in a river downstream of discharge.		Humans	Fish
(d) Humans planting cabbages to eat only to find that the cabbages are being eaten by slugs.		Humans	Slugs
(e) A shrimp that gets food scraps and protection from sea anemones, which appear to be unaffected.		Shrimp	Anemone
(f) Birds follow a herd of antelopes to feed off disturbed insects, antelopes alerted to danger by the birds.		Birds	Antelope

Interspecific Competition

In naturally occurring populations, direct competition between different species (**interspecific competition**) is usually less intense than intraspecific competition because coexisting species have evolved slight differences in their realized niches, even though their fundamental niches may overlap (a phenomenon termed **niche differentiation**). This has been well documented in barnacle species (below). However, when two species with very similar niche requirements are brought into direct competition through the introduction of a foreign species, one usually benefits at the expense of the other, which is excluded (the **competitive**

exclusion principle). In many countries, the introduction of foreign, ecologically aggressive species is implicated in the competitive displacement and decline of many native species (see the examples of mallard ducks and squirrels, below). Displacement of native species by introduced ones is more likely if the introduced competitor is also adaptable and hardy. It can be difficult to provide evidence of decline in a species as a direct result of competition, but it can often be inferred if the range of the native species contracts and that of the introduced competitor shows a corresponding increase.

Competitive Exclusion in Barnacles

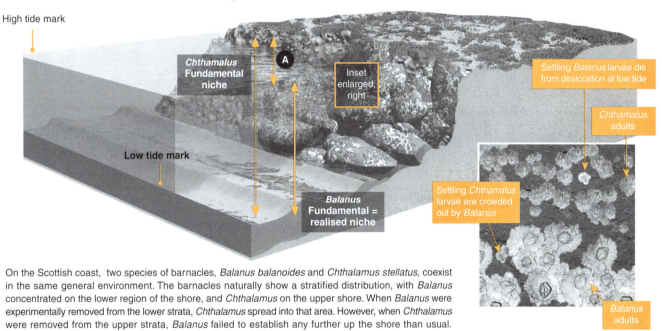

On the Scottish coast, two species of barnacles, *Balanus balanoides* and *Chthalamus stellatus*, coexist in the same general environment. The barnacles naturally show a stratified distribution, with *Balanus* concentrated on the lower region of the shore, and *Chthalamus* on the upper shore. When *Balanus* were experimentally removed from the lower strata, *Chthalamus* spread into that area. However, when *Chthalamus* were removed from the upper strata, *Balanus* failed to establish any further up the shore than usual.

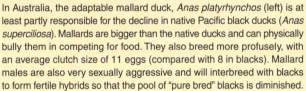

In Australia, the adaptable mallard duck, *Anas platyrhynchos* (left) is at least partly responsible for the decline in native Pacific black ducks (*Anas superciliosa*). Mallards are bigger than the native ducks and can physically bully them in competing for food. They also breed more profusely, with an average clutch size of 11 eggs (compared with 8 in blacks). Mallard males are also very sexually aggressive and will interbreed with blacks to form fertile hybrids so that the pool of "pure bred" blacks is diminished.

The **European red squirrel**, *Sciurus vulgaris*, was the only squirrel species in Britain until the introduction of the **American gray squirrel**, *Sciurus carolinesis*, in 1876. The more adaptable gray squirrel has displaced native red squirrels over much of the British Isles, particularly in the south. Whereas the red squirrels once occupied both coniferous and broad leafed woodland, they are now mostly restricted to coniferous forest and are completely absent from much of their former range.

1. (a) In the example of the barnacles (above), describe what is represented by the zone labelled with the arrow **A**:

(b) Explain the evidence for the barnacle distribution being the result of competitive exclusion:

2. Describe two aspects of the biology of a named introduced species that have helped its success as an invading competitor:

(a)

(b)

Periodicals: The future of red squirrels in Britain

Related activities: Species Interactions, Intraspecific Competition

RA 2

Intraspecific Competition

Some of the most intense competition occurs between individuals of the same species (**intraspecific competition**). Most populations have the capacity to grow rapidly, but their numbers cannot increase indefinitely because environmental resources are finite. Every ecosystem has a **carrying capacity** (K), defined as the number of individuals in a population that the environment can support. Intraspecific competition for resources increases with increasing population size and, at carrying capacity, it reduces the per capita growth rate to zero. When the demand for a particular resource (e.g. food, water, nesting sites, nutrients, or light) exceeds supply, that resource becomes a **limiting factor**. Populations respond to resource limitation by reducing their population growth rate (e.g. through lower birth rates or higher mortality). The response of individuals to limited resources varies depending on the organism. In many invertebrates and some vertebrates such as frogs, individuals reduce their growth rate and mature at a smaller size. In some vertebrates, territoriality spaces individuals apart so that only those with adequate resources can breed. When resources are very limited, the number of available territories will decline.

Intraspecific Competition

Scramble competition in caterpillars

Contest competition in wolves

Display of a male anole

Direct competition for available food between members of the same species is called **scramble competition**. In some situations where scramble competition is intense, none of the competitors gets enough food to survive.

In some cases, competition is limited by hierarchies existing within a social group. Dominant individuals receive adequate food, but individuals low in the hierarchy must **contest** the remaining resources and may miss out.

Intraspecific competition may be for mates or breeding sites, as well as for food. In anole lizards (above), males have a bright red throat pouch and use much of their energy displaying to compete with other males for available mates.

Competition Between Tadpoles of *Rana tigrina*

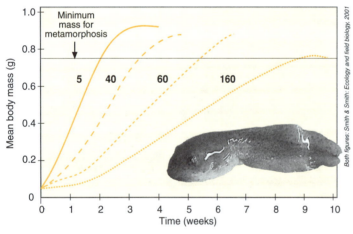

Mean body mass (g) vs Time (weeks). Minimum mass for metamorphosis. Curves labelled 5, 40, 60, 160.

Both figures: Smith & Smith: Ecology and field biology, 2001

Food shortage reduces both individual growth rate and survival, and population growth. In some organisms, where there is a metamorphosis or a series of moults before adulthood (e.g. frogs, crustacean zooplankton, and butterflies), individuals may die before they mature.

The graph (left) shows how the growth rate of tadpoles (*Rana tigrina*) declines as the density increases from 5 to 160 individuals (in the same sized space).

- At high densities, tadpoles grow more slowly, taking longer to reach the minimum size for metamorphosis (0.75 g), and decreasing their chances of successfully metamorphosing from tadpoles into frogs.
- Tadpoles held at lower densities grow faster, to a larger size, metamorphosing at an average size of 0.889 g.
- In some species, such as frogs and butterflies, the adults and juveniles reduce the intensity of intraspecific competition by exploiting different food resources.

1. Using an example, predict the likely effects of **intraspecific competition** on each of the following:

   (a) Individual growth rate: _____

   (b) Population growth rate: _____

   (c) Final population size: _____

2. In the tank experiment with *Rana* (above), the tadpoles were contained in a fixed volume with a set amount of food:

   (a) Describe how *Rana* tadpoles respond to resource limitation: _____

   _____

   (b) Categorize the effect on the tadpoles as density-dependent / density-independent (delete one).

   (c) Comment on how much the results of this experiment are likely to represent what happens in a natural population:

   _____

KEY TERMS: Mix and Match

INSTRUCTIONS: Test your vocabulary by matching each term to its definition, as identified by its preceding letter code.

ALLELOPATHY

AMENSALISM

CARRYING CAPACITY

COMMENSALISM

COMMUNITY

COMPETITION

DEMOGRAPHICS

DENSITY

DISTRIBUTION

EMIGRATION

ENVIRONMENTAL RESISTANCE

EXPLOITATION

EXPONENTIAL GROWTH

IMMIGRATION

K-SELECTION

LIMITING FACTORS

MORTALITY

MUTUALISM

NATALITY

PARASITISM

POPULATION SIZE

r-SELECTION

SIGMOIDAL GROWTH

SURVIVORSHIP CURVE

URBANIZATION

A The relationship in which the presence of one species has a beneficial effect on another but itself is not affected.

B A form of competition between two species in which one is inhibited and the other is not.

C Growth that occurs in multiples based on earlier populations. An accelerating growth rate.

D An interaction between organisms exploiting the same resource.

E A naturally occurring group of different species living within the same environment and interacting together.

F The maximum number of a specific organism that the environment can provide for.

G Selection favoring rapid rates of population increase; especially prominent in species that colonize transient environments.

H Selection that occurs in an environment at or near carrying capacity, favoring the production of a few, highly competitive offspring.

I The birth rate of a population, (usually expressed as the number of births per 1000 individuals).

J The act of leaving the area of one's birth or residence to settle in another area.

K The biotic and abiotic factors that prevent a population from continually increasing in size.

L Interaction in which one species benefits at the expense of another.

M The grouping of populations into particular sets of characteristics, e.g. sex, age etc.

N The act of entering and settling in an area that is different from one's original home.

O A pattern of S-shaped growth, characterized by a lag phase, a phase of rapid growth, and then a stabilizing phase. Also called logistic growth.

P Any factors affecting the maximum number a population can reach.

Q The harmful effect on a plant caused by the release of chemicals into the ground by another plant.

R The total number of individuals of a species within a set habitat or area.

S The redistribution of people from rural areas to urban environments.

T A curve showing the age specific mortality of a population.

U The death rate of a population, (usually expressed as the number of deaths per 1000 individuals).

V Interaction between species in which both participants benefit.

W The number of individuals per unit area.

X The location of individuals in a population within an area.

Y Exploitation involving an organism and its host. The host is detrimentally affected by the relationship, but is not usually killed.

Investigating Ecosystems

Key concepts

▶ Populations are usually too large to assess without sampling.

▶ Common sampling methods include quadrats, transects, mark and recapture, and netting and trapping.

▶ Information about the physical environment is important when investigating ecosystems.

▶ Fieldwork should involve due care and respect of organisms and the environment.

Key terms

age structure
abundance
belt transect
density
direct count
distribution
graph
indicator species
indirect methods
Lincoln index
line transect
mark and recapture
mean
quadrat
qualitative methods
quantitative methods
random sampling
sample
standard deviation

Objectives

☐ 1. Use the **KEY TERMS** to help you understand and complete these objectives.

Sampling Populations   pages 103-114, 117-119

☐ 2. Describe the kind of information that can be gained from population studies including: **abundance**, **density**, age structure, and **distribution**.

☐ 3. Explain why random sampling is important. Describe methods to ensure **random sampling** in field studies.

☐ 4. Describe **quantitative methods** for sampling populations, including: **direct counts**, **quadrats**, **transects**, **mark and recapture** (including the **Lincoln index**), and **netting and trapping**. Describe the advantages and limitations of each method, including suitability to organism and habitat.

☐ 5. Recognize the value of **indirect sampling methods** to population studies.

☐ 6. Describe **qualitative methods** for investigating the distribution of organisms in specific habitats.

☐ 7. Recognize and use appropriate methods to display population data. Calculate simple statistics (e.g. **mean** and **standard deviation)** for sample data.

☐ 8. Calculate and apply simple statistical tests including chi-squared and Student's t test.

☐ 9. Appreciate the role of classification keys in identifying species. Demonstrate an ability to use simple keys to identify plants and animals.

Measuring Abiotic Factors   pages 103-104, 115-116

☐ 10. Explain how abiotic factors influence the distribution and abundance of organisms in a habitat. Explain why population studies invariably involve measuring abiotic factors in the field at the time of population sampling.

☐ 11. Describe methods to measure abiotic factors, including: pH, light, temperature, dissolved oxygen, current speed, conductivity, and total dissolved solids (TDS). Include reference to the relevant units of measurement in each case.

Periodicals:
Listings for this chapter are on page 230

Weblinks:
www.thebiozone.com/
weblink/EnvSci-2764.html

Presentation Media
Environmental Science:
Investigating Ecosystems

Sampling Populations

In most ecological studies, it is not possible to measure or count all the members of a population. Instead, information is obtained through **sampling** in a manner that provides a fair (unbiased) representation of the organisms present and their distribution. This is usually achieved through **random sampling**, a technique in which every possible sample of a given size has the same chance of selection. Most practical exercises in community ecology involve the collection or census of living organisms, with a view to identifying the species and quantifying their abundance and other population features of interest. Sampling techniques must be appropriate to the community being studied and the information you wish to obtain. Any field study must also consider the time and equipment available, the organisms involved, and the impact of the sampling method on the environment. Often indicator species and **species diversity indices** are used as a way of quantifying biodiversity and ecosystem "health". Such indicators can be particularly useful when monitoring ecosystem change and looking for causative factors in species loss.

Quantifying the Diversity of Ecosystems

Reef community:
high density, clumped distribution

The methods we use to sample communities and their constituent populations must be appropriate to the ecosystem being investigated. Communities in which the populations are at low density and have a random or clumped distribution will require a different sampling strategy to those where the populations are uniformly distributed and at higher density. There are many sampling options, each with advantages and drawbacks for particular communities. How would you assess aspects (e.g. species richness, abundance, or distribution) of the reef community above?

Random point sampling

Point sampling: systematic grid

Line and belt transects

Random quadrats

Photo: www.coastal-planning.net

Marine ecologists use quadrat sampling to estimate biodiversity prior to works such as dredging.

Line transects are appropriate to estimate biodiversity along an environmental gradient.

RA

TAG@KU.EDU
MONARCH WATCH
1-888-TAGGING
GHS 831

Tagging has been used for more than 30 years to follow the migration of monarch butterflies. The photograph here depicts an older tagging method, which has largely been replaced by a tag on the underside of the hindwing (inset). The newer method results in better survival and recapture rates and interferes less with flight.

Which Sampling Method?

Field biologists take a number of factors into consideration when deciding on a sampling method for a chosen population or community. The benefits and drawbacks of some common methods are outlined below:

Point sampling is time efficient and good for determining species abundance and community composition. However, organisms in low abundance may be missed.

Transects are well suited to determining changes in community composition along an environmental gradient but can be time consuming to do well.

Quadrats are also good for assessments of community diversity and composition but are largely restricted to plants and immobile animals. Quadrat size must also be appropriate for the organisms being sampled.

Mark and recapture is useful for highly mobile species which are otherwise difficult to record. However, it is time consuming to do well. **Radiotracking** offers an alternative to mark and recapture and is now widely used in conservation to study the movements of both threatened species and pests.

Sensors and Measures

Various meters can be used to quantify aspects of the physical environment, including the pH, temperature, light levels, and turbidity. Meters that measure single factors have now largely been replaced by multi-purpose meters.

Total dissolved solids (TDS) meter: Measures the content of dissolved solids (as ions) in water in mgL^{-1} giving an indication of water quality. The probe measures the conductivity of the water to approximate the level of TDS. TDS can also be measured gravimetrically by evaporating a sample leaving the residue behind.

Quantum light meter: Measures light intensity levels but not light quality (wavelength). Light levels can change dramatically from a forest floor to its canopy. A light meter provides a quantitative measure of these changes, many of which are not detectable with our own visual systems.

All photos: Campus photography University of Waikato

Dissolved oxygen meter: This measures the amount of oxygen dissolved in water (as mgL^{-1}), which gives and indication of water quality and suitability to support organisms such as fish. The **Winkler** method uses a titration of $MnSO_4$, KI, and $K_2S_2O_3$ to determine the concentration of O_2.

Related activities: *Quadrat Sampling, Transect Sampling, Mark and Recapture Sampling, Monitoring Change in an Ecosystem*

RA 2

Using Dataloggers in Field Studies

Usually, when we collect information about populations in the field, we also collect information about the physical environment. This provides important information about the local habitat and can be useful in assessing habitat preference. With the advent of **dataloggers**, collecting this information is straightforward.

Dataloggers are electronic instruments that record measurements over time. They are equipped with a microprocessor, data storage facility, and sensor. Different sensors are used to measure a range of variables in water or air. The datalogger is connected to a computer, and software is used to set the limits of operation (e.g. the sampling interval) and initiate the logger. The logger is then disconnected and used remotely to record and store data. When reconnected to the computer, the data are downloaded, viewed, and plotted. Dataloggers make data collection quick and accurate, and they enable prompt data analysis.

Dataloggers fitted with sensors are portable and easy to use in a wide range of aquatic (left) and terrestrial (right) environments. Different variables can be measured by changing the sensor attached to the logger.

1. Explain why we **sample** populations: _____

_____

2. Describe a sampling technique that would be appropriate for determining each of the following:

    (a) The percentage cover of a plant species in pasture: _____

    (b) The density and age structure of a plankton population: _____

    (c) Change in community composition from low to high altitude on a mountain: _____

3. Explain why it is common practice to also collect information about the physical environment when sampling populations:

_____

_____

Percentage Cover of Mosses and Lichens on Oak Tree

Quadrat 5
Quadrat 4
Quadrat 3
Quadrat 2
Quadrat 1

0   50   100
Percentage cover

- ■ Red stem moss
- ■ Fern moss
- ▦ Snake moss
- ▦ Star moss
- □ Eye brow moss
- ■ Broad leaved star moss
- ▦ Tree moss
- ▦ Lichens (various species)

QUADRAT	1	2	3	4	5
Height (m)	0.4	0.8	1.2	1.6	2.0
Light (arbitrary units)	40	56	68	72	72
Humidity (percent)	99	88	80	76	78
Temperature (°C)	12.1	12.2	13	14.3	14.2

Lichen

Moss

4. The figure (above) shows the changes in vegetation cover along a 2 m vertical transect up the trunk of an oak tree (*Quercus*). Changes in the physical factors light, humidity, and temperature along the same transect were also recorded. From what you know about the ecology of mosses and lichens, account for the observed vegetation distribution:

_____

_____

_____

Quadrat Sampling

Quadrat sampling is a method by which organisms in a certain proportion (sample) of the habitat are counted directly. As with all sampling methods, it is used to estimate population parameters when the organisms present are too numerous to count in total. It can be used to estimate population **abundance** (number), **density**, **frequency of occurrence**, and **distribution**. Quadrats may be used without a transect when studying a relatively uniform habitat. In this case, the quadrat positions are chosen randomly using a random number table.

The general procedure is to count all the individuals (or estimate their percentage cover) in a number of quadrats of known size and to use this information to work out the abundance or percentage cover value for the whole area. The number of quadrats used and their size should be appropriate to the type of organism involved (e.g. grass vs tree).

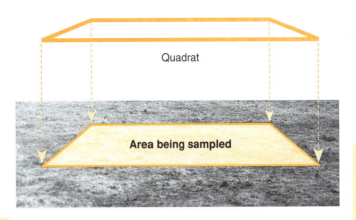

Quadrat

Area being sampled

Investigating Ecosystems

$$\text{Estimated average density} = \frac{\text{Total number of individuals counted}}{\text{Number of quadrats} \times \text{area of each quadrat}}$$

Guidelines for Quadrat Use:

1. The **area of each quadrat** must be known exactly and ideally quadrats should be the same shape. The quadrat does not have to be square (it may be rectangular, hexagonal etc.).

2. **Enough quadrat samples** must be taken to provide results that are representative of the total population.

3. The **population of each quadrat** must be known exactly. Species must be distinguishable from each other, even if they have to be identified at a later date. It has to be decided beforehand what the count procedure will be and how organisms over the quadrat boundary will be counted.

4. The size of the quadrat should be appropriate to the organisms and habitat, e.g. a large size quadrat for trees.

5. The quadrats must be **representative of the whole area**. This is usually achieved by **random sampling** (right).

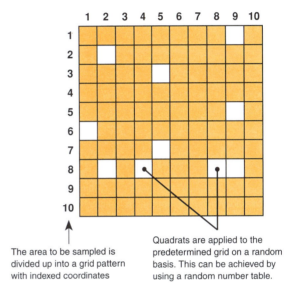

The area to be sampled is divided up into a grid pattern with indexed coordinates

Quadrats are applied to the predetermined grid on a random basis. This can be achieved by using a random number table.

Sampling a centipede population

A researcher by the name of Lloyd (1967) sampled centipedes in Wytham Woods, near Oxford in England. A total of 37 hexagon–shaped quadrats were used, each with a diameter of 30 cm (see diagram on right). These were arranged in a pattern so that they were all touching each other. Use the data in the diagram to answer the following questions.

1. Determine the average number of centipedes captured per quadrat:

   _____

2. Calculate the estimated average density of centipedes per square meter (remember that each quadrat is 0.08 square meters in area):

   _____

3. Looking at the data for individual quadrats, describe in general terms the distribution of the centipedes in the sample area:

   _____

   _____

4. Describe one factor that might account for the distribution pattern:

   _____

   _____

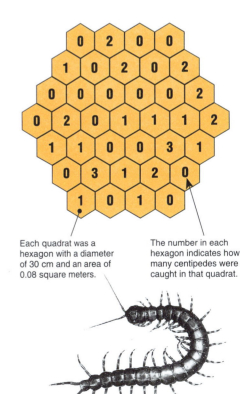

Each quadrat was a hexagon with a diameter of 30 cm and an area of 0.08 square meters.

The number in each hexagon indicates how many centipedes were caught in that quadrat.

Centipede

Related activities: Density and Distribution, Sampling a Leaf Litter Population
Weblinks: Investigating Marine Life, Using Quadrats to Sample

DA 2

Quadrat-Based Estimates

The simplest description of a plant community in a habitat is a list of the species that are present. This qualitative assessment of the community has the limitation of not providing any information about the **relative abundance** of the species present. Quick estimates can be made using **abundance scales**, such as the ACFOR scale described below. Estimates of percentage cover provide similar information. These methods require the use of **quadrats**. Quadrats are used extensively in plant ecology. This activity outlines some of the common considerations when using quadrats to sample plant communities.

What Size Quadrat?

Quadrats are usually square, and cover 0.25 m² (0.5 m x 0.5 m) or 1 m², but they can be of any size or shape, even a single point. The quadrats used to sample plant communities are often 0.25 m². This size is ideal for low-growing vegetation, but quadrat size needs to be adjusted to habitat type. The quadrat must be large enough to be representative of the community, but not so large as to take a very long time to use.

A quadrat covering an area of 0.25 m² is suitable for most low growing plant communities, such as this alpine meadow, fields, and grasslands.

Larger quadrats (e.g. 1 m²) are needed for communities with shrubs and trees. Quadrats as large as 4 m x 4 m may be needed in woodlands.

Small quadrats (0.01 m² or 100 mm x 100 mm) are appropriate for lichens and mosses on rock faces and tree trunks.

How Many Quadrats?

As well as deciding on a suitable quadrat size, the other consideration is how many quadrats to take (the sample size). In species-poor or very homogeneous habitats, a small number of quadrats will be sufficient. In species-rich or heterogeneous habitats, more quadrats will be needed to ensure that all species are represented adequately.

Determining the number of quadrats needed

- Plot the cumulative number of species recorded (on the y axis) against the number of quadrats already taken (on the x axis).

- The point at which the curve levels off indicates the suitable number of quadrats required.

Fewer quadrats are needed in species-poor or very uniform habitats, such as this bluebell woodland.

Describing Vegetation

Density (number of individuals per unit area) is a useful measure of abundance for animal populations, but can be problematic in plant communities where it can be difficult to determine where one plant ends and another begins. For this reason, plant abundance is often assessed using **percentage cover**. Here, the percentage of each quadrat covered by each species is recorded, either as a numerical value or using an abundance scale such as the ACFOR scale.

The ACFOR Abundance Scale

A = Abundant (30% +)

C = Common (20-29%)

F = Frequent (10-19%)

O = Occasional (5-9%)

R = Rare (1-4%)

The ACFOR scale could be used to assess the abundance of species in this wildflower meadow. Abundance scales are subjective, but it is not difficult to determine which abundance category each species falls into.

1. Describe one difference between the methods used to assess species abundance in plant and in animal communities:

_____

2. Identify the main consideration when determining appropriate quadrat size: _____

3. Identify the main consideration when determining number of quadrats: _____

4. Explain two main disadvantages of using the ACFOR abundance scale to record information about a plant community:

(a) _____

(b) _____

Related activities: Sampling Populations, Quadrat Sampling
Weblinks: Ecological Sampling Methods

Sampling a Leaf Litter Population

The diagram on the following page represents an area of leaf litter from a forest floor with a resident population of organisms. The distribution of four animal species as well as the arrangement of leaf litter is illustrated. Leaf litter comprises leaves and debris that have dropped off trees to form a layer of detritus. This exercise is designed to practice the steps required in planning and carrying out a sampling of a natural population. It is desirable, but not essential, that students work in groups of 2–4.

1. **Decide on the sampling method**

   For the purpose of this exercise, it has been decided that the populations to be investigated are too large to be counted directly and a quadrat sampling method is to be used to estimate the average density of the four animal species as well as that of the leaf litter.

2. **Mark out a grid pattern**

   Use a ruler to mark out 3 cm intervals along each side of the sampling area (area of quadrat = 0.03 x 0.03 m). **Draw lines** between these marks to create a 6 x 6 grid pattern (total area = 0.18 x 0.18 m). This will provide a total of 36 quadrats that can be investigated.

3. **Number the axes of the grid**

   Only a small proportion of the possible quadrat positions are going to be sampled. It is necessary to select the quadrats in a random manner. It is not sufficient to simply guess or choose your own on a 'gut feeling'. The best way to choose the quadrats randomly is to create a numbering system for the grid pattern and then select the quadrats from a random number table. Starting at the *top left hand corner*, **number the columns** and **rows** from 1 to 6 on each axis.

4. **Choose quadrats randomly**

   To select the required number of quadrats randomly, use random numbers from a random number table. The random numbers are used as an index to the grid coordinates. Choose 6 quadrats from the total of 36 using table of random numbers provided for you at the bottom of the next page. Make a note of which column of random numbers you choose. Each member of your group should choose a different set of random numbers (i.e. different column: A–D) so that you can compare the effectiveness of the sampling method.

   Column of random numbers chosen: _____

   NOTE: Highlight the boundary of each selected quadrat with coloured pen/highlighter.

5. **Decide on the counting criteria**

   Before the counting of the individuals for each species is carried out, the criteria for counting need to be established.

   There may be some problems here. You must decide before sampling begins as to what to do about individuals that are only partly inside the quadrat. Possible answers include:

   (a) Only counting individuals if they are completely inside the quadrat.

   (b) Only counting individuals that have a clearly defined part of their body inside the quadrat (such as the head).

   (c) Allowing for 'half individuals' in the data (e.g. 3.5 snails).

   (d) Counting an individual that is inside the quadrat by half or more as one complete individual.

   Discuss the merits and problems of the suggestions above with other members of the class (or group). You may even have counting criteria of your own. Think about other factors that could cause problems with your counting.

6. **Carry out the sampling**

   Carefully examine each selected quadrat and **count the number of individuals** of each species present. Record your data in the spaces provided on the following page.

7. **Calculate the population density**

   Use the combined data TOTALS for the sampled quadrats to estimate the average density for each species by using the formula:

   Density =

   $$\frac{\textbf{Total number in all quadrats sampled}}{\textbf{Number of quadrats sampled} \ \ \textbf{X} \ \ \textbf{area of a quadrat}}$$

   Remember that a total of 6 quadrats are sampled and each has an area of 0.0009 m². The density should be expressed as the number of individuals *per square meter* (no. m^{-2}).

   Woodlouse: ☐   False scorpion: ☐

   Centipede: ☐   Leaf: ☐

   Springtail: ☐

8. (a) In this example the animals are not moving. Describe the problems associated with sampling moving organisms. Explain how you would cope with sampling these same animals if they were really alive and very active:

   _____

   _____

   _____

   (b) Carry out a direct count of all 4 animal species and the leaf litter for the whole sample area (all 36 quadrats). Apply the data from your direct count to the equation given in (7) above to calculate the actual population density (remember that the number of quadrats in this case = 36):

   Woodlouse: ☐   Centipede: ☐   False scorpion: ☐   Springtail: ☐   Leaf: ☐

   Compare your estimated population density to the actual population density for each species:

   _____

   _____

   _____

Related activities: Quadrat Sampling, Quadrat-Based Estimates   **PDA 2**

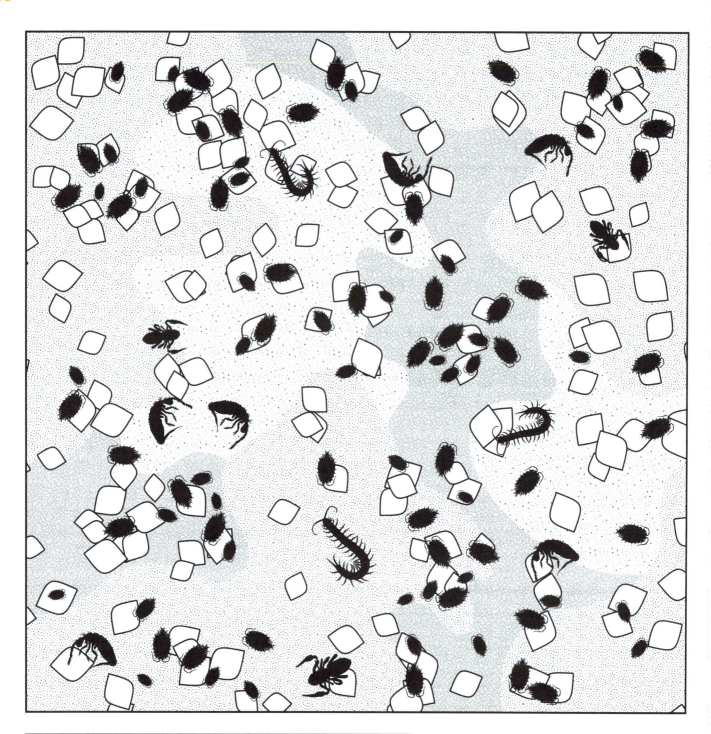

Coordinates for each quadrat	Woodlouse	Centipede	False scorpion	Springtail	Leaf
1:					
2:					
3:					
4:					
5:					
6:					
TOTAL					

Table of random numbers

A	B	C	D
2 2	3 1	6 2	2 2
3 2	1 5	6 3	4 3
3 1	5 6	3 6	6 4
4 6	3 6	1 3	4 5
4 3	4 2	4 5	3 5
5 6	1 4	3 1	1 4

The table above has been adapted from a table of random numbers from a statistics book. Use this table to select quadrats randomly from the grid above. Choose one of the columns (A to D) and use the numbers in that column as an index to the grid. The first digit refers to the row number and the second digit refers to the column number. To locate each of the 6 quadrats, find where the row and column intersect, as shown below:

Example: 5 2   refers to the 5th row and the 2nd column

Transect Sampling

A **transect** is a line placed across a community of organisms. Transects are usually carried out to provide information on the **distribution** of species in the community. This is of particular value in situations where environmental factors change over the sampled distance (**environmental gradient**) or in the transition area between one ecosystem and another (**ecotone**). The usual practice for small transects is to stretch a string between two markers. The string is marked off in measured distance intervals, and the species at each marked point are noted. The sampling points along the transect may also be used for the siting of quadrats, so that changes in density and community composition can be recorded. Belt transects are essentially a form of continuous quadrat sampling. They provide more information on community composition but can be difficult to carry out. Some transects provide information on the vertical, as well as horizontal, distribution of species (e.g. tree canopies in a forest).

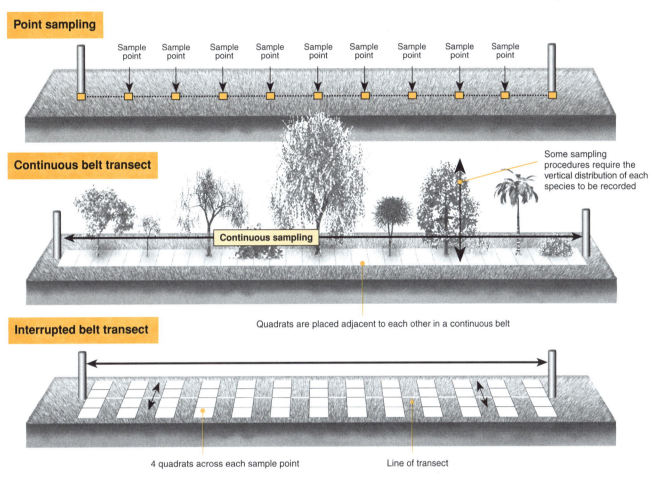

Point sampling

Sample point — Sample point — Sample point — Sample point — Sample point — Sample point — Sample point — Sample point — Sample point

Continuous belt transect

Continuous sampling

Some sampling procedures require the vertical distribution of each species to be recorded

Quadrats are placed adjacent to each other in a continuous belt

Interrupted belt transect

4 quadrats across each sample point   Line of transect

1. Belt transect sampling uses quadrats placed along a line at marked intervals. In contrast, point sampling transects record only the species that are touched or covered by the line at the marked points.

   (a) Describe one disadvantage of belt transects: _____

   _____

   (b) Explain why line transects may give an unrealistic sample of the community in question: _____

   _____

   _____

   (c) Explain how belt transects overcome this problem: _____

   _____

   (d) Describe a situation where the use of transects to sample the community would be inappropriate: _____

   _____

2. Explain how you could test whether or not a transect sampling interval was sufficient to accurately sample a community:

   _____

   _____

   _____

Kite graphs are an ideal way in which to present distributional data from a belt transect (e.g. abundance or percentage cover along an environmental gradient. Usually, they involve plots for more than one species. This makes them good for highlighting probable differences in habitat preference between species. Kite graphs may also be used to show changes in distribution with time (e.g. with daily or seasonal cycles).

3. The data on the right were collected from a rocky shore field trip. Periwinkles from four common species of the genus *Littorina* were sampled in a continuous belt transect from the low water mark, to a height of 10 m above that level. The number of each of the four species in a 1 m² quadrat was recorded.

Plot a **kite graph** of the data for all four species on the grid below. Be sure to choose a scale that takes account of the maximum number found at any one point and allows you to include all the species on the one plot. Include the scale on the diagram so that the number at each point on the kite can be calculated.

An Example of a Kite Graph

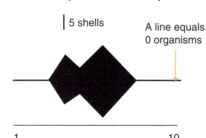

| 5 shells

A line equals
0 organisms

1   10

Distance above water line (m)

Field data notebook

Numbers of periwinkles (4 common species) showing vertical distribution on a rocky shore

Periwinkle species:

Height above low water (m)	L. littorea	L. saxatalis	L. neritoides	L. littoralis
0-1	0	0	0	0
1-2	1	0	0	3
2-3	3	0	0	17
3-4	9	3	0	12
4-5	15	12	0	1
5-6	5	24	0	0
6-7	2	9	2	0
7-8	0	2	11	0
8-9	0	0	47	0
9-10	0	0	59	0

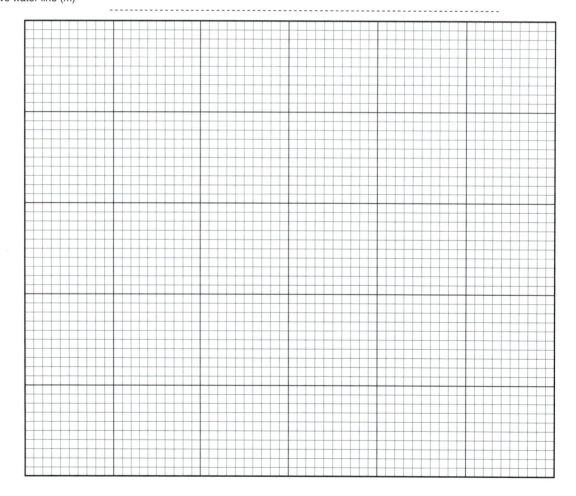

Mark and Recapture Sampling

The mark and recapture method of estimating population size is used in the study of animal populations where individuals are highly mobile. It is of no value where animals do not move or move very little. The number of animals caught in each sample must be large enough to be valid. The technique is outlined in the diagram below.

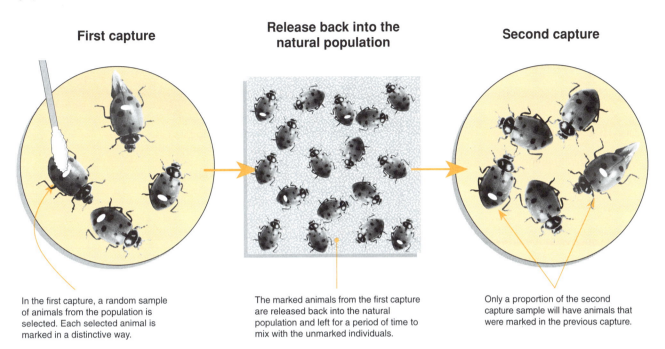

First capture

Release back into the natural population

Second capture

In the first capture, a random sample of animals from the population is selected. Each selected animal is marked in a distinctive way.

The marked animals from the first capture are released back into the natural population and left for a period of time to mix with the unmarked individuals.

Only a proportion of the second capture sample will have animals that were marked in the previous capture.

Investigating Ecosystems

The Lincoln Index

$$\text{Total population} = \frac{\text{No. of animals in 1st sample (all marked)} \quad X \quad \text{Total no. of animals in 2nd sample}}{\text{Number of marked animals in the second sample (recaptured)}}$$

The mark and recapture technique comprises a number of simple steps:

1. The population is sampled by capturing as many of the individuals as possible and practical.

2. Each animal is marked in a way to distinguish it from unmarked animals (unique mark for each individual not required).

3. Return the animals to their habitat and leave them for a long enough period for complete mixing with the rest of the population to take place.

4. Take another sample of the population (this does not need to be the same sample size as the first sample, but it does have to be large enough to be valid).

5. Determine the numbers of marked to unmarked animals in this second sample. Use the equation above to estimate the size of the overall population.

1. For this exercise you will need several boxes of matches and a pen. Work in a group of 2-3 students to 'sample' the population of matches in the full box by using the mark and recapture method. Each match will represent one animal.

(a) Take out 10 matches from the box and mark them on 4 sides with a pen so that you will be able to recognize them from the other unmarked matches later.
(b) Return the marked matches to the box and shake the box to mix the matches.
(c) Take a sample of 20 matches from the same box and record the number of marked matches and unmarked matches.
(d) Determine the total population size by using the equation above.
(e) Repeat the sampling 4 more times (steps b–d above) and record your results:

	Sample 1	Sample 2	Sample 3	Sample 4	Sample 5
Estimated population					

(f) Count the actual number of matches in the matchbox : _____

(g) Compare the actual number to your estimates. By how much does it differ: _____

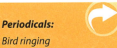

Periodicals:
Bird ringing

Related activities: Sampling Populations,
Sampling Animal Populations

RDA 2

2. In 1919 a researcher by the name of Dahl wanted to estimate the number of trout in a Norwegian lake. The trout were subject to fishing so it was important to know how big the population was in order to manage the fish stock. He captured and marked 109 trout in his first sample. A few days later, he caught 177 trout in his second sample, of which 57 were marked. Use the Lincoln index (on the previous page) to estimate the total population size:

Size of first sample: _____

Size of second sample: _____

Number marked in second sample: _____

Estimated total population: _____

3. Discuss some of the problems with the mark and recapture method if the second sampling is:

(a) Left too long a time before being repeated: _____

_____

_____

(b) Too soon after the first sampling: _____

_____

_____

4. Describe two important assumptions being made in this method of sampling, which would cause the method to fail if they were not true:

(a) _____

_____

_____

(b) _____

_____

_____

5. Some types of animal would be unsuitable for this method of population estimation (i.e. would not work).

(a) Name an animal for which this method of sampling would not be effective: _____

(b) Explain your answer above: _____

_____

_____

6. Describe three methods for marking animals for mark and recapture sampling. Take into account the possibility of animals shedding their skin, or being difficult to get close to again:

(a) _____

(b) _____

(c) _____

7. At various times since the 1950s, scientists in the UK and Canada have been involved in computerized tagging programmes for Northern cod (a species once abundant in Northern Hemisphere waters but now severely depleted). Describe the type of information that could be obtained through such tagging programmes:

_____

_____

_____

_____

Sampling Animal Populations

Unlike plants, most animals are highly mobile and present special challenges in terms of sampling them **quantitatively** to estimate their distribution and abundance. The equipment available for sampling animals ranges from various types of nets and traps (below), to more complex electronic devices, such as those used for radio-tracking large mobile species.

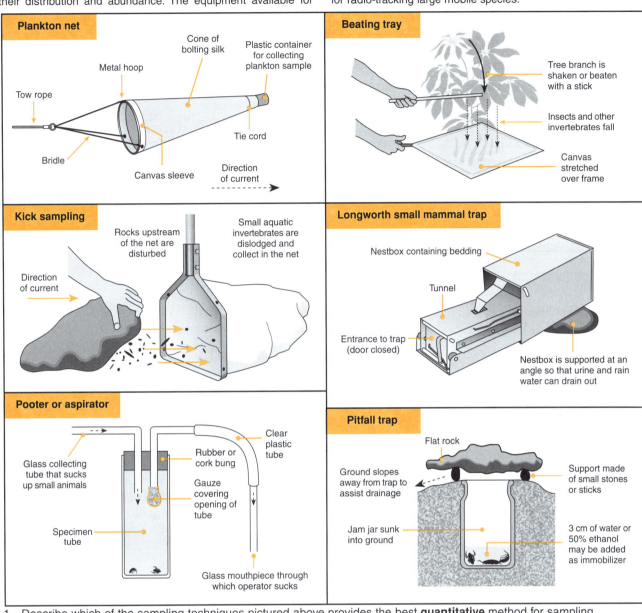

Plankton net
- Tow rope
- Bridle
- Metal hoop
- Canvas sleeve
- Cone of bolting silk
- Plastic container for collecting plankton sample
- Tie cord
- Direction of current

Beating tray
- Tree branch is shaken or beaten with a stick
- Insects and other invertebrates fall
- Canvas stretched over frame

Kick sampling
- Direction of current
- Rocks upstream of the net are disturbed
- Small aquatic invertebrates are dislodged and collect in the net

Longworth small mammal trap
- Nestbox containing bedding
- Tunnel
- Entrance to trap (door closed)
- Nestbox is supported at an angle so that urine and rain water can drain out

Pooter or aspirator
- Glass collecting tube that sucks up small animals
- Rubber or cork bung
- Clear plastic tube
- Gauze covering opening of tube
- Specimen tube
- Glass mouthpiece through which operator sucks

Pitfall trap
- Flat rock
- Ground slopes away from trap to assist drainage
- Support made of small stones or sticks
- Jam jar sunk into ground
- 3 cm of water or 50% ethanol may be added as immobilizer

Investigating Ecosystems

1. Describe which of the sampling techniques pictured above provides the best **quantitative** method for sampling invertebrates in vegetation. Explain your answer:

_____

_____

_____

_____

2. Explain why pitfall traps are not recommended for estimates of population density: _____

_____

_____

3. (a) Explain how mesh size could influence the sampling efficiency of a plankton net: _____

_____

(b) Explain how this would affect your choice of mesh size when sampling animals in a pond: _____

_____

Related activities: Mark & Recapture Sampling, Sampling a Leaf Litter Population

RA 2

Indirect Sampling

If populations are small and easily recognized they may be monitored directly quite easily. However, direct measurement of elusive, easily disturbed, or widely dispersed populations is not always feasible. In these cases, indirect methods can be used to assess population abundance, provide information on habitat use and range, and enable biologists to link habitat quality to species presence or absence. Indirect sampling methods provide less reliable measures of abundance than direct sampling methods, such as mark and recapture, but are widely used nevertheless. They rely on recording the signs of a species, e.g. scat, calls, tracks, and rubbings or markings on vegetation, and using these to assess population abundance. In Australia, the Environmental Protection Agency (EPA) provides a Frog Census Datasheet (below) on which volunteers record details about frog populations and habitat quality in their area. This programme enables the EPA to gather information across Australia.

INFORMATION NEEDED FOR THE FROG CENSUS
- Where you recorded frogs calling; When you made the recordings; and What frogs you recorded (if possible).

Observers Name:
Contact Address:

Post Code:
Telephone Home: _____ Work / Mobile:

Do You Want to be involved next year?(Please Circle)

Location Description (Try to provide enough detail to enable us to find map.
Please use a separate datasheet for each site)

is location the same as in (CIRCLE) 1994 1995 1996 1997

Grid Reference of Location and Type of Map Used:
OR Street Directory Reference:_____ Year and Edition:
Page Number:_____ Grid Reference:
Nearest Town from Location (if known):

Date of Observation (e.g. 8 Sept 1998):
Time Range of Observation (e.g. 8.30-8.40 pm):

HABITAT ASSESSMENT
Habitat Type (please circle one):   pond   dam   stream   drain
                reservoir   wetland   spring   swamp
Comments:

WATER QUALITY and WEATHER
CIRCLE to indicate the condition of the site (you can circle more than one choice).
Water Flow: Still   Flowing Slowly Flowing Quickly
Water Appearance: Clear   Polluted   Frothy Oily
              Muddy
Weather Conditions: 1. Windy / Still
               2. Overcast / Recent Rains / Dry (indicate for 1 AND 2)

FROGS HEARD CALLING
Please indicate your estimate of how many frogs you heard calling (NOTE it is very important to tell us if you heard no frogs)
Number of Calls Heard (circle):
None   One   Few (2-9)   Many (10-50)   Lots (>50)
If you want to test your frog knowledge write the species you heard calling:
Species of Frog(s) Identified: 1._____   2._____
                  3._____   4._____
Comments:

Now we need you to return your datasheet and tape in the postage free post-pak addressed to REPLY PAID 6360 Mr Peter Goonan Environment Protection Agency GPO Box 2607 ADELAIDE SA 5001. We will identify your frog calls and let you the results of your recordings.

Office use only. Please leave blank.
FROG SPECIES PRESENT.

cies Number	Species 1	Species 2	Species 3	Species 4	Species 5
cies Name					
(2 - 9)					
y (10 - 50)					
(>50)					

ENVIRONMENT PROTECTION AGENCY
DEPARTMENT FOR ENVIRONMENT HERITAGE AND ABORIGINAL AFFAIRS

Recording a date and accurate map reference is important

Population estimates are based on the number of frog calls recorded by the observer

To sample nocturnal, highly mobile species, e.g. bats, electronic devices, such as the bat detector above, can be used to estimate population density. In this case, the detector is tuned to the particular frequency of the hunting clicks emitted by specific bat species. The number of calls recorded per unit time can be used to estimate numbers per area.

The analysis of animal tracks allows wildlife biologists to identify habitats in which animals live and to conduct population surveys. Interpreting tracks accurately requires considerable skill as tracks may vary in appearance even when from the same individual. Tracks are particularly useful as a way to determine habitat use and preference.

▶Wombat scat

All animals leave scats (feces) which are species specific and readily identifiable. Scats can be a valuable tool by which to gather data from elusive, nocturnal, easily disturbed, or highly mobile species. Fecal analyses can provide information on diet, movements, population density, sex ratios, age structure, and even genetic diversity.

1. (a) Describe the kind of information that could be gathered from the Frog Census Datasheet:

_____

(b) Identify the benefits of linking a measure of abundance to habitat assessment: _____

_____

2. Describe one other indirect method of population sampling and outline its advantages and drawbacks:

_____

_____

_____

Weblinks: New Zealand Frog Survey

Periodicals:
Bowels of the beasts

Monitoring Change in an Ecosystem

Much of the importance we place on ecosystem change stems ultimately from what we want from that ecosystem. Ecosystems are monitored for changes in their status so that their usefulness can be maintained, whether that use is for agriculture, industry, recreation, or conservation. Never is this so apparent as in the monitoring of aquatic ecosystems. Aquatic environments of all types provide aesthetic pleasure, food, habitat for wildlife, water for industry and irrigation, and potable water. The different uses of aquatic environments demand different standards of **water quality**. For any water body, this is defined in terms of various chemical, physical, and biological characteristics. Together, these factors define the 'health' of the aquatic ecosystem and its suitability for various desirable uses. Water quality is determined by measurement or analysis on-site or in the laboratory. Other methods, involving the use of **indicator species**, can also be used to biologically assess the health of a water body.

Techniques for Monitoring Water Quality

Some aspects of water quality, such as black disk clarity measurements (above), must be made in the field.

The collection of water samples allows many quality measurements to be carried out in the laboratory.

Telemetry stations transmit continuous measurements of the water level of a lake or river to a central control office.

Temperature and dissolved oxygen measurements must be carried out directly in the flowing water.

Water Quality Standards in Aquatic Ecosystems

Water quality variable	Why measured	Standards applied:	
Dissolved oxygen	• A requirement for most aquatic life • Indicator of organic pollution • Indicator of photosynthesis (plant growth)	More than 80% saturation More than 5 gm^{-3}	**(F, FS, SG)** **(WS)**
Temperature	• Organisms have specific temperature needs • Indicator of mixing processes • Computer modeling examining the uptake and release of nutrients	Less than 25°C Less than 3°C change along a stretch of river	**(F)** **(AE, F, FS, SG)**
Conductivity	• Indicator of total salts dissolved in water • Indicator for geothermal input		
pH (acidity)	• Aquatic life protection • Indicator of industrial discharges, mining	Between pH 6 - 9	**(WS)**
Clarity - turbidity - black disk	• Aesthetic appearance • Aquatic life protection • Indicator of catchment condition, land use	Turbidity: 2 NTU Black disk: more than 1.6 m	**(AE, CR, A)**
Color - light absorption	• Aesthetic appearance • Light availability for excessive plant growth • Indicator of presence of organic matter		
Nutrients (Nitrogen, phosphorus)	• Enrichment, excessive plant growth • Limiting factor for plant and algal growth	DIN: less than 0.100 gm^{-3} DRP: less than 0.030 gm^{-3} NO$_3^-$: less than 10 gm^{-3}	**(AE, A)** **(WS)**
Major ions (Mg^{2+}, Ca^{2+}, Na$^+$, K$^+$, Cl$^-$, HCO$_3^-$, SO$_4^{2-}$)	• Baseline water quality characteristics • Indicator for catchment soil types, geology • Water hardness (magnesium/calcium) • Buffering capacity for pH change (HCO$_3^-$)		
Organic carbon	• Indicator of organic pollution • Catchment characteristics	BOD: less than 5 gm^{-3}	**(AE, CR, A)**
Fecal bacteria	• Indicator of pollution with fecal matter • Disease risk for swimming etc.	ENT: less than 33 cm^{-3} FC: less than 200 cm^{-3}	**(CR)**

Standards refer to specific water uses:
AE = aquatic ecosystem protection
A = aesthetic
CR = contact recreation
SG = shellfish gathering
WS = water supply
F = fishery
FS = fish spawning
SW = stock watering

Abbreviations:
NTU = unit of turbidity measurement
DIN = dissolved inorganic nitrogen
DRP = dissolved reactive phosphorus
BOD = biochemical oxygen demand
ENT = enterococci
FC = fecal coliform

Spawning salmon require high oxygen levels for egg survival.

1. Explain why dissolved oxygen, temperature, and clarity measurements are made in the field rather than in the laboratory:

_____

_____

_____

_____

Related activities: Sampling Populations

DA 2

Calculation and Use of Diversity Indices

One of the best ways to determine the health of an ecosystem is to measure the variety (rather than the absolute number) of organisms living in it. Certain species, called **indicator species**, are typical of ecosystems in a particular state (e.g. polluted or pristine). An objective evaluation of an ecosystem's biodiversity can provide valuable insight into its status, particularly if the species assemblages have changed as a result of disturbance.

Diversity can be quantified using a **diversity index (DI)**. Diversity indices attempt to quantify the degree of diversity and identify indicators for environmental stress or degradation. Most indices of diversity are easy to use and they are widely used in ecological work, particularly for monitoring ecosystem change or pollution. One example, which is a derivation of **Simpson's index**, is described below. Other indices produce values ranging between 0 and almost 1. These are more easily interpreted because of the more limited range of values, but no single index offers the "best" measure of diversity: they are chosen on their suitability to different situations.

Simpson's Index for finite populations

This diversity index (DI) is a commonly used inversion of Simpson's index, suitable for finite populations.

$$DI = \frac{N(N-1)}{\Sigma n(n-1)}$$

After Smith and Smith as per IOB.

Where:

- **DI** = Diversity index
- **N** = Total number of individuals (of all species) in the sample
- **n** = Number of individuals of each species in the sample

This index ranges between 1 (low diversity) and infinity. The higher the value, the greater the variety of living organisms. It can be difficult to evaluate objectively without reference to some standard ecosystem measure because the values calculated can, in theory, go to infinity.

Example of species diversity in a stream

The example describes the results from a survey of stream invertebrates. The species have been identified, but this is not necessary in order to calculate diversity as long as the different species can be distinguished. Calculation of the DI using Simpson's index for finite populations is:

Species	No. of individuals
A (Common backswimmer)	12
B (Stonefly larva)	7
C (Silver water beetle)	2
D (Caddis fly larva)	6
E (Water spider)	5
Total number of individuals = 32	

$$DI = \frac{32 \times 31}{(12 \times 11) + (7 \times 6) + (2 \times 1) + (6 \times 5) + (5 \times 4)} = \frac{992}{226} = 4.39$$

A stream community with a high macroinvertebrate diversity (above) in contrast to a low diversity stream community (below).

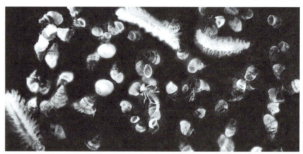

Photos: Stephen Moore

2. Discuss the link between water quality and land use: _____

_____

_____

_____

3. Describe a situation where a species diversity index may provide useful information: _____

_____

_____

4. An area of forest floor was sampled and six invertebrate species were recorded, with counts of 7, 10, 11, 2, 4, and 3 individuals. Using Simpson's index for finite populations, calculate DI for this community:

(a) DI = _____   DI = _____

(b) Comment on the diversity of this community: _____

_____

_____

5. Explain how you could use indicator species to detect pollution in a stream: _____

_____

_____

Radio-tracking

Field work involving difficult terrain, aquatic environments, or highly mobile, secretive, or easily disturbed species, has been greatly assisted in recent years by the use of radio-transmitter technology. Radio-tracking can be used to quickly obtain accurate information about an animal's home range and can provide information about dispersal, distribution, habitat use, and competitive relationships. Radio-tracking is particularly suited to population studies of threatened species (because it is relatively non-invasive) and of pests (because their dispersal and habitat use can be monitored). The information can be used to manage an endangered species effectively or to plan more efficient pest control operations. Satellite transmitters can be used to study migratory movements of large animals and marine species, which are more difficult to follow.

Radio-tracking technology is widely used in conservation work to study animal movements and habitat use. The information allows conservation organizations to develop better strategies for the management of species in the wild or follow the progress of reintroduced captive-bred animals.

A tracking antenna and receiver can be used to pinpoint the location of an animal. Antennae are directional and so can accurately fix an animal's position. They can be mounted on to light aircraft or off-road vehicles to provide mobile tracking over large areas. For work in inaccessible or difficult terrain, portable, hand-held antennae are used.

Australian brush-tailed possums are a major pest in New Zealand where they damage native forests, and prey on native birds. Radio-tracking is used on possums in critical conservation areas to determine dispersal rates, distribution, and habitat use. This allows pest control can be implemented more effectively.

From Bonfil et al 2005.

Tracking Migrations

During 2002 and 2003, a number of great white sharks were radio-tagged in South African waters. The data recovered showed the first ever recorded intercontinental migration by a great white. A female shark known as P12, swam 11 000 km from South Africa to Australia in 99 days with a minimum speed just under 5 kmh^{-1}. Within 9 months she had returned to South African waters, completing a round trip of more than 20 000 km.

1. Describe two applications of radio-tracking technology in endangered species management: _____

_____

_____

_____

2. Explain why radio-tracking might be used to monitor pest species: _____

_____

_____

_____

3. Explain how radio-tracking has increased our knowledge of the movement of marine animals: _____

_____

_____

_____

_____

Related activities: Sampling Animal Populations
Weblinks: Transoceanic Migration of White Sharks

EA 2

Classification Keys

Community analysis is easier and more meaningful if the species sampled can be correctly identified. Classification systems provide a way in which to distinguish and identify species. An organism's classification should include a clear, unambiguous **description**, an accurate **diagram**, and its unique name, denoted by the **genus** and **species**. Classification keys are used to identify an organism and assign it to the correct species (assuming that the organism has already been formally classified and is included in the key). Typically, keys are **dichotomous** and involve a series of linked steps. At each step, a choice is made between two features; each alternative leads to another question until an identification is made. If the organism cannot be identified, it may be a new species, or the key may be inappropriate or need revision. An example of a **dichotomous key** is described below. It describes features for identifying the larvae of various genera within the order Trichoptera (caddisflies). From this key you should be able to assign a generic name to each of the caddisfly larvae pictured.

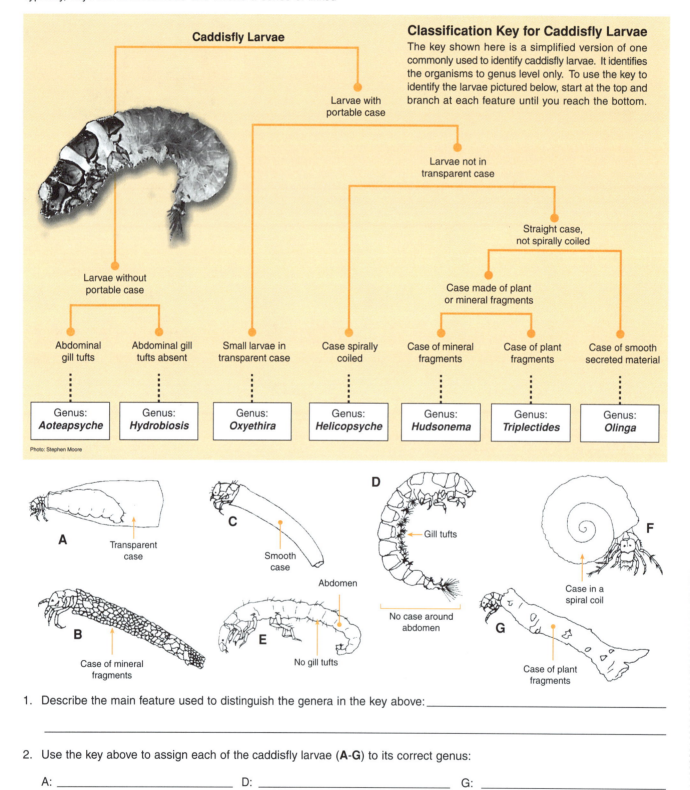

Classification Key for Caddisfly Larvae

The key shown here is a simplified version of one commonly used to identify caddisfly larvae. It identifies the organisms to genus level only. To use the key to identify the larvae pictured below, start at the top and branch at each feature until you reach the bottom.

Caddisfly Larvae

Larvae with portable case

Larvae not in transparent case

Straight case, not spirally coiled

Case made of plant or mineral fragments

Larvae without portable case

| Abdominal gill tufts | Abdominal gill tufts absent | Small larvae in transparent case | Case spirally coiled | Case of mineral fragments | Case of plant fragments | Case of smooth secreted material |

| Genus: *Aoteapsyche* | Genus: *Hydrobiosis* | Genus: *Oxyethira* | Genus: *Helicopsyche* | Genus: *Hudsonema* | Genus: *Triplectides* | Genus: *Olinga* |

Photo: Stephen Moore

A — Transparent case

C — Smooth case / Abdomen

D — Gill tufts / No case around abdomen

F — Case in a spiral coil

B — Case of mineral fragments

E — No gill tufts

G — Case of plant fragments

1. Describe the main feature used to distinguish the genera in the key above: _____

_____

2. Use the key above to assign each of the caddisfly larvae (**A-G**) to its correct genus:

A: _____   D: _____   G: _____

B: _____   E: _____

C: _____   F: _____

Related activities: Keying Out Plant Species

Keying Out Plant Species

Dichotomous keys are a useful tool in biology and can enable identification to the species level provided the characteristics chosen are appropriate for separating species. Keys are extensively used by botanists as they are quick and easy to use in the field, although they sometimes rely on the presence of particular plant parts such as fruits or flowers. Some also require some specialist knowledge of plant biology. The following simple activity requires you to identify five species of the genus *Acer* from illustrations of the leaves. It provides valuable practice in using characteristic features to identify plants to species level.

A Dichotomous Key to Some Common Maple Species

1a Adult leaves with five lobes 2

1b Adult leaves with three lobes 4

    2a Leaves 7.5-13 cm wide, with smooth edges, lacking serrations along the margin. U shaped sinuses between lobes.

        Sugar maple, *Acer saccharum*

    2b Leaves with serrations (fine teeth) along the margin 3

        3a Leaves 5-13 cm wide and deeply lobed.

            Japansese maple, *Acer palmatum*

        3b Leaves 13-18 cm wide and deeply lobed.

            Silver maple, *Acer saccharinum*

        4a Leaves 5-15 cm wide with small sharp serrations on the margins. Distinctive V shaped sinuses between the lobes.

            Red maple, *Acer rubrum*

        4b Leaves 7.5-13 cm wide without serrations on the margins. Shallow sinuses between the lobes.

            Black maple, *Acer nigrum*

A

D

B   Sinus

Lobe

C

E

0 1 2 3 4
cm

1. Use the dichotomous key to the common species of *Acer* to identify the species illustrated by the leaves (drawn to scale). Begin at the top of the key and make a choice as to which of the illustrations best fits the description:

(a) Species A: _____

(b) Species B: _____

(c) Species C: _____

(d) Species D: _____

(e) Species E: _____

2. Identify a feature that could be used to identify maple species when leaves are absent: _____

3. When identifying a plant, suggest what you should be sure of before using a key to classify it to species level:

_____

_____

4. Explain the importance of correctly identifying species when carrying out population studies: _____

_____

_____

KEY TERMS: Mix and Match

INSTRUCTIONS: Test your vocabulary by matching each term to its definition, as identified by its preceding letter code.

AGE STRUCTURE

A A calculated statistic used to express the variability of a population about the mean.

ABUNDANCE

B Sampling methods for aspects of animal population biology (e.g. abundance) that is independent of sighting the animals themselves (e.g. by using the signs such as scat, calls, tracks).

BELT TRANSECT

C The sum of the data divided by the number of data entries (n).

DENSITY

D Sampling method in which the organism sampled is present during the sampling.

DIRECT COUNT

E The number of individuals per unit area.

DISTRIBUTION

F A line across a habitat along which organisms are sampled at set intervals to determine changes in community composition.

GRAPH

G The location of individuals of a population within an area.

INDICATOR SPECIES

H Sampling method used to determine the size of a population in which individuals from a population are marked and released and then recapture after a set period of time.

INDIRECT METHODS

I Species that can be used to infer the health or state of an ecosystem by either their presence, abundance or absence.

LINCOLN INDEX

J Sampling method in which numerical data is recorded, e.g. the number of individuals in an area.

LINE TRANSECT

K Method in which descriptions or observations are recorded in a non-numerical way, e.g. the behavior of individuals.

MARK AND RECAPTURE

L A form of continuous quadrat sampling along a line.

MEAN

M Sampling method using a technique to ensure that every possible sample of a given size has the same chance of selection.

QUADRAT

N A measured and marked region used to isolate a sample area for study.

QUALITATIVE METHODS

O A sub-set of a whole used to estimate the values that might have been obtained if every individual or response was measured.

QUANTITATIVE METHODS

P The number of organisms in a population or area.

RANDOM SAMPLING

Q A diagram which displays numerical information in a way that can be used to identify trends in the data.

SAMPLE

R The structure of a population base upon the number of individuals in a particular age bracket.

STANDARD DEVIATION

S Index which measures the size of a population based on capturing, marking and recapturing individuals in a population.

Land and Water

Land

Agriculture
- The green revolution
- Economic importance of agriculture
- Soil degradation and conservation
- Sustainable forestry
- Pest control systems

Land management
- Deforestation and desertification
- Mining and minerals
- Rangeland management
- City planning and transport
- Soil and ecosystem remediation

Water

Agriculture
- Irrigation
  - see Earth's Systems

Fisheries
- Monitoring and managing fish stocks
- Sustainable yields
- Impact of by-catch on fish stocks
- Environmental effects of fishing
- Aquaculture

Much of the Earth's land is devoted to agriculture or is otherwise intensively used.

Overfishing, intensive water use, and pollution have significantly depleted aquatic resources.

Global Resources

The growing human population is putting pressure on the Earth's limited resources.

Global resources include land, water, minerals, and energy resources.

Sustainable and environmentally sound use of the Earth's resources can help reduce habitat loss and resource depletion.

Energy can be transformed in many ways; some methods are more efficient than others.

Efficient use of energy and energy resources will help reduce future energy demands.

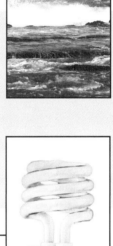

Energy concepts
- Transformation of energy
- Electricity generation

Non renewable energy
- Fossil fuels, extraction, and uses
- Nuclear power generation

Renewable energy
- Wind, water, solar, and geothermal
- Advantages and disadvantages
- Environmental effects

Energy efficiency
- Energy efficiency
- Efficient building design
- Measuring efficiency

Energy conservation
- Economic and environmental importance of efficient energy use
- New technologies
  - hybrid vehicles
  - hydrogen fuel cells
  - future concepts

Energy Generation

Energy Conservation

Energy

Land and Water

Key concepts

▶ Agriculture and forestry require careful management of resources to ensure their long term sustainability.

▶ Intensive farming practices require the input of large amounts of energy and water.

▶ Careful land management and development reduces environmental disturbance.

▶ Many fisheries have been over fished and require intensive management through restrictions or closure.

Key terms

aquaculture

by-catch

chemical pest control

cultivation

desertification

erosion

globalization

green revolution

Integrated pest management

intensive industrialized agriculture

maximum sustainable yield (MSY)

mineral

mining

pests

rangeland

remediation

salinization

soil conservation

soil degradation

stock indicators

subsistence farming

sustainable agriculture

sustainable forestry

trawling

urban development

weeds

Objectives

☐ 1. Use the **KEY TERMS** to help you understand and complete these objectives.

Agriculture and Forestry
pages 123-144

☐ 2. Explain the importance of plants to humans. Identify important cereal crop plants and describe their **cultivation**, and economic and dietary importance. Outline the consequences of crop failure.

☐ 3. Explain what is meant by the **green revolution** and describe how it has improved crop yields. Distinguish between the initial green revolution and the second green revolution (=gene revolution).

☐ 4. Describe and contrast the differences between **subsistence farming** and **intensive industrialized agriculture**.

☐ 5. Explain the term **sustainable agriculture.** Contrast it with **industrialized intensive agriculture**. Your discussion should refer to organic and inorganic farming, pesticide use, energy inputs, amount of land used, and long term sustainability.

☐ 6. Compare and contrast **chemical pest control** and **integrated pest management** (**IPM**), including economic and environmental considerations.

☐ 7. Describe **soil degradation** (including **erosion**) and its effects on the environment. Explain how **soil conservation** methods can prevent soil degradation and loss.

☐ 8. Describe different methods of forestry and their environmental impact. Comment on the sustainability of these methods in different situations.

Use of Land
pages 145-148

☐ 9. Describe the nature of **rangelands** and why they are ecologically valuable. Explain how they can be managed and utilized in a sustainable way.

☐ 10. Discuss the issues surrounding **urban development**. Explain methods for sustainable urban and city development, including efficient city design and transport options.

☐ 11. Outline the formation of **minerals** and **mineral deposits**. Describe their extraction and economic importance.

☐ 12. Describe methods for ecosystem and soil restoration and **remediation**.

Fisheries
pages 149-152

☐ 13. Explain what is meant by **maximum sustainable yield**, including its calculation and its use in fisheries management.

☐ 14. Discuss the ecological impacts of commercial fishing practices with reference to netting, trolling, lining, and trawling. Explain the significance of the **by-catch** to marine ecosystems.

☐ 15. Explain the use of **stock indicators** in measuring the health of a fishery.

☐ 16. Discuss the viability and environmental impact of **aquaculture** as an alternative to fishing natural populations.

Periodicals:

Listings for this chapter are on page 231

Weblinks:

www.thebiozone.com/
weblink/EnvSci-2764.html

Presentation Media
Environmental Science:
Land and Water

The Importance of Plants

Via the process of photosynthesis, plants provide oxygen and are also the ultimate source of food and metabolic energy for nearly all animals. Besides foods (e.g. grains, fruits, and vegetables), plants also provide people with shelter, clothing, medicines, fuels, and the raw materials from which innumerable other products are made.

Plant tissues provide the energy for almost all heterotrophic life. Many plants produce delicious fruits in order to spread their seeds.

Plant tissues can be utilized to provide shelter in the form of framing, cladding, and roofing.

Many plants provide fibers for a range of materials including cotton (above), linen (from flax), and coir (from coconut husks).

Plant extracts, including rubber from rubber trees (above), can be utilized in many ways as an important manufacturing material.

Coal, petroleum, and natural gas are fossil fuels which were formed from the dead remains of plants and other organisms. Together with wood, they provide important sources of fuel.

Plants produce many beneficial and not so beneficial substances (e.g. the cannabis plant above). Over 25% of all modern medicines are derived from plant extracts.

1. Using examples, describe how plant species are used by people for each of the following:

(a) Food: _____

(b) Fuel: _____

(c) Clothing: _____

(d) Building materials: _____

(e) Aesthetic value: _____

(f) "Recreational" drugs: _____

(g) Therapeutic drugs (medicines): _____

2. Outline three reasons for ensuring the protection of native forests:

(a) _____

(b) _____

(c) _____

Land and Water

Related activities: Global Human Nutrition

RA 1

Global Human Nutrition

Globally, 854 million people are undernourished and, despite improvements in agricultural methods and technologies, the number of hungry people in the world continues to rise. The majority of these people live in developing nations, but 9 million live in industrialized countries. Over 6 million people die annually from starvation, while millions of others suffer debilitating diseases as a result of malnutrition. Protein deficiencies (such as kwashiorkor), are common amongst the world's malnourished, because the world's poorest nations consume only a fraction of the world's protein resources, surviving primarily on cereal crops. Political and environmental factors contribute significantly to the world's hunger problem. In some countries, food production is sufficient to meet needs, but inadequate distribution methods cause food shortages in some regions. Advances in agricultural practices (fertilizer and pesticide application, genetically enhanced stock) improve agricultural productivity and food supply, but can have detrimental effects through loss of biodiversity, soil and water pollution, and increased levels of greenhouse gases.

Human Nutritional Requirements

A **balanced diet,** taken from the components below, is essential for human growth, development, metabolism, and good health. In many developing countries, deficiency diseases and starvation are prevalent either because of an absolute scarcity of food or because of inadequate nutrition. In many developed Western nations, an oversupply of cheap, nutritionally poor and highly processed food is contributing to an increase of diet-related diseases such as obesity, diabetes, and heart disease. **Malnutrition** (a lack of specific nutrients), once commonly associated with undernutrition, is now rising in developed nations over consuming on poor quality processed foods.

meat | beans | lentils

Proteins (supplied by beans and pulses, and animal products such as meat and fish) are essential to growth and repair of muscle and other tissues. Unlike animal protein, plant protein is incomplete and sources must be chosen to complement one another nutritionally. Deficiencies result in kwashiorkor or marasmus.

Carbohydrates (right) are supplied in breads, starchy vegetables, cereals, and grains. They form the staple of most diets and provide the main energy source for the body.

Fats (left) and oils provide an energy source and are important for absorption of fat soluble vitamins.

Minerals (inorganic elements) and **vitamins** (essential organic compounds) are both required for numerous normal body functions. They are abundant in fruit and vegetables (right)

Agricultural Practices

Essentially, there are two broadly different types of agriculture: industrialized, or high-input, agriculture and traditional or subsistence agricultural systems. These categories exclude the hunter-gatherer societies, such as the Inuit, which collect food directly from the wild using methods of foraging and hunting with little or no domestication of target foodstuffs.

Subsistence agriculture is low technology, low-input farming where only enough food is grown to supply the family unit. It has minimal environmental impact, but can be unsustainable in densely populated areas. Subsistence agriculture occurs mostly in Africa, Asia and South America, and parts of the Pacific (e.g. Niue, left).

Industrialized, intensive agriculture produces high yields per unit of land at cheaper prices to the consumer, but has a large environmental impact because of high inputs of energy, fertilizers, and pesticides. **Wheat production** (left) and animal "factory farming" are examples. Rice production is also an example of intensive agriculture, but remains largely traditional (not mechanized) in many parts of the world.

Plantation agriculture is a form of industrialized agriculture practised mainly in tropical countries solely for the production of a high value cash crop for sale in developed countries. Typical crops include bananas (left), cotton, coffee, sugarcane, tobacco, and cocoa.

1. Discuss the differences between subsistence and industrialized agriculture with respect to relative inputs of land, labor, financial capital, and fossil fuel energy:

_____

_____

_____

_____

_____

2. *One of the likely effects of a global fuel crisis would be food shortage.* Explain this statement: _____

_____

_____

_____

The Green Revolution

Since the 1950s, most increases in global food production have come from increased yields per unit area of cropland rather than farming more land. The initial **green revolution** increased the intensity and frequency of cropping, using high inputs of fertilizers, pesticides, and water to increase yields in improved varieties. The **second green revolution** began in the 1960s and improved production by further developing high yielding crop varieties. The countries whose crop yields per unit of land area have increased during the two green revolutions are illustrated below. Several

agricultural research centers and **seed** or **gene banks** also play a key role in developing high yielding crop varieties. Most of the world's gene banks store the seeds of the hundred or so plant species that collectively provide approximately 90% of the food consumed by humans. However, some banks are also storing the seeds of species threatened with extinction or a loss of genetic diversity. Producing more food on less land is an important way of protecting biodiversity by saving large areas of natural habitat from being used to grow food.

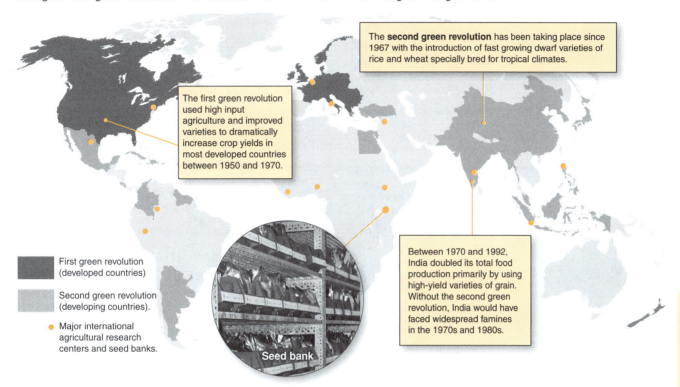

The **second green revolution** has been taking place since 1967 with the introduction of fast growing dwarf varieties of rice and wheat specially bred for tropical climates.

The first green revolution used high input agriculture and improved varieties to dramatically increase crop yields in most developed countries between 1950 and 1970.

Between 1970 and 1992, India doubled its total food production primarily by using high-yield varieties of grain. Without the second green revolution, India would have faced widespread famines in the 1970s and 1980s.

First green revolution (developed countries)

Second green revolution (developing countries).

● Major international agricultural research centers and seed banks.

Seed bank

High-input, intensive agriculture uses large amounts of fossil fuel energy, water, commercial inorganic fertilizers, and pesticides to produce large quantities of single crops (monocultures) from relatively small areas of land. At some point though, outputs diminish or even decline.

There are approximately 30 000 plant species with parts suitable for human consumption, but just three grain crops (wheat, rice, and corn) provide more than half the calories the world's population consumes. These crops have been the focus of the second green revolution.

Increased yields from industrialized agriculture depend on the extensive use of fossil fuels to run machinery, produce and apply fertilizers and pesticides, and pump water for irrigation. Since 1950, the use of fossil fuels in agriculture has increased four-fold.

1. Explain how the technologies of the first and second green revolutions differ: _____

_____

_____

_____

_____

_____

_____

Periodicals:
Sowing a gene revolution,
Back to the future of cereals

Related activities: *Global Human Nutrition, Cereal Crop Production, The Impact of Farming* **Weblinks:** *Green Revolution: Curse or Blessing?*

A 2

The second green revolution (also called the **gene revolution**) is based on further developments in **selective breeding** and **genetic engineering**. It has grown rapidly in scope and importance since it began in 1967. Initially, it involved the development of fast growing, high yielding varieties of rice, corn, and wheat, which were specially bred for tropical and subtropical climates to meet global food demand. More recently, genetically modified seeds have been used to create plants with higher yields and specific tolerances (e.g. pest resistance, herbicide tolerance, or drought tolerance). GM seed is also used to improve the nutritional quality of crops (e.g. by increasing protein or vitamin levels), or to produce plants for edible vaccine delivery.

Recent Crop Developments

Winged bean

Upland rice

A new potential crop plant is the tropical winged bean (*Psophocarpus*). All parts of the plant are edible, it grows well in hot climates, and it is resistant to many of the diseases common to other bean species.

Most green revolution breeds are "high-responders", requiring optimum levels of water and fertilizer before they realise their yield potential. Under sub-optimal conditions they may not perform as well as traditional varieties.

Improving Rice Crops

Rice is the world's second most important cereal crop, providing both a food and an income source to millions of people worldwide. Traditional rice strains lack many of the essential vitamins and minerals required by humans for good health and are susceptible to crop failure and low yields if not tended carefully. Advances in plant breeding, biotechnology, and genetic engineering (below) have helped to overcome these problems.

IR-8 rice

The second green revolution produced a high-yielding, semi-dwarf variety of rice called **IR-8** (above) in response to food shortages. IR-8 was developed by cross breeding two parental strains of rice and has shorter and stiffer stalks than either parent, allowing the plant to support heavier grain heads without falling over. More recently, a new improved variety, '**super rice**' has been developed to replace IR-8. Yields are expected to be 20% higher.

Wheat

Maize

Improvements in crop production have come from the modification of a few, well known species. Future research aims to maintain genetic diversity in high-yielding, disease resistant varieties.

A century ago, yields of maize (corn) in the USA were around 25 bushels per acre. In 1999, yields from hybrid maize were five to ten times this, depending on the growing conditions.

Genetically modified organisms (**GMO**s) are becoming more common in crop production. **Golden rice** is genetically engineered to contain high levels of beta-carotene, which is converted in the body to vitamin A. This allows better nutrient delivery to people in developing countries where rice is the staple food. Other areas of research include improving the resistance of rice to insects, bacteria, and herbicides, improving yields, and delivering edible hepatitis and cholera vaccines in the rice.

2. The second green revolution is also known as the gene revolution:

(a) Discuss the differences between the development of IR-8 rice and golden rice: _____

_____

_____

_____

_____

(b) Discuss the advantages of the gene revolution: _____

_____

_____

_____

(c) Discuss the disadvantages of the gene revolution: _____

_____

_____

_____

Cereal Crop Production

Agricultural ecosystems may be industrialized (high-input) or traditional. Industrialized agriculture uses large amounts of fossil fuel energy, water, fertilizers, and pesticides to increase net production (crop yield). Despite the high diversity of edible plants, the world's population depends on just 30 crops for 95% of its food. Four crops: wheat, rice, maize, and potato, account for a bigger share than all other crops combined. Since 1950, most of the increase in global food production has resulted from increased yields per unit of farmed land. This increase was termed the **green revolution**. More recently, a second green revolution has being taking place, with the use of fast growing, high yielding varieties of rice, corn, and wheat, specially bred for tropical and subtropical climates. Producing more food from less land increases the per capita food production while at the same time protecting large areas of potentially valuable agricultural land from development. Although food production has nearly tripled since the 1950s, the rate of this increase has started to slow, and soil loss and degradation are taking a toll on formerly productive land. Sustainable farming practices provide one way in which to reduce this loss of productivity.

Wheat (*Triticum* spp.)

Wheat is the most important world cereal crop and is extensively grown in temperate regions. Bread (common) wheat is a soft wheat with a high gluten (protein) content. It is cultivated for the grain, which is used both whole or ground. Durum wheat is a hard (low gluten) wheat used primarily for the manufacture of pasta. Key areas for wheat production are the prairies of Canada and the USA, Europe, and Russia (the former Soviet wheat belt). The economic stability of many nations is affected by the trade in wheat and related commodities. **New developments**: Wheat cultivars are selected for particular nutritional qualities or high yield in local conditions. Research focuses on breeding hardy, disease resistant, and high yielding varieties.

Maize (corn, *Zea mays*)

Maize is a widely cultivated tropical and subtropical C_4 cereal crop, second only to wheat in international importance as a food grain. The USA corn belt produces nearly half the world's maize. Some is exported, but now 85% is used within the USA as animal feed (as grain and silage). Maize is also a major cereal crop in Africa but is second to rice in importance in Asian countries. Nutritionally, maize is poor in the essential amino acids tryptophan and lysine. Recent breeding efforts have been aimed at addressing these deficiencies. **New developments**: Plant breeding has produced high lysine hybrid varieties with better disease resistance and higher yields. Most countries have cultivars suited to local conditions.

Rice (*Oryza sativa*)

Rice is the basic food crop of monsoon Asia. It is highly nutritious and requires relatively little post-harvest processing. The most common paddy (*japonica*) varieties are aquatic and are often grown under irrigation. Its cultivation is labor intensive. Upland (*indica*) varieties have similar requirements to other cereal crops. Most rice is grown in China, mainly for internal consumption. Other major producers include India, Pakistan, Japan, Thailand and Vietnam. **New developments**: Much effort has gone into producing fast growing, disease resistant, high yielding cultivars which will crop up to 3 times a season. Genetic engineering to increase tolerance to high salinity is extending the range for cultivation in the upland varieties of rice.

Sorghum (*Sorghum bicolor*)

Sorghum is a frost-sensitive, tropical C_4 plant, well adapted to arid conditions. It has low soil nutrition and water requirements, reflecting its origin in the sub-Saharan Sudan region of Africa. Sorghum is now widely cultivated in Africa, the middle East to India and Burma, and parts of Australia, the Americas and Southern Europe. It is nutritious and is used as a human foodstuff in Asia and Africa. In other regions, it is used mainly as animal feed and as an industrial raw material (for oil, starch, and fiber). **New developments**: New hybrids are high yielding, low-growing, and ripen uniformly. Further breeding aims to improve grain quality, and combine high yield properties with the disease resistance of the African wild stocks.

World Production of Major Food Crops

World production of wheat

World production of maize

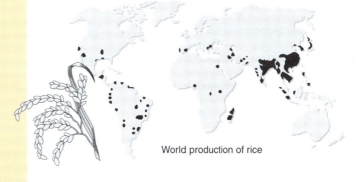

World production of rice

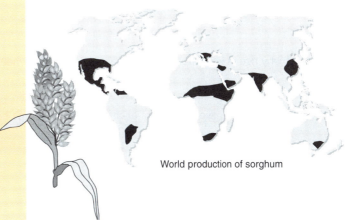

World production of sorghum

Land and Water

© Biozone International 2007-2011
Photocopying Prohibited

Periodicals: The adaptations of the cereals

Related activities: *Global Human Nutrition, The Green Revolution*
Weblinks: *FAO: Crop and Grassland Service*

A 2

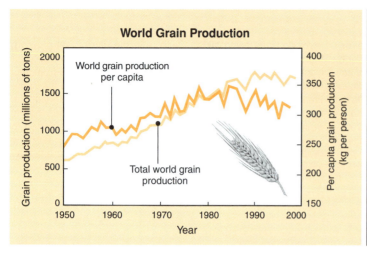

World Grain Production

Grain production (millions of tons) vs Year (1950–2000), with lines for *World grain production per capita* and *Total world grain production*. Per capita grain production (kg per person) on right axis.

Cropping properties of major world crop plants

Crop plant	Yield (kg grain ha⁻¹)	Specific requirements for growth
Maize	1000 - 4000	Warm, frost free climate, fertile soil, drought intolerant
Wheat	1000 - 14 500	Adapted to a wide range of temperate climates and soils
Rice	4500 (paddy) 1500 (indica)	Tropical, paddy varieties are aquatic, drought intolerant
Sorghum	300 - 2000. As high as 6500 for irrigated hybrids	Wide range of soils. Drought tolerant. Grown in regions too dry for maize.

Sorghum is able to grow well in the very hot, dry regions of tropical Africa and central India. Adaptations include:

- A **dense root system** that is very efficient at extracting water from the soil.
- A thick **waxy cuticle** that prevents evaporative water loss through the leaf surface.
- The presence of special cells (called **motor cells**) on the underside of the leaf that cause the leaf to roll inwards in dry conditions. This traps moist air in the rolled leaf and reduces water loss.
- Reduced number of sunken stomata on leaves.

Maize grows well where temperature and light intensity are high. Adaptations include:

- Maize has an additional photosynthetic pathway (the **C_4 pathway**), which is absent in most cooler climate plants. The C_4 pathway allows maize to fix CO_2 at low levels as a four-carbon molecule. This molecule is used to boost CO_2 in the regular C_3 pathway. In tropical conditions, the C_4 pathway allows photosynthesis to continue at high rates (primarily by inhibiting photorespiration).
- The roots are shallow, so maize often has small **aerial roots** at the base of the stem to increase their ability to withstand buffeting by wind.

Most of the **rice** in southeast Asia is grown partly submerged in paddy fields. Adaptations include:

- The stem of a rice plant has **large air spaces** (hollow aerenchyma) running the length of the stem. This allows oxygen to penetrate through to the roots which are submerged in water.
- The roots are also very shallow, allowing access to oxygen that diffuses into the surface layer of the waterlogged soil.
- When oxygen levels fall too low, the root cells respire anaerobically, producing ethanol. Ethanol is normally toxic to cells, but the root cells of rice have an unusually high tolerance to it.

1. Explain how crop yields were increased in:

   (a) The first green revolution: _____

   (b) The second green revolution (in the last 30 years): _____

2. Suggest a reason for the decline in per capita production of grain in the last decade: _____

   _____

3. Comment on the importance of wheat as a world food crop: _____

   _____

4. (a) Suggest when sorghum is a preferable crop to maize: _____

   _____

   (b) Suggest why rice is less important as an export crop than wheat or maize: _____

   _____

5. Briefly describe two adaptive features of each of the cereal crops below:

   (a) Rice: _____

   _____

   (b) Maize: _____

   _____

Chemical Pest Control

Pest control refers to the regulation or management of a species defined as a pest because of perceived detrimental effects on other species, the environment, or the economy. Pests can be managed through **biological controls**, which exploit natural existing ecological relationships, and **chemical controls** (pesticides). Opponents of pesticide use believe that the harmful effects of pesticides outweigh the benefits, especially given an increasing resistance to pesticides by target organisms. When pesticide resistance develops, more frequent applications and larger doses are often recommended. This leads to a **pesticide treadmill**, where farmers pay more and more for a pest control program that becomes less and less effective.

Biomagnification of DDT in an aquatic ecosystem

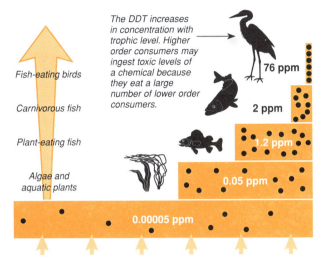

The DDT increases in concentration with trophic level. Higher order consumers may ingest toxic levels of a chemical because they eat a large number of lower order consumers.

Fish-eating birds — 76 ppm

Carnivorous fish — 2 ppm

Plant-eating fish — 1.2 ppm

Algae and aquatic plants — 0.05 ppm

0.00005 ppm

DDT enters the lake as runoff from farmland sprayed with the insecticide.

Pesticides, radioactive isotopes, heavy metals, and industrial chemicals such as PCBs can be taken up by organisms via their food or be absorbed from the surrounding medium. The **toxicity** of a chemical is a measure of how poisonous it is to both target and non-target organisms. Its **specificity** describes how selective it is in targeting a pest, while its **persistence** describes how long it stays in the environment. Many highly persistent pesticides show progressive concentration in food chains. This undesirable feature of their use is called **biomagnification**.

Pesticide type	Examples	Environmental persistence	Bioaccumulation
Insecticides			
Organochlorines	*DDT*, dieldrin*	2-15 yrs	Yes
Organophosphates	*Malathion*	1-2 weeks/years	No
Carbamates	*Carbaryl*	Days to weeks	No
Botanicals	*Pyrethrum, camphor*	Days to weeks	No
Microbials	*Microorganisms*	Days to weeks	No
Fungicides			
Various chemicals	*Methyl bromide*	Days	No
Herbicides			
Contact[§] chemicals	*Paraquat*	Days to weeks	No
Systemic[¶] chemicals	*2,4-D, 2,4,5-T, glyphosphate*	Days to weeks	No
Soil sterilants	*Butylate*	Days	No
Fumigants			
Various chemicals	*Methyl bromide*	Years	Yes

* Now banned in most developed countries
¶ Systemic chemicals: Effective when absorbed into general circulation
§ Contact chemicals: Effective after contact with surface tissue

Source of data: Miller (2000) Living in the Environment, Brooks/Cole

C. Benticat et al, Evolutionary Biology 104(8), 8 April 2008

LD50

The **LD50 (Lethal Dose 50%)** is a test to determine how much of a specific substance is required to kill 50% of a test population. The lower the figure, the more toxic the substance. The species tested, their relative health, and the mode of administration (oral, intravenous, or surface) can all influence the outcome. LD50 is calculated over a specific test period, so it does not provide information about low level, long term exposure to a substance.

The mosquito *Culex quinquefasciatus* (right) can carry the West Nile virus, which is fatal in up to 15% of cases. In 2009, 663 cases were reported in the United States. LD50 testing is routinely carried out to calculate the effectiveness of current and new insecticides against *C. quinquefasciatus* (graph right).

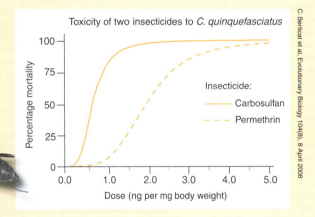

Toxicity of two insecticides to *C. quinquefasciatus*

Insecticide:
— Carbosulfan
- - - Permethrin

(y-axis: Percentage mortality, 0 to 100)
(x-axis: Dose (ng per mg body weight), 0.0 to 5.0)

CDC

---

1. Explain why top consumers are most at risk of the toxic effects of pesticide **biomagnification**: _____

_____

2. Explain why persistence is an important property to consider when using a pesticide: _____

_____

3. (a) State the LD50 for the insecticide carbosulfan against *C. quinquefasciatus*: _____

   (b) State the LD50 for the insecticide permethrin against *C. quinquefasciatus*: _____

4. Identify which insecticide *C. quinquefasciatus* has a greater chance of developing resistance to and explain why:

_____

_____

Related activities: The Impact of Farming, Integrated Pest Management
Weblinks: Biocontrol Information Center, Integrated Pest Management

RDA 2

Pesticide Resistance

Insecticides are pesticides used to control insects considered harmful to humans, their livelihood, or environment. Insecticides have been used for hundreds of years, but their use has proliferated since the advent of synthetic insecticides (e.g. DDT) in the 1940s. **Insecticide resistance** develops when the target species becomes adapted to the effects of the control agent and it no longer controls the population effectively. Resistance can arise through a combination of behavioral, anatomical, biochemical, and physiological mechanisms, but the underlying process is a form of **natural selection**, in which the most resistant organisms survive to pass on their genes to their offspring. To combat increasing resistance, higher doses of more potent pesticides are sometimes used. This drives the selection process, so that increasingly higher dose rates are required to combat rising resistance. The increased application may also kill useful insects and birds, reducing biodiversity and leading to bioaccumulation in food chains. This cycle of increasing resistance in response to increased doses is made worse by the development of **multiple resistance** in some insect pest species. Insecticides are used in medical, agricultural, and environmental applications, so the development of resistance has serious environmental and economic consequences.

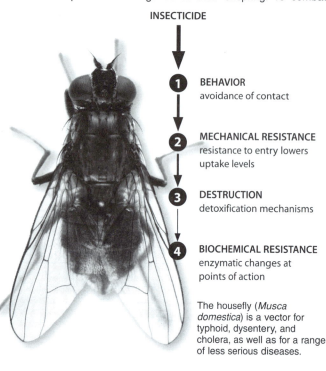

INSECTICIDE

1 BEHAVIOR
avoidance of contact

2 MECHANICAL RESISTANCE
resistance to entry lowers uptake levels

3 DESTRUCTION
detoxification mechanisms

4 BIOCHEMICAL RESISTANCE
enzymatic changes at points of action

The housefly (*Musca domestica*) is a vector for typhoid, dysentery, and cholera, as well as for a range of less serious diseases.

Mechanisms of Resistance in Houseflies

Insecticide resistance in houseflies can arise through a combination of mechanisms. (1) Increased sensitivity to an insecticide will cause the pest to avoid a treated area. (2) The *Pen* gene confers stronger physical barriers, decreasing the rate at which the chemical penetrates the cuticle. (3) Chemical changes within the insect's body can render the pesticide harmless, and (4) structural changes to the target enzymes make the pesticide ineffective. No single mechanism provides total immunity, but together they transform the effect from potentially lethal to insignificant.

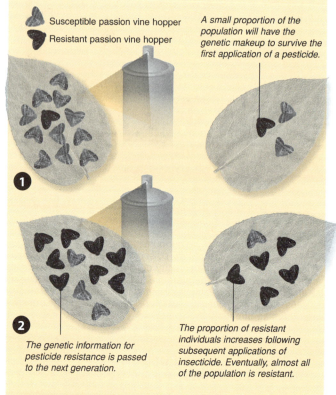

Susceptible passion vine hopper

Resistant passion vine hopper

A small proportion of the population will have the genetic makeup to survive the first application of a pesticide.

1

The genetic information for pesticide resistance is passed to the next generation.

2

The proportion of resistant individuals increases following subsequent applications of insecticide. Eventually, almost all of the population is resistant.

The Development of Resistance

The application of an insecticide can act as a potent selection pressure for resistance in pest insects. The insecticide acts as a selective agent, and only individuals with greater natural resistance survive the application to pass on their genes to the next generation. These genes (or combination of genes) may spread through all subsequent populations.

1. Give two reasons why widespread insecticide resistance can develop very rapidly in insect populations:

   (a) _____

   (b) _____

2. Explain how repeated insecticide applications acts as a selective agent for evolutionary change in insect populations:

   _____

   _____

3. With reference to synthetic insecticides, discuss the implications of insecticide resistance to human populations:

   _____

   _____

   _____

   _____

Related activities: Chemical Pest Control, Integrated Pest Management

Integrated Pest Management

Integrated Pest Management is an approach to pest control that uses a combination of both chemical, biological, and mechanical controls. The aim of most IPM programs is to reduce crop damage by pests to economically tolerable levels rather than total pest eradication. Well managed IPM programs can have outstanding success and are generally recognized as providing economically and ecologically sound alternatives to conventional pest management methods. IPM can be slower to take effect than conventional controls and expert knowledge of crop and pest ecology is required to obtain the best results. Well designed IPM programs can reduce costs and pesticide use by 50-90%. IPM can also reduce fertilizer use, and slow the development of pesticide resistance. IPM emphasises the use of ecologically sensitive pesticides which tend to be specific to the target pest but harmless to non-target species. They are less likely to cause resistance, and are non-persistent and cost effective.

Crop monitoring (ongoing)

Careful management of crops and monitoring of pest levels. When damage is unacceptable, farmers implement control measures to bring pest levels back to acceptable levels.

Recording and evaluation · Soil preparation · Planting · Harvesting · **IPM Cycle** · Climate forecasting · Pest trapping · Chemical controls · Biological controls · Cultivation controls · Monitoring pest damage

Stage 1: Cultivation controls

Cultivation controls, e.g. hand, hot water, or flame weeding, or vacuuming up pests, start the pest control program.

Stage 2: Biological controls

Sex attractants and biological controls, e.g. natural predators, are used to reduce pest populations. The Colorado potato beetle (above) is controlled using a fungal pathogen combined with release and conservation of the beetle's natural predators.

Stage 3: Targeted pesticides

Small amounts of narrow spectrum pesticides are applied only if other methods do not achieve adequate control. A variety of chemicals may be used at different times to slow the development of pest resistance and preserve natural predator populations.

Land and Water

Indonesia: An international success story

- In 1986, the Indonesian government banned the use of 57 of 66 pesticides used on rice and phased out pesticide subsidies over two years. The money saved from subsidy reduction was used to launch a nationwide program of IPM.

- Between 1987 and 1992, pesticide use fell by 65%, rice production rose by 15%, and 250 000 farmers were trained in IPM.

- By 1993 the program had saved the Indonesian government over $1.2 billion in pesticide costs; enough to fund IPM.

1. Compare and contrast the basic aims of **integrated pest management** and **chemical pest control**:

_____

_____

_____

_____

Biological Control of Greenhouse Whitefly
(*Trialeurodes vaporariorum*)

Biological control is an important part of IPM. It uses natural predators, parasites, or pathogens to target pest species, as illustrated by the example of whitefly control below. Adult whiteflies resemble tiny moths about 3 mm long. Their young appear as scales on the undersides of plants where they feed by sucking the sap. Whitefly can over-winter in a glasshouse on crops or weeds where the scales (immobile nymph and pupal stages) can withstand frosts. The young excrete a sticky honeydew on which sooty molds develop. The mold reduces the amount of light reaching the leaves, thereby reducing photosynthetic rate and crop yield. Two biocontrol agents are in common use for whitefly. The ladybird *Delphastus* feeds voraciously on the eggs and larvae of whitefly, consuming up to 150 whitefly eggs a day. The tiny parasitic wasp *Encarsia formosa* parasitizes the whitefly scale and also feeds on them directly, further helping to reduce the whitefly numbers.

Delphastus can consume up to 150 whitefly eggs in a day.

Adult whitefly *produce 30-500 eggs in just 1-2 months.*

Photos: Dr. John Dale, Defenders Ltd

Encarsia can parasitize up to 300 whitefly scales in 30 days.

Pupa

Adult

Once the whitefly nymphs settle they become immobile.

2. Describe the main features of an IPM program, briefly stating the importance of each:

(a) _____

_____

(b) _____

_____

(c) _____

_____

(d) _____

_____

3. (a) Explain the general principle underlying the **biological control** of pests: _____

_____

_____

(b) Explain what precautions should be taken when implementing a biocontrol program: _____

_____

_____

4. Explain how IPM can help build greater environmental health for a farm: _____

_____

_____

_____

_____

_____

_____

_____

Soil Degradation

Soil is a rather fragile resource and can be easily damaged by inappropriate farming practices. Some soils, such as those under the Amazon rainforest, are very vulnerable to human interference. Attempts to clear the forest and bring it into agricultural production are proving a disaster. These soils are very thin and nutrient poor; after only a few years farming they may be abandoned due to poor production. Overgrazing and deforestation may cause **desertification**. Chemically intensive agricultural practices call for ever-increasing doses of herbicides, insecticides, fungicides, and fertilizers. These often result in high crop yields, but produce soils that are compacted and lacking structure. Healthy soils are 'alive' with a diverse community of organisms, including bacteria, fungi, and invertebrates. These organisms improve soil structure and help to create **humus**. Repeated chemical applications kill soil organisms and eventually result in a soil that is hard, lacking in organic material, and unproductive.

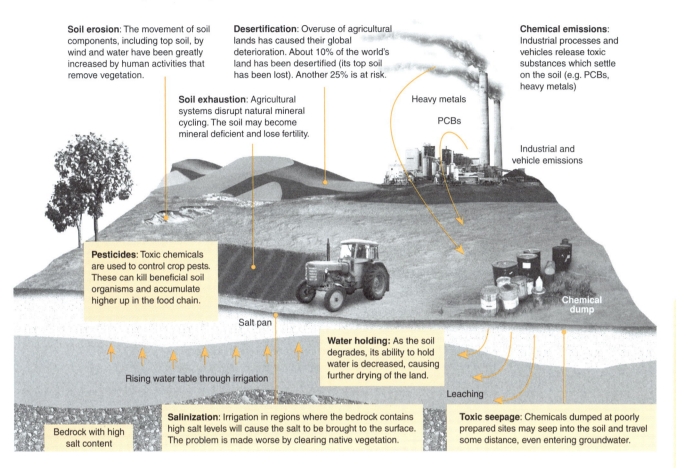

Soil erosion: The movement of soil components, including top soil, by wind and water have been greatly increased by human activities that remove vegetation.

Desertification: Overuse of agricultural lands has caused their global deterioration. About 10% of the world's land has been desertified (its top soil has been lost). Another 25% is at risk.

Chemical emissions: Industrial processes and vehicles release toxic substances which settle on the soil (e.g. PCBs, heavy metals)

Soil exhaustion: Agricultural systems disrupt natural mineral cycling. The soil may become mineral deficient and lose fertility.

Heavy metals

PCBs

Industrial and vehicle emissions

Pesticides: Toxic chemicals are used to control crop pests. These can kill beneficial soil organisms and accumulate higher up in the food chain.

Chemical dump

Salt pan

Water holding: As the soil degrades, its ability to hold water is decreased, causing further drying of the land.

Rising water table through irrigation

Leaching

Bedrock with high salt content

Salinization: Irrigation in regions where the bedrock contains high salt levels will cause the salt to be brought to the surface. The problem is made worse by clearing native vegetation.

Toxic seepage: Chemicals dumped at poorly prepared sites may seep into the soil and travel some distance, even entering groundwater.

Land and Water

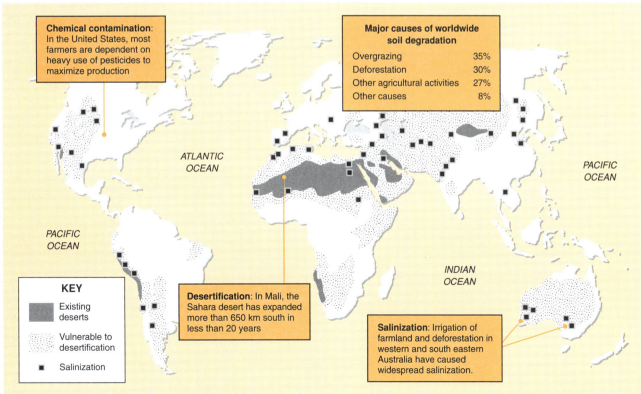

Chemical contamination: In the United States, most farmers are dependent on heavy use of pesticides to maximize production

Major causes of worldwide soil degradation

Overgrazing	35%
Deforestation	30%
Other agricultural activities	27%
Other causes	8%

ATLANTIC OCEAN

PACIFIC OCEAN

PACIFIC OCEAN

INDIAN OCEAN

KEY

Existing deserts

Vulnerable to desertification

Salinization

Desertification: In Mali, the Sahara desert has expanded more than 650 km south in less than 20 years

Salinization: Irrigation of farmland and deforestation in western and south eastern Australia have caused widespread salinization.

Periodicals:
Quick and Dirty

Related activities: Chemical Pest Control, The Impact of Farming, Reducing Soil Erosion **Weblinks**: *Soil Erosion and Conservation, Soil Degradation Maps*

The problem of disposing of unwanted agricultural chemicals has reached major proportions in developed countries. Chemical dumps (such as the one illustrated above) suffer from deterioration, with the contents spilling from rusting drums and entering the ground water system.

The high use of pesticides in developed countries is claimed to be necessary by growers to maintain high levels of production. This often comes at the cost of destroying the natural predators of pest species. Pesticides can accumulate in the soil and enter the ground water system.

Human activities such as overgrazing livestock on pasture and deforestation may cause regional climate changes and a marked reduction in rainfall. This in turn may lead to the formation of a desert environment or the encroachment of an existing desert onto formerly arable land.

1. For question 1 circle the letter with the correct answer:

   Soil erosion is caused by
   A.   Wind and flowing water
   B.   The loss of trees and surface cover
   C.   Poor grazing and tillage practices
   D.   All of A, B, and C

2. Explain how human induced salinization develops: _____

   _____

   _____

3. Describe alternative farming practices that do not use chemically intensive methods for:

   (a) Nutrient enrichment: _____

   _____

   _____

   (b) Pest control: _____

   _____

   _____

4. The synthetic insecticide DDT was in wide use after 1945 by farmers around the world. In the 1970s, the use of this chemical was banned by most Western countries. It remains as a residue in soils and waterways.

   (a) Explain why this chemical was banned: _____

   _____

   _____

   (b) Explain why the use of synthetic pesticides is becoming increasingly uneconomic: _____

   _____

   _____

5. Discuss the features of **desertification**, outlining its causes and the ways in which it may be averted or reversed:

   _____

   _____

   _____

   _____

Reducing Soil Erosion

Good soil is vital for productive agriculture. Most modern cropping techniques use heavy machinery to turn over the remnants of harvested crops, break up the soil, and smooth it flat to form a planting surface. This leaves the soil exposed, and large volumes of topsoil can be lost through wind or rain before there is sufficient crop cover to protect it. Even when a crop is fully established, there may still be exposed ground from which soil can be lost. Alternative planting techniques such as **minimum tillage farming**, **terracing**, **contour plowing**, **windbreaks,** and **intercropping** reduce the exposure of soil to the elements.

Crops are often planted parallel to the slope of the land so that machinery can move through them easily. This orientation produces channels down which water can easily flow, taking valuable top soil with it.

Plowing and planting across, rather than down, slopes produces contours that slow water runoff and reduce soil loss by up to 50%. Water has more time to settle into the soil, reducing the amount of irrigation required.

Terracing converts a slope into broad strips, slowing or preventing water and soil runoff and reducing erosion. This technique is commonly used in paddy fields. Terraces also help to control flooding downstream.

Windbreaks reduce soil erosion by reducing wind speed close to the ground. They also reduce water loss, and so lower irrigation requirements. Windbreaks placed near drainage ditches help to reduce erosion because the tree roots stabilize soil at the edge of the ditch.

Agroforestry is a combination of agriculture and forestry. Crops or stock are raised on the same land as a stand of woody perennials. Biodiversity levels are often higher than in conventional agricultural systems, and soil loss is much reduced.

Cropping system	Average annual soil loss (tha⁻¹)	Percent rain runoff
Bare soil	41.0	30
Continuous corn	19.7	29
Continuous wheat	10.1	23
Rotation: corn, wheat, clover	2.7	14
Continuous grass	0.3	12

Soil erosion is significantly reduced when the vegetative cover over the soil is maintained (above). Continuous cover can be achieved by using machinery to plant crops directly into the soil, along with fertilizers and pesticides, beneath the existing ground cover.

1. List four agricultural methods that help to reduce soil loss: _____

_____

2. Explain how terracing and contour plowing reduce soil loss compared to plowing parallel to the slope:

_____

_____

_____

3. Explain how maintaining vegetative cover reduces soil erosion: _____

_____

_____

4. Discuss the effects of traditional intensive cropping versus alternative cropping systems on soil erosion:

_____

_____

_____

_____

© Biozone International 2007-2011
Photocopying Prohibited

Periodicals:
Our good Earth

Related activities: Soil Degradation
Weblinks: Soil Erosion and Conservation

A 3

The Impact of Farming

Global crop production depends on soil, yet soil loss via erosion and pollution threatens ecosystems throughout the world. As the world population grows and more land is cultivated for agriculture, sustainable farming practices will become essential to our continued survival. Current industrialized farming practices are considered unsustainable, even though they increase yields from relatively small amounts of land. Over-use of inorganic fertilizer, erosion of top soil, and high water demands are the leading causes of this unsustainability. Finding solutions is not easy; if farmers suddenly stopped using inorganic fertilizers, the world would experience widespread famine. The implications of two contrasting farming practices are outlined below.

High Input Agriculture

Intensive farming techniques flourished after World War II. They are based on **high-yielding hybrid cultivars** and large inputs of **inorganic fertilizers**, **chemical pesticides**, and **farm machinery**. Intensive systems increased crop yields to up to four times those produced using the lower input methods of five decades ago. Large areas planted in monocultures (single crops) are typical. Irrigation and fertilizer programs are often extensive to allow for the planting of several crops per season. Given adequate irrigation and continued fertilizer inputs, yields from intensive farming are high. Over time, these yields decline as soils are eroded or cannot recover from repeated cropping. These problems can be alleviated with good crop management.

Intensive agriculture relies on the heavy use of irrigation, inorganic fertilizers (produced using fossil fuels), pesticides, and farm machinery. Such farms may specialize in a single crop for many years.

Environmental Considerations

- Regular pesticide use to reduce the numbers of insect pests.

- Mammals and birds may be affected by **bioaccumulation** of pesticides and loss of invertebrate food sources.

- Regular fertilizer applications required to achieve high yields.

- Poor soil retention of fertilizer and high rates of leaching.

- Lack of vegetated borders create an impoverished habitat and expose fields to wind and water.

- A monoculture regime leads to reduced biodiversity.

Low Input Agriculture

Organic farming is a form of **sustainable agriculture** based on avoiding the use of chemical pest controls and inorganic fertilizers. It relies on mixed (crop and livestock) farming and crop management, combined with the use of environmentally friendly pest controls (e.g. biological controls and flaming), and livestock and green manures. Farm practices include **crop rotation** and **intercropping**, in which two or more crops are grown at the same time on the same plot, often maturing at different times. These plots can provide food, fuel, and natural pest control and fertilizers on a sustainable basis. Yields are often, although not always, lower than from high input systems, but the produce can fetch high prices, and input costs are reduced.

Some traditional farms use low-input agricultural practices similar to those used in modern organic farming. However, many small farming units find it difficult to remain economically viable.

Environmental Considerations

- Pesticides do not reside nor accumulate in food chains.

- Produce is pesticide free and produced in a sustainable way.

- Alternative pest controls reduce the dependence on pesticides.

- Vegetated borders increase habitat and species diversity and reduce soil loss by reducing exposure.

- Crop rotation reduces pest and disease load on land.

- More land require cultivation to achieve the same yields, so less land can be left unfarmed for conservation purposes.

1. (a) Discuss the advantages and disadvantages of high input agriculture: _____

_____

_____

_____

_____

(b) Discuss how sustainable agricultural practices could address some of these disadvantages: _____

_____

_____

Related activities: Chemical Pest Control, Reducing Soil Erosion

Agricultural Practices

Producing food from a limited amount of land presents several challenges: to maximize yield while minimizing losses to disease and pests, to ensure sustainability of the practice, and (in the case of animals) to meet certain standards of welfare and safety. Industrialized intensive agricultural systems meet these demands by using high inputs of energy to obtain high yields per unit of land farmed. Such systems apply not just to crop plants, but to animals too, which are raised to slaughter weight at high densities in confined areas (a technique called **factory farming**). **Sustainable agriculture** refers to the long-term ability of a farm to produce food without irreversibly damaging ecosystem health. Two key issues in sustainable agriculture are **biophysical** and

socio-economic. Biophysical issues center on soil health and the biological processes essential to crop productivity. Socio-economic issues center on the long-term ability of farmers to manage resources, such as labor, and obtain inputs, such as seed. Sustainable agriculture relies on good soil conservation practices, and the use of manure, compost, and other forms of organic matter over inorganic fertilizers. It also uses an integrated program of pest management, emphasizing biological and physical means of pest control and using chemical controls only as a last resort. Such regimes are increasingly proving more profitable than high-input systems because less money is spent on inputs of irrigation water, fertilizers, and pesticides.

Some Features of Industrialized Agriculture

Antibiotics are used in the intensive farming of **poultry** for egg and meat production. Proponents regard antibiotics as an important management tool to prevent, control, and treat disease, allowing farmers to raise healthy animals and produce safe food.

The application of inorganic fertilizers has been a major factor in the increased yields of industrialized agriculture. However, excessive application can lead to undesirable enrichment of water bodies and contamination of groundwater.

Fertilizers can be sprayed using aerial topdressing in inaccessible areas.

Pesticides and fungicides are used extensively to control crop pests and diseases in industrialized agriculture. Indiscriminate use of these leads to increased resistance to commonly used chemicals and contamination of land and water.

Clearing land of trees for agriculture can lead to slope instability, soil erosion, and land degradation.

Antibiotics are used to treat diseases such as mastitis in dairy cattle. Milk must be withheld until all antibiotic residues have disappeared.

Feedlots are a type of confined animal feeding operation which is used for rapidly feeding livestock, notably cattle (above left), up to slaughter weight. Diet for stock in feedlots are very dense in energy to encourage rapid growth and deposition of fat in the meat (marbling). As in many forms of factory farming, antibiotics are used to combat disease in the crowded environment.

Land and Water

1. Explain the need for each if the following in industrialized intensive agriculture:

   (a) Pesticides: _____

   _____

   (b) Fertilizers: _____

   _____

   (c) Antibiotics: _____

   _____

2. Explain where the energy in intensive agricultural practices is used: _____

   _____

   _____

   _____

   _____

Related activities: The Impact of Farming

A 3

Some Features of Sustainable Agriculture

Sustainable agricultural practices are economically viable and environmentally sound. Increasingly, farmers are investigating methods by which they can earn a reasonable living from the land, while remaining less reliant on government subsidies, and petroleum and chemical inputs. As in intensive farming, there are many approaches to sustainable agriculture. That pictured here is just one.

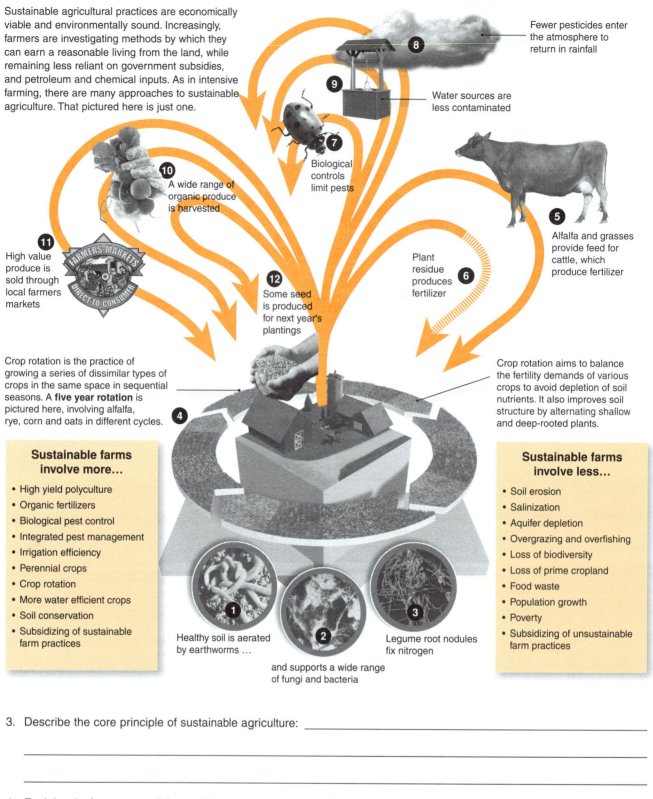

8 Fewer pesticides enter the atmosphere to return in rainfall

9 Water sources are less contaminated

7 Biological controls limit pests

10 A wide range of organic produce is harvested

11 High value produce is sold through local farmers markets

5 Alfalfa and grasses provide feed for cattle, which produce fertilizer

6 Plant residue produces fertilizer

12 Some seed is produced for next year's plantings

Crop rotation is the practice of growing a series of dissimilar types of crops in the same space in sequential seasons. A **five year rotation** is pictured here, involving alfalfa, rye, corn and oats in different cycles.

4

Crop rotation aims to balance the fertility demands of various crops to avoid depletion of soil nutrients. It also improves soil structure by alternating shallow and deep-rooted plants.

Sustainable farms involve more...
- High yield polyculture
- Organic fertilizers
- Biological pest control
- Integrated pest management
- Irrigation efficiency
- Perennial crops
- Crop rotation
- More water efficient crops
- Soil conservation
- Subsidizing of sustainable farm practices

Sustainable farms involve less...
- Soil erosion
- Salinization
- Aquifer depletion
- Overgrazing and overfishing
- Loss of biodiversity
- Loss of prime cropland
- Food waste
- Population growth
- Poverty
- Subsidizing of unsustainable farm practices

1 Healthy soil is aerated by earthworms ...

2 and supports a wide range of fungi and bacteria

3 Legume root nodules fix nitrogen

3. Describe the core principle of sustainable agriculture: _____

_____

_____

4. Explain why farmers practising sustainable agriculture can find it more profitable than intensive farming in the long term:

_____

_____

5. Explain why farming in the near future will most probably be a mix of industrialized and sustainable farming practices:

_____

_____

_____

_____

Forestry

The idea of **sustainable forestry** followed acknowledgement of the damage done by unrestricted logging of old growth forests. For forestry to be sustainable, demand for timber must be balanced with the regrowth of seedlings. Sustainable forestry allows timber demands to be met without over-exploiting the timber-producing trees. Different methods for logging are used depending on the type of forest being logged. This allows the various services provided by forests to remain undisrupted. These services include providing shelter for wildlife, acting to reduce water runoff by absorbing excess rainwater, and moderating the local climate.

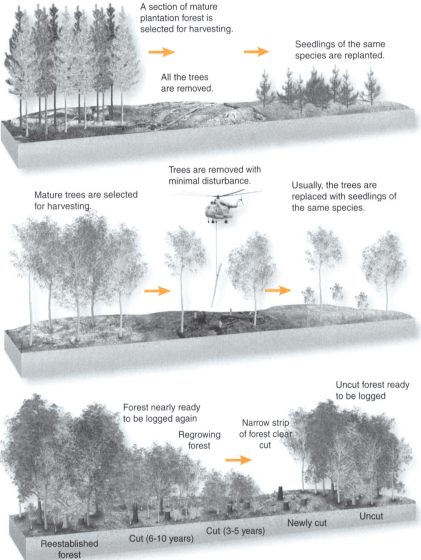

A section of mature plantation forest is selected for harvesting.

Seedlings of the same species are replanted.

All the trees are removed.

Trees are removed with minimal disturbance.

Mature trees are selected for harvesting.

Usually, the trees are replaced with seedlings of the same species.

Uncut forest ready to be logged

Forest nearly ready to be logged again

Regrowing forest

Narrow strip of forest clear cut

Newly cut

Uncut

Reestablished forest

Cut (6-10 years)

Cut (3-5 years)

Clear Cutting

A section of a mature forest is selected (based on tree height, girth, or species), and all the trees are removed. During this process the understorey is destroyed. A new forest of economically desirable trees may be planted. In plantation forests, the trees are generally of a single species and may even be clones. Clear cutting is a very productive and economical method of managing a forest, however it is also the most damaging to the natural environment. In plantation forests, this may not be of concern and may not affect sustainability, but clear cutting of old growth forests causes enormous ecological damage.

Selective Logging

A mature forest is examined, and trees are selected for removal based on height, girth, or species. These trees are felled individually and directed to fall in such a way as to minimize the damage to the surrounding younger trees. The forest is managed in such a way as to ensure continual regeneration of young seedlings and provide a balance of tree ages that mirrors the natural age structure.

Strip Cutting

Strip cutting is a variation of clear cutting. Trees are clear cut out of a forest in strips. The strip is narrow enough that the forest on either side is able to reclaim the cleared land. As the cleared forest reestablishes (3-5 years) the next strip is cut. This allows the forest to be logged with minimal effort and damage to forest on either side of the cutting zone, while at the same time allowing the natural reestablishment of the original forest. Each strip is not cut again for around 30 years, depending on regeneration time.

Old growth forests are climax communities. They have remained undisturbed by natural events and human interference for many hundreds of years. Old growth forests are ecologically significant because of their high biodiversity, and they are often home to endangered or endemic species. Larger forests also play a part in climate modification.

Second growth forests result from secondary ecological succession after a major forest disturbance such as fire or logging. At first, these forests may have quite different characteristics from the original community, especially if particular tree species were removed completely by logging. As the forest develops, the trees are often of the same age so that a single canopy develops.

Commercial plantations (tree farms) are specifically planted and grown for the production of timber or timber based products. These forests are virtual monocultures containing a specific timber tree, such as *Pinus radiata* (Monterey or radiata pine). These trees have often been selectively bred to produce straight-trunked, uniform trees that grow quickly and can be easily harvested and milled.

1. Suggest which logging method best suits the ideas of sustainability and explain your answer: _____

_____

Forests and Fires

Fires are a part of natural forest development and may occur as a result of lighting strikes, the concentration of heat on dry tinder, or by human activities. For many years, these natural fires were extinguished by fire services or prevented by education campaigns, but this led to a build up of flammable material in forested areas.

(1) In natural, unmodified environments, fires tend to be brief and small. They burn out relatively quickly, removing material near the surface.

(4) The build up of debris can eventually lead to small fires quickly forming wildfires, which devastate large tracts of forest.

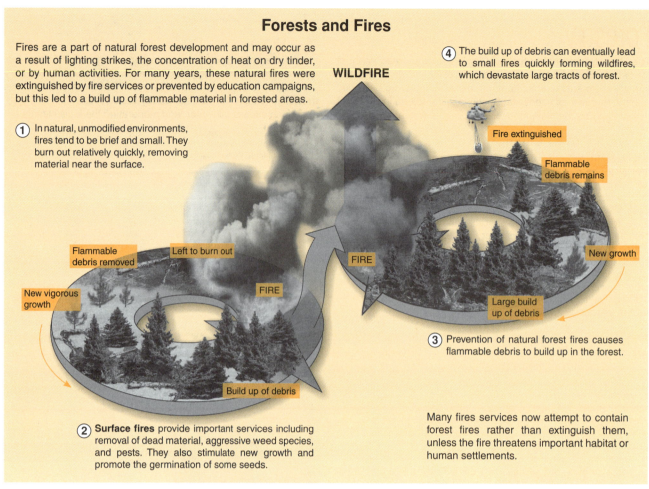

WILDFIRE

Fire extinguished

Flammable debris remains

New growth

Flammable debris removed

Left to burn out

FIRE

New vigorous growth

FIRE

Large build up of debris

Build up of debris

(3) Prevention of natural forest fires causes flammable debris to build up in the forest.

(2) **Surface fires** provide important services including removal of dead material, aggressive weed species, and pests. They also stimulate new growth and promote the germination of some seeds.

Many fires services now attempt to contain forest fires rather than extinguish them, unless the fire threatens important habitat or human settlements.

Part of forest management is to reduce the occurrence of large, serious fires. **Controlled burns** are designed to remove excess flammable material in a section of forest, and so significantly reduce the risk of a wildfire. This is done is colder seasons where the risk of the burn becoming uncontrollable is reduced. The controlled burns also help to stimulate new growth.

Controlled burns are carried out to prevent small **surface fires** from becoming crown fires or out of control wildfires. Surface fires burn debris close to the ground and can be of benefit to a forest. **Crown fires** are large, extremely hot forest fires that often destroy large trees and forests. **Ground fires** are fires that burn material underground (such as peat) but may emerge to cause surface fires.

2. Describe the advantages and disadvantages of each type of logging method: _____

_____

_____

_____

_____

3. Explain the importance of old growth forests: _____

_____

_____

4. (a) Distinguish between, ground fires, surface fires, and crown fires: _____

_____

_____

(b) Describe the benefits of controlled burns: _____

_____

_____

Managing Rangelands

Rangelands are large, relatively undeveloped areas populated by grasses, grass-like plants, and scrub. They are usually semi-arid to arid areas and include grasslands, tundra, scrublands, coastal scrub, alpine areas, and savanna. Globally, rangelands cover around 50% of the Earth's land surface. The US has about 3.1 million km^2 of rangeland, of which 1.6 million km^2 is privately owned. Rangelands cover 80% of Australia, mostly as the outback, but only 3% of Australia's population live in rangeland areas. Rangelands are often used to graze livestock such as sheep and cattle but, because they occur in low-rainfall areas, they do not regenerate rapidly. Careful management is required to prevent damage and soil loss as a result of overgrazing.

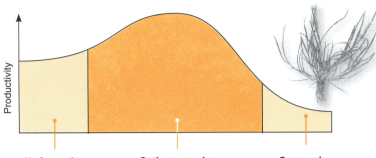

Undergrazing
Net productivity is reduced because standing dead material leaves little room for new growth to come through.

Optimum grazing
Old material is removed so new growth can come through, but enough growing material is left to allow recovery.

Overgrazing
Too much material is removed and new growth can not become established. Plants die and erosion occurs.

Grasses (left) grow continuously from a basal meristem, so the leaf can be cropped without causing growth to stop. This allows a field to be grazed in a near-continuous fashion. Grazing by animals stimulates grass to grow and removes dead material. Grasslands cropped at their optimum capacity can be much more productive than if left uncropped (left).

Overgrazing occurs when too many animals are grazed for too long on a section of pasture and the grass does not have enough time between cropping to regrow. Overgrazing may destroy the meristem, in which case plant regeneration stops. Exposed soils may become colonized by invasive species (below) or eroded by wind and rain.

Effect of Grazing on Plant Species Composition

Ungrazed

Moderate grazing

Overgrazed

Species reaction to grazing

 Decreasers   Increasers   Invaders

Intensive grazing causes changes in the species composition. Species that perform better under grazing will increase their range, while others will reduce their range. Grazing also opens gaps in plant distribution, which allows invasive species to establish or increase in range.

Total Net Primary Production and Efficiency of Grazed and Ungrazed Grasslands			
		Net production (kcal m^{-2})	Efficiency (%)
Grazed	Desert	1081	.13
	Shortgrass plains	3761	.80
	Mixed grasslands	2254	.51
	Prairie	3749	.77
Ungrazed	Desert	1177	.16
	Shortgrass plains	2721	.57
	Mixed grasslands	2052	.47
	Prairie	2220	.44

From Ecology and Field Biology, R. Smith

1. Explain how carefully managed grazing on a rangeland can increase its productivity: _____

_____

_____

2. Describe the effect of grazing on the diversity of rangeland plants: _____

_____

_____

3. Explain why rangelands can easily become overgrazed: _____

_____

_____

4. Discuss the relationship between a rangeland's productivity and the number of animals grazed on the land:

_____

_____

_____

_____

_____

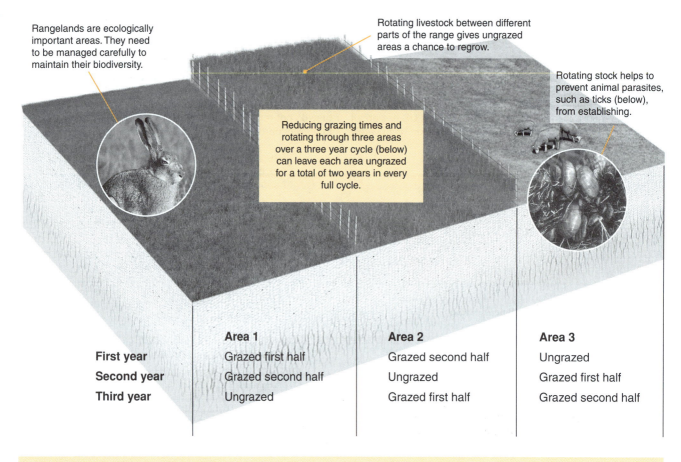

Rangelands are ecologically important areas. They need to be managed carefully to maintain their biodiversity.

Rotating livestock between different parts of the range gives ungrazed areas a chance to regrow.

Rotating stock helps to prevent animal parasites, such as ticks (below), from establishing.

Reducing grazing times and rotating through three areas over a three year cycle (below) can leave each area ungrazed for a total of two years in every full cycle.

	Area 1	Area 2	Area 3
First year	Grazed first half	Grazed second half	Ungrazed
Second year	Grazed second half	Ungrazed	Grazed first half
Third year	Ungrazed	Grazed first half	Grazed second half

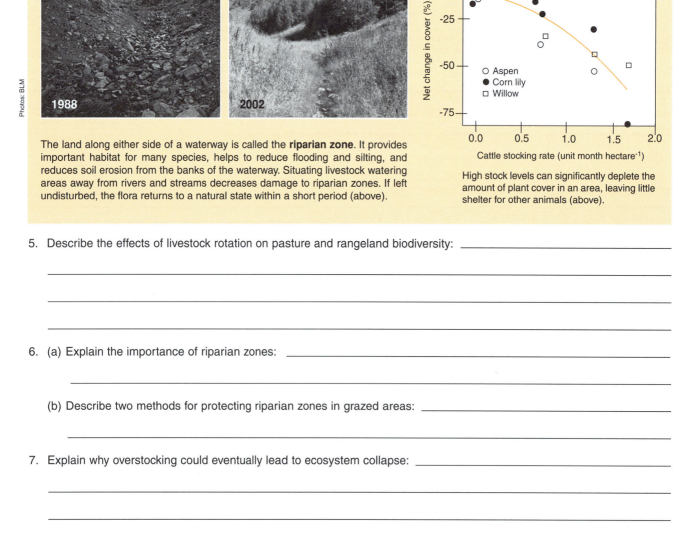

Photos: BLM

1988

2002

The land along either side of a waterway is called the **riparian zone**. It provides important habitat for many species, helps to reduce flooding and silting, and reduces soil erosion from the banks of the waterway. Situating livestock watering areas away from rivers and streams decreases damage to riparian zones. If left undisturbed, the flora returns to a natural state within a short period (above).

Net change in cover (%)

○ Aspen
● Corn lily
□ Willow

Cattle stocking rate (unit month hectare^{-1})

High stock levels can significantly deplete the amount of plant cover in an area, leaving little shelter for other animals (above).

5. Describe the effects of livestock rotation on pasture and rangeland biodiversity: _____

_____

_____

_____

6. (a) Explain the importance of riparian zones: _____

_____

(b) Describe two methods for protecting riparian zones in grazed areas: _____

_____

7. Explain why overstocking could eventually lead to ecosystem collapse: _____

_____

_____

City Planning

Cities are urban centres of population and commerce. The population that defines a city varies from country to country, but it is commonly in the tens of thousands. Cities can be modelled along three types of plan: concentric, sector, or multi-nuclei, but the history and geography of an area results in many variations of these. Unordered city growth and inefficient sprawl are prevented by planning regulations dictating zones where certain developments can occur. This also prevents the mixing of incompatible activities (e.g. residential with heavy industry). Each planning zone has its own set of regulations for development. Modern city planning must integrate many factors including sustainable development, aesthetics (how something looks), safety, transport, and environmental considerations (e.g. environmental protection and minimizing pollution). A well designed city can enhance the economic and social aspects of a community.

Concentric Rings

Concentric cities have the central business district (CBD) surrounded by industrial areas, with residential areas on the outer rings. In developed Western cities, the affluent residential areas are on the outskirts of the city and poorer high density housing is closer to the inner city. In developing countries, this pattern of distribution is often reversed, with affluent areas close to the central city and slums and shanty towns on the outskirts.

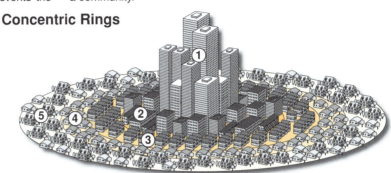

Sector City

Sector cities locate the bulk of industrial and commercial areas in the city center. Other sectors assigned to specific purposes (e.g. transport) are developed around them. This design often occurs because affluent areas are built around desirable features (such as scenic areas or waterfronts). Industry and high density housing are built close to transportation routes for easy transport of goods and workers.

Multi-Nuclei City

Multi-nuclei cities are probably the closest representation to the majority of the world's cities. They are built around multiple centers or satellite towns rather than a central CBD. As the city expands, the distance between the CBD and outlying areas becomes greater, and workers often have to commute long distances from their homes to their place of work. As the population grows, satellite areas become larger and more influential. They develop their own commercial and industrial areas. Business may shift from the CBD to the satellite areas because there is more land for expansion, lower rents, and often better access to the work force. The CBD may become diminished and lose influence.

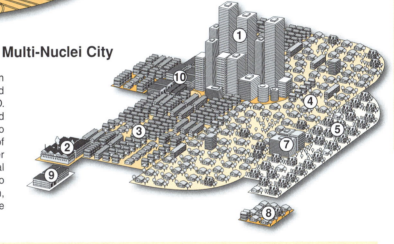

Key to City Zones

1. Central business district (CBD)
2. Heavy industry and manufacturing
3. High density, low rent residential
4. Medium density residential
5. Low density, high rent residential
6. Recreation and entertainment
7. Outlying commercial area
8. Satellite town/suburb
9. Satellite industrial area
10. Light industry/commercial

1. Explain why few cities completely match the models above: _____

_____

2. Describe some disadvantages of urban sprawl: _____

_____

Periodicals:
The rise of vertical farms

Building Sustainable Cities

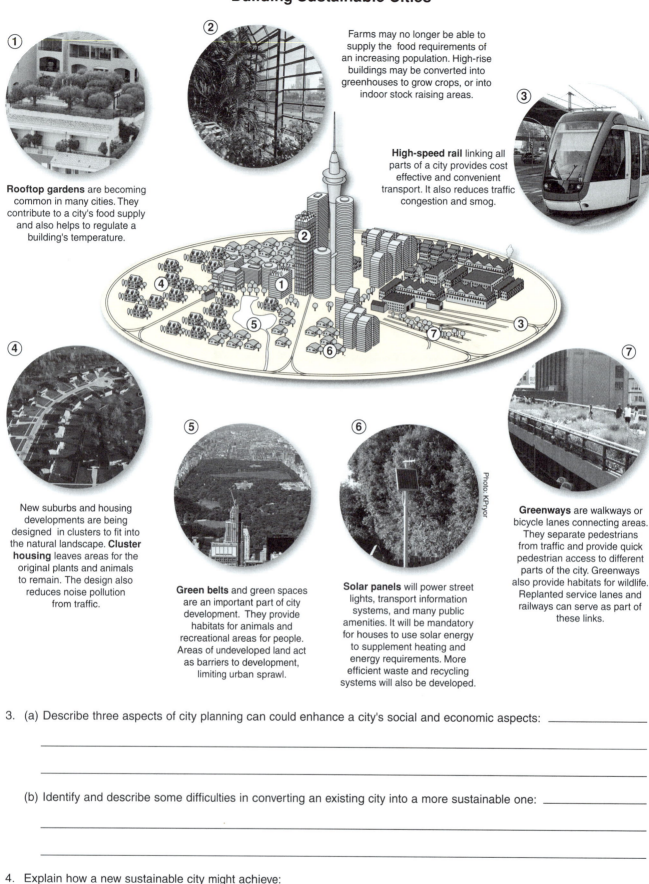

Rooftop gardens are becoming common in many cities. They contribute to a city's food supply and also helps to regulate a building's temperature.

Farms may no longer be able to supply the food requirements of an increasing population. High-rise buildings may be converted into greenhouses to grow crops, or into indoor stock raising areas.

High-speed rail linking all parts of a city provides cost effective and convenient transport. It also reduces traffic congestion and smog.

New suburbs and housing developments are being designed in clusters to fit into the natural landscape. **Cluster housing** leaves areas for the original plants and animals to remain. The design also reduces noise pollution from traffic.

Green belts and green spaces are an important part of city development. They provide habitats for animals and recreational areas for people. Areas of undeveloped land act as barriers to development, limiting urban sprawl.

Solar panels will power street lights, transport information systems, and many public amenities. It will be mandatory for houses to use solar energy to supplement heating and energy requirements. More efficient waste and recycling systems will also be developed.

Greenways are walkways or bicycle lanes connecting areas. They separate pedestrians from traffic and provide quick pedestrian access to different parts of the city. Greenways also provide habitats for wildlife. Replanted service lanes and railways can serve as part of these links.

Photo: KPryor

Photo: Beyond My Ken

3. (a) Describe three aspects of city planning can could enhance a city's social and economic aspects: _____

_____

_____

(b) Identify and describe some difficulties in converting an existing city into a more sustainable one: _____

_____

_____

4. Explain how a new sustainable city might achieve:

(a) Efficient transport: _____

_____

(b) Ecological balance: _____

_____

Transportation

Efficient movement around and between cities is often limited by the **geography**, **design**, and **planning** of the transport system. To be efficient, public transport systems need a high population density and must be able to transport people to within a short walk of their destination. In many cities, extensive light rail systems are used to achieve this. Roads, especially busy highways, have a significant impact on local ecosystems, contributing to pollution and forming dangerous barriers for animals to cross. Thousands of animals are killed each year crossing roads. Roads are especially problematic if they intersect territories or migration routes. The construction of wildlife crossings provide a partial solution to this problem.

Eco-friendly Transport

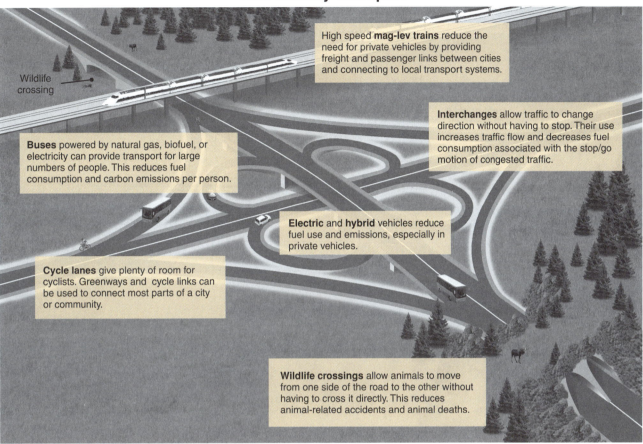

High speed **mag-lev trains** reduce the need for private vehicles by providing freight and passenger links between cities and connecting to local transport systems.

Wildlife crossing

Interchanges allow traffic to change direction without having to stop. Their use increases traffic flow and decreases fuel consumption associated with the stop/go motion of congested traffic.

Buses powered by natural gas, biofuel, or electricity can provide transport for large numbers of people. This reduces fuel consumption and carbon emissions per person.

Electric and **hybrid** vehicles reduce fuel use and emissions, especially in private vehicles.

Cycle lanes give plenty of room for cyclists. Greenways and cycle links can be used to connect most parts of a city or community.

Wildlife crossings allow animals to move from one side of the road to the other without having to cross it directly. This reduces animal-related accidents and animal deaths.

Land and Water

Transport system	Private vehicle	Bus	Train	Plane
Advantages	• Convenient, all hours transport • Personalized • Access most locations • Especially useful in low population areas	• Flexible access to many locations • Useful for short to medium distance journeys. • Low proportional operating costs if used in large numbers	• Fast transport over medium to long distances • Low pollution per person • Able to haul large volumes of people and freight	• Fast transport over long distances • Low pollution per person • Able to cross all geographic barriers
Disadvantages	• Expensive to run and maintain • Produce large amounts of pollution per person • Congest the roads • High risk of accident or injury	• Run to timetables, but can be delayed due to traffic congestion • Can cost more to maintain than they earn • Can be slow to reach destinations because of its many stops	• Runs to inflexible time-tables • Expensive to run and maintain • Produce heavy vibration and some noise	• Fixed and inflexible schedules • Can be uncomfortable over long distances • Produce large amounts of localized noise • Expensive to run and maintain

1. Explain how effective transport systems can reduce congestion and pollution: _____

_____

_____

2. Explain the need for all four of the transport systems above: _____

_____

_____

_____

Related activities: City Planning

A 2

Environmental Remediation

As land becomes increasingly scarce, there is a greater incentive and requirement to redevelop land previously used for other purposes. For example, farmland near cities is often developed for residential use and abandoned industrial sites and landfills are often redeveloped into housing, parks, or commercial areas. Chemicals once used on these lands could present a risk to humans through contamination of soil or groundwater, or release of noxious gases. Before land can be redeveloped, it must undergo **environmental remediation**. This is the removal of contaminants in order to make the area safe for human health. The method of remediation used depends on the extent and type of contamination (below). For example, polluted top soil can be removed and treated off-site, or plants and bacteria may be placed *in situ* to absorb and break down the contaminants. A treated area is monitored over many years to ensure that no further leaching of contaminants occurs.

Methods of Remediation

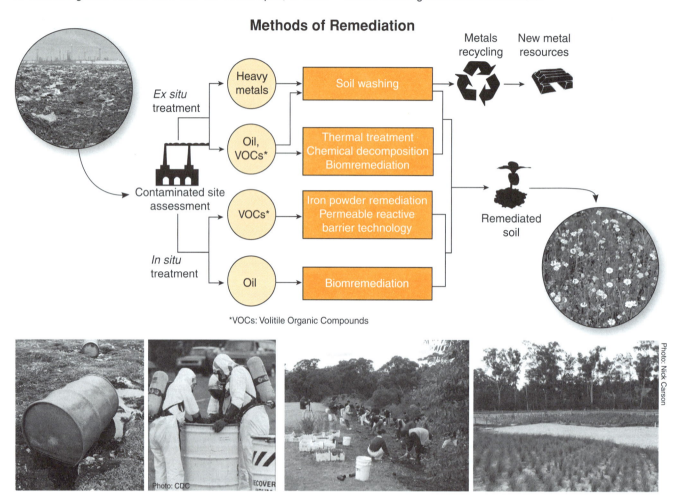

*VOCs: Volitile Organic Compounds

Contaminated sites in the US are classified as **Brownfields** or **Superfund** sites. Brownfields are industrial, urban, or commercial parcels of land that can be used again after remediation. Superfund sites are highly toxic abandoned sites that the Environmental Protection Agency (EPA) has identified for extensive remediation, e.g. Love Canal in Niagara Falls. They fall under the Comprehensive Environmental Response, Compensation and Liability Act (CERCLA).

The EPA offers a number of grants for environmental assessment, cleanup, and job training activities related to contaminated sites. The level of environmental remediation achieved depends upon the extent and nature of the contamination. Even after many years of remediation, some sites can never be made safe enough for humans to occupy. CERCLA allows the EPA to force the responsible parties to perform cleanups or reimburse the government for EPA-lead cleanups. When no responsible party can be identified, CERCLA authorizes the EPA to clean up sites itself.

1. Explain the purpose of environmental remediation: _____

_____

_____

2. Describe some benefits of remediation: _____

_____

_____

_____

3. Choose a contaminated Superfund site from the EPA's national priorities list (*www.epa.gov/superfund/sites/index.htm*). On a separate piece of paper, identify the cause of the contamination and outline the methods used to clean up the site. Discuss the likelihood of a successful outcome and the implications of the outcome to the local community:

Related activities: Types of Pollution, Chernobyl Accident, Bhopal Disaster
Weblinks: Superfund Sites Where You Live

Mining and Minerals

Humans have long utilized many of the minerals contained within the Earth. **Minerals** are naturally occurring solid chemical substances formed through natural geological processes. **Metals** are minerals that conduct heat and energy. They often have a shiny appearance. When minerals are concentrated in an area that makes them economically worth extracting, they are called **ore deposits**. Most of the Earth's high quality, easily accessible ore deposits have been mined, leaving only more inaccessible deposits left to extract. Some low quality ore deposits, previously uneconomical to extract, may require mining in the future as mineral resources become depleted. As the cost of extraction and processing becomes higher and the mineral becomes more scarce, the value of the ore increases, which in turn increases the cost of products containing the mineral.

The formation of minerals and metals deposits varies, but generally involves three stages: formation, transport, and concentration. For example, the formation of gold and silver is associated with **volcanic activity.** The metals are transported in geothermal water (above) and precipitate out as deposits when the water cools.

Mineral deposits may be eroded and the minerals washed into streams, where they are sorted by sedimentary processes. Dense particles fall to the streambed first, forming **placer** deposits. These deposits are important sources of valuable minerals such as gold, platinum, tin, and iron.

The evaporation of mineral-rich waters concentrates mineral salts. Many common salts, including NaCl (table salt) are harvested by evaporative mining (above). The sun and wind evaporate water from shallow pools, leaving mounds of salt crystals behind.

Peak Minerals

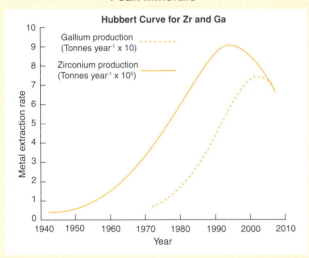

Hubbert Curve for Zr and Ga

- Gallium production (Tonnes year^{-1} x 10)
- Zirconium production (Tonnes year^{-1} x 10^5)

Metal extraction rate (y-axis: 0–10)
Year (x-axis: 1940–2010)

In 1956, geophysicist M.K. Hubbert developed a logistic distribution curve to predict the peak and decline of oil production. His theory proposed that, for any non-renewable resource, the rate of extraction will fit a bell shaped curve. The production rates of many of the mineral resources mined today match a **Hubbert Curve**. Indeed many of the rare minerals used in today's high-tech devices, including cell phones, high efficiency solar cells, and hydrogen fuel cell technology appear to have already reached their peak production rates and are now beginning to decline.

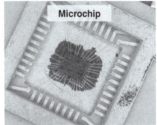

Microchip

Gold bars

Minerals have many applications. Precious metals and minerals (e.g. gold, platinum, diamonds) are relatively rare and have a high economic value. They can be made into jewellery or traded as currency. The strength of many metals makes them useful material for construction (e.g. iron). Conductive properties make them essential in many high-tech devices.

Habitat is destroyed to make way for mining activities

Land disturbance causes accelerated erosion

Mining is associated with many environmental problems including erosion, environmental contamination from chemicals, and habitat destruction. In most countries, mining operations must follow strict procedures to minimize the risk of environmental damage.

1. Describe a use for each of the following metals or minerals:

   (a) Gold: _____

   (b) Iron: _____

   (c) Gallium: _____

2. From the graphs, determine the length of time left before the depletion of:

   (a) Gallium reserves: _____

   (b) Zirconium reserves: _____

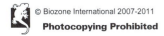
Periodicals:
Earth audit

Related activities: Oil, Coal
Weblinks: Excavating and Refining Gold

A 3

Globalization

The Tragedy of the Commons

Garrett Hardin proposed the **Tragedy of the Commons** in 1968 to describe how over-exploitation of a resource may occur. It proposes that when there is no clear ownership of a natural resource, the users overexploit it to the point where it becomes depleted. Hardin's original example was based on a group of herders sharing land to graze their cows. Each herder continues to place cows on the land until the carrying capacity is exceeded. Each individual herder initially benefits, but eventually the land is damaged from overgrazing and the group as a whole (the common) suffers. The tragedy of the commons can be applied to modern issues of sustainability including overfishing, deforestation, human population growth, pollution, habitat destruction, and resource depletion.

Advantages of Globalization

> Access to new resources and ways of thinking.
> Increased awareness of global environmental issues.
> Greater access to global markets with fewer restrictions (e.g. reduced tariffs, more free trade agreements).
> Greater understanding of cultural differences.
> Greater travel opportunities allows exposure to other societies and cultures.

Disadvantages of Globalization

> Increased consumerism and consumption of goods and resources.
> Exploitation of the workforce in developing countries.
> Exploitation of resources, especially in developing countries, to meet global demand.
> Financial disasters occur on a larger scale (i.e. global rather than regional).
> Potential loss of regional cultural beliefs and customs.

Globalization refers to the transformation of local or regional markets or societies into global ones. It involves the **migration** of people and spread of **trade**, **information**, and **technology** past their traditional national borders. Globalization is not new. In the past, culture and ideas were distributed together with goods along trade routes. Modern globalization began around the same time as the Industrial Revolution, but is usually associated with the rise of large multinational corporations and the reduction of trade restrictions between many countries over the last 30 years. The global export of Western ideas and culture through mass media (film, radio, television and the Internet) has increased the rate of globalization. Some powerful groups have been set up to advance globalization and development. Some of the advantages and disadvantages of these are discussed below left.

Globalization has been driven partly by measures taken after World War II, in which large organizations were set up to rebuild ruined countries. These organizations now work to develop trade between countries. They include:

- The **World Bank** provides financial and technical assistance to developing countries to promote social and economic progress. 182 countries are members.
- The **International Monetary Fund** (IMF) is a global organization with 187 member countries. Its goal is to aid global growth and economic stability by providing financial aid to member countries.
- The **World Trade Organization** (WTO) helps countries negotiate trade deals so producers, exporters, and importers can conduct their business efficiently on a global scale. 153 countries are members.
- The **United Nations** (UN) is a global organization committed to maintaining international peace and security, economic development, and human rights. It has 192 member countries.

1. Describe purpose of the following organizations:

   (a) The World Bank: _____

   (b) The IMF: _____

   (c) The UN: _____

   (d) The WTO: _____

2. Describe the impact of globalization on the environment: _____

   _____

   _____

   _____

3. Explain how the Tragedy of the Commons can be applied on both local and global scales: _____

   _____

   _____

   _____

Weblinks: *Globalization 101*

Periodicals: Time to rethink everything

Ecological Impacts of Fishing

Fishing is an ancient human tradition that satisfies our need for food, and is economically, socially, and culturally important. Today, it is a worldwide resource extraction industry. Several decades of overfishing in all of the world's oceans has pushed commercially important species (such as cod) into steep decline. The United Nation's Food and Agriculture Organization (FAO) reports that almost seven out of ten of the ocean's commercially targeted marine fish stocks are either fully or heavily exploited (44%), over-exploited (16%), depleted (6%), or very slowly recovering from previous overfishing (3%). The **maximum sustainable yield** has been exceeded by too many fishing vessels catching too many fish, often using wasteful and destructive methods.

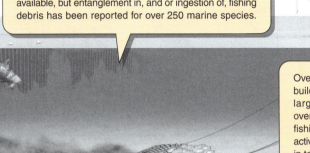

Lost fishing gear (particularly drift nets) threatens marine life. Comprehensive data on **ghost fishing** impacts is not available, but entanglement in, and or ingestion of, fishing debris has been reported for over 250 marine species.

Over-capitalization of the fishing industry has led to the build up of excessive fishing fleets, particularly of the large scale vessels. This has led to widespread overfishing (with many fish stocks at historic lows and fishing effort at unprecedented highs). Not only are the activities of these large vessels ecologically unsustainable in terms of fish stocks but, on average, for every calorie of fish caught, a fishing vessel uses 15 calories of fuel.

Bottom trawls and dredges cause large scale physical damage to the seafloor. Non-commercial, bottom-dwelling species in the path of the net can be uprooted, damaged, or killed, turning the seafloor into a barren, unproductive wasteland unable to sustain marine life. An area equal to half the world's continental shelves is now trawled every year. In other words, the world's seabed is being scraped 150 times faster than the world's forests are being clear-cut.

Due to the limited selectivity of fishing gear, millions of marine organisms are discarded for economic, legal, or personal reasons. Such organisms are defined as **by-catch** and include fish, invertebrates, protected marine mammals, sea turtles, and sea birds. Depending on the gear and handling techniques, some or all of the discarded animals die. A recent estimation of the worldwide by-catch is approximately 30 million tons per year, which is about one third of the estimated 85 million tons of catch that is retained each year.

Land and Water

Longline fishing (mainly for tuna) results in the death of 100 000 albatrosses and petrels every year in the southern Pacific alone. Six of the world's twenty albatross species are in serious decline and longline fishing is implicated in each case.

Photo: Jane Ussher

Over-harvesting of abundant species, or removal of too many reproductive individuals from a population, can have far reaching ecological effects. Modern boats, with their sophisticated fish-finding equipment, have the ability to catch entire schools of fish.

NOAA

Fish farming, once thought to be the solution to the world's overfishing problems, actually accelerates the decline of wild fish stocks. Many farmed fish are fed meal made from wild fish, but it takes about one kilo of wild fish to grow 300 g of farmed fish. Some forms of fish farming destroy natural fish habitat and produce large scale effluent flows.

1. Explain the term **over-exploitation** in relation to commercial fisheries management: _____

   _____

2. Define the term **by-catch**: _____

   _____

© Biozone International 2007-2011
Photocopying Prohibited

Periodicals: Oceans of nothing

Related activities: Fisheries Management
Weblinks: The Impact of Fishing Methods on the Environment

RDA 3

The Peruvian Anchovy Fishery: An Example of Over-Exploitation

Before 1950, fish in Peru were harvested mainly for human consumption. The total annual catch was 86 000 tonnes. In 1953, the first fish meal plants were developed. Within nine years, Peru became the number one fishing nation in the world by volume; 1700 purse seiners exploited a seven month fishing season and Peru's economy was buoyant.

In 1970, fearing a crash, a group of scientists in the Peruvian government issued a warning. They estimated that the sustainable yield was around 9.5 million tonnes, a number that was being surpassed. The government decided to ignore this; due to the collapse of the Norwegian and Icelandic herring fisheries the previous year, Peru was the dominant player in the lucrative anchovy market. In 1970, the government allowed a harvest of 12.4 million tonnes. In 1971, 10.5 million tonnes were harvested. In 1972, the combination of environmental changes (El Niño) and prolonged overfishing led to a complete collapse of the fishery, which has never recovered.

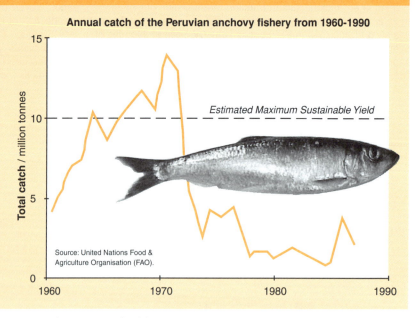

Annual catch of the Peruvian anchovy fishery from 1960-1990

Estimated Maximum Sustainable Yield

Source: United Nations Food & Agriculture Organisation (FAO).

3. Using an example, explain why a catch over the **maximum sustainable yield** will result in the collapse of a fishery:

_____

_____

_____

4. Use the graph showing the relationship between age, biomass, and stock numbers in a commercially harvested fish population (below, right) to answer the following questions:

(a) State the optimum age at which the animals should be harvested:

_____

(b) Identify the age range during which the greatest increase in biomass occurs:

_____

(c) Suggest what other life history data would be required by fisheries scientists when deciding on the management plan for this population:

_____

_____

_____

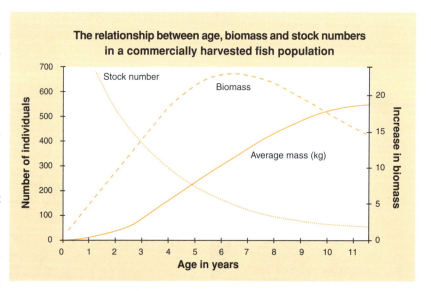

The relationship between age, biomass and stock numbers in a commercially harvested fish population

Stock number

Biomass

Average mass (kg)

5. Discuss three methods by which fish populations can be conserved: _____

_____

_____

6. (a) Outline two advantages of marine fish farming: _____

_____

(b) Outline two disadvantages of marine fish farming: _____

Fisheries Management

The stock of North Sea cod (*Gadus morhua*) is one of the world's six large populations of this economically important species. As one of the most intensively studied, monitored, and exploited fish stocks in the North Sea, it is considered a highly relevant indicator of how well sustainable fisheries policies are operating. Stocks of commercially fished species must be managed carefully to ensure that the catch (take) does not undermine the long term sustainability of the fishery. This requires close attention to **stock indicators**, such as catch per unit of fishing effort, stock recruitment rates, population age structure, and spawning biomass. Currently, the North Sea cod stock is below safe biological limits and stocks are also depleted in all waters adjacent to the North Sea, where the species is distributed. Recent emergency measures plan to arrest this decline.

Total international landings of North Sea cod

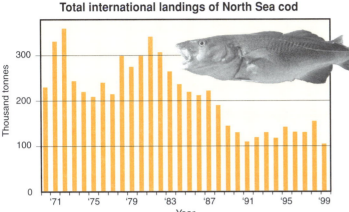

Recruitment and spawning stock biomass of North Sea cod

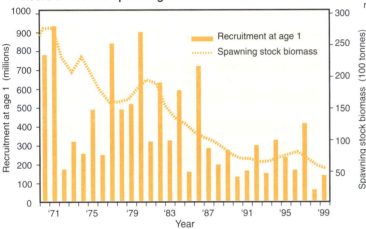

The state of the fishery

- Fishing mortality has increased gradually, and has been above the precautionary limit (that considered to be a safe take) since 1980 (left).

- Recruitment has been generally poor since 1987 (below, left).

- The number of spawning adults has fallen to levels below those required to recruit new individuals into the stock (below, left).

- ICES (the International Council for the Exploration of the Sea) advised that the spawning stock biomass (an indicator of the number of breeding adults) reached a new historic low in 2001, and that the risk of stock collapse is high.

What has been done?

- A large part of the North Sea was closed for cod fishing between February and April 2001, to protect juvenile cod .

- The TAC has been set at approximately half that set for the year 2000. Further regulations, such as increasing net mesh size and reducing the volume of fish discarded, are planned, and will further restrict the effort of fishing fleets until (if) the stock recovers.

- The ICES has recommended a recovery plan that will ensure recovery of the spawning stock to a level of more than 150 000 t. Reductions in TAC alone are insufficient to stop the declines.

Some important definitions

Stock: The part of the population from which catches are taken in a fishery

Stock recruitment: The entry of juvenile fish into the fish stock

Total Allowable Catch (TAC): The catch that can be legally taken from the stock

Stock collapse: Population level at which the fish stock cannot recover

Sources: European Environmental Agency (EEA), CEFAS (The Centre for Environment, Fisheries, and Aquaculture Science), and the ICES.

1. It has been known for more than a decade that the stock of cod in the North Sea has been declining drastically and that fishing takes were not sustainable. With reference to the data above, discuss the evidence to support this statement:

_____

_____

_____

2. Using the information provided above for guidance, describe the state the North Sea cod fishery, summarizing the main points below. If required, develop these as a separate report. Identify:

(a) The location of the fishery: _____

(b) The current state of the fishery (including stock status, catch rates, TAC, and quota): _____

_____

(c) Features of the biology of cod that are important in the management of the fishery (list): _____

_____

(d) Methods used to assess sustainability (list): _____

(e) Management options for the fishery (list): _____

_____

_____

© Biozone International 2007-2011
Photocopying Prohibited

Related activities: Ecological Impacts of Fishing

Weblinks: Starfish, Fisheries and the Environment

RDA 3

Land and Water

Sustainable Yield

$$SY = \left(\frac{Total\ biomass}{Energy} at\ time\ t1 \right) - \left(\frac{Total\ biomass}{Energy} at\ time\ t \right)$$

= (annual growth and recruitment) - (annual death and emigration)

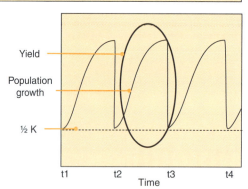

Photo:NIWA

Sustainable yield (SY) refers to the number or weight of fish that can be removed by fishing without reducing the stock biomass from year to year. It assumes that the environmental conditions remain the same and do not contribute to fluctuations in biomass levels. Maintaining a **maximum sustainable yield** (MSY) relies on obtaining precise data about a population's age structure, size, and growth rates. If the MSY is incorrectly established, unsustainable quotas may be set, and fish stock may become depleted.

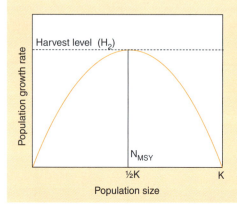

The orange roughy fishery in New Zealand is an example of the consequences of incorrect estimates of MSY. Scientists believed the fish (above) grew quickly and matured early, so their initial estimates of population size and growth rates were too high. They subsequently found that the fish have low productivity and are slow to mature and breed. High quotas allowed too many fish to be taken, and the fishery could not be sustained. It went into serious decline, although careful management since has seen some recovery.

The theoretical maximum sustainable yield (N_{MSY}) occurs when a population is at half the carrying capacity (½K). At this point, the population growth rate will also be at its maximum. Under ideal conditions, harvesting at this rate (H_2) should be able to continue indefinitely. However, the growth rate of a population is likely to fluctuate from year to year. If a population has below-average growth for several years while the take remains the same, there is a high risk of population collapse because an ever-increasing proportion of the population will be taken with each harvest.

3. Explain why it is essential to have accurate estimates of population age structure, size and growth rate when determining a maximum sustainable yield:

_____

_____

_____

4. Explain the implications to the population of the following scenarios:

a) The population size is over estimated: _____

_____

b) The population growth rate is over-estimated: _____

_____

c) Initial studies of the age structure incorrectly show there is a greater proportion of mature fish than younger fish.

_____

_____

5. Discuss the statement "*Harvesting at the maximum sustainable yield puts the target population on a knife edge*.":

_____

_____

_____

_____

Key Terms: Mix and Match

INSTRUCTIONS: Test your vocabulary by matching each term to its definition, as identified by its preceding letter code.

AQUACULTURE

BY-CATCH

CHEMICAL PEST CONTROL

CULTIVATION

DESERTIFICATION

GLOBALIZATION

GREEN REVOLUTION

INTEGRATED PEST MANAGEMENT

MACRONUTRIENTS

MAXIMUM SUSTAINABLE YIELD

MINERAL

PESTS

RANGELAND

REMEDIATION

SOIL CONSERVATION

SOIL DEGRADATION

STOCK INDICATOR

SUBSISTENCE FARMING

SUSTAINABLE AGRICULTURE

SUSTAINABLE FORESTRY

URBAN DEVELOPMENT

WEEDS

A Unwanted plants that are growing within a particular area of land or water.

B Agricultural practice that has long term viability at its current production level.

C The exchanges between, and merging of, global markets, cultures and ideas.

D Forestry management system that enables the long term removal of timber from a forest.

E The deterioration of arable or forested land into desert as a result of overgrazing and lack of irrigation and climate change.

F Organisms which are unwanted by humans because of the damage they cause to crops or stored goods.

G Organisms caught during a fishing operation that are not of the targeted species.

H Chemical elements and compounds needed by organisms in large quantities.

I Arid or semiarid land that supports a mix of grasses or low shrubs and may be used for grazing.

J The largest possible yield that can be obtained from a population which can then be replaced by the growth rate of that population.

K The sudden increase in crop production due to the availability of synthetic fertilizers and better production capabilities since the 1950s.

L The change in rural land to residential and commercial properties usually attached to or close to city boundaries.

M The damage and loss of topsoil, humus and nutrients from the land due to poor or inappropriate farming practices.

N Marker or unit that can be used to measure the abundance of a wild stock such as cod.

O Farming practice in which a farmer grows only the food that is needed for his immediate family rather than for the market place.

P The use of both chemical and biological control methods to control crop pests.

Q The removal of pollutants and contaminants from an environment so that it can be safely used for another purpose or restored.

R The farming of aquatic organisms for profit, either indoors in tanks or outdoors in confined ponds or estuaries.

S The use of methods that actively reduce the amount of both soil and nutrients lost from the soil during crop production.

T The planting and growing of plant crops on arable land.

U A naturally occurring homogenous inorganic solid that has a definite chemical composition, crystalline, structure, colour, and hardness.

V The control of crop pests using synthetic insecticides.

Land and Water

Weblinks: Ecological Footprint

Energy

Key concepts

▶ Energy can not be created or destroyed, it is simply transformed from one form to another.

▶ Non-renewable resources provide immediate low cost power in the short term.

▶ Renewable energy technology is rapidly becoming more efficient and more reliable.

▶ Increasing the efficiency of energy usage can dramatically reduce energy demands.

Key terms

biofuel
CAFE regulations
coal
energy conservation
fossil fuel
geothermal energy
hydroelectric power
hydrogen fuel cell
industrial revolution
natural gas
non-renewable energy
nuclear fission
nuclear fusion
nuclear power
oil
photovoltaic cell
renewable energy
solar energy
thermodynamics
watt
wave energy
wind energy
wind turbine

Objectives

☐ 1. Use the **KEY TERMS** to help you understand and complete these objectives.

Energy   pages 155, 172-174

☐ 2. Recall basic energy concepts, forms of energy, **energy transformation** and laws of **thermodynamics**. Recall that energy is lost from the system at each transformation. *Appreciate that the terminology associated with energy in the popular media is frequently a shorthand parlance for types of energy transformations associated with human application, e.g. energy production, energy consumption, energy producer etc.*

☐ 3. Describe the different methods of **electricity generation**.

☐ 4. Summarize the history of human energy use, including reference to the **industrial revolution** and our dependence on the **fossil fuels**: **coal**, **oil**, and **natural gas**.

☐ 5. Outline current and future global energy demands.

☐ 6. Examine the need for greater efficiency of energy exploitation, including considering: reducing and using waste heat, saving energy in industry and transport with reference to the **Corporate Average Fuel Economy** (CAFE) regulations, use of hybrid vehicles, and reducing energy usage in buildings.

Sources of Non-Renewable Energy   pages 156-162

☐ 7. Describe the methods of coal and oil extraction and the effects of these on the environment.

☐ 8. Discuss the advantages and disadvantages of using coal and oil as a source of energy. Include considerations of economic and environmental impacts, and efficiency with which usable forms of energy are produced.

☐ 9. Describe the process of **nuclear power** generation. Discuss its advantages and disadvantages, and short and long term environmental effects.

☐ 10. Explain how the principles of sustainability can be applied to extending the lifetime of **non-renewable** resources.

Sources of Renewable Energy   pages 163-171

☐ 11. Discuss the production of **hydroelectric power**, its capacity to produce electricity, and its effect on the environment.

☐ 12. Describe the production of electricity from and potential future use of **solar energy**, **wind energy**, **wave** and **tidal energy**, **geothermal energy**, **biofuels**, and **hydrogen fuel cells**.

☐ 13. Describe the advantages and disadvantages of solar energy, wind energy, wave energy, geothermal energy, biofuels, and hydrogen fuel cells.

Periodicals:
Listings for this chapter are on page 231

Weblinks:
www.thebiozone.com/
weblink/EnvSci-2764.html

Presentation Media
Environmental Science:
Energy

Using Energy Transformations

Most commercial electricity is generated by transforming **kinetic energy** into **electrical energy.** This is usually achieved by using kinetic energy to turn a turbine attached to a magnet or electromagnet housed inside a large set of wire coils (or vice versa) (the generator). Moving the magnet through the coils produces electricity by a process called **electromagnetic induction**. The difference between most forms of electricity generation is the method employed to turn the turbine. Energy comes in many forms, from **potential** (stored) energy to kinetic (movement) energy. Energy can be **transformed** easily between these forms. A rock at the top of a hill has gravitational potential energy. Giving it a push so that it rolls down the hill converts the gravitational potential energy into kinetic energy, along with some sound and heat. Energy is lost from a system (normally as heat due to friction) whenever energy is transformed from one form into another. Removing causes of energy loss improves the efficiency of the device being used. Generally, the fewer steps involved in energy transformation, the less energy will be lost from the system.

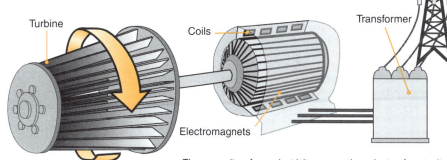

Turbine — Coils — Electromagnets — Transformer

The capacity of an electricity generation plant refers to its instantaneous power output. For example, a plant rated at 1000 MW has the ability to produce 1000 megawatts (1000 megajoules per second) of electricity at any one point in time.

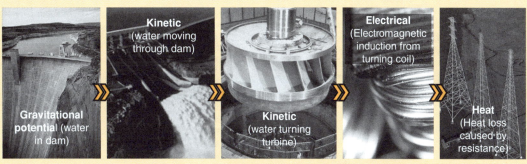

Gravitational potential (water in dam) → **Kinetic** (water moving through dam) → **Kinetic** (water turning turbine) → **Electrical** (Electromagnetic induction from turning coil) → **Heat** (Heat loss caused by resistance)

An energy chain can be used to describe where the energy used to generate electricity comes from (and goes to). The number of steps in the chain depends on the form of energy being used and the type of energy generation.

Photovoltaic cells (or solar cells) are increasingly being used in the production of electricity on a small scale. The solar cell is able to produce electricity directly from the Sun's energy without the need for a turbine.

1. Describe the process by which electricity is commercially generated: _____

_____

_____

_____

2. Explain why no form of electricity generation can ever be 100% efficient: _____

_____

_____

3. For each of the following create an energy chain to show the energy transformations in the generation of electricity:

(a) Geothermal power generation: _____

_____

(b) Coal fired power station: _____

_____

(c) Nuclear power station: _____

_____

Energy

Related activities: Non-Renewable Resources, Renewable Energy

RA 2

Non-Renewable Resources

The Earth contains enormous mineral resources, which are able to be obtained and used with relative ease to produce usable energy. The most commonly used of these are the **fossil fuels**, i.e. **coal**, **oil** and **natural gas.** These are can be burnt immediately to produce heat energy, or they can be refined to provide for a variety of energy or material needs. As well as fossil fuels, **radioactive** minerals can be mined and concentrated, and the energy they produce harnessed to provide electrical energy.

Around 85% of the world's energy needs comes from burning fossil fuels, with around 5% coming from **nuclear energy.** The distribution of mineral use globally is not uniform. For example, 79% of nuclear power stations are found in just ten countries. Moreover, the world's twenty wealthiest countries use more than half the world's commercial energy supply yet constitute less than a fifth of the world's population. In contrast, many poorer nations lack easy access to energy resources.

Non-Renewable Energy Resources from the Earth's Crust

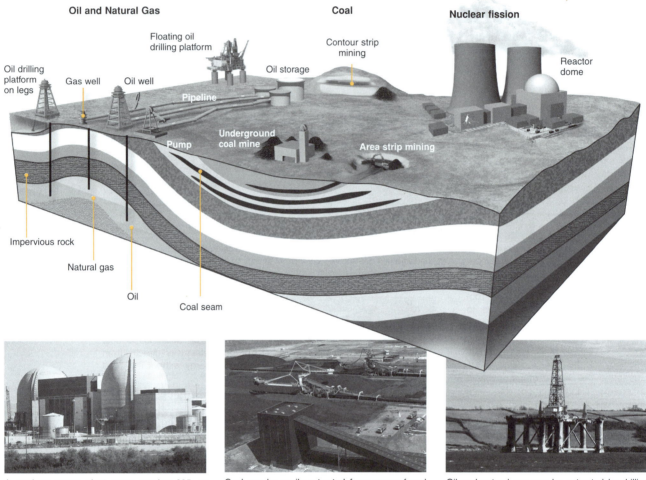

A nuclear power plant uses uranium-235 or plutonium-239 as fuel in a controlled nuclear fission reaction to release energy for propulsion, heat, and electricity generation. Nuclear power does not release CO_2, but safe storage and disposal of nuclear waste remains a challenge.

Coal can be easily extracted from seams found near the surface. This causes a large amount of disruption to the landscape. Coal from deeper seams can be extracted by underground mining, which causes little surface disruption provided there is no land subsidence.

Oil and natural gas can be extracted by drilling into a reservoir and pumping the contents to the surface. Many large reservoirs are found offshore, along the continental shelves. Special drilling platforms can be towed out by boats and anchored the reservoir.

1. Explain why coal, oil, natural gas and nuclear fuels such as uranium are non-renewable: _____

_____

_____

_____

2. Describe some of the issues associated with extracting energy resources from the Earth's crust: _____

_____

_____

_____

_____

Related activities: Oil, Coal, Nuclear Power

Periodicals:
Ice on fire

Oil

Oil is formed from the remains of algae and zooplankton which settled to the bottom of shallow seas and lakes about the same time as the coal forming swamps. These remains were buried and compressed under layers of nonporous sediment. The process, although continuous, occur so slowly that oil (and coal) is essentially non-renewable. Crude oil can be refined and used for an extensive array of applications including fuel, road tar, plastics, and cosmetics.

Oil and Natural Gas

Oil and natural gas are both composed of a mixture of hydrocarbons and are generally found in the same underground reservoirs. **Natural gas** is generally defined as a mixture of hydrocarbons with four or fewer carbon atoms in the chain (as these are gaseous at standard temperatures and pressures). **Oil** is defined as the mixture of hydrocarbons with five or more carbon atoms in the chain.

Major World Oil Reserves

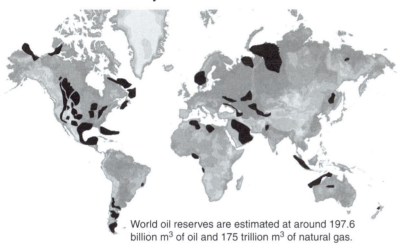

World oil reserves are estimated at around 197.6 billion m^3 of oil and 175 trillion m^3 of natural gas.

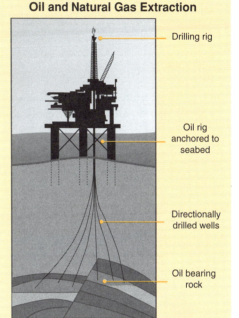

Oil and Natural Gas Extraction

- Drilling rig
- Oil rig anchored to seabed
- Directionally drilled wells
- Oil bearing rock

Oil and natural gas reservoirs are found using a number of techniques including echolocation, gravitational and magnetic fluctuations, and geological surveys. A well is drilled once a reservoir has been located. Steerable drill heads allow multiple wells to be drilled without having to move the platform.

Natural gas is often found in the same reservoirs as oil. Drilling rigs require specialized facilities to store the gas. Because of this, much natural gas is either vented, or reinjected to maintain pressure in the reservoir.

Transport of natural gas requires specialized equipment. Liquid natural gas (LNG) tankers are able to cool the gas to -162°C and transport it as a liquid (saving space). Gas can also be piped to shore if facilities are nearby.

Oil may be found in materials that make extraction through conventional drilling impossible. These **non conventional oils** (e.g. oil shale) are often mined in the same way as coal and the oil washed from them.

Crude and **heavy oils** require refining before use. Crude oil is separated into different sized fractions by a **distillation tower**. Heavy oils may be heated under pressure to break them into smaller more usable molecules.

Energy

1. Describe the difference in the composition of natural gas and oil: _____

_____

_____

2. Describe how oil-bearing rocks are found and exploited: _____

_____

_____

3. Explain why natural gas is often reinjected into the main oil reservoir: _____

_____

_____

_____

Periodicals:
The Canadian oil boom:
Scraping bottom

Related activities: Non-Renewable Resources
Weblinks: Coal and Oil Formation

A 2

World Oil Production and Consumption

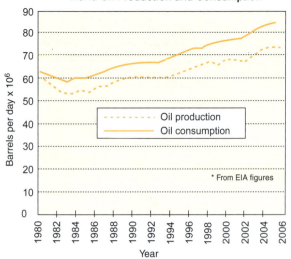

* From EIA figures

Oil	
Advantages	Disadvantages
Large supply	Many reserves are offshore and difficult to extract
High net energy gain	High CO_2 production
Can be refined to produce many different fuel types	Potential for large environmental damage if spilled
Easy to transport	Rate of use will use up reserves in near future

*Note: The difference between consumption and production figures are due to changes in stock and the consumption of additives which increase the volume of the resulting fuel.

Oil Refining

Oil is refined in a fractionating or distillation tower by **fractional distillation**. The tower is around 400°C at the bottom, but cools towards the top to less than 100°C. Crude oil is pumped into the bottom of the distillation tower and evaporates. The oil vapor cools and condenses as it travels up the tower. Long chain hydrocarbons condense near the bottom of the tower while short chain hydrocarbons condense near the top.

Short chain hydrocarbons find use in portable lighters. Butane is commonly used in cigarette lighters and camp stoves. Propane is commonly used for larger barbecue grills.

Petrol and diesel are formed from hydrocarbons with between 6 and 12 C atoms. They provide a high energy, easily combustible fuel that, being a liquid, is easily stored and transported.

Mid length hydrocarbon chains (about 15 C atoms) are used as jet fuel. They are less volatile and less flammable than shorter chain hydrocarbon fuels while providing high energy per unit volume.

Long chain hydrocarbons may be heated to split them into shorter chains (to boost the fractions of petrol and diesel produced), or used in lubricating oil, heavy fuel oil, waxes, and tar.

4. Examine the graph of oil consumption and production:

   (a) Describe the trend of the line graphs: _____

   (b) Describe the trend in the data from the year 2000 to 2006: _____

   _____

   _____

   _____

5. Describe some of the advantages and disadvantages of using oil: _____

   _____

   _____

   _____

6. Explain how crude oil is refined: _____

   _____

   _____

   _____

Coal

Coal is formed from the remains of terrestrial plant material buried in vast shallow swamps during the carboniferous period (359 to 299 million years ago) and subsequently compacted under sediments to form a hard black material. Coal accounts for the majority of the world's energy needs and is used for domestic and industrial purposes. Coal reserves are in the billions of tonnes, but removing it from the ground requires large amounts of energy and causes intense disturbance of the surrounding landscape. Burning coal produces vast quantities of greenhouse gases and pollutants, contributing to smog and global warming.

Surface Mining

Surface mining (e.g. strip mining) is used when the coal bed is found close to the surface. **Overburden** (the layers of earth above the coal bed) is removed by heavy machinery and may be stored for later remediation. **Area strip mining** removes coal in long strips. Overburden from the new strip is used to fill the previous one. **Contour strip mining** is similar but is used on steeper terrain, following the contours of the land.

Surface mining causes a vast amount of disturbance to the local environment. The land itself is disturbed and the machinery used contributes to noise and visual pollution. Land mined in this way can be quickly eroded by heavy rains, and sediments (often laden with toxic substances) can be washed into streams and rivers.

Surface mines can be restored once the mining operation is complete, although this does not always happen. Restoration does not always return the mine to its former states either. Open pit mines may be left to fill with water to create a lake where once there was not.

Subsurface Mining

Subsurface mining uses two main methods. **Room and pillar** mining removes large areas of coal but leaves behind coal pillars than help support the roof of the mine. **Long wall mining** uses machines that move along the coal face. Coal falls on to a conveyer as it is cut from the seam and is taken to the surface. As the machine moves forward the space behind is allowed to collapse.

Subsurface mining causes far less land disturbance than surface mining. However, it is far more dangerous and much of the coal is left in the ground. Risks include roof collapse, build up of explosive or toxic gases, and lung diseases from inhaling fine dust. Although less land is disturbed by digging, land subsidence can leave ripples or holes in the land above.

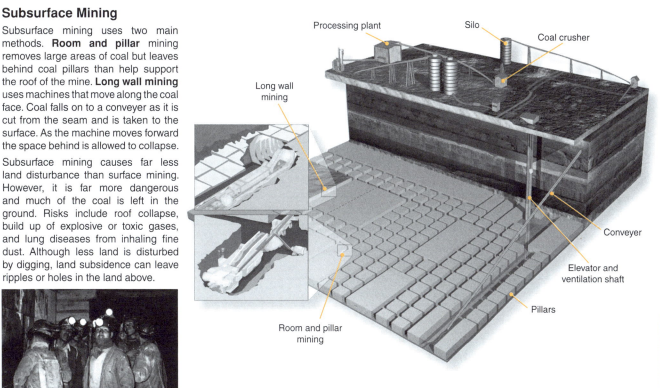

Processing plant · Silo · Coal crusher · Long wall mining · Conveyer · Elevator and ventilation shaft · Pillars · Room and pillar mining

1. For each of the following mining methods, explain the reason for its use and give an advantage and disadvantage:

    (a) Surface mining: _____

    _____

    _____

    _____

    (b) Subsurface mining: _____

    _____

    _____

    _____

Related activities: *Non-Renewable Resources*

Weblinks: *Coal and Oil Formation*

Photo: Wojsyl

The longer coal has been **buried** and **compressed,** the better it is as a fuel. Coals compressed under high pressure and temperatures form **anthracite**, the highest grade of coal. **Peat** (above), the lowest grade of coal, forms under minimal pressure and still has a high moisture content. Intermediate grades include **lignite** and **bituminous** coal.

Coal is pulverized and used to fuel thermal power stations. In developing countries it is often used for home heating and cooking. This can lead to health problems if furnaces or stoves are not properly vented and coal ash handled carefully, as coal can contain many toxic substances.

Major World Coal Reserves

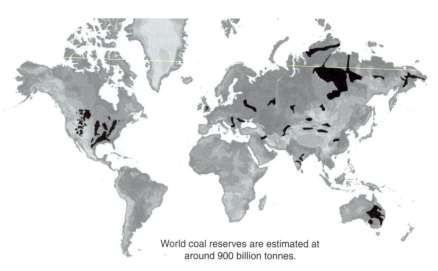

World coal reserves are estimated at around 900 billion tonnes.

Coal	
Advantages	Disadvantages
Huge supplies (at least 500 years worth)	High CO_2 production when burned
High net energy yields.	High particle pollution from soot
Can be used to produce syngas and converted to other fuels (e.g. gasoline).	Low grade coals produce high pollution and contribute to acid rain
Relatively easy to extract when near to surface	High land disturbance through mining
Important in industry as coke (reducer)	

2. Describe some of the detrimental environmental effects of both surface and subsurface mining: _____

_____

_____

_____

_____

3. Explain why anthracite is a better fuel than peat: _____

_____

_____

_____

4. Discuss the advantages and disadvantages of coal: _____

_____

_____

_____

5. In the United States, the EPA conducted a detailed study of 20 potentially toxic substances from coal burning electric utilities. It concluded that, with the possible exception of mercury, there were no compelling health risks from burning coal. In many developing countries, emissions from burning coal are a serious problem for health due to exposure to arsenic, fluorine, radioactive particles (uranium and thorium), and carcinogenic organic compounds.

Discuss the statement above. Explain why burning coal in the United States presents little or no health risks, while developing countries experience many health problems from burning coal.

_____

_____

_____

_____

Nuclear Power

Nuclear power accounts for about 5% of the world's production of usable energy but 14% of world electricity because virtually all of it is used for electricity production. Nuclear **fission** reactors are currently the only reactor type used to produce commercial electricity, although there are a number of reactor designs. Nuclear power reactors first began to be developed for industry in the 1950s and there are now more than 400 reactors throughout the world, with most located in the USA and western Europe. The popularity of nuclear power stations declined during the 1970s and 80s due to high costs and two high profile accidents. Currently, with better technology available and growing concerns over climate change and energy shortages, nuclear power is being reexamined as a cost effective option for electricity production.

Nuclear Power Station

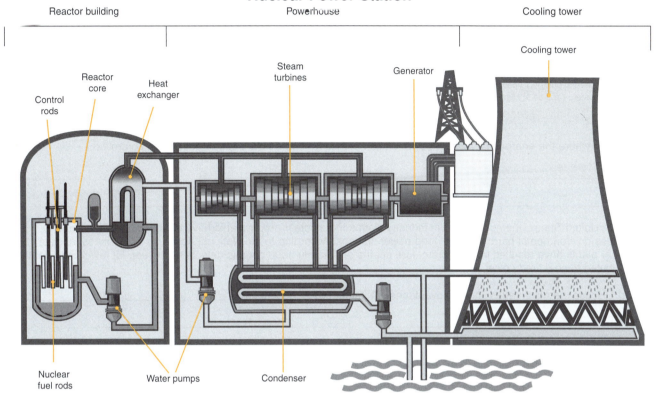

Reactor building   Powerhouse   Cooling tower

Control rods — Reactor core — Heat exchanger — Steam turbines — Generator — Cooling tower

Nuclear fuel rods — Water pumps — Condenser

A nuclear power station consists of a reactor building, powerhouse, and cooling tower(s). The reactor building houses the reactor core, which consists of a series of nuclear fuel rods set between removable control rods. Heat produced in the reactor is passed through a heat exchanger to heat water to steam which drives the turbines and generator. Steam then passes into a condenser which is cooled by water pumped from the cooling tower.

Nuclear Fission

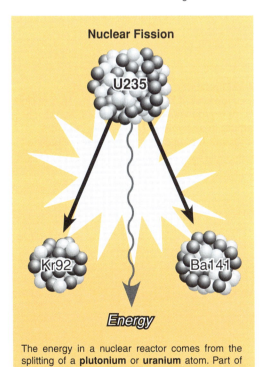

U235

Kr92   Ba141

Energy

The energy in a nuclear reactor comes from the splitting of a **plutonium** or **uranium** atom. Part of the mass of the atom is converted into energy. The energy released is used to heat a heat sink (water or a metal or molten salt) surrounding the reactor.

Nuclear Power Generation	
Advantages	Disadvantages
Large potential fuel supply	High start up costs
Little fuel is needed so supplies last a long time	Disposal of waste presents major technical and environmental problems
Low air pollution (low CO_2 emissions)	Risk of catastrophic environmental disaster if accident occurs
Little land required	Technology can be adapted to develop nuclear weapons
Large amount of energy generated	Potential terrorist target

Photo: USDE

The energy produced by nuclear reactions is enormous. **Uranium** subjected to fission produces around three million times as much energy as an equal mass of coal. However only a small percentage of this energy is used in nuclear power plants.

Kurchatov Inst.

The potential disasters that nuclear power stations present were shown in 1986 when the number 4 reactor at **Chernobyl** exploded, spreading radioactive material over a wide area and causing the evacuation of the city of Pripyat.

Periodicals:
Can nuclear power compete?

Related activities: Non-Renewable Resources, Chernobyl Accident
Weblinks: How it Works

A 3

Energy

Fukushima Nuclear Crisis

On March 11, 2011 the Fukushima Nuclear Power Station, 220 km north of Tokyo, suffered multiple reactor failures after a 9.0 magnitude earthquake and 10 m high tsunami. Coolant pumps failed with a possible partial meltdown of at least three reactors. Heat generated by the fuel rod meltdown caused reactor water to boil to steam, exposing the fuel rods to air and causing production of hydrogen gas. Venting the gas from each of the three separate reactor containment vessels led to explosions that destroyed the outer reactor buildings. The containment vessels of reactors 2 and 3 may have been damaged during the explosions, leading to radiation spikes. In last resort efforts to cool the fuel rods engineers pumped seawater into the coolant system (info as at March 17, 2011).

Reactor 3: Hydrogen explosion destroyed top half of building. Containment vessel possibly damaged

Reactor 1: Hydrogen explosion blew off top of building. Containment vessel undamaged.

Reactor 4: Fire in nuclear fuel storage pond. Spent fuel may have been exposed. High levels of radiation detected.

Reactor 2: Containment vessel possibly damaged in explosion and leaking. Coolant pumps damaged. Fuel rods exposed.

Schematic of Fukushima Daiichi Nuclear Plant

1. Explain where the energy in a nuclear power station comes from and how it is harnessed and controlled:

   _____

   _____

2. In the United States, the nuclear power industry claims that nuclear power plants have resulted in no fatalities and far less environmental harm that coal fired power stations. According to the National Academy of Sciences, nuclear power plants have resulted in 6000 premature deaths and nearly 4000 genetic defects each year, far lower than deaths attributed to coal fired power stations.

   (a) Discuss the advantages and disadvantages of nuclear power generation: _____

   _____

   _____

   _____

   (b) Explain why many people dislike the idea of nuclear power plants despite all of a nuclear power plants inbuilt safety features:

   _____

   _____

   _____

3. Present day nuclear reactors require a total of around 70 000 tonnes of natural uranium a year. At this rate of consumption, the known global supplies of uranium will last around 70 years. However, it is estimated nearly 10.5 million tonnes of uranium deposits are still undiscovered. Better refining of uranium, or reprocessing spent material, could reduce requirements by 50%. There is an estimated 4.5 billion tonnes of uranium in seawater. Fast breeder reactors, which are currently uneconomic and difficult to control, use only 1% of the uranium fuel used today and use virtually all their wastes as fuel.

   Calculate the length of time the uranium fuel supply will last based on:

   (a) Undiscovered uranium: _____

   (b) Undiscovered uranium plus better refining and reprocessing: _____

   (c) Extracting uranium from seawater: _____

   (d) Using known reserves with fast breeder reactors: _____

4. After many years of its unpopularity, many electrical companies were considering a return to nuclear power. Discuss how the crisis at Fukushima may affect these considerations.

   _____

   _____

   _____

Renewable Energy

There are a number of drivers behind the demand for alternative methods for power generation. There has been a steady decrease in easily obtainable non-renewable energy resources and a steady rise in their cost and use. Coupled with these reasons, the environmental damage caused by nuclear waste and burning fossil fuels has created a strong public demand for renewable, environmentally friendly sources of energy. However, taking advantage of renewable energy resources involves making

changes to infrastructure and meeting large start-up costs. Many developing nations may find this beyond their abilities, although small items such as solar cookers may become common in rural areas. Renewable energy technologies are rapidly becoming more efficient and less expensive. They are often as efficient on small scales as on large ones, and it is likely that they will soon become far more common for "off the grid" domestic energy generation, especially for lighting and heating water.

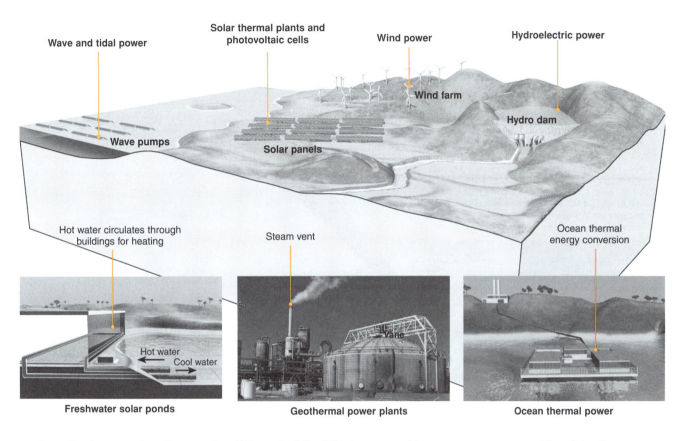

Wave and tidal power · Solar thermal plants and photovoltaic cells · Wind power · Hydroelectric power · Wave pumps · Wind farm · Solar panels · Hydro dam

Hot water circulates through buildings for heating · Steam vent · Ocean thermal energy conversion

Hot water · Cool water · Vane

Freshwater solar ponds · **Geothermal power plants** · **Ocean thermal power**

1. Describe the type of environment in which each of the following renewable energy resources would work best:

(a) Solar: _____

(b) Wave: _____

(c) Wind: _____

(d) Hydro: _____

(e) Geothermal: _____

2. Explain why renewable energy is likely to become the predominant energy source in the future: _____

© Biozone International 2007-2011
Photocopying Prohibited

Energy

Wind Power

Wind power has be used for many years to provide mechanical energy for running water pumps or machinery. Today it is mainly used to produce electricity. Wind power is becoming increasingly reliable and cost effective as the technology develops and turbines are able to operate in a range of conditions and wind speeds. Globally, wind power is steadily increasing in generation capacity, but wind is a variable energy provider. Fluctuations in power availability begin to become discernible when it makes up more than 20% of a nation's power output, meaning output can not be matched to changes in demand.

Wind farms often cover large areas of land but turbines can be designed to operate at sea and, on a smaller scale, along highway edges. Turbines range in size from just a meter across, to the world's current largest at 198 m tall and 126 m in diameter, with a generation capacity of 7 MW. Larger 10 MW turbines are already being planned.

At the end of 2009, the power output from wind turbines was around 1.5% of the global production of usable energy. Many European countries now use wind power to generate a substantial proportion of national power requirements. Denmark, for example, produces around 20% of its required power by wind. Currently, the European Union and the United States are the biggest producers of wind energy.

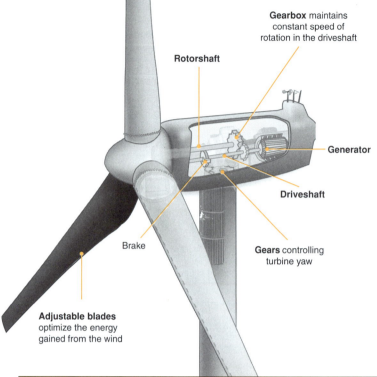

Gearbox maintains constant speed of rotation in the driveshaft

Rotorshaft

Generator

Driveshaft

Brake

Gears controlling turbine yaw

Adjustable blades optimize the energy gained from the wind

Wind Power	
Advantages	Disadvantages
No emissions	Production of visual and noise pollution
Little ground disturbance during or after construction	Requires steady winds
Compact and transportable to most locations	Can interfere with the flight paths of flying animals
Can be located in many areas (even at sea)	Much of actual cost to user is repaying start up costs.
	Back up systems required in low winds

1. Explain why wind power works best when it makes up only a minor portion of national electricity requirements:

_____

_____

_____

2. Discuss the advantages and disadvantages of wind power: _____

_____

_____

_____

_____

3. A typical wind turbine produces around 2.3 MW. The average house uses 30 kWh per day. Calculate the following:

(a) The minimum number of wind turbines required to power a town of 20 000 households: _____

(b) The total cost of the wind turbines in 3a above at a rate of $1000 per kilowatt installed: _____

(c) The number of wind turbines required to replace a 120 MW coal fired power station: _____

Related activities: Renewable Energy
Weblinks: Wind Energy Basics

Periodicals:
Where the wind blows

© Biozone International 2007-2011
Photocopying Prohibited

Hydroelectricity

Hydroelectricity accounts for around 20% of global electricity production. Electricity is produced by utilizing the **kinetic energy** of water stored in reservoirs behind **dams**. Water is directed along pipes into the powerhouse where it drives turbines connected to a generator. The larger the volume of water and the further it has to fall, the greater the amount of energy it contains. Large dams can therefore produce large amounts of electricity. The generation of electricity itself produces no CO_2 emissions or other air pollution, but the construction of the dam requires massive amounts of energy and labor and often requires river diversions. Construction of large hydroelectric dams is highly controversial because creating a reservoir behind the dam often requires the submergence of towns and land. Dams constructed inefficiently can also fill up with silt and gradually reduce in generation capacity.

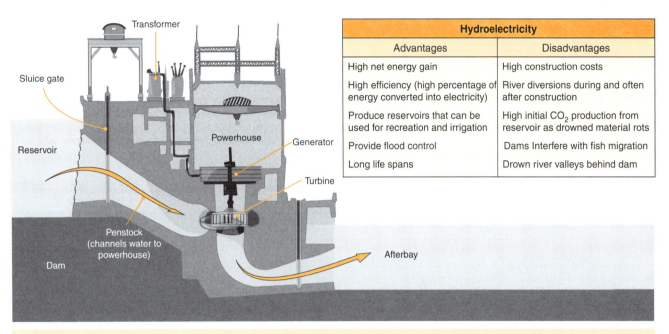

Hydroelectricity	
Advantages	Disadvantages
High net energy gain	High construction costs
High efficiency (high percentage of energy converted into electricity)	River diversions during and often after construction
Produce reservoirs that can be used for recreation and irrigation	High initial CO_2 production from reservoir as drowned material rots
Provide flood control	Dams Interfere with fish migration
Long life spans	Drown river valleys behind dam

The Yangtze River

1987

2006

Silt from Yangtze River

Siberian Crane

The **Three Gorges Dam** (above) on the Yangtze river, China, is 2.3 km wide and 101 m high, with a reservoir 660 km long. It has a generation capacity of 22 500 MW. The construction of the Three Gorges Dam in China caused the river water level to rise by 100 m, and required 1.2 million people to be relocated.

Dams reduce flood damage by regulating water flow downstream. However, they also prevent deposition of fertile silts. Flooding land behind the dam to create a reservoir seriously disrupts the feeding areas of wading birds.

Colorado River

A number of dams are found along the Colorado River, which runs from Colorado through to Mexico. The two largest hydroelectric dams on the river are the Glen Canyon Dam and the Hoover Dam. Together these dams have a generation capacity of over 3000 MW and provide irrigation and recreation for thousands of people. Both dams control water flow through the Colorado River and were controversial even before their construction.

The construction of **Glen Canyon Dam** effectively ended the annual flooding of the Colorado River. This has allowed invasive plants to establish and has caused the loss of many camping beaches as new silt is trapped behind the dam. The reduced flow rate of the river has severely affected native fish stocks. Controlled floods held in 1996 and 2004 have had beneficial effects on the downstream ecosystems.

Hoover Dam, which impounds Lake Mead, has a generation capacity of over 2000 MW. Water from Lake Mead serves more than 8 million people in Arizona, Nevada, and California. The dam has had a major effect on the Colorado delta, which has reduced in size from around 800 000 hectares to barely 73 000 hectares. Native fish populations have also been reduced.

Energy

Related activities: Renewable Energy

Weblinks: How Hydroelectric Power is Made

1. (a) Explain how hydroelectric dams are used to generate electricity: _____

    _____

    _____

    _____

   (b) Describe the relationship between water volume, height of the dam and electricity production: _____

    _____

    _____

    _____

2. Large scale hydroelectric power uses a high dam built across a river to block the water flow and create a reservoir. Water moving through pipes is used to turn large turbines. Small scale hydroelectric power uses only a small dam and no reservoir. The flow of the water directly from the stream is used to turn the turbine. Pumped-storage hydroelectric power uses excess power from power stations to pumped water to a storage dam at a high level. This is released later when more electricity is needed.

   (a) Explain why small scale hydroelectric power has less environmental impact on the environment than larger schemes:

    _____

    _____

    _____

   (b) Explain how pumped-storage hydroelectric power can help electricity production during periods of high demand:

    _____

    _____

    _____

    _____

   (c) Explain why pumped-storage hydroelectric power is an efficient use of electricity resources: _____

    _____

    _____

    _____

3. Using specific examples, describe some advantages and disadvantages of large scale hydroelectric dams:

    _____

    _____

    _____

    _____

    _____

4. Discuss the following statement: "*Hydroelectric power produces clean, environmentally friendly electricity*":

    _____

    _____

    _____

    _____

    _____

    _____

Solar Power

The energy reaching the Earth from the Sun is in the order of trillions upon trillions of joules per day, far more than all of humanity uses in an entire year. This energy can be harnessed in many ways to create electricity. Currently, most large scale methods of generating electricity from sunlight involve **concentrating** sunlight to heat a fluid, which will turn water to steam to drive a turbine. Solar power stations based on concentrating sunlight include the **central receiver system** (also known as a **power tower**), **distributed receiver system,** and **parabolic dishes**. Other designs include solar ponds and photovoltaic cells.

Distributed receiver systems use parabolic troughs to focus light into a thin beam. The beam of light heats oil in a pipe running along the focal point of the trough. The oil is used to heat water to steam to drive a turbine.

Parabolic reflector dishes focus light onto a Stirling engine at the dish's focal point. This is connected to a generator, which produces electricity directly. Each dish tracks the Sun at the most efficient angle.

Solar energy can be used directly to heat water (above) or air. Water heaters mounted on the roof of a house can dramatically reduce the amount of electricity needed to provide hot water and so lower household electricity bills.

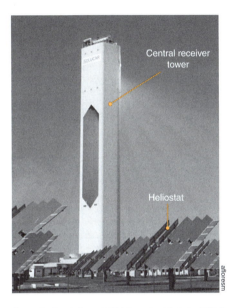

A **central receiver system** uses mirrors, called heliostats, to focus the Sun's rays onto a central tower. The focused light is used to heat water or molten salts, which are pumped up into the central tower. These heat water to steam to drive a turbine and create electricity. Power stations that use molten salts as the heating fluid operate at between 500ºC and 800ºC and are able to store heat for operation overnight.

Solar Pond

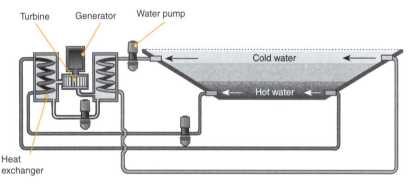

Solar ponds produce a thermal gradient between the top and bottom of the pool. Hot water is pumped into a heat exchanger, causing enclosed water or gas to heat up and flow past a turbine to a second heat exchanger where it is cooled down again.

Solar Power	
Advantages	Disadvantages
Low or no CO_2 emissions	Ground shaded by large solar panels
Relatively high net energy gain	Back up systems required
Small photovoltaic cells are portable and can power many applications	Large land area needed for commercial scale production
Unlimited energy source during fine weather	High sunshine hours required
	High start up costs

1. (a) Describe some advantages of using solar energy to produce electricity: _____

_____

_____

(b) Describe some disadvantages of using solar energy to produce electricity: _____

_____

_____

2. Explain why solar energy could provide almost limitless energy for humans to use: _____

_____

_____

Solar cells

Electricity is produced when a photon of light hits a semiconducting material (such as silicon) and knocks an electron loose. The electron is captured and forced to travel in one direction around a circuit, and so produces direct current electricity.

The efficiency of a photovoltaic cell depends partially on the material from which it is made, as this affects its ability to absorb photons, capture electrons, and pass electrons through an electrical circuit. Currently the most efficient solar cells are around 40% efficient.

Photovoltaic cells (solar cells) produce electricity directly from light. Advances in this technology have made these smaller and more efficient. There are no emissions or fuel costs once they are installed. Large power stations of 60 MW have been built.

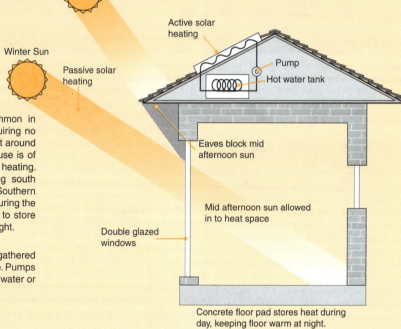

Solar Heating

Passive solar heating is becoming more common in houses. It can efficiently heat a home while requiring no electrical input and no equipment for moving heat around the house. The design and placement of the house is of great importance when using solar energy for heating. Houses placed with their main windows facing south in Northern Hemisphere and north in the Southern Hemisphere gain large amounts of solar energy during the day. Double glazed windows and insulation help to store this energy to keep the house warm during the night.

Active solar heating uses pumps to circulate heat gathered from a rooftop collector to various parts of a house. Pumps may circulate water through a tank to provide hot water or through a heat exchanger to feed radiators.

3. Explain how solar energy can be used to provide electricity even at night: _____

_____

_____

_____

_____

4. Explain the difference between passive and active solar heating: _____

_____

_____

_____

_____

5. Discuss how a house could meet all its energy demands from solar energy: _____

_____

_____

_____

_____

_____

_____

_____

Geothermal Power

Geothermal power stations operate where **volcanic activity** heats groundwater to steam. Bores drilled into the ground release this steam and transfer it via insulated pipes to a separator where the dry steam is separated and directed to turbines. Wet steam and waste dry steam are then condensed to water and reinjected into the **geothermal reservoir** to maintain the pressure and ground water supply. Geothermal power stations often operate at near full capacity, providing a **base load**, which other power sources can top up. Geothermal fields must be carefully managed to prevent the depletion of the reservoir and subsidence of nearby land.

Geothermal energy is produced by the fission of radioactive material deep in the Earth. This causes an enormous amount of heat that heats groundwater when close to the surface, producing a geothermal reservoir.

Geothermal power stations often provide base load supplies. This is the minimum continuous electrical supply for an area and is supplied by power stations that can operate constantly at near full capacity.

Geothermal power is only around 20% efficient. However, waste hot water from the power plant can be used to heat other industrial operations, such as heating ponds for producing tropical shrimp in temperate environments.

Steam fields are often large and steam must be sent along specially designed pipes that can expand and contract up to several meters in various weather conditions.

Geothermal heat pumps are now installed in many houses. These use a small pump to circulate fluid inside pipes from the roof and floor space of a house into the ground. In summer, this transfers heat from the house to the ground, cooling the house. In winter, it transfers heat from the ground into the house. Geothermal heat pumps do not have to be used in geothermal areas, they simply use the relatively constant temperature of the ground.

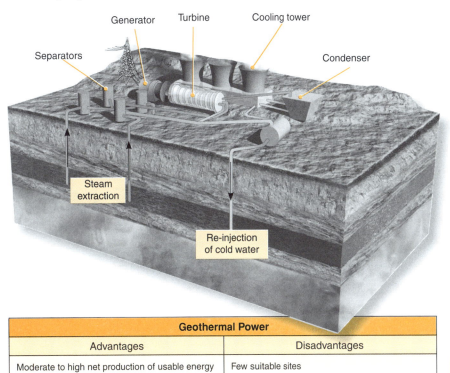

Generator • Turbine • Cooling tower • Separators • Condenser • Steam extraction • Re-injection of cold water

Geothermal Power	
Advantages	Disadvantages
Moderate to high net production of usable energy	Few suitable sites
Moderate CO_2 emissions	Easily depleted if not carefully managed
Low cost (in suitable areas)	Noise and odour pollution
Low environmental impact if managed correctly	Land subsidence possible

1. Explain why geothermal electricity is currently only viable in a few places on Earth: _____

_____

_____

2. Explain why geothermal reservoirs used for electricity production must be carefully managed: _____

_____

_____

3. Explain why geothermal power plants can be used as baseload supplies: _____

_____

_____

Periodicals:
Going underground

Related activities: Renewable Energy

A 2

Energy

Ocean Power

An enormous amount of energy is stored in the world's oceans. Twice daily, tides move huge amounts of water up and down the coasts of the continents, while billions of joules of energy are converted when waves meet the shoreline. Many of the world's energy problems could potentially be solved by harnessing this energy. However, there are many problems involved in building tidal or wave harnessing machines. They often require certain shoreline contours and features of the seabed, together with regularly spaced and sized swells. They must also be able to withstand the relentless and often unpredictable movement of the sea and constant immersion in seawater. Many designs have been proposed to exploit various types of seawater movement, however it is not expected that ocean power will contribute much to world energy needs in the near future.

Machines to Harness Tidal or Wave Energy

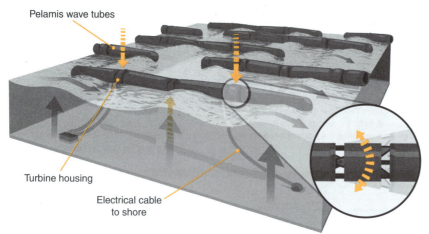

Pelamis wave tubes

Turbine housing

Electrical cable to shore

Tidal barrages have the potential to produce vast amounts of electricity. However, they are extremely expensive to build (in the order of $billions), require several meters of tidal difference, and potentially destroy the estuaries across which they are built.

1 Sluice gates opened as the tide comes in.

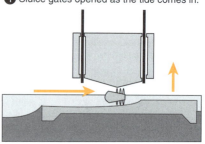

The regular motion of waves can be used to drive a number of turbine types. **Wave tubes** (above) use the up-down motion of waves to drive turbines situated inside articulated power modules. Other designs use the vacuum produced by wave movement to drive wind turbines placed parallel to the water's surface. Suitable sites for these devices are limited and often they only operate within specific wave heights and frequencies, making them inefficient in many situations. Designs must also be able to withstand freak waves, storms, and the corrosive nature of seawater.

2 The gates are closed at the tide's highest point.

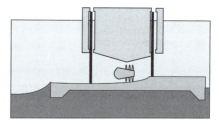

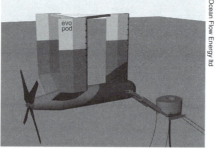

Ocean Flow Energy ltd

Ocean thermal energy conversion (OTEC) power plants use the temperature difference between shallow and deep waters to drive turbines. Warm shallow water is used to vaporize a volatile liquid, which passes via a turbine to a condenser cooled by cool deep water. These plants are only around 3-7% efficient, because the temperature difference is small and energy is required to drive water pumps.

Estuaries, channels, and deep rivers often provide the right conditions for many types of ocean power schemes. The currents produced by the moving water can be used to drive underwater turbines in much the same way as wind drives wind turbines. However debris caught in the current causes continual damage to these types of devices and most, such as the evopod (above), are still experimental.

3 The gates are opened at low tide and the water flowing through drives the turbines like a normal hydroelectric dam.

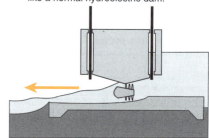

1. Describe the technical problems associated with producing energy from the sea: _____

_____

_____

_____

2. Describe the potential benefits of harnessing ocean power: _____

_____

_____

3. Explain why ocean power is unlikely to ever produce much of the world's energy: _____

_____

_____

A 2

Related activities: Renewable Energy
Weblinks: Wave Power

Periodicals:
Turning the tide

© Biozone International 2007-2011
Photocopying Prohibited

Biofuels

Fuels made from biological processes have been used for many years. In many regions dried animal dung is used to fuel fires. More recently there has been a move to produce more commercial quantities of renewable biofuels for use in transport and industry. **Biofuels** include ethanol, **gasohol** (a blend of petrol and ethanol), methanol, and diesel made from a blend of plant oils and traditional diesel oil. **Biogas** (methane) is an important renewable gas fuel made by fermenting wastes in a digester.

Gasohol

Gasohol is a blend of finished motor gasoline containing alcohol (generally ethanol but sometimes methanol). In Brazil, gasohol consists of 24% ethanol mixed with petrol.

Advantages

- Cleaner fuel than petrol
- Renewable resource
- Creates many jobs in rural areas

Disadvantages

- Ethanol burns hotter than petrol so petrol engines tend to overheat and they need to be modified
- Fuel tank and pipes need coating to prevent corrosion by ethanol
- Fuel consumption 20% greater compared with petrol

Sources of biomass for ethanol production

- Sugar cane (ethanol is produced in this way in Brazil).
- Corn starch (in the USA).
- Grass, certain waste materials (paper, cardboard), and from wood. Fast-growing hardwood trees can be treated to release cellulose. Once released, it may be converted to simple glucose by hydrolytic enzymes and then fermented to produce ethanol.

Biogas

Methane gas is produced by anaerobic fermentation of organic wastes such as sewage sludge at sewage waste treatment stations, animal dung, agricultural wastes, or by the rotting contents of landfill sites.

Stages in methane production

Saprophytic bacteria (facultative anaerobes) break down fats, proteins, and polysaccharides.

Acid-forming bacteria break down these monomers to short-chain organic acids.

Methanogen bacteria (strict anaerobes) produce methane gas.

Biogas

Biogas
Methane: 50-80%
CO_2: 15-45%
Water: 5%

Digester

Small scale fermenter

Sources: *Biological Sciences Review*, Sep 2000, pp.27-29; *Biologist*, Feb 1998, pp. 17-21; Microorganism & Biotechnology, 1997, Chenn, P. (John Murray Publishers).

Comparisons of Renewable and Non-Renewable Energy

	Capital cost per kW	Electricity cost per kW	Advantage	Disadvantage
Biomass	Low	Medium	Readily available resources	Often inefficient
Geothermal	High	Low	No-low emissions	Few accessible sites
Hydroelectric	Medium	Low	Medium to high net energy gain	River flow restrictions and damming
Solar	High	High	No emissions Can be made portable	Large amount of sunlight needed
Wave/Tidal	High	High	No emissions	Few dependable sires
Wind	Medium	Medium	No emissions	Not fully dependable
Coal	Low	Low	High net energy gain	High greenhouse emissions
Natural gas	Low	High	High net energy gain	High greenhouse emissions
Nuclear	High	Low	No emissions	Radioactive waste

1. Explain the nature of the following renewable fuels:

(a) Biogas: _____

_____

(b) Gasohol: _____

_____

2. Describe two disadvantages of using pure ethanol as a motor fuel: _____

_____

_____

3. Use the table above to explain why non-renewable energy sources has until recently been favored over renewable energy sources:

_____

_____

_____

Related activities: Renewable Energy

A 2

Current and Future Energy

The Earth's current total energy consumption is around 4.72×10^{17} (472 quadrillion) BTUs per year (about 500 trillion joules). The demand for energy is expected to increase by at least 50% by 2050, partly because of the increase in technology and its requirements for energy and partly because of the expected increase in the human population to around 9-10 billion. The majority of this increase in demand is expected to occur in developing countries. Fossil fuels will not be able to keep up with energy demands beyond 2030, so there is a growing emphasis on the development of new energy sources.

World Energy Demands

Quadrillion BTUs (British Thermal Units)

EIA figures 2010

1980 1985 1990 1995 2000 2005 2010 2015 2020 2025 2030

Predicted future energy needs

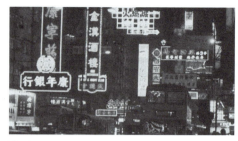

The increase in demand for energy is driven by an increase in demand for technology and an increase in population. However, large future increases in energy demand may be offset by advances in energy efficiency.

Future Energy Solutions

Energy use in the near future will come from a mix of renewable and non-renewable sources. Renewable energy use will become more common as technology improves and costs decrease. There may be a move away from large scale energy providers, with households using solar (above) and possibly wind energy to provide electricity to power lights and heat water.

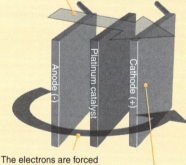

H_2 molecules have electrons removed at the anode by reacting with a platinum catalyst

Anode (-)

Platinum catalyst

Cathode (+)

The electrons are forced to move around a circuit, creating electricity.

H^+ ions pass through the catalyst and react with O_2 to form H_2O

Hydrogen fuel cells are expected to appear on the market soon to power vehicles, although the lack of hydrogen fuelling stations is a major obstacle to use. Hydrogen sources are also a problem, with oil required to supply hydrogen from hydrocarbons, or energy needed to split water to hydrogen and oxygen.

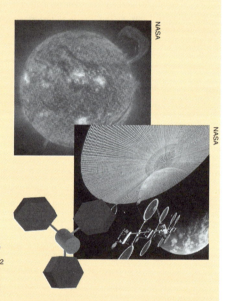

NASA

Distant future energy solutions may include **nuclear fusion** (joining H atoms to form He) power stations, giant solar energy collectors in space, and even nanomotors, which extract energy from the slightest movements.

1. Describe the trend in global energy demand: _____

_____

2. Explain where this demand in energy comes from: _____

_____

_____

3. For any one of the future energy solutions, list some possible problems that will need to be overcome before it becomes a common form of energy generation:

_____

_____

_____

_____

Related activities: Energy Conservation
Weblinks: Fuel Cells

Periodicals:
High hopes for hydrogen

Energy Conservation

An **energy conservation** drive is required to make better use of the energy resources we have. Developed nations waste large amounts of energy. In the United States, 84% of commercial energy is wasted, 41% as unavoidable waste and 43% through the use of energy inefficient systems and poorly designed and insulated buildings. Traditionally, the solution for our global energy requirements has been to produce more energy, but a more **energy efficient** solution is now in demand. Energy efficiency involves improving products or systems so that they do more work and waste less energy, thus conserving energy overall. General improvements in efficiency can be achieved by reducing energy use, improving the energy efficiency of processes, appliances, and vehicles, and increased use of public transport. Energy experts also advise that producing and using the most economical energy sources first, before moving on to more expensive forms, conserves both energy and resources.

Energy Efficiency at Home

Most of the energy used in domestic or commercial buildings is for heating, air conditioning, and lighting. Most buildings are highly energy inefficient, leaking energy as heat. New technologies and products enable the construction of energy efficient buildings (below), or **superinsulated** homes, saving the home owner money and reducing carbon dioxide emissions. Superinsulated homes are often constructed from strawbales or sheltered (in part) by earth. Superinsulated buildings are designed to leak no heat, and gain heat from intrinsic heat sources (such as waste heat from appliances or the body heat of the occupants).

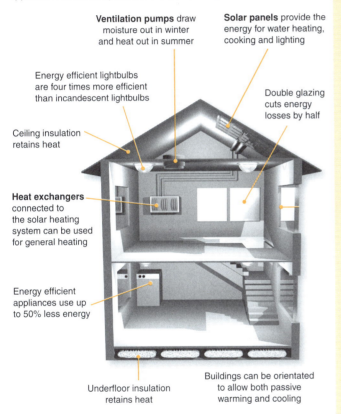

Ventilation pumps draw moisture out in winter and heat out in summer

Solar panels provide the energy for water heating, cooking and lighting

Energy efficient lightbulbs are four times more efficient than incandescent lightbulbs

Double glazing cuts energy losses by half

Ceiling insulation retains heat

Heat exchangers connected to the solar heating system can be used for general heating

Energy efficient appliances use up to 50% less energy

Underfloor insulation retains heat

Buildings can be orientated to allow both passive warming and cooling

Energy Efficiency in Transportation

20% of the world's global energy is used for transportation, 90% of which is wasted because it can not be utilized by internal combustion engines. The **Corporate Average Fuel Economy (CAFE)** regulation is designed to improve the fuel economy of cars and light trucks sold in the US. In 2002, fuel economy was 14% better than it would have been without the standards in place. The use of lighter, stronger materials in car manufacturing, coupled with improved aerodynamics and the inclusion of heavier vehicles into the CAFE regulation, will also aid fuel efficiency.

Hybrid vehicles (right) use two or more different power sources for propulsion, with the combination of combustion engine and electric batteries being the most common. Energy savings are gained by capturing the energy released during braking, storing energy in the batteries, using the electric engine during idling, and using both the petrol and electric motors for peak power needs (which reduces fuel consumption).

Yellow Cab

Rail — 1 575 BTU (27 passengers per vehicle)

Private car — 2 130 BTU (1.59 ppv)

Bus — 2 696 BTU (9.2 ppv)

Transportation energy data book ed. 29 2010

British thermal units (BTU) used per passenger kilometer

The total transport efficiency of a vehicle depends on its fuel efficiency and the number of people it is transporting. Buses usually carry less than half their maximum capacity while private cars use less fuel per kilometer. Rail is the most efficient public transport.

Energy

---

1. Discuss methods of increasing energy efficiency in the home and in transport: _____

   _____

   _____

   _____

2. (a) Calculate the number of passengers a bus would need to regularly carry to at least equal the efficiency of a car:

   _____

   (b) Aeroplanes use around 180 500 BTU per kilometer but carry around 98 people per trip. Calculate the BTU per passenger kilometer for an aeroplane:

   _____

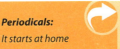

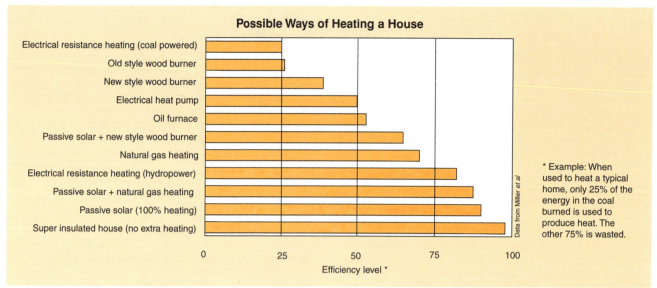

Possible Ways of Heating a House

Electrical resistance heating (coal powered)
Old style wood burner
New style wood burner
Electrical heat pump
Oil furnace
Passive solar + new style wood burner
Natural gas heating
Electrical resistance heating (hydropower)
Passive solar + natural gas heating
Passive solar (100% heating)
Super insulated house (no extra heating)

Efficiency level *

Data from Miller et al

* Example: When used to heat a typical home, only 25% of the energy in the coal burned is used to produce heat. The other 75% is wasted.

A move towards more energy efficient systems for industrial and domestic use has been driven by the demand for and costs of energy increasing, and by a decreasing availability of natural energy stores. Improvements in energy use help to slow the use of resources but can also help the individual save on electrical and heating bills, although the start up costs for efficient technology such as LED lights can be considerable.

Incandescent bulb

Out with the old...

THE FIGURES: EFFICIENCY

Incandescent light bulbs turn as little as 5% of the electrical energy they receive into light. Newer compact fluorescent light bulbs (CFLs) turn around 22% of the energy they receive into light while light emitting diode (LED) lamps turn more than 50% of the energy they receive into light. Incandescent light bulbs, while cheap, only last around 1200 hours while CFLs and LEDs last around 10 000 and 50 000 hours respectively. Over the lifetime of one LED lamp, thousands of dollars could be saved on the cost of new light bulbs and electrical bills, as well as lowering the energy output requirements of the local power stations.

CFL bulb

... in with the new

THE DISADVANTAGES

Disadvantages of CFL lights include the use of mercury inside the bulb. LEDs suffer from the production of bright white light instead of the soft yellow of incandescent bulbs. This can be solved by mixing the colors of LEDs used.

LED bulb

Wiki commons

3. Explain why simply building new power stations is no longer seen as an acceptable solution to increased energy demands:

_____

_____

_____

_____

_____

4. (a) An LED light bulb typically costs around $15 while a CFL costs $4 and an incandescent bulb $1. Over 50 000 hours of light bulb use, calculate the cost of light bulbs alone when using an LED bulb, a CFL or an incandescent bulb:

_____

_____

(b) An LED, CFL, and incandescent bulb use 0.006kW, 0.014kW and 0.06kW of energy per hour respectively while electricity may cost $0.2 per kWh. Over 50 000 hours, calculate the cost of running an LED bulb, a CFL, and an incandescent bulb:

_____

_____

(c) If a household changes 20 light fittings from incandescent to LED lights, calculate the savings it will make over 50 000 hours of light bulb use compared to if it had changed to CFLs or remained incandescent light bulbs:

_____

_____

5. In groups, discuss the reasons why people may not wish to change all the light bulbs in their house at once (or at all):

KEY TERMS: Mix and Match

INSTRUCTIONS: Test your vocabulary by matching each term to its definition, as identified by its preceding letter code.

BIOFUEL

CAFE REGULATIONS

COAL

ENERGY CONSERVATION

FOSSIL FUEL

GEOTHERMAL POWER

HYDROELECTRIC POWER

HYDROGEN FUEL CELL

INDUSTRIAL REVOLUTION

NATURAL GAS

NON-RENEWABLE ENERGY

NUCLEAR FISSION

NUCLEAR FUSION

NUCLEAR POWER

OIL

PHOTOVOLTAIC CELL

RENEWABLE ENERGY

SOLAR ENERGY

THERMODYNAMICS

WATT

WAVE ENERGY

WIND ENERGY

WIND TURBINE

A   Fossil fuel consisting of methane, ethane, propane and butane that is used as a high energy fuel.

B   A type of battery that utilizes the energy produced from the redox reaction between hydrogen and oxygen.

C   The use of sunlight to produce usable energy, often in the form of heat.

D   The production of electricity using materials that can be replaced or regenerated within a short time span.

E   The time during the 19th and 20th centuries in which scientific breakthroughs led to the mechanization of industry, resulting in a rise in technology and living standards.

F   Black sedimentary rock, consisting primarily of carbon. Formed from the buried and compressed remains of ancient swamps and is now used as a high energy fuel.

G   Fuel produced millions of years ago by the burying and compression of organic matter.

H   Energy produced by using the motion of waves to drive turbines.

I   Energy produced from using radioactive material to heat water to steam to drive a turbine connected to a generator.

J   A branch of physics that deals with the principles and relationships concerning the conversion and conservation of energy.

K   Fuel that is formed from renewable organic compounds, often in the form of waste material such as animal dung or wood pulp.

L   The splitting of a heavy atom causing the generation of large amounts of energy and lighter atoms.

M   Device that uses the force of the wind to turn rotors connected to a generator to produce electrical energy.

N   Energy produced by using the force of wind to drive turbines.

O   Electrical cell that is able to convert sunlight directly into electrical energy.

P   Liquid made from hydrocarbons that was formed from the buried remains of marine or lake living planktonic organisms.

Q   The Corporate Average Fuel Economy. A regulation designed to improve the fuel economy of cars sold in the USA.

R   Energy produced by using water passing through a dam to turn turbines connected to generators.

S   The use of energy in such a way that it expends the minimum amount necessary to achieve a purpose.

T   Energy derived from heat produced by volcanic activity.

U   The joining of hydrogen atoms to form helium, generating large amounts of energy.

V   Energy produced by using fuels that cannot be replaced unless over geologic time scales.

W   The unit of power. Equal to one joule of energy per second.

Energy

Pollution

Types of Pollution

Air pollution
- Sources of air pollution
- Formation and effects of smog
- Major air pollutants
- Effects on the environment

Water pollution
- Sources of water pollution
- Effects on the environment
- Oil spills

Impacts and Treatment

Treating pollution
- Sewage treatment and disposal
- Waste management systems
- Monitoring water quality

Impacts of pollution
- Clean up costs and economic impact
- Environmental effects
- Health effects
- Environmental and Industrial disasters

Pollution has wide ranging and detrimental effects on aquatic and terrestrial environments.

Treating the environmental and health effects of pollution is costly and often difficult.

Pollution and Global Change

Human activities have a global effect. Pollution and habitat destruction continue to damage vast areas of the Earth.

Strategies aimed at slowing these global changes are being implemented in places, but it could be many years before the benefits are seen.

Human induced greenhouse gas emissions are leading to global climate change.

The harmful effects of human activity can be prevented or reduced through conservation.

Ozone
- Formation of stratospheric ozone
- Depletion by CFCs
- Environmental effects of ozone depletion
- Strategies for reducing ozone loss

Global warming
- Causes of climate change
- Impacts of climate change
- Reducing the rate of climate change

Loss of biodiversity
- Habitat loss
- Exploitation
- Pollution
- Endangered species

Maintaining biodiversity
- Conservation efforts
- Nature reserves
- Laws and treaties

Climate Change

Conserving Biodiversity

Global Change

Pollution

Key concepts

► Pollutants come from a variety of sources and activities.

► There are environmental, health, and economic costs of pollution.

► Many pollutants have a long term effect on health and the environment.

► Reducing both usage of materials and waste greatly reduces pollution.

Key terms

acid rain

atmospheric pollution

biological oxygen demand

non-point source pollution

direct costs

environmental remediation

eutrophication

indicator organism

indirect costs

integrated waste management

noise pollution

organic effluent

oil spill

photochemical smog

point source pollution

pollution

recycling

sewerage

sewage

sewage treatment

toxicant

waste management

Objectives

☐ 1. Use the **KEY TERMS** to help you understand and complete these objectives.

Types of Pollution   pages 178-186

☐ 2. Explain what is meant by water pollution, distinguishing between **point source pollution** and **non-point source pollution**.

☐ 3. Describe the effect of **organic effluent** (e.g. sewage or milk) and fertilizer run-off (nitrates and phosphates) on aquatic ecosystems.

☐ 4. Explain the causes of **atmospheric pollution**, distinguishing between natural and anthropogenic sources.

☐ 5. Identify the causes of **noise pollution** and describe its effects on human health and the environment.

☐ 6. Discuss measures for treating, preventing, and reducing pollutants, including **sewage treatment**, **waste management,** and **environmental remediation**, for example, following **oil spills**.

Impact of Pollution   pages 187- 202

☐ 7. Describe the impacts of human activities on the environment. Recognize that these impacts are largely the result of resource use, rapid population growth, and **urbanization**.

☐ 8. Describe the origin, cause, and global distribution of **acid rain**.

☐ 9. Discuss the economic impacts of **pollution**, including consideration of **direct** and **indirect costs**.

☐ 10. Describe some of the health effects of water, land, and atmospheric pollution.

☐ 11. Recognize that effective waste management and pollution control systems are costly but that this cost is offset by the benefits gained by reducing pollution and waste.

☐ 12. Describe some of the causes of major oil spills and discuss their immediate and longer term environmental and economic effects. Describe clean up methods and explain the reasons for the use of specific methods in particular situations.

Periodicals:
Listings for this chapter are on page 231

Weblinks:
www.thebiozone.com/
weblink/EnvSci-2764.html

Presentation Media
*Environmental Science:
Pollution and Global Change*

Types of Pollution

Any addition to the air, water, soil, or food that threatens the survival, health, or activities of organisms is called **pollution**. **Pollutants** can enter the environment naturally (e.g. from volcanic eruptions) or through human activities. Most pollution from human activity occurs in or around urban and industrial areas and regions of industrialized agriculture. Pollutants may come from single identifiable **point sources**, such as power plants, or they may enter the environment from diffuse or **non-point sources**, such as through land runoff. While pollutants often contaminate the areas where they are produced, they can also be carried by wind or water to other areas. Commonly recognized forms of pollution include air and water pollution, but other less obvious forms of pollution, including light and noise pollution, are also the result of concentrations of human activity. Some global phenomena, such as **global warming** and **ozone depletion** are the result of pollution of the Earth's stratosphere.

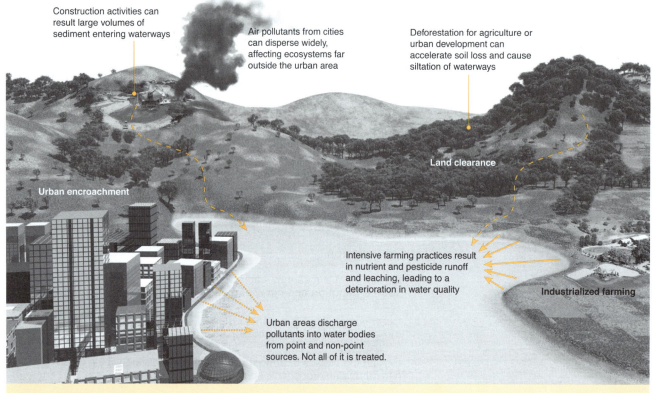

Construction activities can result large volumes of sediment entering waterways

Air pollutants from cities can disperse widely, affecting ecosystems far outside the urban area

Deforestation for agriculture or urban development can accelerate soil loss and cause siltation of waterways

Land clearance

Urban encroachment

Intensive farming practices result in nutrient and pesticide runoff and leaching, leading to a deterioration in water quality

Industrialized farming

Urban areas discharge pollutants into water bodies from point and non-point sources. Not all of it is treated.

Fertilizers, herbicides, and pesticides are major contaminants of soil and water in areas where agriculture is industrialized. Fertilizer runoff and leaching adds excess nitrogen and phosphorus to ground and surface water and leads to **cultural euthrophication**.

Soil contamination occurs via chemical spills, leaching, or leakage from underground storage. The runoff from mining and metal processing operations can carry radioactive waste and heavy metals such as mercury, cadmium, and arsenic.

Together with vehicle exhausts, power plants and industrial emissions are a major source of air pollution. SO_2 and NO_2 from these primary sources mix with water vapor in the atmosphere to form acids which may be deposited as rain, snow, or dry acid.

1. Identify the main sources of each of the following pollutants:

   (a) Pesticides and herbicides in waterways: _____

   (b) Sewage: _____

   (c) Oxides of sulfur and nitrogen: _____

   (d) Sedimentation and siltation of waterways: _____

2. Explain the impact of urbanization on the pollution load in a given region: _____

   _____

   _____

Related activities: Water Pollution, Atmospheric Pollution, Soil Degradation
Weblinks: Impact of Ozone Depletion and Pollution

Water Pollution

Water pollution can occur as a result of contamination from many sources, from urban and industrial to agricultural. Pollutants may first enter the groundwater where they are difficult to detect and manage. Some enter surface waterways directly through runoff from the land, but most are deliberately discharged at single (point) sources. Some pollutants alter the physical state of a water body (its temperature, pH, or turbidity). Others involve the addition of potentially harmful substances. Even substances that are beneficial at a low concentration may cause problems when their concentration increases. One such form of pollution involves excessive nutrient loading of waterways by organic effluent. This causes accelerated enrichment (**cultural eutrophication**) of water bodies and results in excessive weed and algal growth. It also increases the uptake of dissolved oxygen by the microorganisms that decompose the organic matter in the effluent. This reduces the amount of dissolved oxygen available to other aquatic organisms and may cause the death of many. An indicator of the polluting capacity of an effluent is known as the **biological oxygen demand** or **BOD**. This is measured as the weight (mg) of oxygen used by one liter of sample effluent stored in darkness at 20°C for five days. Developing global and national initiatives to control water pollution is important because many forms of water pollution cross legislative boundaries. The US is the world's largest user of water but loses about 50% of the water it withdraws. Water conservation is required to enable more effective use of water, reduce the burden on wastewater systems, decrease pollution of surface and groundwater, and slow the depletion of aquifers.

Sources of Water Pollution

Sediment pollution: Soil erosion causes soil particles to be carried into waterways. Apart from erosion destroying the topsoil, the increased sediment load may cause choking of waterways, buildup behind dams, and the destruction of aquatic habitats.

Sewage: Water containing human wastes, soaps and detergents from toilets, washing machines, and showers are discharged into waterways such as rivers, lakes and the sea. Without treatment this may lead to outbreaks of disease such as cholera.

Disease-causing agents: Disease-causing microbes from infected animals and humans can be discharged into waterways. This is particularly a problem during floods when human waste may mix with drinking water, causing the spread of disease.

Inorganic plant nutrients: Fertilizer runoff from farmland adds nitrogen and phosphorus to waterways. This nutrient enrichment accelerates the natural process of **eutrophication**, causing algal blooms and prolific aquatic weed growth, which can lead to the suffocation of aquatic animals.

Organic compounds: Synthetic, often toxic, compounds, may be released into waterways from oil spills, the waste products of manufacturing processes (e.g. dioxin, PCBs, phenols, and DDT) and the application of agrichemicals. These can build up in the food chain and poison human consumers.

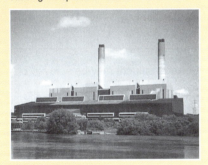

Thermal pollution: Many industrial processes, including thermal power generation (above), release heated water into river systems. The increase in water temperature reduces oxygen levels and may harm the survival of river species as all as creating thermal barriers to fish movement.

Radioactive substances: Mining and refinement of radioactive metals may discharge radioactive materials. Accidental spillages from nuclear power stations, such as the Chernobyl accident of 1986, may contaminate land and water causing genetic defects, especially in developing fetuses.

Kurchatov Inst.

Inorganic chemicals: Acid drainage from mines and acid rain can severely alter the pH of waterways. Runoff from open-caste mining operations can be loaded with poisonous heavy metals such as mercury, cadmium, and arsenic which can cause severe nerve damage and other health problems.

Detecting Pollution

Water pollution can be monitored in several ways. The nutrient loading can be assessed by measuring the **BOD**. **Electronic probes** and **chemical tests** can identify the absolute levels of various inorganic pollutants (e.g. nitrates, phosphates, and heavy metals). The presence of **indicator species** can give an indication of the pollution status for a waterway. This method relies on an understanding of the *tolerance levels* to pollution of different species that should be living in the waterway (e.g. worms, insect larvae, snails, and crustaceans).

Pollution

Related activities: *Monitoring Change in an Ecosystem, Sewage Treatment*
Weblinks: *Caring For Our Water*

RA 2

1. Explain the term **cultural eutrophication** and its primary cause: _____

   _____

2. Describe three uses of water for each of the following areas of human activity:

   (a) Domestic use: _____

   _____

   (b) Industrial use: _____

   _____

   (c) Agricultural use: _____

   _____

3. (a) Explain what is meant by the term **biological oxygen demand** (BOD) as it is related to water pollution:

   _____

   _____

   _____

   (b) Describe how human use of a water body could create a very high BOD: _____

   _____

   (c) Describe the likely effect of a high BOD on the invertebrates and fish living in a small lake: _____

   _____

   _____

   (d) Explain why, when measuring BOD, that the sample is kept in darkness: _____

   _____

4. Sewage effluent may be sprayed onto agricultural land to irrigate crops and plantations of trees:

   (a) Describe an advantage of utilizing sewage in this way: _____

   _____

   (b) Describe a major drawback of using sewage effluent in this way: _____

   _____

   (c) Suggest an alternative treatment or use of the effluent: _____

5. When studying aquatic ecosystems, the species composition of the community (its biodiversity) in different regions of a water body or over time is often recorded. In general terms, suggest how a change in species composition of an aquatic community could be used to indicate water pollution:

   _____

   _____

   _____

   _____

   _____

   _____

   _____

   _____

Sewage Treatment

Once water has been used by household or industry, it becomes sewage. **Sewage** includes toilet wastes and all household water, but excludes storm water, which is usually diverted directly into waterways. In some cities, the **sewerage** and stormwater systems may be partly combined, and sewage can overflow into surface water during high rainfall. When sewage reaches a treatment plant, it can undergo up to three levels of processing (purification). Primary treatment is little more than a mechanical screening process, followed by settling of the solids into a sludge. Secondary sewage treatment is primarily a biological process in which aerobic and anaerobic microorganisms are used to remove the organic wastes. Advanced secondary treatment targets specific pollutants, particularly nitrates, phosphates, and heavy metals. Before water is discharged after treatment, it is always disinfected (usually by chlorination) to kill bacteria and other potential pathogens.

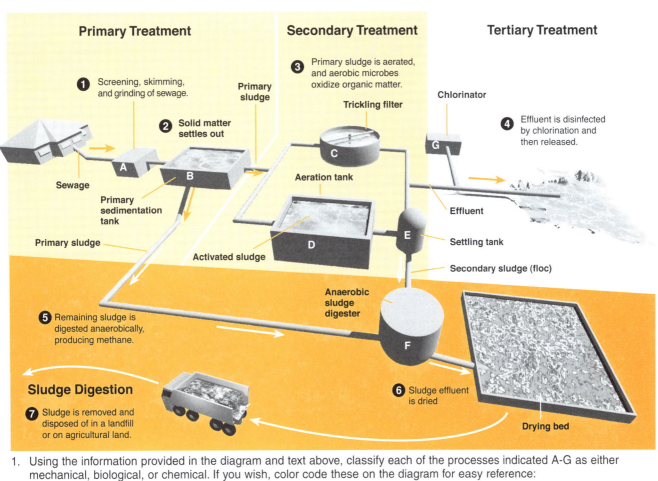

Primary Treatment

❶ Screening, skimming, and grinding of sewage.

❷ Solid matter settles out

Sewage

Primary sedimentation tank

Primary sludge

A

B

Primary sludge

Secondary Treatment

❸ Primary sludge is aerated, and aerobic microbes oxidize organic matter.

Trickling filter

C

Aeration tank

Activated sludge

D

Anaerobic sludge digester

E

F

Tertiary Treatment

Chlorinator

❹ Effluent is disinfected by chlorination and then released.

G

Effluent

Settling tank

Secondary sludge (floc)

❻ Sludge effluent is dried

Drying bed

Sludge Digestion

❺ Remaining sludge is digested anaerobically, producing methane.

❼ Sludge is removed and disposed of in a landfill or on agricultural land.

1. Using the information provided in the diagram and text above, classify each of the processes indicated A-G as either mechanical, biological, or chemical. If you wish, color code these on the diagram for easy reference:

A: _____   D: _____   G: _____

B: _____   E: _____

C: _____   F: _____

2. Using the diagram above for reference, investigate the sewage treatment process in your own town or city, identifying the specific techniques and problems of waste water management in your area. Make a note of the main points to cover in the space provided below, and develop your discussion as a separate report. Identify:

(a) Your urban area and treatment station: _____

(b) The volume of sewage processed: _____

(c) The degree of purification: _____

(d) The treatment processes used (list): _____

(e) The discharge point(s): _____

(f) Problems of waste water management: _____

_____

(g) Future options or plans: _____

_____

Periodicals:
The activated sludge process

Related activities: Types of Pollution, Water Pollution

RA 2

Pollution

Waste Management

The disposal of solid and hazardous waste is one of the most urgent problems of today's industrialized societies. Traditionally, solid waste has been disposed of in open dumps and, more recently, in sanitary, scientifically designed landfills. Even with modern designs and better waste processing, landfills still have the potential to contaminate soil and groundwater. In addition, they occupy valuable land, and their siting is often a matter of local controversy. More and more today, city councils and local authorities support the initiatives for the reduction, reuse, and recycling of solid wastes. At the same time, they must develop strategies for the safe disposal of hazardous wastes, which pose an immediate or potential threat to environmental and human health. A programme of integrated waste management (below) combines features of traditional waste management with new techniques to reduce and incinerate wastes. Such schemes will form the basis of effective waste management in the future.

Components of Integrated Waste Management

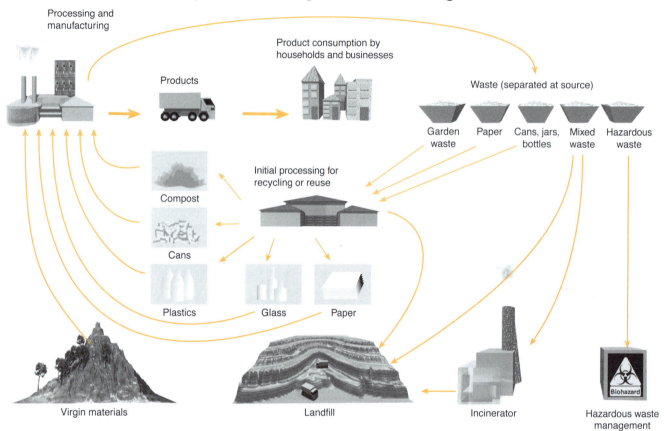

1. The diagram provides an overview of an **idealized management system** for waste materials from households and industries. It provides a starting point for comparing how different waste products could be disposed of or processed. Using the information provided for guidance, investigate the disposal, recycling, and post-waste processing options for each of the waste products listed below. List the important points in the spaces provided, including reference to disposal methods and particular problems associated with these, processing or recycling (if relevant), and useful end-products (if relevant). If required, develop this list, or part of it, as a separate report:

   (a) Glass, plastic and paper waste: _____

   _____

   _____

   (b) Metals and their alloys, e.g. aluminum, tin and steel: _____

   _____

   _____

   (c) Organic waste: _____

   _____

   (d) Hazardous waste (including medical): _____

   _____

2. Identify a waste product that is not part of an integrated waste management program: _____

Periodicals:
Making landfill history

Reducing Waste

Industrialized and developing countries produce vast quantities of waste each year as part of their industrial nature. Three main types of waste can clearly be identified: solid, liquid, and gaseous. Each of these can be further divided into other types such as domestic, industrial, medical, or hazardous. Much of the waste produced by industrialized countries contains valuable resources, which could be used again if properly processed. As resources become scarcer and competition for them grows, both individuals and companies are beginning to explore ways of reusing waste material. The reduction of solid waste presents a great challenge because its components can often be difficult to separate or break down.

Composting is a simple way in which biodegradable waste, such as food scraps and garden waste, can be broken down and its nutrients returned to the earth. Composting is possible in almost every household, even those without a yard. A common trend today is to have small worm farms or cultured composts for kitchen scraps in small containers on or under kitchen benches. Outdoors, compost can be made in purpose built containers or simply in a pile in the corner of the yard.

Reusing an object or material in an unchanged form is the simplest way of reducing waste. A growing number of retail outlets and are offering their customers the choice of buying reusable shopping bags, while others now charge extra if customers use plastic bags. In the UK, these methods reduced the use of supermarket plastic bags from 10 billion in 2006 to 6 billion in 2010. In New Zealand, Foodstuffs supermarket chains reduced plastic bag use by 23% in two years, saving nearly 700 tonnes of plastic each year.

Not everything can be reused as it is. **Recycling** broken or otherwise useless material stops waste building up in the home and at the same time can reduce the energy and resource requirements of industry. Materials such as glass and metals can be recycled relatively easily by being melted and reshaped, saving the energy required to mine and process the ores. Plastics may be chemically treated to break them into their monomer components or they can be heated and reformed.

Recycling is the last of the three Rs of waste reduction. The priority of **reduce**, **reuse**, and **recycle** is based on reducing the volume of raw materials used, reusing products already manufactured (such as shopping bags and bottles), and recycling what can not be reused. What cannot be recycled is then dealt with as true waste. However, in theory virtually everything can be recycled in some way.

Energy Cost of Reusable vs Disposable Cups

Cup type	Cup mass (gcup^{-1})	Material specific energy (MJkg^{-1})	Energy per cup (MJcup^{-1})
Ceramic	292	48	14
Plastic	59	107	6.3
Glass	199	28	5.5
Paper	8.3	66	0.55
Foam	1.9	104	0.20

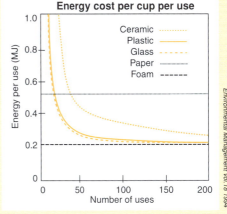

Energy cost per cup per use

The manufacture of reusable items, such as ceramic cups, uses a large amount of energy. Energy is also used in heating water and manufacturing detergent to wash them. Disposable foam or paper cups require little energy to produce and none for cleaning. The graph above illustrates how many uses it takes before recyclable items (glass, plastic, or ceramic) reach the same energy per cup value as single use items (paper and foam). It does not account for the cost of disposal.

1. Explain why composting is a useful and inexpensive way of dealing with organic waste: _____

_____

_____

2. Explain why recycling metals is particularly energy saving: _____

_____

_____

3. Estimate the energy used per use after 100 uses of:

(a) A foam cup: _____

(b) A ceramic cup: _____

(c) A plastic cup: _____

Noise Pollution

Pollution does not necessarily have to be chemical in its nature. With the development of industry, technology, and large human populations comes an increase in noise. Noise pollution is a growing issue in many areas, not just in cities, which are noisy places simply by their nature, but also in areas where noise or very loud persistent sounds are uncommon.

Cities are very noisy places with the constant drone of machinery and traffic audible throughout day and night. This persistent noise can create excessive stresses on people and, in extreme cases, can lead to insomnia or psychosis.

Away from cities, noise can still be a problem. Wind turbines produce high levels of noise from the vibrations of the rotating blades. Most of this noise is at a low frequency, penetrating buildings and causing annoyance to nearby residents.

Noise from the engines and sonar of ships can travel through vast areas of ocean and is known to interfere with the sonar and communication of whales. This can make it difficult for them to navigate and may be factor in strandings.

Getting One Back

Photo: NOAA

When a new marina was opened in Sausalito, California, 1980, many people sleeping in house boats had their nights disturbed by a loud persistent throbbing that seemed to be coming from under the water. Many people blamed secret night-time pumping of untreated sewage into the bay or other industrial machinery. Eventually the source of the noise was found to be the tiny toadfish (or midshipman fish). During the breeding season, the males produce the loud throbbing noise at night to attract mates.

Cause of sound	dB
Blue whale call	160
Space shuttle at launch	
Artillery fire	140
Small arms fire	
Jet aircraft at take-off	120
Rock concert	
Chain saw	100
Lawn mower	
Alarm clock	80
Busy traffic	
Normal conversation	60
Moderate rainfall	
Quiet room	40
Isolated desert night	
Whisper	20
Normal breathing	
	0

Acceptable noise levels for urban environments are set by the local councils. Careful planning of suburban areas can reduce the amount of noise pollution. Measures such as separating industrial and residential areas decreases clashes between industrial and residential expectations of noise levels. Noise pollution can be reduced by better design and insulation of equipment, houses, and buildings.

Sound levels are measured in decibels (dB). The scale is logarithmic so that 30 dB has ten times more energy than 20dB and one hundred times more than 10 dB. Exposure to noise levels above 85 dB can cause permanent hearing loss, while pain is experienced at around 120 dB.

1. Describe some of the effects of noise pollution: _____

_____

_____

2. Describe some ways in which noise pollution can be reduced: _____

_____

_____

3. Identify some sources of noise pollution in your community: _____

_____

4. Calculate how many times more sound energy than a quiet room each of the following has:

(a) Normal conversation: _____ (b) Artillery fire: _____

Atmospheric Pollution

Air pollution consists of gases, liquids, or solids present in the atmosphere at levels high enough to harm living things (or cause damage to materials). Human activities make a major contribution to global air pollution, although natural processes can also be responsible. Lightning causes forest fires, oxidizes nitrogen and creates ozone, while erupting volcanoes give off toxic and corrosive gases. Air pollutants can be divided into primary and secondary pollutants. **Primary pollutants** are emitted directly from the source, while **secondary pollutants** form when primary pollutants

react in the atmosphere (e.g. acid rain). Air pollution tends to be concentrated around areas of high population density, particularly in Western industrial and post-industrial societies. In the last few decades there has been a massive increase in air pollution in parts of the world that previously had little, such as Mexico city and some of the large Asian cities. Air pollution does not just exist outdoors. The air enclosed in spaces such as cars, homes, schools, and offices may have significantly higher levels of harmful air pollutants than the air outdoors.

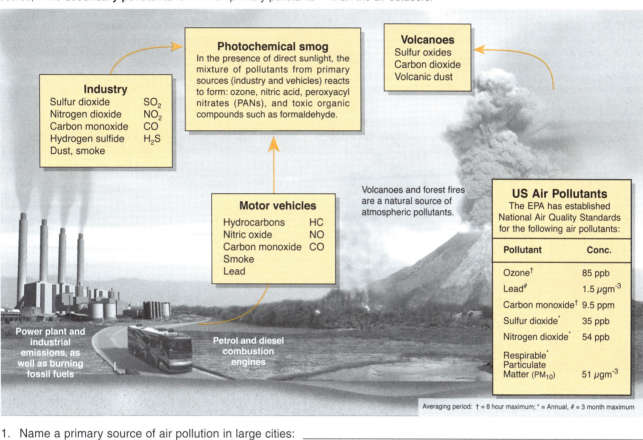

1. Name a primary source of air pollution in large cities: _____

2. A major cause of air pollution is the burning of fossil fuels to supply energy for domestic or industrial purposes. Identify four fossil fuels, their application, and describe a negative environmental effect of their use:

    (a) _____

    (b) _____

    (c) _____

    (d) _____

3. One way of monitoring the level of air pollution is to make regular inspections of what are called 'biological indicators', such as lichen, in the environment.

    (a) Giving an example, explain the role of **biological indicators**: _____

    _____

    _____

    _____

    (b) Explain how **lichen** could be used as a biological indicator: _____

    _____

    _____

    _____

Pollution

Related activities: Monitoring Change in an Ecosystem, Types of Pollution, Global Warming, Stratospheric Ozone Depletion, Acid Rain

RA 2

Health officials are paying increasing attention to the *sick building syndrome*. This air pollution inside office buildings can cause eye irritations, nausea, headaches, respiratory infections, depression and fatigue. Gases, ozone and microbes are implicated.

Aircraft contribute to atmospheric pollution with their jet exhaust at high altitude (at 10 000 m). The cabin environment of aircraft is also often polluted. Some passengers may spread infections (e.g. TB and SARS) through the recirculated cabin air.

Automobiles are the single most important contributor of air pollutants in large cities, producing large amounts of carbon monoxide, hydrocarbons, and nitrous oxides. Some countries require cars to have **catalytic converters** fitted to their exhausts.

4. Complete the table below summarizing the main types of air pollutants:

Pollutant	Major sources	Environmental effects	Human health effects	Prevention or control
Carbon monoxide				Fit cars with catalytic converters and keep well tuned.
Hydrogen sulfide	Burning fuels, oil refineries, wood pulp processing.			
Sulfur oxides				Use alternative, sulfur free fuels such as natural gas and LPG.
Nitrogen oxides		Forms photochemical smog. Retards plants growth.		
Smoke				
Lead			Causes convulsions, coma and damage to the nervous system.	
Ozone				Fit cars with catalytic converters to reduce the amount of NO_x and volatile hydrocarbons emitted.
Hydrocarbons	Incomplete combustion.			

5. **Sick building syndrome** affects large office buildings where the workers are breathing in an air conditioned atmosphere. The pollutant gases are released from the materials and equipment in the office, while disease-causing microbes may live in the heating, air conditioning and ventilation ducts.

(a) Explain what is meant by the term 'sick building syndrome': _____

_____

(b) Suggest a way of reducing this form of indoor pollution: _____

_____

(c) A more extreme example of indoor pollution has been recently diagnosed on long distance flights in modern passenger jets with their pressurized cabin atmospheres. Explain why this situation is potentially more threatening than sick building syndrome, particularly when taking into account that most modern jets recirculate most cabin air:

_____

_____

Acid Rain

Acid rain is not a new phenomenon. It was first noticed last century in regions where the industrial revolution began. Buildings in areas with heavy industrial activity were being worn away by rain. Acid rain, more correctly termed **acid deposition**, can fall to the Earth as rain, snow or sleet, as well as dry, sulfate-containing particles that settle out of the air. It is a problem that crosses international boundaries. Gases from coal-burning power stations in England fall as acid rain in Norway and Sweden, emissions from the United States produce acid deposition in Canada, while

Japan receives acid rain from China. The effect of this fallout is to produce lakes that are so acid that they cannot support fish, and forests with sickly, stunted tree growth. Acid rain also causes the release of heavy metals (e.g. cadmium and mercury) into the food chain by affecting the solubility of the metal salt or oxide (solubility changes with pH. Acids also react with metals to form soluble salts. Changes in species composition of aquatic communities may be used as **biological indicators** measuring the severity of acid deposition.

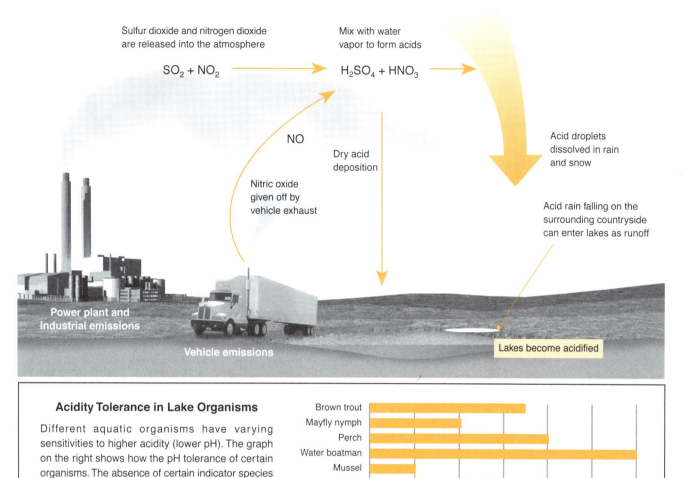

Acidity Tolerance in Lake Organisms

Different aquatic organisms have varying sensitivities to higher acidity (lower pH). The graph on the right shows how the pH tolerance of certain organisms. The absence of certain indicator species from a waterway can provide evidence of pollution in the recent past as well as the present.

1. Describe the effect of acid deposition on communities of living organisms: _____

2. Study the graph illustrating the acidity tolerance of lake organisms (above).

(a) State which species is the most **sensitive** to acid conditions: _____

(b) State which species is the most **tolerant** of acid conditions: _____

(c) Explain how you could use these kinds of measurements as an indicator of the ecological state of a lake:

3. Describe some of the measures that could be taken to reduce acid emissions: _____

4. Explain why these measures are slow to be implemented: _____

Related activities: Monitoring Change in an Ecosystem, Types of Pollution, Atmospheric Pollution, Ocean Acidification

DA 2

Pollution

Toxicants in the Home

People are often surprised by the number of dangerous chemical pollutants in their homes, even when excluding chemicals such as pesticides and cleaning agents. Many of these chemicals are used as preservatives or are created during the use of an appliance. Others are part of the fabric of clothes or carpet. Exposure to low levels over many years has the potential to cause costly and dangerous health problems, although countries are now beginning to more closely regulate these chemicals.

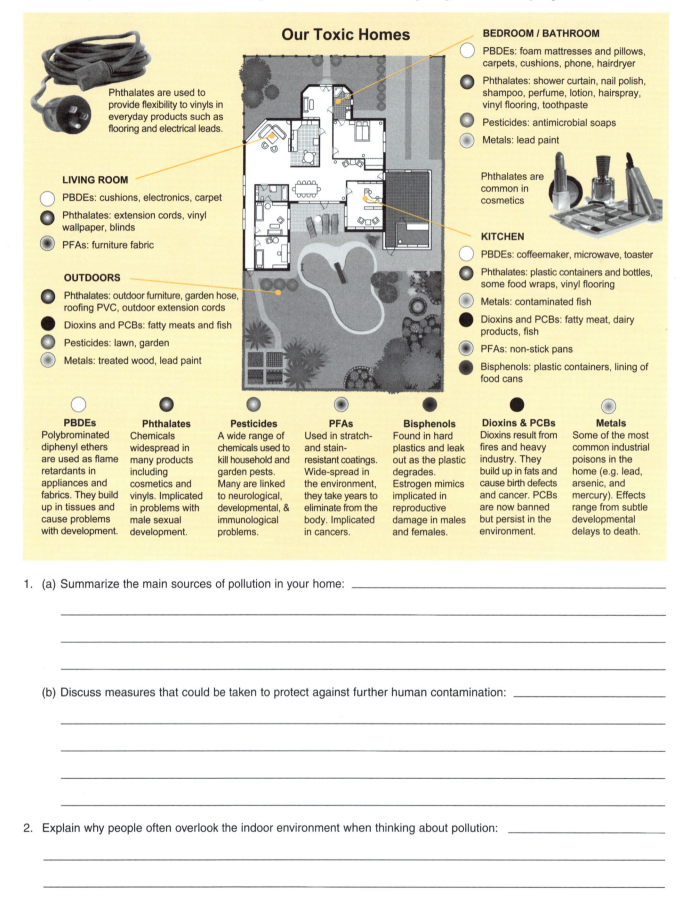

Our Toxic Homes

Phthalates are used to provide flexibility to vinyls in everyday products such as flooring and electrical leads.

LIVING ROOM
- PBDEs: cushions, electronics, carpet
- Phthalates: extension cords, vinyl wallpaper, blinds
- PFAs: furniture fabric

OUTDOORS
- Phthalates: outdoor furniture, garden hose, roofing PVC, outdoor extension cords
- Dioxins and PCBs: fatty meats and fish
- Pesticides: lawn, garden
- Metals: treated wood, lead paint

BEDROOM / BATHROOM
- PBDEs: foam mattresses and pillows, carpets, cushions, phone, hairdryer
- Phthalates: shower curtain, nail polish, shampoo, perfume, lotion, hairspray, vinyl flooring, toothpaste
- Pesticides: antimicrobial soaps
- Metals: lead paint

Phthalates are common in cosmetics

KITCHEN
- PBDEs: coffeemaker, microwave, toaster
- Phthalates: plastic containers and bottles, some food wraps, vinyl flooring
- Metals: contaminated fish
- Dioxins and PCBs: fatty meat, dairy products, fish
- PFAs: non-stick pans
- Bisphenols: plastic containers, lining of food cans

PBDEs	Phthalates	Pesticides	PFAs	Bisphenols	Dioxins & PCBs	Metals
Polybrominated diphenyl ethers are used as flame retardants in appliances and fabrics. They build up in tissues and cause problems with development.	Chemicals widespread in many products including cosmetics and vinyls. Implicated in problems with male sexual development.	A wide range of chemicals used to kill household and garden pests. Many are linked to neurological, developmental, & immunological problems.	Used in stratch- and stain-resistant coatings. Wide-spread in the environment, they take years to eliminate from the body. Implicated in cancers.	Found in hard plastics and leak out as the plastic degrades. Estrogen mimics implicated in reproductive damage in males and females.	Dioxins result from fires and heavy industry. They build up in fats and cause birth defects and cancer. PCBs are now banned but persist in the environment.	Some of the most common industrial poisons in the home (e.g. lead, arsenic, and mercury). Effects range from subtle developmental delays to death.

1. (a) Summarize the main sources of pollution in your home: _____

    _____

    _____

    _____

   (b) Discuss measures that could be taken to protect against further human contamination: _____

    _____

    _____

    _____

    _____

2. Explain why people often overlook the indoor environment when thinking about pollution: _____

    _____

    _____

    _____

Related activities: Health Effects of Pollution

Health Effects of Pollution

The effects of pollution on health depends on concentration and type of pollutant and extent of exposure. People living in cities are usually more exposed to pollutants than those in rural areas, although those living in or near intensively farmed areas using fertilizers and pesticides can also be exposed to high levels of toxins. While it is difficult to avoid some pollutants, such as carbon monoxide from busy traffic, others such as cigarette smoke, can be more easily avoided.

Air Pollution

Air pollutants, such as lead, severely affect nerve function. CO reduces the blood's ability to carry oxygen and results in headaches, and impaired thinking and reflexes. SO_2, NO_x and O_3 detrimentally affect respiratory function.

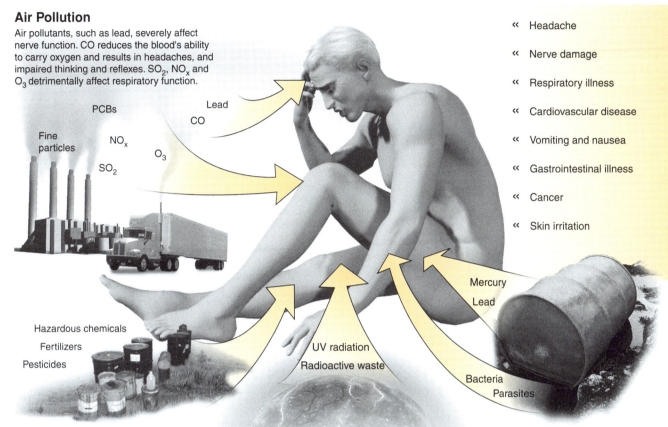

PCBs
Lead
CO
Fine particles
NO_x
O_3
SO_2

Hazardous chemicals
Fertilizers
Pesticides

UV radiation
Radioactive waste

Mercury
Lead

Bacteria
Parasites

« Headache

« Nerve damage

« Respiratory illness

« Cardiovascular disease

« Vomiting and nausea

« Gastrointestinal illness

« Cancer

« Skin irritation

Soil Contamination

Pesticides based on organophosphates are extremely toxic to humans and other mammals. Fertilizers can cause methemoglobinemia, cancer, and respiratory illness.

Radiation

UV radiation from the sun causes thousands of cases of melanoma skin cancer every year, while radioactive waste can cause cancer and genetic defects in fetuses.

Water Pollution

Heavy metals such as mercury and lead can cause nerve damage, while bacteria such as cholera or parasites such as giardia cause intestinal illness.

Toxic gases and ultra-fine particles produced by industry cause lung diseases. In the USA, air pollution causes up to 200 000 deaths and costs $150 million to treat per year.

Water polluted by fertilizers, pesticides, heavy metals, and untreated sewage can cause serious health issues. In some countries, barely 5% of sewage is treated.

Higher levels of UV radiation as a result of stratospheric ozone deletion could cause an extra 300 000 cases of skin cancer and 1.5 million extra cases of cataracts per year.

1. Identify three types pollutants people are often exposed to and their effects on human health: _____

_____

_____

_____

2. Discuss the social and economic costs of these pollutants: _____

_____

_____

_____

Pollution

Related activities: Types of Pollution, Water Pollution, Air Pollution

A 3

The Economic Impact of Pollution

Although there is an economic cost to pollution, placing a monetary value on it is difficult and controversial. The various sectors involved (health officials, economists, and industry) often disagree about how to estimate the cost of pollution, as it is difficult to assign monetary values to environment, health, and human life. It can also be difficult to determine the economic impact of pollution because, while a region as a whole may benefit from the economic activities of a polluter, specific groups within the region may suffer. Some economic costs associated with pollution are more easily determined than others. **Direct** costs (e.g. cleaning up an oil spill) are easily calculated, but **indirect costs** (e.g. estimating revenue losses) or **repercussion costs** (e.g. loss of public confidence) can be harder to quantify. **Cost-benefit analysis** is used to assess the cost of controlling pollution. The short-term and long-term costs and benefits for a variety of pollution control measures are compared and used to determine whether a control or regulation should be put in place. Environmental regulations, taxes, and pollution quotas are commonly used to control levels of pollution and to promote sustainable use of resources and the environment.

The Costs of Environmental Clean-Up

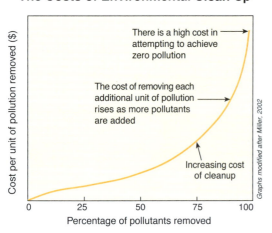

There is a high cost in attempting to achieve zero pollution

The cost of removing each additional unit of pollution rises as more pollutants are added

Increasing cost of cleanup

Cost per unit of pollution removed ($) / Percentage of pollutants removed

Graphs modified after Miller, 2002

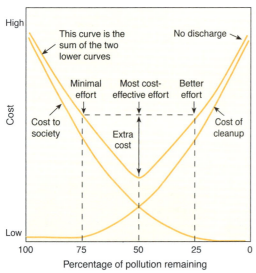

This curve is the sum of the two lower curves

No discharge

Minimal effort — Most cost-effective effort — Better effort

Cost to society

Extra cost

Cost of cleanup

Cost / Percentage of pollution remaining

In December 2007, a barge collided with the *Hebei Spirit* oil tanker, spilling almost 11 000 tonnes of oil into the Yellow Sea off the coast of Korea. Warm weather, wind, and wave conditions dispersed the oil, producing a 33 km oil slick that affected 300 km of the coastline of the ecologically significant Taean region. This region is home to one of Asia's largest wetlands. It is used by migratory birds, contains a maritime park and hundreds of sea farms, and includes many beautiful beaches popular with tourists. A comprehensive and rapid clean up was achieved using over 200 000 people and a number of expert international teams. The immediate cost of the environmental clean-up (US$330 million) was relatively easy to determine. However, the full costs, including costs due to the long-term effects of pollutants on the environment, lost revenue from contaminated aquaculture activities, and reduced tourism, are more difficult to estimate.

As a comparison, the *Hebei Spirit* oil spill is one third the size of the 1989 *Exxon Valdez* oil spill, which cost US$2.5 billion to clean up. The environmental impacts from the *Exxon Valdez* oil spill are still being felt in Prince William Sound today.

Cleaning up shoreline   Dead seabirds after the *Exxon-Valdex* oil spill

Photo courtesy of Exxon Valdez Oil Spill Trustee Council

GRAPHS: The cost of removing pollutants rises sharply as more pollutants are removed (top left), until the cleanup costs exceed the harmful costs of the pollution. The point at which the costs of the pollution and the costs of clean-up are equal marks the break-even point. This point is determined by separately plotting the clean-up cost and the cost of the pollution to society. The two curves are then added together to reveal the total costs (below left).

1. With reference to the **break-even point**, explain why total pollutant removal is often not cost effective:

   _____

   _____

   _____

2. Describe the following costs associated with a named major pollution incident: _____

   (a) Direct costs: _____

   _____

   _____

   (b) Indirect costs: _____

   _____

   _____

Exxon Valdez Oil Spill

Oil is arguably one of the most important chemicals in human economics. It provides power for transport and electricity, and the raw materials for many consumer products, including plastics. Billion of dollars a year are spent on removing it from the ground and billions more in revenue made from its sale. However, crude oil is a very toxic substance and removing it from reservoirs is fraught with difficulty and danger. Some of the greatest man-made environmental disasters have occurred because of the search for and transport of oil. Oil tankers carry huge volumes of crude oil over the seas and are some of the largest ships afloat. As a result there is enormous potential for disaster if one is grounded. The grounding of the *Exxon Valdez* is one of the most infamous examples.

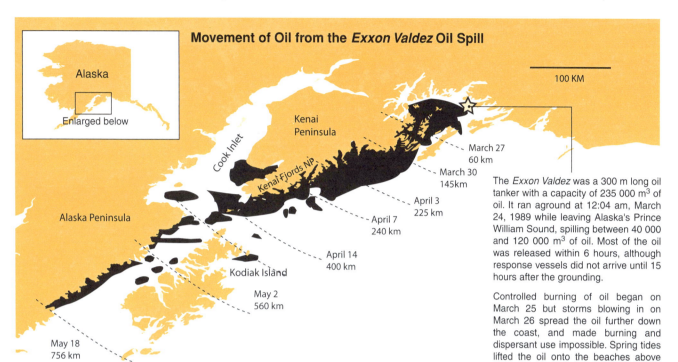

Movement of Oil from the *Exxon Valdez* Oil Spill

Alaska

Enlarged below

100 KM

Cook Inlet

Kenai Peninsula

Kenai Fjords N/P

Alaska Peninsula

Kodiak Island

March 27
60 km

March 30
145km

April 3
225 km

April 7
240 km

April 14
400 km

May 2
560 km

May 18
756 km

The *Exxon Valdez* was a 300 m long oil tanker with a capacity of 235 000 m^3 of oil. It ran aground at 12:04 am, March 24, 1989 while leaving Alaska's Prince William Sound, spilling between 40 000 and 120 000 m^3 of oil. Most of the oil was released within 6 hours, although response vessels did not arrive until 15 hours after the grounding.

Controlled burning of oil began on March 25 but storms blowing in on March 26 spread the oil further down the coast, and made burning and dispersant use impossible. Spring tides lifted the oil onto the beaches above the normal wave action. On April 10 another storm blew oil ashore in the Kenai Fjords National Park.

Diagram source: Exxon Valdez Oil Spill Trustee Council

NOAA

US Navy

The were several causes of the disaster. The crew of the *Exxon Valdez* had not had their mandatory rest period and were fatigued. They had also failed to manoeuvre the ship correctly (probably due to fatigue), and the radar system that could have informed the crew of a collision had not been repaired and was not operating.

The clean-up operation was made more difficult by the remote location of the oil spill. Food, equipment, and shelter had to be brought in for up to 11 000 workers, along with fuel and dispersant equipment for 1400 vessels and 85 aircraft. The clean up stopped in September due to the approach of the Alaskan winter, but was restarted in April 1990.

357 sea otters were treated after the spill, at an estimated cost of US$51 000 per otter. Fisheries in the area were closed, including black cod and Pacific herring. It is estimated that around 87% of the herring's spawning grounds were oiled. Mollusks were found to contain higher than normal levels of aromatic chemicals after the spill.

Approximately a quarter of a million seabirds, 2800 sea otters, 300 harbor seals, 250 bald eagles, 22 killer whales, and countless fish were killed in the first weeks of the spill. Oil can still be found 20 years later, not far beneath the surface of many of the affected beaches, despite one of the biggest clean up operations in US history.

1. (a) Explain how the *Exxon Valdez* spill could have been avoided: _____

_____

_____

(b) Describe some of the effects of the spill: _____

_____

(c) Explain why the clean up of this spill was particularly difficult: _____

_____

_____

Pollution

Periodicals:
In the wake of the spill

Related activities: Water Pollution, Oil

A 3

Niger Delta Oil

The Niger Delta is situated in the south of Nigeria. It covers an area of around 70 000 km^2 (including the surrounding wetlands) and is home is nearly 30 million people. The associated forests and wetlands are some of the most biologically diverse in Africa, but the delta also contains the continent's greatest concentration of oil. This has lead to a number of environmental and humanitarian issues. Many parts of the Niger Delta have become heavily polluted with oil from drilling and recovery operations and, although billions of dollars of oil is recovered each year, very little has made its way to the local communities, many of whom still live in poverty.

Nigeria is the largest oil producing nation in Africa, with proven reserves of around 36 billion barrels. Oil is the country's main export earner, accounting for nearly 90% of export earnings. It also accounts for around 80% of the federal government's revenue. A number or oil companies operate within the delta, producing over 2 million barrels per day.

Oil has been removed from the delta for the past fifty years, but the oil industry in Africa has had little regulation because of regional conflicts and poor government management. Successive governments have failed to ensure money from the oil companies reaches the local communities. Local communities and environmental groups accuse the oil industry of causing an environmental catastrophe by using drilling practices that disregard the environment or the community. WWF UK estimates that 1.5 million tonnes of oil has been spilt in the delta over the past fifty years.

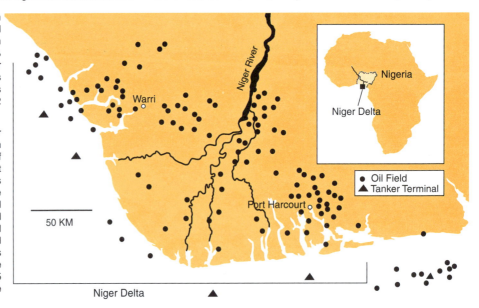

Niger Delta

- Oil Field
▲ Tanker Terminal

Fisheries in the delta have been devastated by regular oil spills, and ground and drinking water have been contaminated. Many of the traditional fishing grounds in the Niger Delta have been polluted by oil and pesticides or heavily depleted by over-fishing. Fishermen are having to go further out to sea to fish. Those who can not have had their livelihoods ruined.

Many old or corroding oil pipelines crisscross the delta. Locals accuse oil companies of poor maintenance and slow response to oil leaks and spills. In 2009, Shell Oil admitted to spilling 14 000 tonnes of oil into the delta. Oil companies claim conflict in the region as the cause of the oil spills, with damage to oil pipelines caused by bombings or theft and vandalism, although local communities dispute this.

Flaring is one of the major causes of pollution in the delta. Natural gas that can not be separated from the oil easily is burnt off, producing smoke, acid rain, and CO_2. Gas flares are a major source of greenhouse gases, including methane, and also produce soot, which covers the surrounding area. Flaring was forbidden in Nigeria in 2005 but large volumes of gas are still burnt.

1. Describe some of the environmental effects associated with oil drilling in the Niger Delta: _____

_____

_____

2. Explain why communities living in the Niger Delta feel ignored by the oil companies and the government:

_____

_____

3. Discuss the issues associated with oil drilling in regions where there is internal conflict or political instability:

_____

_____

_____

_____

Related activities: *Exxon Valdez Oil Spill, Deepwater Horizon Oil Spill, Cleaning Up Oil Spills*

Deepwater Drilling

As technology improves and the demand for oil increases, oil companies are now beginning to drill oil wells much further from shore than was once possible. Floating oil platforms are now able to operate in water thousands of meters deep, thereby accessing sites once thought impossible to reach. From 1996 to 2009, the maximum operating depth of offshore floating platforms increased from about 1000 m to over 3000 m. This increase in drilling depth produces a new suite of potential problems. Drilling rigs require powerful thrusters and mooring lines to maintain their position in strong ocean currents, and they must be built larger and stronger to be able to handle the extra weight of the larger drilling equipment. The risks of environmental disaster also rise the further from shore and the deeper an oil rig drills. A blowout of a well 2000 m or more below sea level has the potential to devastate large areas of ocean because to the difficulty in accessing the wellhead. This was demonstrated on April 20, 2010, when the oil rig *Deepwater Horizon* exploded and sank after a blowout at the Macondo well site. The well took six months to seal.

Deep Water Drilling Platforms in the Gulf of Mexico

There are some 3500 oil and gas platforms in the Gulf of Mexico, most located offshore from Texas, Louisiana, and Mississippi.

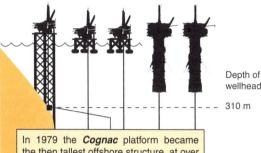

Depth of wellhead

— 310 m

In 1979 the **Cognac** platform became the then tallest offshore structure, at over 380 m tall. At that time, it was the deepest working oil rig.

Deepwater Horizon was destroyed while working the Macondo well at 1544 m. Just months before, the rig set a new record for drilling the deepest oil well extending to over 10 680 m below sea level.

— 1544 m

Thunder Horse, the world's biggest offshore platform is currently operating in more than 1900 m of water 240 km southeast of New Orleans.

— 1928 m

The **Perdido** spar platform has operated in some of the deepest waters of any platform yet and drilled some of the deepest wells. Its Tobago wellhead is nearly 3000 m below sea level.

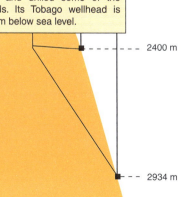

— 2400 m

— 2934 m

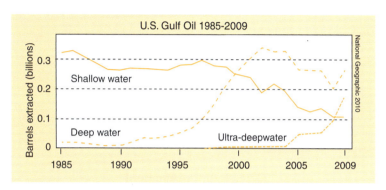

U.S. Gulf Oil 1985-2009 — National Geographic 2010. Shallow water, Deep water, Ultra-deepwater. Barrels extracted (billions).

Oil production has moved into deeper and deeper water due to an improvement in technology and oil reserves in shallow water tapering off. Some rigs are now capable of drilling to a total depth of more than 10 000 m.

Huge crews and support networks are needed to operate drilling rigs and the equipment that services them. In the Gulf area alone, an estimated 107 000 jobs are linked to the oil and gas industry, producing an annual revenue of almost US$63 billion a year. Money is also invested in the construction of the gigantic oil rigs with some costing more than $1 billion to build.

1. Explain why oil drilling rigs are now capable of operating in extremely deep water:

2. Explain why oil companies are exploring for oil in progressively deeper water:

3. Describe the issues associated with ultra-deepwater oil wells:

Pollution

Deepwater Horizon Oil Spill

The **Deepwater Horizon** was an offshore, ultra-deepwater oil drilling rig situated in the Gulf of Mexico and most notable for drilling the deepest oil well to date (the **Tiber** well). On April 20, 2010, a blowout caused a massive explosion that killed 11 crew and was followed by an inferno that destroyed and ultimately sunk the rig. The riser pipe from the wellhead ruptured at a depth of 1500 m and oil gushed into the Gulf of Mexico, creating an oil slick that covered over 6 500 km^2.

The Gulf of Mexico is surrounded by the United States in the north and west, Mexico in the south, and the island of Cuba in the east. Its shores contain many important wildlife areas, especially the Mississippi Delta and the wetlands around Florida. Its waters provide extremely rich fishing, with shrimp, oysters, and finfish being the major catches.

The *Deepwater Horizon* spill site was located about 80 km from shore. At its most intense, oil was escaping into the Gulf at a rate of nearly 10 000 m^3 per day. The well was sealed with a cap on July 15, three months after the initial explosion. The final concrete plug was put into place on September 19.

Protective booms were placed around sensitive wetland and marine areas, including eight national parks, which are home to many birds and thousands of other marine and wetland species. Despite these precautions, shifting currents still washed thousands of liters of oil ashore.

Oil slick April 29

Oil slick

Mississippi delta

Former rig site.

NASA

Causes of the Accident

Preliminary investigations into the disaster identified a series of equipment failures:

- The cement and casings within the well were not fitted and used correctly. This allowed natural gas to enter the riser, causing the blowout.

- The blowout preventer (BOP) on the *Deepwater Horizon* could not be activated and so failed to seal the well. BOPs are fitted to the riser pipes that lead from the wellhead to the surface. They are designed to seal the wellhead in the event of an accident.

- A safety switch, known as a deadman's switch, should have activated the BOP automatically, but failed to do so.

- The *Deepwater Horizon* lacked an acoustic switch, which could have activated the BOP remotely. Acoustic switches are not mandatory in the US, but they are in various other countries.

Oil was not detected for two days after the explosion, before the oil rig sank. Estimates of the flow rate of the oil after the sinking (which may have caused the riser pipe to rupture) ranged from 160 m^3 per day initially to more than 10 000 m^3. At least 780 000 m^3 of oil was estimated to have leaked into the Gulf, many times more than the volume of oil spilled from the *Exxon Valdez*.

USCG

Deepwater Horizon after explosion

Largest Recorded Oil Spills (m^3)

Forbes/National Geographic 2010

Kuwait oil fields 906 200	
Deepwater Horizon 780 000	
Ixotoc I 531 000	
Atlantic Empress/Aegean Captain 350 000	
ABT Summer 305 200	
Fergana valley 333 000	
Nowruz oil field 302 000	
Castillo de Beliver 286 200	
Amoco Cadiz 254 400	
Odyssey 162 000	
Exxon Valdez 40 000	Not one of the largest spills ever, but ecologically significant.

The *Deepwater Horizon* oil spill is now one of the largest oil spills in history. The largest ever oil spill, in the Kuwait oil fields, was deliberate, carried out by the Iraqi military just before the Coalition liberation of Kuwait in 1991.

1. Describe the events that caused oil to spill from the Mocondo wellhead into the Gulf of Mexico: _____

_____

_____

_____

_____

Related activities: Oil Spills and Wildlife, Cleaning up Oil Spills
Weblinks: 2010 Gulf of Mexico Oil Spill

Periodicals:
The meaning of the mess

Stopping the Flow

BP faced a number of challenges in stopping the flow of oil into the Gulf of Mexico from the broken riser pipe. The extreme depth of the well (1500 m) causes problems with both temperature and pressure. At this depth, Remote Operated Vehicles (ROVs) must carry out any work and a fleet of ships are required to support the operations.

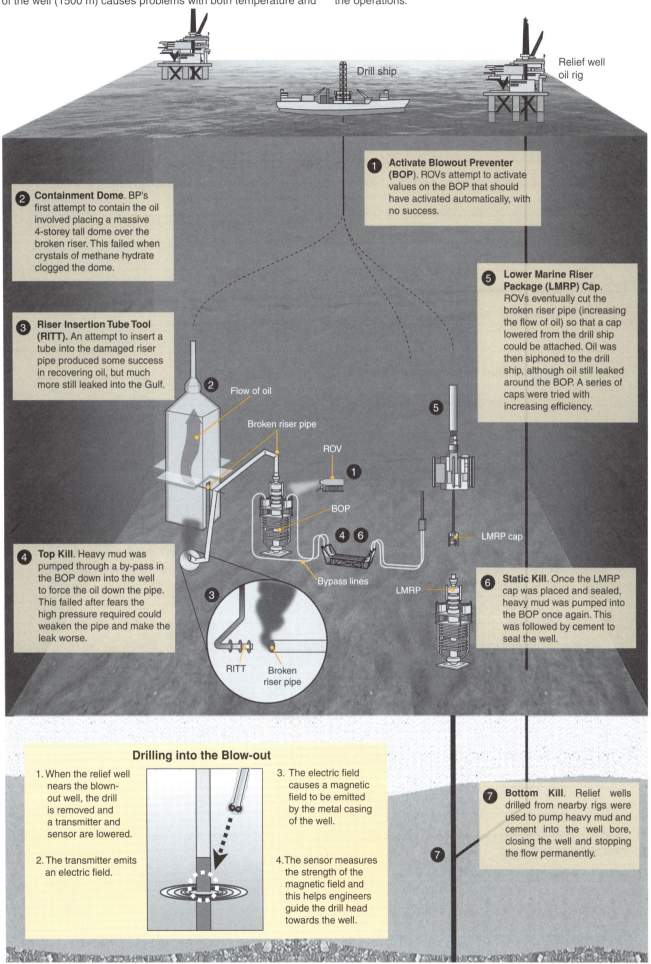

Drill ship

Relief well oil rig

① Activate Blowout Preventer (BOP). ROVs attempt to activate values on the BOP that should have activated automatically, with no success.

② Containment Dome. BP's first attempt to contain the oil involved placing a massive 4-storey tall dome over the broken riser. This failed when crystals of methane hydrate clogged the dome.

③ Riser Insertion Tube Tool (RITT). An attempt to insert a tube into the damaged riser pipe produced some success in recovering oil, but much more still leaked into the Gulf.

⑤ Lower Marine Riser Package (LMRP) Cap. ROVs eventually cut the broken riser pipe (increasing the flow of oil) so that a cap lowered from the drill ship could be attached. Oil was then siphoned to the drill ship, although oil still leaked around the BOP. A series of caps were tried with increasing efficiency.

Flow of oil

Broken riser pipe

ROV

BOP

LMRP cap

Bypass lines

LMRP

④ Top Kill. Heavy mud was pumped through a by-pass in the BOP down into the well to force the oil down the pipe. This failed after fears the high pressure required could weaken the pipe and make the leak worse.

③ RITT — Broken riser pipe

⑥ Static Kill. Once the LMRP cap was placed and sealed, heavy mud was pumped into the BOP once again. This was followed by cement to seal the well.

Drilling into the Blow-out

1. When the relief well nears the blown-out well, the drill is removed and a transmitter and sensor are lowered.

2. The transmitter emits an electric field.

3. The electric field causes a magnetic field to be emitted by the metal casing of the well.

4. The sensor measures the strength of the magnetic field and this helps engineers guide the drill head towards the well.

⑦ Bottom Kill. Relief wells drilled from nearby rigs were used to pump heavy mud and cement into the well bore, closing the well and stopping the flow permanently.

Pollution

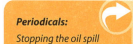 *Periodicals:*
Stopping the oil spill

2. Explain why estimates of the oil flow rate from the wellhead varied so widely: _____

_____

_____

3. Explain the purpose of the blowout preventer: _____

_____

_____

4. (a) Calculate how many times more oil was spilt from the *Deepwater Horizon* oil spill than from the *Exxon Valdez*:

_____

(b) Explain why oil spills from drilling platforms have the potential to be much larger than spills from oil tankers:

_____

_____

_____

5. Explain why ROVs are needed to work at the wellhead on deepwater oil rigs: _____

_____

_____

6. Explain why the containment dome failed to stem the oil spill: _____

_____

_____

_____

7. (a) Describe the methods involved in the top kill attempt: _____

_____

_____

(b) Explain why the top kill attempt failed: _____

_____

_____

8. (a) Describe the method used in the bottom kill attempt: _____

_____

_____

_____

(b) Describe how the engineers from the relief well located the blown out well bore: _____

_____

_____

9. Explain why several progressively more complicated methods were used in attempting to stem the flow of oil, before the relief well was completed:

_____

_____

_____

_____

Oil Spills and Wildlife

The coastlines of Louisiana, Mississippi, and Florida are important and delicate ecosystems. Their estuaries, marshes and wetlands provide habitat for a range of species including oysters, mudcrabs, and many seabirds, and they act as shelter for fish fry before they return to the ocean. The Gulf itself is home to many important commercial fish species and to 70% of the US shrimping industry. The oil leaked from the Macondo well site placed all of these habitats at risk and many may remain so for many years to come.

Location of Spill Site and Threatened Wildlife Sanctuaries

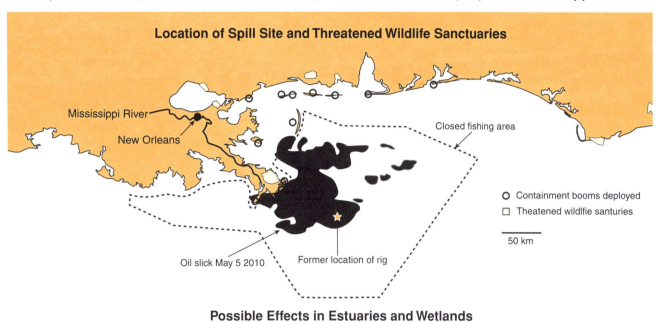

Mississippi River

New Orleans

Closed fishing area

○ Containment booms deployed

□ Theatened wildlfie santuries

50 km

Oil slick May 5 2010

Former location of rig

Possible Effects in Estuaries and Wetlands

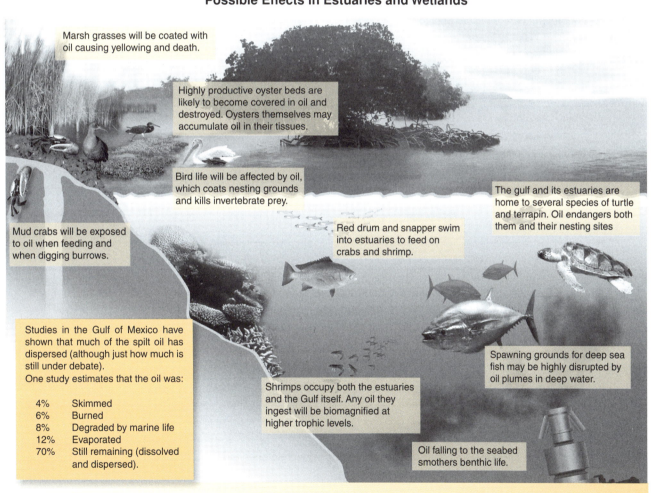

Marsh grasses will be coated with oil causing yellowing and death.

Highly productive oyster beds are likely to become covered in oil and destroyed. Oysters themselves may accumulate oil in their tissues.

Bird life will be affected by oil, which coats nesting grounds and kills invertebrate prey.

The gulf and its estuaries are home to several species of turtle and terrapin. Oil endangers both them and their nesting sites

Mud crabs will be exposed to oil when feeding and when digging burrows.

Red drum and snapper swim into estuaries to feed on crabs and shrimp.

Studies in the Gulf of Mexico have shown that much of the spilt oil has dispersed (although just how much is still under debate).
One study estimates that the oil was:

4%	Skimmed
6%	Burned
8%	Degraded by marine life
12%	Evaporated
70%	Still remaining (dissolved and dispersed).

Shrimps occupy both the estuaries and the Gulf itself. Any oil they ingest will be biomagnified at higher trophic levels.

Spawning grounds for deep sea fish may be highly disrupted by oil plumes in deep water.

Oil falling to the seabed smothers benthic life.

Effects of Crude Oil on Wildlife

Physical contact: Fur and feathers become matted with oil, causing them to lose their ability to insulate. Flotation is reduced, increasing the risk of drowning.

Toxic contamination: Vapors from the oil may damage the lungs and the nervous system. Ingestion can cause damage to the stomach and intestinal tract.

Destruction of food sources and habitat: Predators may be put off food tasting or smelling of oil. Contaminated habitat may affect nesting or hatching.

Reproductive problems: Oil can seal the pores in birds eggs, preventing gas exchange. It also affects embryonic development, causing long term defects.

Periodicals:
Accidental Laboratory

Related activities: Deepwater Horizon Oil Spill, Cleaning Up Oil Spills

Pollution

A 3

Ecosystem Recovery Time

The rate of ecosystem recovery after an oil spill depends on the habitat involved, the local climate and conditions, and the type of oil spilled.

Florida Barge, Cape Cod
1969 **700 000 L**

Salt marshes and estuaries

IXTOC I, Bay of Campeche, Gulf of Mexico
1979 **530 million L**

Sandy beaches that protected lagoons

Years after spill

0   5   10   15   20   40

(Florida Barge)

Invertebrates and grasses killed off. Birds and fish heavily affected.

Slow return of species as oil breaks down.

Health of marshes returning but growth and survival of crabs impaired. Undegraded oil still present.

Species still affected by residues. Crabs dig shallower burrows and show slowed responses to predators.

(IXTOC I)

0   5

Wildlife on barrier islands heavily affected. Heavy oiling of beaches but shellfish mostly survive.

Shrimp and squid fisheries closed due to oil contamination. This allows populations to recover.

Little evidence of spill or harm done. A few hardened oil deposits persist.

1. Describe how the nature of oil results in it causing such large ecological problems: _____

_____

_____

_____

_____

2. Describe some immediate effects of oil on the wildlife it comes in contact with: _____

_____

_____

_____

_____

3. (a) Explain why it is difficult to predict the effects of oil spills on ecosystems: _____

_____

_____

_____

_____

(b) Explain why the size of the oil spill does is not necessarily linked to the magnitude of the ecological effect:

_____

_____

_____

_____

_____

4. Explain why oil spills are rarely just ecological disasters but economic ones too: _____

_____

_____

_____

_____

_____

Cleaning up oil spills

Oil spills can be extremely difficult to clean up due to the sticky nature of the oil. Heavy crude is one of the most difficult substances to clean as it forms thick, viscous slicks that are difficult to disperse. The environment also plays major part in the clean up; warm temperatures contribute to the evaporation of large quantities of volatile compounds from the oil and allow bacteria to quickly break it down. Wave action also helps to oxygenate and degrade the oil. Human efforts include confining and burning large slicks, using chemical dispersants, and cleaning beaches with steam or digging up sand and removing it for remediation.

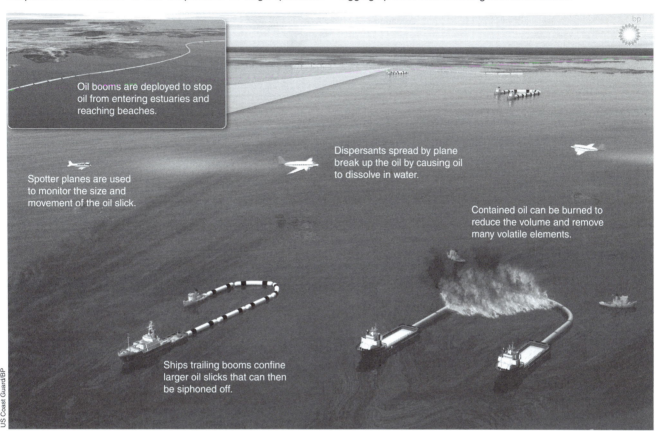

Oil booms are deployed to stop oil from entering estuaries and reaching beaches.

Spotter planes are used to monitor the size and movement of the oil slick.

Dispersants spread by plane break up the oil by causing oil to dissolve in water.

Contained oil can be burned to reduce the volume and remove many volatile elements.

Ships trailing booms confine larger oil slicks that can then be siphoned off.

US Coast Guard/BP

All images: US Coast Guard

Floating booms designed to stop oil movement are used to protect sensitive areas. During the Gulf clean-up more than 550 km of booms were deployed.

Oil captured by skimmer boats is set alight to reduce its volume, although this causes dense plumes of smoke. Around 38 000 m^3 of oil was burned in the Gulf.

Oil that reaches the beach may need to be dug up and removed for remediation. On accessible beaches, large graders can be used to scrape up large amounts of sand and oil and remove it from the beach. New sand may be brought in to maintain the beach.

Chemical dispersants are dropped from the air to clear the surface slick, but were also injected into the oil at the Mocondo wellhead to try to disperse the oil before it reached the surface. The long term effect of using dispersant this way is not known.

Hot water and steam are used to clean rocks and beaches. This method was used during the *Exxon Valdez* clean up but not during the Gulf clean up as it has the potential to do more harm than good by killing rock dwelling organisms such as barnacles.

Water quality tests are carried out on a regular basis to track the progress of the oil. Bacteria in the Gulf waters provide natural bioremediation and began to quickly break down the oil. A large plume of oil in deep water appears to have been dispersed by bacterial action.

Skimmer boats collect oil floating on the surface. This can be burnt or siphoned off and processed using centrifuges to separate the oil and water.

Pollution

Related activities: Water Pollution, Deepwater Horizon Oil Spill, Exxon Valdez Oil Spill, Oil

A 2

Natural Degradation of Oil

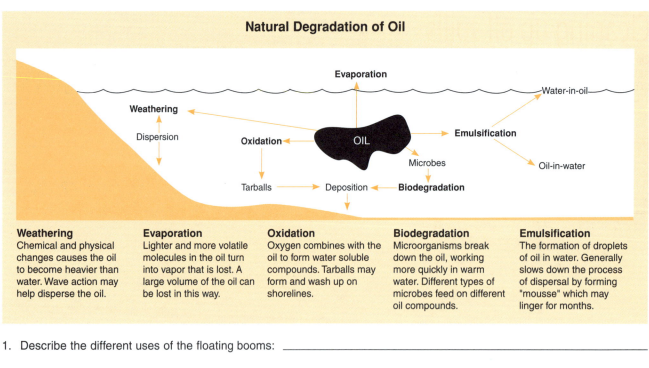

Weathering
Chemical and physical changes causes the oil to become heavier than water. Wave action may help disperse the oil.

Evaporation
Lighter and more volatile molecules in the oil turn into vapor that is lost. A large volume of the oil can be lost in this way.

Oxidation
Oxygen combines with the oil to form water soluble compounds. Tarballs may form and wash up on shorelines.

Biodegradation
Microorganisms break down the oil, working more quickly in warm water. Different types of microbes feed on different oil compounds.

Emulsification
The formation of droplets of oil in water. Generally slows down the process of dispersal by forming "mousse" which may linger for months.

1. Describe the different uses of the floating booms: _____

   _____

   _____

2. Explain why collected oil is burnt at the surface, and the effects of this: _____

   _____

   _____

   _____

3. Explain how dispersants work and issues involved in using them: _____

   _____

   _____

   _____

4. Explain why using steam to clean oil from beaches was not used in the Gulf clean up: _____

   _____

   _____

   _____

5. Describe the effects of the following natural processes on the oil:

   (a) Biodegradation: _____

   _____

   (b) Emulsification: _____

   _____

   (c) Evaporation: _____

   _____

   (d) Oxidation: _____

   _____

   (e) Weathering: _____

   _____

Chernobyl Accident

On April 26 1986, operators at the **Chernobyl** nuclear power plant, then in the Soviet controlled state of Ukraine, began a test that would lead to the largest nuclear accident in history. The accident caused the meltdown of the number 4 reactor core and resulted in an explosion that spread radioactive material over a wide area. The nearby town of **Pripyat** was evacuated. Over 350,000 people were relocated over the next twenty years. The accident was the result of a series of human errors and poorly designed equipment.

The Accident

The accident resulted from the failure of a safety test designed to test the power plant's ability to continue to generate electricity to run cooling pumps during a total power loss. Similar tests had already been carried out on the reactor. All had failed to show its ability to generate sufficient electricity to bridge the minute long gap between a power failure and the emergency generators restoring full power. The test was to be carried out during a maintenance shutdown of the number 4 reactor.

Operator error during the reactor shutdown caused instability in the reactor core. As the test proceeded, power output fell below that required to run the coolant pumps. This caused a positive feedback loop with ever-increasing power levels. Although an emergency shutdown was initiated, the system was too slow to prevent the coolant from flashing to steam. A design flaw in the control rods enhanced the problem. An initial explosion caused control rods to jam so that they could not be inserted into the reactor. A few seconds later, power levels reached an estimated 30 GW (far beyond operating capacity) causing a second, much larger explosion that destroyed the reactor.

Cause of the Accident

The failure of the experiment and the subsequent explosion were due to:

- The postponement of the test by several hours so that senior operators were no longer on site.
- Extremely small operational safety margins.
- Inexperienced operators being in control of the test.
- Human error.
- Poor design of reactor control rods.
- Poor design for overall control of the nuclear reaction.

Environmental Effects

Radioactive particles released by the explosion fell across a large area surrounding the plant, killing much of the nearby forest. In particular, an area of pine forest (known as Red Forest) received an extremely large dose of radioactive particles. The pine forest was bulldozed and buried after the pines died. Winds blew radioactive material over a large part of Europe. Radioactivity in surrounding waterways fell rapidly due to dilution and deposition, but wildlife around the area have suffered higher than normal rates of mutation, with many animals dying from thyroid disease. Much of the radioactivity is now concentrated in the soil.

The exclusion zone around the power plant has essentially become a wildlife refuge due to the evacuation of residents immediately following the disaster. Ecological succession has returned much of the land to forest or open meadow.

Because of the long half-lives of many of the radioactive particles released, the area around Chernoybl will be contaminated for many years, possibly generations to come.

Kurchatov Inst.

Site of reactor core

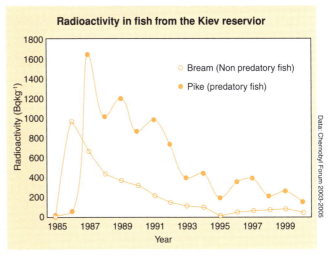

Radioactivity in fish from the Kiev reservoir

○ Bream (Non predatory fish)
● Pike (predatory fish)

Data: Chernobyl Forum 2003-2005

Other Nuclear Accidents		
Reactor	Cause	Effect
Kyshtym (USSR)	Poor nuclear fuel storage facilities.	Explosion releases high levels of radiation. 200 people die from cancer.
Windscale (Great Britain)	Incorrect temperature gauge readings.	Reactor fire. Large radiation leak.
Three Mile Island (United States)	Human error, mechanical fault.	Partial meltdown. No environmental effects.
Mihama (Japan)	Steam leak.	5 workers killed. No environmental effects.

1. Explain why the Chernobyl reactor explosion was a "disaster waiting to happen": _____

   _____

   _____

2. Describe some of the effects of the radioactivity: _____

   _____

   _____

3. Explain why predatory fish like pike contain much higher levels of radiation than non-predatory fish: _____

   _____

   _____

Pollution

Related activities: Water pollution, Air Pollution
Weblinks: Long Shadow of Chernobyl

A 3

Bhopal Disaster

Many industrial disasters can be traced back to the need to increase revenue and regain the often vast sums of money involved. Industrial plants often operate twenty-four hours a day to increase production and plant efficiency. Cost cutting measures may reduce safety margins. Factors such as these were instrumental in the disaster at the Union Carbide factory in Bhopal, India. On the night of December 2-3 1984, the chemical methyl-isocyanate, was leaked from the plant, killing more than 4000 people and injuring tens of thousands of others. Poor maintenance and a lack of safety were primarily to blame.

Bhopal Disaster

The Union Carbide plant was built for the production of the pesticide **carbaryl** (trade name Sevin). The pesticide is non-toxic in vertebrates and does not persist in the environment. However several of the chemicals used to make carbaryl are highly toxic and must be handled and stored with extreme care.

The disaster occurred when water entered a tank containing the intermediate chemical methyl isocyanate. The resulting exothermic reaction raised the temperature in the tank to over 200°C. Pressure inside the tank caused toxic gases to be vented covering parts of the city. The gas cloud caused the immediate deaths of over 4000 people. Another 4000 died within a week and 8000 died in the following years. Between 200 000 and 500 000 people received minor to major injuries.

Cause of the Disaster

The disaster was caused by many factors, including:

- Hazardous intermediate chemicals were stored rather than used immediately.
- Poor plant maintenance.
- Failure of safety systems due to poor condition; gas scrubbers, flare towers, and water curtains under repair or insufficient.
- Safety systems, including refrigeration, were turned off.
- Plant location near to densely populated residential areas.

At the time, Union Carbide (which is now owned by the Dow Chemical Company) maintained that the disaster was the result of sabotage. However, in June 2010, eight officials from the operation were convicted of negligence by the Indian government.

Effects of the Disaster

Animal and plant life around the plant were also severely affected by the toxic gas, although there is little research into this.

After the disaster, the plant was shut down and the site cleaned up. However, toxic chemicals including mercury, lead, chloroform, and dichloromethane are still stored at the site and continue to leak into soil and water. Repeated tests confirm chemical levels hundreds to thousands of times higher than would normally be expected.

The Indian government estimated the economic cost of the disaster at almost $4 billion. In 1989, Union Carbide agreed to an out of court settlement of $470 million. It was also ordered by the Indian supreme court to fund a hospital dedicated to treating disaster victims. The maximum compensation received by individuals affected in the tragedy was about US$3000.

Area of Bhopal Affected by Gas Leak

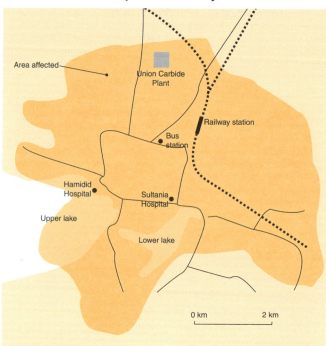

Luca Frediani

1. Calculate the approximate area covered by the gas leak: _____

_____

2. Explain how the plant originally provided a beneficial service to Bhopal and India: _____

_____

_____

3. Give two reasons for the disaster and explain how they could have been avoided: _____

_____

_____

_____

_____

_____

Related activities: Water Pollution, Air Pollution

KEY TERMS: Mix and Match

INSTRUCTIONS: Test your vocabulary by matching each term to its definition, as identified by its preceding letter code.

ACID RAIN

ATMOSPHERIC POLLUTION

BIOLOGICAL OXYGEN DEMAND

DIRECT COSTS

EUTROPHICATION

INDICATOR ORGANISM

INDIRECT COSTS

INTEGRATED WASTE MANAGEMENT

NOISE POLLUTION

NON-POINT SOURCE POLLUTION

ORGANIC EFFLUENT

OIL SPILL

PHOTOCHEMICAL SMOG

POINT SOURCE POLLUTION

POLLUTION

RECYCLING

SEWAGE TREATMENT

TOXICANT

A Pollution that enters a system through diffuse, poorly defined entrances, such a chemicals dropped by a crop duster.

B Management process that uses many different methods of waste processing to effectively deal with waste products.

C Process of accelerated enrichment of water ways, often by nitrogenous materials such as fertilizers.

D Precipitation with a pH below 6. It is caused by sulfur dioxide and nitrogen dioxide dissolving in water vapor.

E The pollution of the air by fine particles and gases including CO, CO_2, O_3 and NO_2.

F The adding of unwanted, damaging or often harmful chemicals to a system.

G Pollution that can be identified as emanating from a specific place, such as a pipe or drain.

H Costs that are indirectly related to or caused by an industry or pollution event, e.g. the loss of business due to a negative public image.

I Organism whose presence, absence or abundance can be used as a determination of the health of the habitat being studied.

J Costs that are directly related to or caused by an industry or pollution event, e.g. the cost of clean up.

K Liquid sewage or other organic waste, e.g. milk, produced by living organisms and discharged before processing.

L The mass (in milligrams) of oxygen used by one liter of sample effluent stored in darkness at 20°C for five days.

M Environmental pollution consisting of persistent, bothersome, or harmful noise which may interfere with communication, recreation, work, or sleep.

N The loss of oil from a contained environment.

O Type of air pollution caused by the action of sunlight on hydrocarbons, nitrogen oxides and other pollutants from emitted by motor vehicles and industry.

P The use of waste or old material to provide all or part of the raw material for new products.

Q A chemical compound typically produced by human activity that has a harmful effect on an organism.

R The process of using mechanical, biological, and chemical treatments to separate, process, and purify biological and domestic waste.

Pollution

A 2

Global Change

Key concepts

► Human activities can interfere with the environment on both a local and on a global scale.

► Global warming and climate change have severe effects on the environment.

► Human activities have caused the Earth to lose much of its biodiversity.

► Species and resources can be managed sustainably.

Key terms

biodiversity

carbon credit

climate change

deforestation

endangered species

ex-situ conservation

extinction

global warming

globalization

greenhouse effect

greenhouse gas

habitat restoration

Indicator organism

in-situ conservation

national park

ocean acidification

ozone depletion

seedbank

stratospheric ozone

threatened species

ultraviolet radiation

Objectives

☐ 1. Use the **KEY TERMS** to help you understand and complete these objectives.

Stratospheric Ozone   pages 205-206

☐ 2. Describe the role of stratospheric ozone in absorbing **ultraviolet** (UV) **radiation.** Outline the effects of UV radiation on living organisms.

☐ 3. Discuss the cause of stratospheric **ozone depletion**, its effects and efforts to reduce the rate of depletion.

☐ 4. Distinguish between stratospheric ozone and localized ozone pollution in the lower atmosphere.

Global Warming   pages 207-214

☐ 5. Explain what is meant by **global warming** and distinguish it from the **greenhouse effect**. Discuss measures to reduce global warming or its impact.

☐ 6. Describe the origins and relative effects of **greenhouse gases**.

☐ 7. Discuss effects of global warming on various environments and the plants and animals that inhabit them.

☐ 8. Explain the cause and effects of **ocean acidification**.

Loss of Biodiversity   pages 215-228

☐ 9. Explain what is meant by **biodiversity** and discuss the importance of preserving and managing it.

☐ 10. Identify regions of naturally occurring high biodiversity and describe the importance of these.

☐ 11. Use examples to help distinguish between a **threatened** and an **endangered species**.

☐ 12. Describe the role of national parks and reserves in preserving biodiversity.

☐ 13. Discuss the use of both **in-situ** and **ex-situ** conservation methods and the advantages and disadvantages of each.

Periodicals:
Listings for this
chapter are on page 231

Weblinks:
www.thebiozone.com/
weblink/EnvSci-2764.html

Presentation Media
Environmental Science:
Pollution and Global Change

Stratospheric Ozone Depletion

In a band of the upper stratosphere, 17-26 km above the Earth's surface, exists a thin veil of renewable **ozone** (O_3). This ozone absorbs about 99% of the harmful incoming UV radiation from the sun and prevents it from reaching the Earth's surface. Apart from health problems, such as increasingly severe sunburns, increase in skin cancers, and more cataracts of the eye (in both humans and other animals), an increase in UV-B radiation is likely to cause immune system suppression in animals, lower crop yields, a decline in the productivity of forests and surface dwelling plankton, more smog, and changes in the global climate. Ozone is being depleted by a handful of human-produced chemicals (ozone depleting compounds or ODCs). The problem of **ozone depletion** was first detected in 1984. Researchers discovered that ozone in the upper stratosphere over Antarctica is destroyed during the Antarctic spring and early summer (September–December). Rather than a "hole", it is more a

thinning, where ozone levels typically decrease by 50% to 100%. In 2000, the extent of the hole above Antarctica was the largest ever, but depletion levels were slightly less than 1999. Severe ozone loss has also been observed over the Arctic. During the winter of 1999-2000, Arctic ozone levels were depleted by 60% at an altitude of 18 km, up from around 45% in the previous winter. The primary cause for ozone depletion appears to be the increased use of chemicals such as chloro-fluoro-carbons (**CFCs**). Since 1987, nations have cut their consumption of ozone-depleting substances by 70%, although the phaseout is not complete and there is a significant black market in CFCs. **Free chlorine** in the stratosphere peaked around 1999 and is projected to decline for more than a century. Ozone loss is projected to diminish gradually until around 2050 when the polar ozone holes will return to 1975 levels. It will take another 100-200 years for full recovery to pre-1950 levels.

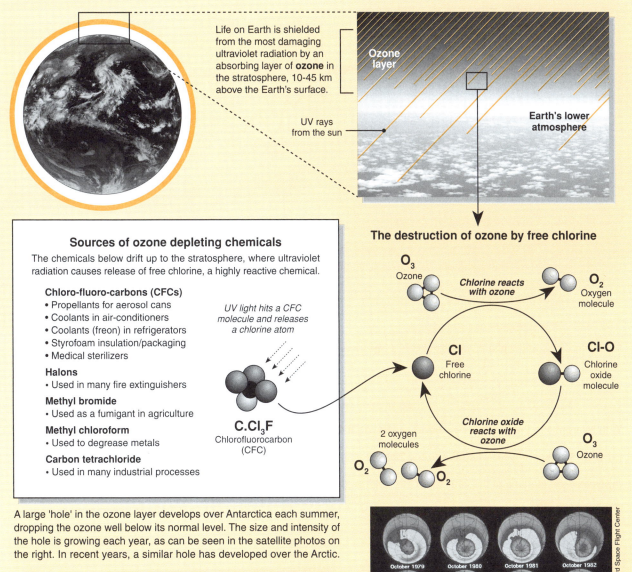

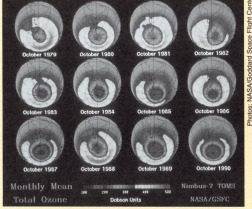

A large 'hole' in the ozone layer develops over Antarctica each summer, dropping the ozone well below its normal level. The size and intensity of the hole is growing each year, as can be seen in the satellite photos on the right. In recent years, a similar hole has developed over the Arctic.

Dobson Unit (DU): A measurement of **column ozone** levels (the ozone between the Earth's surface and outer space). In the tropics, ozone levels are typically between 250 and 300 DU year-round. In temperate regions, seasonal variations can produce large swings in ozone levels. These variations occur even in the absence of ozone depletion. **Ozone depletion** refers to reductions in ozone below normal levels after accounting for seasonal cycles and other natural effects. For a graphical explanation, see NASA's TOMS site: *http://toms.gsfc.nasa.gov/teacher/basics/dobson.html*

Related activities: The Atmosphere and Climate
Weblinks: Impact of Ozone Depletion and Pollution

RDA 2

Characteristics of the ozone 'hole'

The ozone 'hole' (stratospheric ozone depletion) can be characterized using several measures. The five graphs on this page show how the size and intensity of the hole varies through the course of a year, as well as how the phenomenon has progressed over the last two decades. An explanation of the unit used to measure ozone concentration (Dobson units) is given on the opposite page. Graphs 2 and 5 illustrate readings taken between the South Pole (90° south) and 40° latitude.

Data supplied by NASA's Goddard Space Flight Center and the National Oceanic and Atmospheric Administration (NOAA) in the USA.

Graph 1: Ozone hole altitude profile

Legend:
- August 7, 1997
- September 9, 1997
- October 10, 1997

X-axis: Ozone partial pressure (mPa)
Y-axis: Altitude (km)

Graph 2: Antarctic ozone hole area (<220 DU, 40° – 90° South)

Area = North America
Area = Antarctica
Legend: 1993, 1992
X-axis: Time of year (Jul–Dec)
Y-axis: Average area (million km²)

Graph 3: Change in area of the Antarctic ozone hole*

Area = North America
Area = Antarctica
X-axis: Year (1980–2000)
Y-axis: Average area (million km²)

Graph 4: Antarctic ozone hole minimum values* (60° – 90° S)

X-axis: Year (1980–2000)
Y-axis: Dobson Units

Graph 5: Antarctic ozone hole minimum values (40° – 90° South)

Legend: 1992, 1979
X-axis: Time of year (Feb–Nov)
Y-axis: Dobson Units

* Date range in which samples were collected in each year: 7 Sep–13 Oct
The ozone 'hole' is defined as region with less than 220 Dobson units

Sources: NASA Goddard Space Flight Center; NOAA / CMDL

1. Describe some of the damaging effects of excessive amounts of ultraviolet radiation on living organisms:

_____

_____

2. Explain how the atmospheric release of CFCs has increased the penetration of UV radiation reaching the Earth's surface:

_____

_____

3. With reference to the graphs (1-5 above) illustrating the characteristics of the stratospheric ozone depletion problem:

(a) State the time of year when the ozone 'hole' is at its greatest geographic extent: _____

(b) Determine the time of the year when the 'hole' is at its most depleted (thinnest): _____

(c) Describe the trend over the last two decades of changes to the abundance of stratospheric ozone over Antarctica:

_____

_____

(d) Describe the changes in stratospheric ozone with altitude between August and October 1997 in Graph 1 (above):

_____

4. Discuss some of the political and commercial problems associated with reducing the use of ozone depleting chemicals:

_____

_____

_____

Global Warming

The Earth's atmosphere comprises a mix of gases including nitrogen, oxygen, and water vapor. Small quantities of carbon dioxide (CO_2), methane, and a number of other 'trace' gases are also present. The term 'greenhouse effect' describes the natural process by which heat is retained within the atmosphere by these 'greenhouse gases', which act as a thermal blanket around the Earth, letting in sunlight, but trapping the heat that would normally radiate back into space. The greenhouse effect results in the Earth having a mean surface temperature of about 15°C, 33°C warmer than it would have without an atmosphere. About 75% of the natural greenhouse effect is due to water vapor. The next most significant agent is CO_2. Fluctuations in the Earth's

surface temperature as a result of climate shifts are normal, and the current period of warming climate is partly explained by the recovery after the most recent ice age that finished 10 000 years ago. However since the mid 20th century, the Earth's surface temperature has been increasing. This phenomenon is called global warming and the majority of researchers attribute it to the increase in atmospheric levels of CO_2 and other greenhouse gases emitted into the atmosphere as a result of human activity (i.e. it is anthropogenic). Nine of the ten warmest years on record were in the 2000s (1998 being the third warmest on record). Global surface temperatures in 2005 set a new record but are now tied with 2010 as being the hottest years on record.

Solar energy is absorbed as heat by Earth, where it is radiated back into the atmosphere

Most heat is absorbed by CO_2 in the stratosphere and radiated back to Earth

Sources of 'Greenhouse Gases'

Carbon dioxide
- Exhaust from cars
- Combustion of coal, wood, oil
- Burning rainforests

Methane
- Plant debris and growing vegetation
- Belching and flatus of cows

Chloro-fluoro-carbons (CFCs)
- Leaking coolant from refrigerators
- Leaking coolant from air conditioners

Nitrous oxide
- Car exhaust

Tropospheric ozone*
- Triggered by car exhaust (smog)

*Tropospheric ozone is found in the lower atmosphere (not to be confused with ozone in the stratosphere)

Greenhouse gas	Tropospheric conc.		Global warming potential *(compared to CO_2)*¶	Atmospheric lifetime *(years)*§
	Pre-industrial 1750	Present day (2008*)		
Carbon dioxide	280 ppm	383.9 ppm	1	120
Methane	700 ppb	1796 ppb	25	12
Nitrous oxide	270 ppb	320.5 ppb	310	120
CFCs	0 ppb	0.39 ppb	4000+	50-100
HFCs‡	0 ppb	0.045 ppb	1430	14
Tropospheric ozone	25 ppb	34 ppb	17	hours

ppm = parts per million; **ppb** = parts per billion; ‡Hydrofluorcarbons were introduced in the last decade to replace CFCs as refrigerants; * Data from July 2007-June 2008. ¶ Figures contrast the radiative effect of different greenhouse gases relative to CO_2 over 100 years, e.g. over 100 years, methane is 25 times more potent as a greenhouse gas than CO_2 § How long the gas persists in the atmosphere. *Source: CO_2 Information Analysis Centre, Oak Ridge National Laboratory, USA.*

This graph shows how the mean temperature for each year from 1860-2010 (bars) compares with the average temperature between 1961 and 1990. The black line represents the fitted curve and shows the general trend indicated by the annual data. Most anomalies since 1977 have been above normal; warmer than the long term mean, indicating that global temperatures are tracking upwards. The decade 2001-2010 has been the warmest on record.

Source: Hadley Center for Prediction and Research

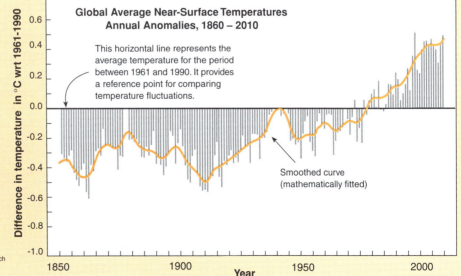

This horizontal line represents the average temperature for the period between 1961 and 1990. It provides a reference point for comparing temperature fluctuations.

Smoothed curve (mathematically fitted)

Periodicals:
Global warming

Related activities: The Atmosphere and Climate, Types of Pollution, Effects of Global Warming   *Weblinks:* The Greenhouse Effect

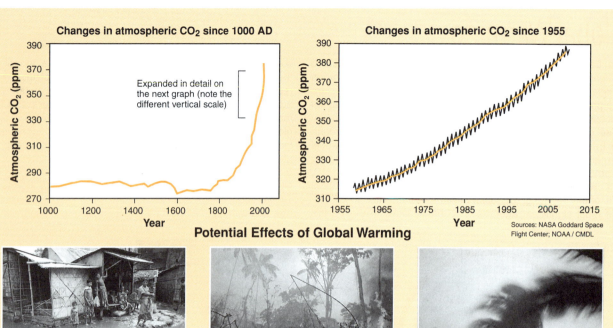

Changes in atmospheric CO₂ since 1000 AD

Expanded in detail on the next graph (note the different vertical scale)

Changes in atmospheric CO₂ since 1955

Sources: NASA Goddard Space Flight Center; NOAA / CMDL

Potential Effects of Global Warming

Sea levels are expected to rise by 50 cm by the year 2100. This is the result of the thermal expansion of ocean water and melting of glaciers and ice shelves. Warming may also expand the habitat for many pests, e.g. mosquitoes, shifting the range of infectious diseases.

Forests: Higher temperatures and precipitation changes could increase forest susceptibility to fire, disease, and insect damage. Forest fires release more carbon into the atmosphere and reduces the size of carbon sinks. A richer CO2 atmosphere will reduce transpiration in plants.

Weather patterns: Global warming may cause regional changes in weather patterns such as El Niño and La Nina, as well as affecting the intensity and frequency of storms. Driven by higher ocean surface temperatures, high intensity hurricanes now occur more frequently.

Water resources: Changes in precipitation and increased evaporation will affect water availability for irrigation, industrial use, drinking, and electricity generation.

Agriculture: Climate change may threaten the viability of important crop-growing regions. Paradoxically, climate change can cause both too much and too little rain.

The ice-albedo effect: Ice has a stabilizing effect on global climate, reflecting nearly all the sun's energy that hits it. As polar ice melts, more of that energy is absorbed by the Earth.

1. Calculate the increase (as a %) in the 'greenhouse gases' between the pre-industrial era and the 2008 measurements (use the data from the table, see facing page). **HINT**: The calculation for carbon dioxide is: $(383.9 - 280) \div 280 \times 100 =$

   (a) Carbon dioxide: _____ (b) Methane: _____ (c) Nitrous oxide: _____

2. Explain the zig-zag nature of the atmospheric CO₂ graph to the above right. _____

   _____

   _____

3. Explain the greenhouse effect and why it is an important process: _____

   _____

   _____

4. Discuss some of the effects global warming will have on human life styles: _____

   _____

   _____

   _____

   _____

Effects of Global Warming

Climate warming is not only an environmental issue; its consequences are interconnected globally and it has implications for economic growth, food security, and world health. A rise in average global temperatures puts greater pressure on species already at risk to adapt, and rates of species loss will accelerate. At least 40% of the world's economy and 80% of the needs of the poor are derived from biological resources, yet the capacity of the current systems to adapt to climate changes puts these resources at risk. The effect on climate change on agriculture and food security depends on a combination of many factors. Higher temperatures can stress plants but will also prolong growing seasons and allow a wider range of crops to be grown. Higher levels of CO_2 speed plant growth and increase resilience to water stress, but warmer temperatures will also extend the range of pests and diseases. Overall, changes in rainfall, increased frequency of severe climatic events, and more soil erosion will influence patterns of agriculture and disease incidence. Humans will have to prepare appropriately for these changes.

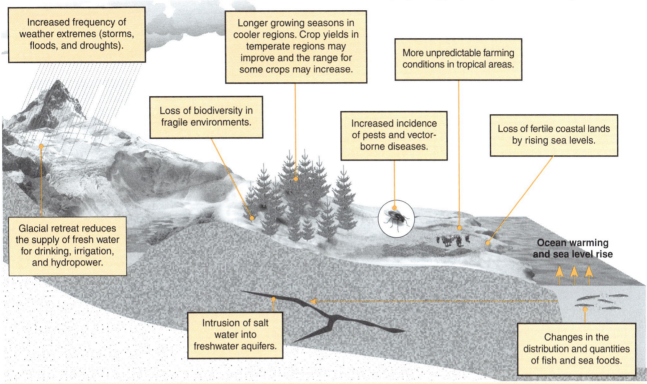

Increased frequency of weather extremes (storms, floods, and droughts).

Longer growing seasons in cooler regions. Crop yields in temperate regions may improve and the range for some crops may increase.

More unpredictable farming conditions in tropical areas.

Loss of biodiversity in fragile environments.

Increased incidence of pests and vector-borne diseases.

Loss of fertile coastal lands by rising sea levels.

Glacial retreat reduces the supply of fresh water for drinking, irrigation, and hydropower.

Ocean warming and sea level rise

Intrusion of salt water into freshwater aquifers.

Changes in the distribution and quantities of fish and sea foods.

Effects of increases in temperature on crop yields

Studies on the grain production of rice have shown that maximum daytime temperatures have little effect on crop yield. However minimum night time temperatures lower crop yield by as much as 5% for every 0.5°C increase in temperature.

Source: Peng S. *et.al.* PNAS 2004

Possible effects of increases in temperature on crop damage

Source: Currano *et.al.* PNAS 2007

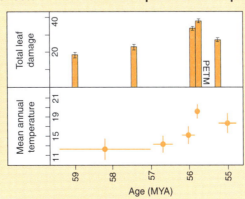

The fossil record shows that global temperatures rose sharply around 56 million years ago. Studies of fossil leaves with insect browse damage indicate that leaf damage peaked at the same time as the Paleocene Eocene Thermal Maximum (PETM). This gives some historical evidence that as temperatures increase, plant damage caused by insects also rises. This could have implications for agricultural crops.

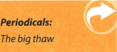

Periodicals:
The big thaw

Related activities: Global Warming

RA 2

Effects of increases in temperature on animal populations

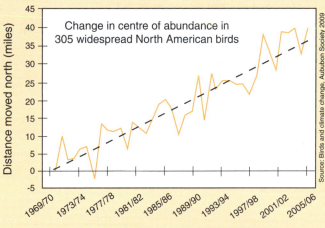

Change in centre of abundance in 305 widespread North American birds

Distance moved north (miles)

Source: Birds and climate change, Aububon Society 2009

A number of studies indicate that animals are beginning to be affected by increases in global temperatures. Data sets from around the world show that birds are migrating up to two weeks earlier to summer feeding grounds and are often not migrating as far south in winter.

Animals living at altitude are also affected by warming climates and are being forced to shift their normal range. As temperatures increase, the snow line increases in altitude pushing alpine animals to higher altitudes. In some areas of North America this has resulting the local extinction of the North American pika (*Ochotona princeps*).

Wiki Commons

1. Global warming is likely to affect the physical environment as well as both the plants and animals inhabiting it:

   (a) Describe some of the likely effects of global warming on physical aspects of the environment: _____

   _____

   _____

   (b) Describe the effects that global warming may have on plant crops: _____

   _____

   _____

   (c) Suggest how farmers might be able to adjust to these changes: _____

   _____

   _____

   (d) Describe how increases in global temperatures have affected some migratory birds: _____

   _____

   _____

   (e) Explain how these changes in migratory patterns might affect food availability for these populations: _____

   _____

   _____

   (f) Explain how global warming could lead to the local extinction of some alpine species: _____

   _____

   _____

   _____

2. Discuss the historical evidence that insect populations are affected by global temperature: _____

   _____

   _____

   _____

Ice Sheet Melting

The surface temperature of the Earth is in part regulated by the amount of ice on its surface, which reflects a large amount of heat into space. However, the area and thickness of the polar sea-ice is rapidly decreasing. From 1980 to 2008 the Arctic summer sea-ice minimum almost halved, decreasing by more than 3 million square kilometers. This melting of sea-ice can trigger a cycle where less heat is reflected into space during summer, warming seawater and reducing the area and thickness of ice forming in the winter. At the current rate of reduction, it is estimated that there may be no summer sea-ice left in the Arctic by 2050.

Arctic sea-ice summer minimum
1980: 7.8 million km²

Arctic sea-ice summer minimum
2007: Record low: 4.33 million km²

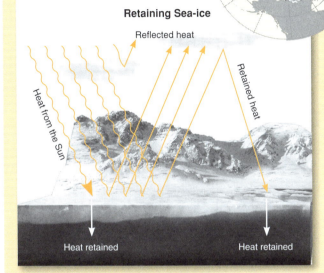

Retaining Sea-ice

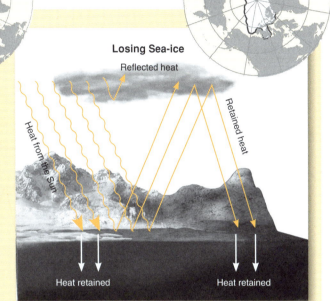

Losing Sea-ice

The **albedo** (reflectivity of sea-ice) helps to maintain its presence. Thin sea-ice has a lower albedo than thick sea-ice. More heat is reflected when sea-ice is thick and covers a greater area. This helps to regulate the temperature of the sea, keeping it cool.

As sea-ice retreats, more non-reflective surface is exposed. Heat is retained instead of being reflected, warming both the air and water and causing sea-ice to form later in the autumn than usual. Thinner and less reflective ice forms and perpetuates the cycle.

The temperature in the Arctic has been above average every year since 1988. Coupled with the reduction in summer sea-ice, this is having dire effects on Arctic wildlife such as polar bears, which hunt out on the ice. The reduction in sea-ice reduces their hunting range and forces them to swim longer distances to firm ice. Studies have already shown an increase in drowning deaths of polar bears.

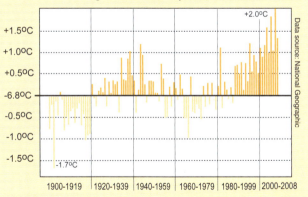

Average* Arctic air temperature fluctuations

Data source: National Geographic

*Figure shows deviation from the average annual surface air temperature over land. Average calculated on the years 1961-2000.

1. Explain how low sea-ice albedo and volume affects the next year's sea-ice cover: _____

_____

_____

2. Discuss the effects of decreasing summer sea-ice on polar wildlife: _____

_____

_____

_____

Periodicals:
Arctic land grab

Related activities: Global Warming

A 2

Ocean Acidification

The oceans act as a **carbon sink,** absorbing much of the CO_2 produced by burning fossil fuels. When CO_2 reacts with water it forms carbonic acid, which decreases the pH of the oceans. This could have major effects on marine life, especially shell making organisms. Ocean acidification is relative term, referring to the oceans becoming less basic as the pH decreases.

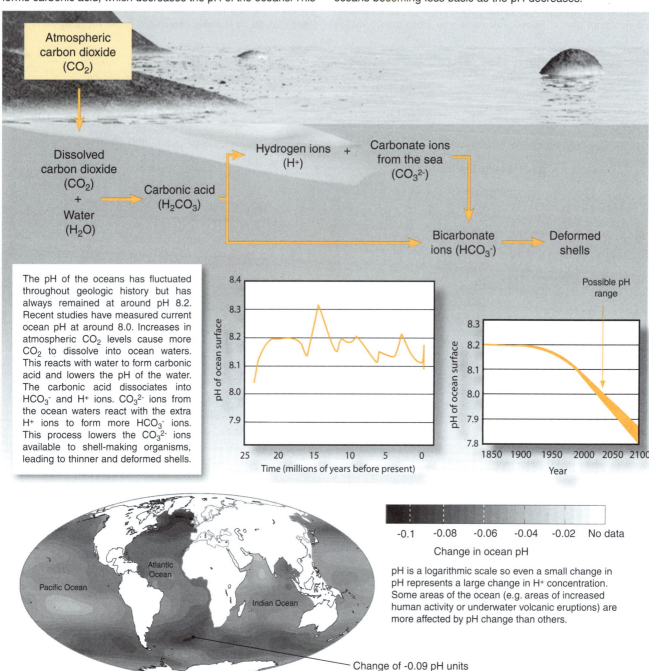

Atmospheric carbon dioxide (CO_2)

Dissolved carbon dioxide (CO_2) + Water (H_2O) → Carbonic acid (H_2CO_3) → Hydrogen ions (H^+) + Carbonate ions from the sea (CO_3^{2-}) → Bicarbonate ions (HCO_3^-) → Deformed shells

The pH of the oceans has fluctuated throughout geologic history but has always remained at around pH 8.2. Recent studies have measured current ocean pH at around 8.0. Increases in atmospheric CO_2 levels cause more CO_2 to dissolve into ocean waters. This reacts with water to form carbonic acid and lowers the pH of the water. The carbonic acid dissociates into HCO_3^- and H^+ ions. CO_3^{2-} ions from the ocean waters react with the extra H^+ ions to form more HCO_3^- ions. This process lowers the CO_3^{2-} ions available to shell-making organisms, leading to thinner and deformed shells.

pH of ocean surface / Time (millions of years before present)

Possible pH range / pH of ocean surface / Year

-0.1 -0.08 -0.06 -0.04 -0.02 No data
Change in ocean pH

pH is a logarithmic scale so even a small change in pH represents a large change in H^+ concentration. Some areas of the ocean (e.g. areas of increased human activity or underwater volcanic eruptions) are more affected by pH change than others.

Change of -0.09 pH units

For questions 1 to 4, circle the letter with the correct answer:

1. Ocean acidification is the process of:

   A. The pH of the oceans rising
   B. The oceans absorbing CO_2
   C. Decreasing concentrations of HCO_3^- ions
   D. The oceans becoming less alkaline

2. Ocean acidification has the effect of:

   A. Increasing the CO_2 absorbed by the oceans
   B. Dissolving seashells
   C. Decreasing the CO_3^{2-} ions available to shell making organisms
   D. Increasing the pH of the oceans

3. The oceanic area most affected by ocean acidification is:

   A. The Indian Ocean, near Australia
   B. The North Atlantic Ocean, near Greenland
   C. The North Pacific near Japan
   D. The Southern Ocean, near Antarctica

4. Even allowing for error, ocean pH in 2100 is predicted to be:

   A. 7.8 Below
   B. 7.9
   C. The same as presently
   D. About the same as 22 mya

5. Describe the relationship between ocean acidity and ocean pH: _____

Related activities: Acid Rain, Effects of Global Warming

Periodicals: Sea life in peril as oceans turn acid

© Biozone International 2007-2011
Photocopying Prohibited

Carbon Trading

Reducing carbon dioxide emissions is a challenge in a world mostly powered by carbon based fossil fuels. One of the proposed strategies to deal with carbon dioxide emissions is the carbon trading scheme based on **carbon credits**. Certain parts of industry, such as forestry and farming, can produce carbon credits by growing plant material. Other companies can buy these carbon credits to offset the carbon dioxide they produce. Each 1000 kg of carbon dioxide is given a credit and these may be bought or sold on an exchange. The value of the carbon credit depends on the demand for and the quality of the credit.

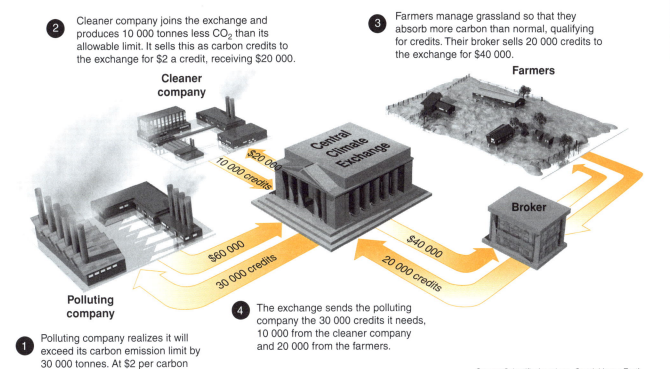

2 Cleaner company joins the exchange and produces 10 000 tonnes less CO_2 than its allowable limit. It sells this as carbon credits to the exchange for $2 a credit, receiving $20 000.

3 Farmers manage grassland so that they absorb more carbon than normal, qualifying for credits. Their broker sells 20 000 credits to the exchange for $40 000.

Farmers

Cleaner company

Central Climate Exchange

$20 000
10 000 credits

Broker

$60 000
30 000 credits

$40 000
20 000 credits

Polluting company

1 Polluting company realizes it will exceed its carbon emission limit by 30 000 tonnes. At $2 per carbon credit, it pays the exchange $60 000.

4 The exchange sends the polluting company the 30 000 credits it needs, 10 000 from the cleaner company and 20 000 from the farmers.

Source: Scientific American, *Special Issue Earth 3.0., Solutions for Sustainable Progress*, 18(5), 2008

Advantages of trading carbon credits	Disadvantages of trading carbon credits
• Caps the amount of carbon dioxide emissions produced. • Makes polluting companies pay a penalty. • May force companies to become more efficient. • Companies that are less polluting or more efficient can sell their extra credits for financial benefit.	• Like any stock market, prices will fluctuate. Very high or low prices will remove incentives to use trade credits. • Many credits are not regulated and may not actually be producing any offsets at all. • The scheme may give large, highly profitable companies a free rein to pollute as they can easily afford credits with expenses being passed on to the consumer.

1. Explain how farmlands are able to generate carbon credits: _____

_____

_____

_____

2. Explain the process of trading credits: _____

_____

_____

3. Discuss the advantages and disadvantages of a carbon trading system: _____

_____

_____

_____

_____

Periodicals:
Carbon cowboys

Related activities: Global Warming, Carbon Capture and Storage
Weblinks: How Does the Emission Trading Scheme Work?

A 2

Carbon Capture and Storage

Coal and oil fired power stations produce around 60% of the world's electricity needs and have traditionally been a major source of air pollution. Even power stations using high quality coal and oil release huge volumes of CO_2 into the atmosphere. This is beginning to be addressed by systems that capture the CO_2 produced so that it can be stored or used for other purposes.

Schematics of Possible Carbon Capture Systems

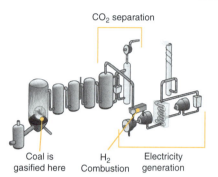

CO₂ separation

Coal is gasified here

H₂ Combustion

Electricity generation

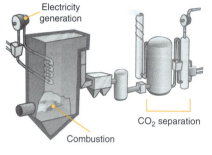

Electricity generation

CO₂ separation

Combustion

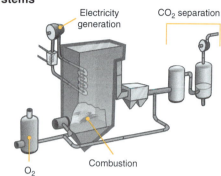

Electricity generation

CO₂ separation

O₂ concentration

Combustion

Pre-combustion capture: The coal is converted to CO_2 and H_2 using a gasification process, The CO_2 is recovered while the H_2 gas is combusted.

Post combustion capture: CO_2 is washed from the flue gas after combustion. It is then passed to a desorber to re-gasify the CO_2, where it is then compressed for storage.

Oxyfuel combustion: Concentrated O_2 is used in the furnace, producing only CO_2 gas in the flue gas. This is then compressed for storage.

Storing Captured CO_2

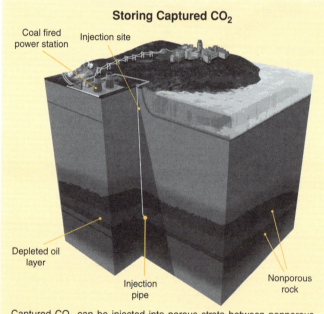

Coal fired power station

Injection site

Depleted oil layer

Injection pipe

Nonporous rock

Captured CO_2 can be injected into porous strata between nonporous layers. Power stations near to injection sites can pipe the recovered CO_2 to the injected well. Other stations will need to transport the CO_2 to the site. The transportation of the CO_2 will, however, produce less CO_2 than that captured by the power station.

Carbon dioxide can be stored by injecting it into depleted oil wells or other deep geological formations, releasing it into deep ocean waters or reacting it with minerals to form carbonates which can be stored as solids. The CO_2 can also be used as a starting point for the production of synthetic fuels.

USGS

There are a number of potential risks associated with CO_2 storage. Deep ocean storage risks lowering ocean pH, while storing CO_2 in geological formations risks sudden release of large quantities of CO_2 if the rock proves unstable. This could be deadly to nearby animal life.

1. Describe the differences and similarities in the three types of carbon dioxide capture systems: _____

_____

_____

2. Describe how captured carbon dioxide might be used or stored: _____

_____

_____

3. Discuss some of the potential problems with capturing and storing carbon dioxide: _____

_____

_____

_____

Related activities: Carbon Trading, Ocean Acidification
Weblinks: What is Carbon Capture and Storage?

Periodicals:
Cleaning up coal

© Biozone International 2007-2011
Photocopying Prohibited

Loss of Biodiversity

The species is the basic unit by which we measure biological diversity or **biodiversity**. Biodiversity is not distributed evenly on Earth, being consistently richer in the tropics and concentrated more in some areas than in others. Conservation International recognises 25 **biodiversity hotspots**. These are biologically diverse and ecologically distinct regions under the greatest threat of destruction. They are identified on the basis of the number of species present, the amount of **endemism**, and the extent to which the species are threatened. More than a third of the planet's known terrestrial plant and animal species are found in these 25 regions, which cover only 1.4% of the Earth's land area. Unfortunately, biodiversity hotspots often occur near areas of dense human habitation and rapid human population growth. Most are located in the tropics and most are forests. Loss of biodiversity reduces the stability and resilience of natural ecosystems and decreases the ability of their communities to adapt to changing environmental conditions. With increasing pressure on natural areas from urbanisation, roading, and other human encroachment, maintaining species diversity is paramount and should concern us all today.

Biodiversity Hotspots

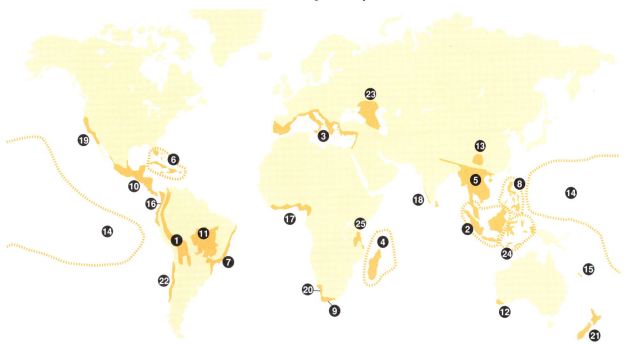

Threats to Biodiversity

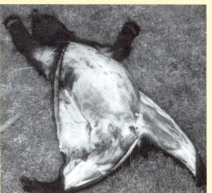

Habitat destruction is one of the greatest threats to willife. Deliberate destruction, such as logging, removes thousands of hectares of habitat a year, but accidental destriction, such as oil spills and industrial accidents, can be almost as bad.

Illegal trade in species (for food, body parts, or for the exotic pet trade) is pushing some species to the brink of extinction. Despite international bans on trade, illegal trade in primates, parrots, reptiles, and big cats (among others) continues.

Pollution and the pressure of human populations on natural habitats threatens biodiversity in many regions. Environmental pollutants may accumulate through food chains or cause harm directly, as with this bird trapped in oil.

1. Use your research tools (e.g. textbook, internet, or encyclopaedia) to identify each of the 25 biodiversity hotspots illustrated in the diagram above. For each region, summarise the characteristics that have resulted in it being identified as a biodiversity hotspot. Present your summary as a short report and attach it to this page of your workbook.

2. Identify the threat to biodiversity that you perceive to be the most important and explain your choice:

_____

_____

_____

Related activities: Ecosystem Stability, Endangered Species, The Impact of Alien Species

RA 2

Tropical Deforestation

Tropical rainforests prevail in places where the climate is very moist throughout the year (200 to 450 cm of rainfall per year). Almost half of the world's rainforests are in just three countries: **Indonesia** in Southeast Asia, **Brazil** in South America, and **Zaire** in Africa. Much of the world's biodiversity resides in rainforests. Destruction of the forests will contribute towards global warming through a large reduction in photosynthesis. In the Amazon, 75% of deforestation has occurred within 50 km of Brazil's roads. Many potential drugs could still be discovered in rainforest plants, and loss of species through deforestation may mean they will never be found. Rainforests can provide economically sustainable crops (rubber, coffee, nuts, fruits, and oils) for local people.

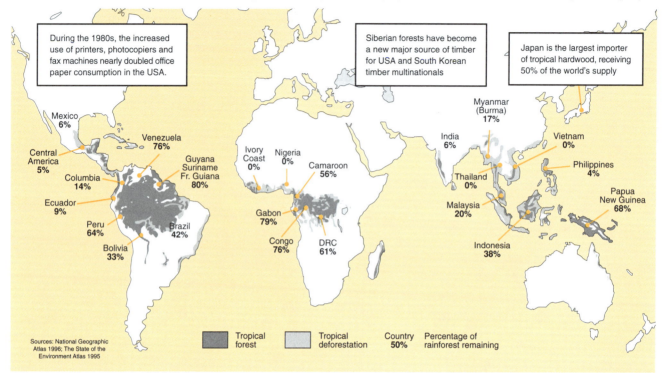

During the 1980s, the increased use of printers, photocopiers and fax machines nearly doubled office paper consumption in the USA.

Siberian forests have become a new major source of timber for USA and South Korean timber multinationals

Japan is the largest importer of tropical hardwood, receiving 50% of the world's supply

Mexico 6%
Central America 5%
Columbia 14%
Ecuador 9%
Peru 64%
Bolivia 33%
Venezuela 76%
Guyana Suriname Fr. Guiana 80%
Brazil 42%
Ivory Coast 0%
Nigeria 0%
Camaroon 56%
Gabon 79%
Congo 76%
DRC 61%
Myanmar (Burma) 17%
India 6%
Thailand 0%
Malaysia 20%
Vietnam 0%
Philippines 4%
Papua New Guinea 68%
Indonesia 38%

Sources: National Geographic Atlas 1996; The State of the Environment Atlas 1995

| | Tropical forest | | Tropical deforestation | Country 50% | Percentage of rainforest remaining |

The felling of rainforest trees is taking place at an alarming rate as world demand for tropical hardwoods increases and land is cleared for the establishment of agriculture. The resulting farms and plantations often have shortlived productivity.

Huge forest fires have devastated large amounts of tropical rainforest in Indonesia and Brazil in 1997/98. The fires in Indonesia were started by people attempting to clear the forest areas for farming in a year of particularly low rainfall.

The building of new road networks into regions with tropical rainforests causes considerable environmental damage. In areas with very high rainfall there is an increased risk of erosion and loss of topsoil.

1. Describe three reasons why tropical rainforests should be conserved:

(a) _____

(b) _____

(c) _____

2. Identify the three main human activities that cause tropical deforestation and describe their detrimental effects:

_____

_____

_____

Related activities: Loss of Biodiversity

Periodicals:
The last of the Amazon

The Impact of Alien Species

Alien species is a term used to describe those organisms that have evolved at one place in the world and have been transported by humans, either intentionally or in advertently, to another region. Some of these alien species are beneficial, e.g. introduced agricultural plants and animals, and Japanese clams and oysters (the mainstays of global shellfish industries). **Invasive species** are those alien species that have a detrimental effect on the ecosystems into which they have been imported. They number in their hundreds with varying degrees of undesirability to humans. Humans have brought many exotic species into new environments for use as pets, food, ornamental specimens, or decoration, while others have hitched a ride with cargo shipments or in the ballast water of ships. Some have been deliberately introduced to control another pest species and have themselves become a problem. Some of the most destructive of all alien species are aggressive plants, e.g. mile-a-minute weed, a perennial vine from Central and South America, miconia, a South American tree invading Hawaii and Tahiti, and *Caulerpa* seaweed, the aquarium strain now found in the Mediterranean. Two animal aliens, one introduced unintentionally and other deliberately, are described below.

Brushtail Possum

A deliberate introduction

The brushtail possum (*Trichosurus vulpecula*) was deliberately introduced to New Zealand from its native Australia in the 1800s to supply the fur trade. In the absence of natural predators and with an abundance of palatable food, possums have devastated New Zealand's flora and fauna. They are voracious omnivores where they selectively feed on the most vulnerable plant parts and eat the eggs and nestlings of birds, and compete with native species for food. There are now more than 70 million of them and they are widespread throughout the country. Possums also carry bovine tuberculosis and pose a risk to livestock in regions bordering farmed lands.

Red Imported Fire Ant

An accidental invasion

Red fire ants (*Solenopsis invicta*) were accidentally introduced into the United States from South America in the 1920s and have spread north each year from their foothold in the Southeast. Red fire ants are now resident in 14 US states where they displace populations of native insects and ground-nesting wildlife. They also damage crops and are very aggressive, inflicting a nasty sting. The USDA estimates damage and control costs for red fire ants at more than $6 billion a year. Red fire ants lack natural control agents in North America and thrive in disturbed habitats such as agricultural lands, where they feed on cereal crops and build large mounded nests.

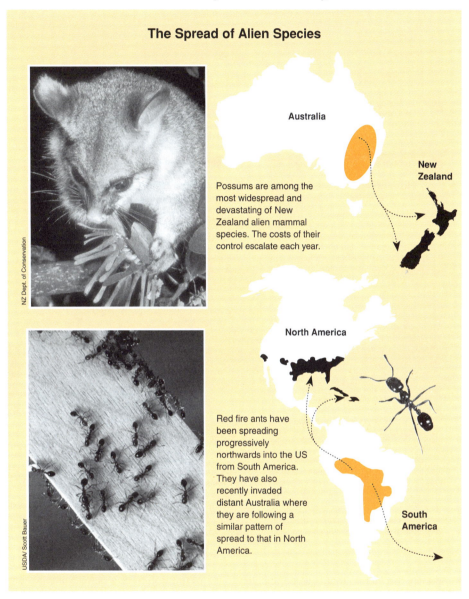

The Spread of Alien Species

NZ Dept. of Conservation

USDA / Scott Bauer

Australia

New Zealand

Possums are among the most widespread and devastating of New Zealand alien mammal species. The costs of their control escalate each year.

North America

Red fire ants have been spreading progressively northwards into the US from South America. They have also recently invaded distant Australia where they are following a similar pattern of spread to that in North America.

South America

1. Give an example of an alien species and discuss the impact it has had on a named ecosystem:

_____

_____

_____

_____

2. Explain why many alien species become invasive when introduced to a new area: _____

_____

_____

_____

Related activities: *Interspecific Competition, Integrated Pest Management*
Weblinks: *Fire Ants Invade and Evolve*

RA 2

Endangered Species

Species under threat of severe population loss or extinction are classified as either **endangered** or threatened. An endangered species is one with so few individuals that it is at high risk of local extinction, while a threatened (or vulnerable) species is likely to become endangered in the near future. While **extinctions** are a natural phenomenon, the rapid increase in the rates of species extinction in recent decades is of major concern. It is estimated that every day up to 200 species become extinct as a result of human activity. Even if a species is preserved from extinction, remaining populations may be too small to be genetically viable. Human population growth, rising non-sustainable resource use, poverty, and lack of environmental accountability are the underlying causes of premature extinction of organisms. The two biggest direct causes are habitat loss, fragmentation, or degradation and the accidental or deliberate introduction of non-native species into ecosystems.

Causes of Species Decline

Commercial and "scientific" whaling

Hunting and Collecting

Species may be hunted or collected legally for commercial gain often because of poor control over the rate and scale of hunting. Some species are hunted because they interfere with human use of an area. Illegal trade and specimen collection threatens the population viability of some species.

Clear felling of native rainforest

Habitat Destruction

Natural habitat can be lost through clearance for agriculture, urban development and land reclamation, or trampling and vegetation destruction by introduced pest plants and animals. Habitats potentially suitable for a threatened species may be too small and isolated to support a viable population.

Weasel with stolen egg   DoC

Introduced Exotic Species

Introduced predators (e.g. rats, mustelids, and cats) prey on endangered birds and invertebrates. Introduced grazing and browsing animals (e.g. deer, goats) damage sensitive plants and trample vegetation. Weeds may out-compete endemic species.

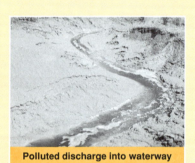

Polluted discharge into waterway

Pollution

Toxic substances released by humans into the environment, e.g. from industry, cause harm directly or accumulate in food chains. Estuaries, wetlands, river systems and coastal ecosystems near urban areas are particularly vulnerable.

Case Study: Black Rhinoceros

Black rhinoceros *(Diceros bicornis)* were once plentiful throughout much of Africa. Now, only remnant populations remain. In Kenya, 98% of the population was lost in only 17 years.

Dehorning programs (above) carried out in Zimbabwe in 1991 have not halted the slaughter. Large numbers of dehorned rhinos are still being shot; conservationists suspect that a trader with a large stockpile of horn is trying to cause rhinoceros extinction in order to increase the horn's value.

1. Identify the factors that have contributed to the **extinction** of one named animal species: _____

_____

2. Describe two good reasons why any species should be preserved from extinction:

   (a) _____

   _____

   (b) _____

   _____

3. (a) Name an **endangered species** from your own country: _____

   (b) Describe the probable cause of its decline: _____

   _____

Related activities: Loss of Biodiversity, Conservation of African Elephants, Nature Reserves

Extinction

Extinction is an important process in evolution as it provides opportunities, in the form of vacant niches, for the development of new species. Most species that have ever lived are now extinct. The species alive today make up only a fraction of the total list of species that have lived on Earth throughout its history. Extinction is a natural process in the life cycle of a species. Background extinction is the steady rate of species turnover in a taxonomic group (a group of related species). The duration of a species is thought to range from as little as 1 million years for complex larger organisms, to as long as 10-20 million years for simpler organisms. Superimposed on this constant background extinction are catastrophic events that wipe out vast numbers of species in relatively brief periods of time in geological terms. The diagram below shows how the number of species has varied over the history of life on Earth. The number of species is indicated on the graph by families; a taxonomic group comprising many genera and species. There have been five major extinction events and two of these have been intensively studied by palaeontologists.

Major Mass Extinctions

The Permian extinction
(225 million years ago)

This was the most devastating mass extinction of all. Nearly all life on Earth perished, with 90% of marine species and probably many terrestrial ones also, disappearing from the fossil record. This extinction event marks the **Paleozoic-Mesozoic** boundary.

The Cretaceous extinction
(65 million years ago)

This extinction event marks the boundary between the Mesozoic and Cenozoic eras. More than half the marine species and many families of terrestrial plants and animals became extinct, including nearly all the dinosaur species (the birds are now known to be direct descendants of the dinosaurs).

Megafaunal extinction
(10 000 years ago)

This mass extinction occurred when many giant species of mammal died out. This is known as the Pleistocene overkill because their disappearance was probably hastened by the hunting activities of prehistoric humans. Many large marsupials in Australia and placental species elsewhere became extinct.

The sixth extinction
(now)

The current mass extinction is largely due to human destruction of habitats (e.g. coral reefs, tropical forests) and pollution. It is considered far more serious and damaging than some earlier mass extinctions because of the speed at which it is occurring. The increasing human impact is making biotic recovery difficult.

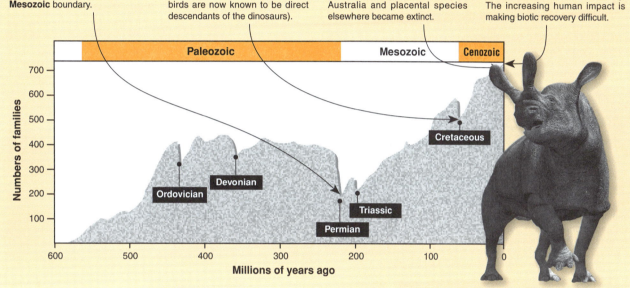

Threatened and Endangered Animal Populations

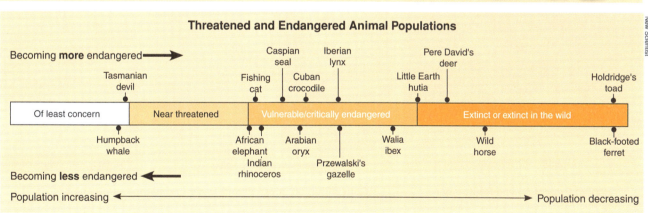

New Scientist

1. Explain how the most recent extinction is different from other mass extinctions: _____

_____

_____

_____

_____

_____

In-Situ Conservation

One of the concerns facing conservationists today is the rapidly accelerating rate at which species are being lost. In 1992, the **Convention on Biological Diversity** was adopted in Rio de Janeiro. It is an international treaty and its aims are to conserve biodiversity, use biodiversity in a sustainable way, and ensure that the benefits of genetic resources are shared equitably. Various strategies are available to protect at-risk species and help the recovery of those that are threatened. *In-situ* methods focus on ecological restoration and legislation to protect ecosystems of special value. Ecological restoration is a long term process and usually involves collaborative work between institutions with scientific expertise and the local communities involved.

Every country in the world has endangered species, some more than others. In the United States alone there are at least 1000 species of threatened or endangered animals and over 500 species of endangered plants. In 1973, the **Endangered Species Act** (**ESA**) became law in the US. Its purpose is to protect species and the ecosystems on which they depend. The act is administered by the US Fish and Wildlife Service and the National Oceanic and Atmospheric Administration. As a result of this and other efforts, species such as the snowy egret, white tailed deer, and wild turkey, which were all critically endangered by the early 1900s, are common once again.

A major New Zealand strategy is the protection and restoration of **mainland islands.** These are sites of ecological importance which are used to rebuild native populations of animals and plants. Methods include predator proof fencing around large tracts of forest, pest control, species translocations, and public education and volunteer programs.

Advantages of *in-situ* conservation

- Species left in the protected area have access to their natural resources and breeding sites.
- Species will continue develop and evolve in their natural environment without human influence, thus conserving their natural behavior.
- *In-situ* conservation is able to protect more species at once and allow them greater space than those in captivity.
- *In-situ* conservation protects larger breeding populations.
- *In-situ* conservation is less expensive and requires fewer specialized facilities than captive breeding.

Disadvantages of *in-situ* conservation

- It is difficult to control illegal exploitation of *in-situ* populations (especially in remote areas).
- Habitats that shelter *in-situ* populations may need extensive restoration, including pest eradication and ongoing control.
- Populations may continue to decline during restoration.

In-situ conservation requires a lot of effort initially to restore sites and eradicate pests.

Woodland-pond restoration (UK)

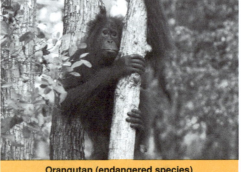

Orangutan (endangered species)

Confiscated ivory, Kenya

Habitat Protection and Restoration

Most countries have a system of reserve lands focused on ecosystem conservation. These areas aim to protect and restore habitats of special importance and they may be intensively managed through pest and weed control, revegetation, reintroduction of threatened species, and site specific management practices (such as coppicing).

Convention on International Trade in Endangered Species (CITES)

CITES is an international agreement between governments which aims to ensure that trade in species of wild animals and plants does not threaten their survival. CITES comprises more than 150 member nations and includes virtually all important wildlife producing and consuming countries. Trade in over 40,000 species is controlled or prohibited depending on their level of threat. In 1989, CITES imposed a global ban on the international trade in ivory and ivory products (above) in a move that has helped enormously in reducing the slaughter of elephants.

1. Explain why *in-situ* conservation commonly involves both ecosystem restoration and legislation to protect species:

_____

_____

_____

_____

Related activities: Loss of Biodiversity, Ex-Situ Conservation

Periodicals: Conflicted conservation

Ex-Situ Conservation

Ex-situ conservation methods operate away from the natural environment and are particularly useful where species are critically endangered. Zoos, aquaria, and botanical gardens are the most conventional vehicles for *ex-situ* conservation. They house and protect specimens for breeding and, where necessary and possible, they reintroduce them into the wild to restore natural populations. Many zoos and botanical gardens support or finance in both *in-situ* and *ex-situ* conservation efforts and collaborate with each other in exchanging animals or plants to maintain genetically diverse breeding groups conservation efforts. The maintenance of seedbanks by botanic gardens and breeding registers by zoos has been particularly important in ensuring that these efforts to conserve species are not impaired by problems of inbreeding. Some animal species respond more favorably to captive breeding and relocation efforts than others. Those implementing captive breeding programmes are faced with balancing the needs of the animals in captivity, while not inadvertently selecting for features that make survival in the wild less likely.

Captive Breeding and Relocation

Individuals are captured and bred under protected conditions. If breeding programs are successful and there is suitable habitat available, captive individuals may be relocated to the wild where they can establish natural populations. Zoos now have an active role in captive breeding. There are problems with captive breeding; individuals are inadvertently selected for fitness in a captive environment and their survival in the wild may be compromised. this is especially so for marine species. However, for some taxa, such as reptiles, birds, and small mammals, captive rearing is very successful.

Above: England is home to a rare sub-species of sand lizard (Lacerta agilis). it is restricted to southern heathlands and the coastal sand dunes of north west England. The UK Herpetological Conservation Trust is the lead partner in the action plan for this species and Chester Zoo hosts a captive breeding colony.

Right: A puppet 'mother' shelters a takahe chick. Takahe, a rare rail species native to New Zealand, were brought back from the brink of extinction through a successful captive breeding programme.

In New Zealand, introduced predatory mammals, including weasels and stoats, have decimated native bird life. Relocation of birds on to predator-free islands or into areas that have been cleared of predators has been instrumental in the recovery of some species such as the North Island kokako. Sadly, others have been lost forever.

The Important Role of Zoos and Aquaria

As well as keeping their role in captive breeding programmes and as custodians of rare species, zoos have a major role in public education. They raise awareness of the threats facing species in their natural environments and engender public empathy for conservation work. Modern zoos tend to concentrate on particular species and are part of global programmes that work together to help retain genetic diversity in captive bred animals.

Above: The okapi is a species of rare forest antelope related to giraffes. Okapi are only found naturally in the Ituri Forest, in the northeastern rainforests of the Democratic Republic of Congo (DRC), Africa, an area at the front line of an ongoing civil war. A okapi calf was born to Bristol Zoo Gardens in 2009, one of only about 100 okapi in captivity.

1. Describe the key features of *ex-situ* conservation methods: _____

2. Explain why some animal species are more well suited to *ex-situ* conservation efforts than others:

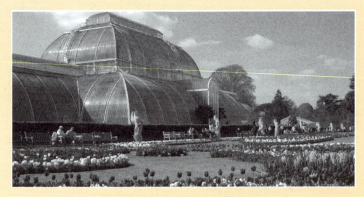

The Role of Botanic Gardens

Botanic gardens have years of collective expertise and resources and play a critical role in plant conservation. They maintain seed banks, nurture rare species, maintain a living collection of plants, and help to conserve indigenous plant knowledge. They also have an important role in both research and education. The Royal Botanic Gardens at Kew (above) contain an estimated 25,000 species, 2700 of which are classified by the ICUN as rare, threatened, or endangered. Kew Gardens are involved in both national and international projects associated with the conservation of botanical diversity and are the primary advisors to CITES on threatened plant species. Kew's Millennium Seed Bank partnership is the largest *ex situ* plant conservation project in the world; working with a network in over 50 countries they have banked 10% of the world's wild plant species.

Seedbanks and Gene Banks

Seedbanks and gene banks around the world have a role in preserving the genetic diversity of species. A seedbank (above) stores seeds as a source for future planting in case seed reserves elsewhere are lost. The seeds may be from rare species whose genetic diversity is at risk, or they may be the seeds of crop plants, in some cases of ancient varieties no longer used in commercial production.

3. Describe three key roles of zoos and aquaria and explain the importance of each:

(a) _____

_____

(b) _____

_____

(c) _____

_____

4. Explain the importance of gene and seed banks, both to conservation and to agriculture: _____

_____

_____

_____

5. Compare and contrast *in-situ* and *ex-situ* methods of conservation, including reference to the advantages and disadvantages of each approach:

_____

_____

_____

_____

_____

_____

_____

_____

_____

_____

Nature Reserves

Conservation on a national scale generally involves setting up reserves or protected areas to slow the loss of biodiversity. **Nature reserves** may be designated by government institutions in some countries or by private landowners. The different types of nature reserves, e.g. wildlife, scenic and scientific reserves, and National Parks, all have varying levels of protection depending upon country and local laws. **National parks** are usually located in places which have been largely undeveloped, and they often feature areas with exceptional ecosystems such as those with endangered species, high biodiversity, or unusual geological

features. Canada's National Parks are a country-wide system of representative natural areas of Canadian significance. They are protected by law for public understanding, appreciation, and enjoyment, while being maintained for future generations. National parks have existed in Canada for well over a century. Some 11% of public lands (336 000 km²) of the USA are in National Parks and Preserves, which protect natural resources, while allowing restricted activities. National wildlife refuges form a network across the USA, with at least one in every state. They provide habitat for endangered species, migratory birds, and big game.

Parks and Reserves in North America

Alaska contains more than half of the total acreage of the park system. It is rich in diversity and shelters a wealth of wildlife.

Mountain bighorn sheep (*Ovis canadensis*) exist mostly in small, isolated populations within their former vast range. Thes populations are at risk of local extinction.

The **gray wolf** (*Canis lupus*) inhabits tundra and open forests throughout Canada and Alaska. More recently, they have been reintroduced into parts of their former range in Northwestern Montana, Central Idaho, and the Greater Yellowstone.

Mountain lions (*Felis concolor*) have a wide distribution throughout northwestern Canada and USA. Their range is continuing to expand eastwards.

Hawaii
Hawaii's federal domain Haleakala National Park (1) is known for its immense crater and rare plants, including the endemic silversword (right). Hawaii Volcanoes National Park (2) has two of the world's most active volcanoes.

Bison (*Bison bison*) have been released into parks and refuges of open woodlands and prairies in North America.

Greater prairie chicken (*Dipsosaurus dorsalis*) inhabit the creosote-bush desert of central USA. Critically imperiled in Illinois, Iowa, Missouri, Texas and Wyoming.

■ Wildlife refuges
■ National Parks

The **Canada goose** (*Branta canadensis*) is North America's commonest goose inhabiting ponds, lakes, bays, estuaries and grasslands throughout Canada and in 49 of the 50 US states.

1. Discuss the importance of national parks and reserves, including conservation, recreational and tourism uses:

_____

_____

_____

_____

_____

_____

Related activities: In-Situ Conservation, Endangered Species, Conservation of African Elephants, Loss of Biodiversity

RA 3

Both New Zealand and Australia protect large land and marine areas as national parks or nature reserves. In New Zealand, national parks are administered by the **Department of Conservation** (DoC). New Zealand also has many offshore islands that are used as predator free sanctuaries for rebuilding populations of threatened species. Many of these have restricted access, with permits required for visitors. Australia's **National Reserve System** comprises over 9300 protected areas including national parks, indigenous lands, and privately protected land. It is governed by a scientific framework based on obtaining a *"comprehensive, adequate and representative system of protected areas"*.

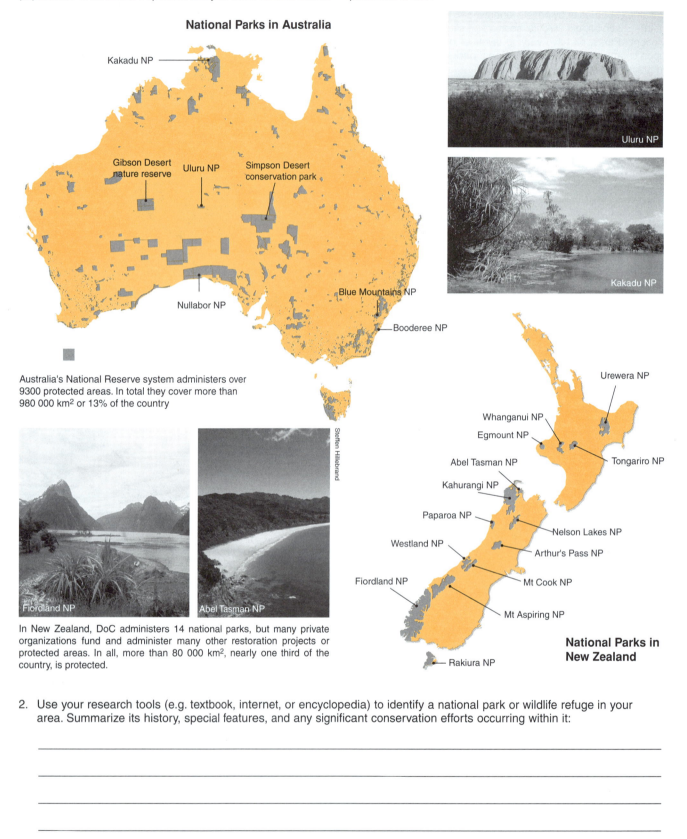

National Parks in Australia

Kakadu NP

Gibson Desert nature reserve
Uluru NP
Simpson Desert conservation park

Nullabor NP

Blue Mountains NP

Booderee NP

Uluru NP

Kakadu NP

Australia's National Reserve system administers over 9300 protected areas. In total they cover more than 980 000 km² or 13% of the country

Fiordland NP

Abel Tasman NP

Steffen Hillebrand

In New Zealand, DoC administers 14 national parks, but many private organizations fund and administer many other restoration projects or protected areas. In all, more than 80 000 km², nearly one third of the country, is protected.

Urewera NP

Whanganui NP
Egmount NP
Abel Tasman NP
Kahurangi NP
Paparoa NP
Westland NP
Fiordland NP

Tongariro NP

Nelson Lakes NP
Arthur's Pass NP
Mt Cook NP
Mt Aspiring NP

Rakiura NP

National Parks in New Zealand

2. Use your research tools (e.g. textbook, internet, or encyclopedia) to identify a national park or wildlife refuge in your area. Summarize its history, special features, and any significant conservation efforts occurring within it:

_____

_____

_____

_____

_____

_____

_____

_____

The UK's natural environment has a long history of human exploitation and is highly modified as a result. Few areas have escaped modification. The main government agencies for conservation in the UK are **English Nature** (England), **Scottish Nature Heritage** (Scotland), and **The Countryside Council for Wales** (Wales). These agencies are supported by a number of voluntary organizations that provide an additional source of expertise, labor, and finance for assisting conservation work.

Protected Habitats in the United Kingdom

National Parks: There are currently 7 National Parks in England and 3 in Wales. While Scotland and Northern Ireland do not have National Parks, they do have essentially equivalent areas in the form of Regional Parks (Scotland) and Areas of Outstanding Beauty (Northern Ireland). Legislation permits some farming, forestry and quarrying within these parks.

Sites of Special Scientific Interest (SSSIs): These are notified by the government agency because of their plants, animals, or geological or physiographical features. In England, about 40% are owned or managed by public bodies or by the Crown (e.g. Ministry of Defence).

Environmentally Sensitive Areas (ESAs): These are areas in the UK whose environmental significance is a result of particular farming practices. If these methods change, then the ecological value of the area will decline. To preserve these areas, restrictions are imposed on the practices allowed.

National Nature Reserves (NNRs): These are sites which have been assigned as reserves under government legislation. They are either owned or controlled by government agencies or held by approved non-governmental organizations.

Marine Nature Reserves (MNRs): In England, these are declared by the Secretary of State for the Environment. At present there two: one in England and one in Wales.

Condition of SSSIs (March 2002)

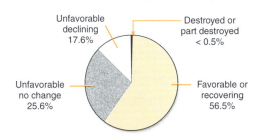

Unfavorable declining 17.6%

Destroyed or part destroyed < 0.5%

Unfavorable no change 25.6%

Favorable or recovering 56.5%

National Parks in the United Kingdom

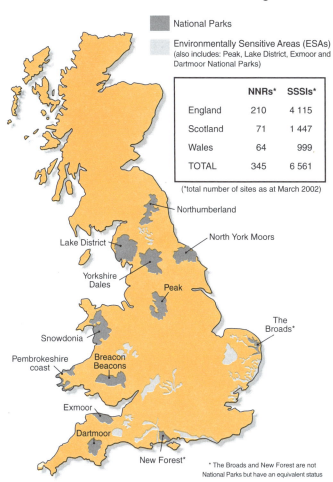

■ National Parks

□ Environmentally Sensitive Areas (ESAs) (also includes: Peak, Lake District, Exmoor and Dartmoor National Parks)

	NNRs*	SSSIs*
England	210	4 115
Scotland	71	1 447
Wales	64	999
TOTAL	345	6 561

(*total number of sites as at March 2002)

Northumberland
North York Moors
Lake District
Yorkshire Dales
Peak
Snowdonia
The Broads*
Pembrokeshire coast
Breacon Beacons
Exmoor
Dartmoor
New Forest*

* The Broads and New Forest are not National Parks but have an equivalent status

The Role of Non-Governmental Organizations

Private organizations and charities play an important role in protecting natural areas. They supplement the role of public departments and increase the area under protection while keeping public costs down. **The Nature Conservancy** is one such organization. The mission of the Conservancy is to preserve the plants, animals, and natural communities that represent the diversity of life on Earth, by protecting the lands and waters they need to survive. With donations from over a million members, the Conservancy has purchased over 69 000 km^2 in the USA and a further 470 000 km^2 outside the USA (an area greater than the combined size of Costa Rica, Honduras and Panama). Larger nature reserves usually promote conservation of biodiversity more effectively than smaller ones, with **habitat corridors** for wildlife and **edge effects** also playing a part.

The Great Sand Dunes National Park in Colorado was in part created by the influence and funds of the Nature Conservancy. It covers 340 km^2.

3. Explain why private organizations play such an important role in conservation: _____

_____

_____

_____

_____

_____

Conservation of African Elephants

Both African and Asian elephant species are under threat of extinction. The International Union for the Conservation of Nature (**IUCN**) has rated the Asian elephant as endangered and the African elephant as vulnerable. In India, the human pressure on wild habitat has increased by 40% in the last 20 years. Where elephants live in close proximity to agricultural areas they raid crops and come into conflict with humans. The ivory trade represents the greatest threat to the African elephant. Elephant tusks have been sought after for centuries as a material for jewellery and artworks. In Africa, elephant numbers declined from 1.3 million to 600 000 during the 1980s. At this time, as many as 2000 elephants were killed for their tusks every week. By the late 1980s, elephant populations continued to fall in many countries, despite the investment of large amounts of money in fighting poaching. From 1975 to 1989 the ivory trade was regulated under CITES, and permits were required for international trading. Additional protection came in 1989, when the African elephant was placed on *Appendix I* of CITES, which imposed a ban on trade in elephant produce. In 1997 Botswana, Namibia, and Zimbabwe, together with South Africa in 2000, were allowed to transfer their elephant populations from Appendix I to Appendix II, allowing limited commercial trade in raw ivory. In 2002, CITES then approved the sale, to Japan, of legally stockpiled ivory by Namibia, South Africa, and Botswana. African countries have welcomed this decision, although there is still great concern that such a move may trigger the reemergence of a fashion for ivory goods and illegal trade.

Two subspecies of African elephant *Loxodonta africana* are currently recognized: the **savannah elephant** *(L. a. africana)* and the less common **forest elephant** *(L. a. cyclotis)*. Recent evidence from mitochondrial DNA indicates that they may, in fact, be two distinct species.

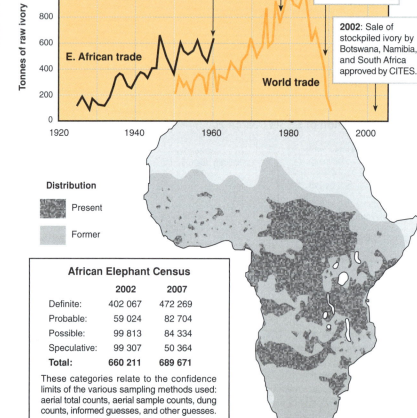

1960: From 1960 onwards, figures for African exports are unreliable because of political unrest.

1975: CITES intervention which regulated the trade in ivory

1989: World wide ban on trade in ivory

2002: Sale of stockpiled ivory by Botswana, Namibia, and South Africa approved by CITES.

Distribution

- Present
- Former

In 1989 the Kenyan government publicly burned 12 tonnes of confiscated ivory. With the increased awareness, the United States and several European countries banned ivory imports. The photo above shows game wardens weighing confiscated ivory tusks and rhinoceros horns.

African Elephant Census

	2002	2007
Definite:	402 067	472 269
Probable:	59 024	82 704
Possible:	99 813	84 334
Speculative:	99 307	50 364
Total:	**660 211**	**689 671**

These categories relate to the confidence limits of the various sampling methods used: aerial total counts, aerial sample counts, dung counts, informed guesses, and other guesses.

Source: **African Elephant Database (IUCN)**; (2002/2007) The website can be accessed via *Bio Links* from Biozone's website.

1. Outline the action taken in 1989 to try and stop the decline of the elephant populations in Africa: _____

_____

_____

2. In early 1999, Zimbabwe, Botswana and Namibia were allowed a one-off, CITES-approved, experimental sale of ivory to Japan. This involved the sale of 5446 tusks (50 tonnes) and earned the governments approximately US$5 million.

   (a) Suggest why these countries wish to resume ivory exports: _____

   _____

   (b) Suggest two reasons why the legal trade in ivory is thought by some to put the remaining elephants at risk:

   _____

   _____

Related activities: Endangered Species

Conservation and Sustainability

Conservation is a term describing the management of a resource so that it is maintained into the future. It encompasses resources of all kinds, from plant and animal populations to mineral resources. Resource conservation has become an important theme in the twenty-first century as the rate of resource use by the expanding human population increases markedly. **Sustainability** refers to the management so that the system or resource is replenished at least at same rate at which it is used. Sustainability is based on the idea of using resources within the capacity of the environment. As such, it allows for managed development and resource use. In contrast, **preservation** aims to keep untouched resources or habitats in their pristine state, without human interference.

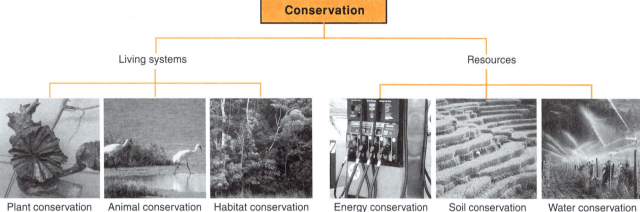

| Plant conservation | Animal conservation | Habitat conservation | Energy conservation | Soil conservation | Water conservation |

The conservation of living systems focuses heavily on the management of endangered species so that their numbers remain stable or increase over time. Many living systems have no directly measurable economic value but are important for global biodiversity. Many people also support the moral value of conserving as many living systems as possible and that humans do not have the right to exterminate other organisms.

Conservation of resources focuses on the efficient use of resources so that remaining stocks are not wasted. Many of these resources are scarce or economically important so require prudent use. Others are damaging to the environment and it is better to use less of them. In recent decades, there has been a growing acknowledgement that humans cannot afford to continue to waste natural resources.

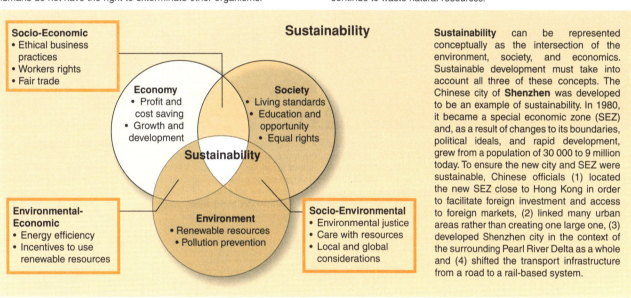

Sustainability can be represented conceptually as the intersection of the environment, society, and economics. Sustainable development must take into account all three of these concepts. The Chinese city of **Shenzhen** was developed to be an example of sustainability. In 1980, it became a special economic zone (SEZ) and, as a result of changes to its boundaries, political ideals, and rapid development, grew from a population of 30 000 to 9 million today. To ensure the new city and SEZ were sustainable, Chinese officials (1) located the new SEZ close to Hong Kong in order to facilitate foreign investment and access to foreign markets, (2) linked many urban areas rather than creating one large one, (3) developed Shenzhen city in the context of the surrounding Pearl River Delta as a whole and (4) shifted the transport infrastructure from a road to a rail-based system.

1. Explain the relationship between conservation and sustainability: _____

_____

_____

2. Explain how conservation differs from preservation and describe situations in which each might be appropriate:

_____

_____

_____

3. Discuss the impact of society and economy on the conservation of living systems and resources:

_____

_____

_____

Related activities: Nature Reserves, Endangered Species

A 3

Saving the Black Robin

There have been many environmental disasters as a direct or indirect result of human operations. However, humans have also been at the forefront of some great environmental achievements as well. New Zealand is home to many endangered birds, one of the most famous being the Chatham Island black robin (*Petroica traversi*). By 1976, there were just seven of these birds left, restricted to one tiny island off the coast of the Chatham Islands, themselves

over 800 km east of mainland New Zealand. As a result of a concerted rescue effort by New Zealand's Wildlife Service (later to become the Department of Conservation) the species was brought back from the brink of extinction. There are now well over 200 birds on two islands. Many of the techniques used during this recovery project, such as cross fostering, were new and have since been used in the conservation of other endangered species.

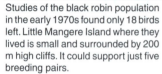

Studies of the black robin population in the early 1970s found only 18 birds left. Little Mangere Island where they lived is small and surrounded by 200 m high cliffs. It could support just five breeding pairs.

The creation of a helicopter landing pad on the island to assist in crayfishing and landing muttonbird hunters, resulted in the island's habitat deteriorating and the black robin population dropped to 9.

A team led by Don Merton arrived on the island in 1976 to begin moving the remaining birds to another site. By this time the black robin population had dropped to just 7, of which only 2 were female.

Two pairs and a single male bird were captured and transferred across a channel just 100 m wide by dinghy to Mangere Island, which supported a small but healthier forested area at one end of the island.

Although the transferred population settled into their new environment and began to breed, deaths were still high. By 1979 there were only five birds left. Cross fostering of chicks was introduced in 1981.

Removing eggs from the black robins' nests induced them to lay again. The removed eggs were placed in the nests of a similar species, the Chatham Island warbler. In this way, multiple clutches of eggs could be produced in one season.

Fostering was also attempted using the more closely related **Chatham Island tomtit** on South East Island. This proved to be more successful than fostering with the Chatham Island warbler. By 1986, there were 38 black robins on two islands.

The black robin population now numbers over 200, all of which can be traced back to just one female, named Old Blue. Although numbers remain stable, there is little genetic diversity in the gene pool and it remains critically endangered.

1. Explain why the black robin was in danger of extinction: _____

_____

_____

_____

2. Describe the methods used to increase the population size of black robin: _____

_____

_____

_____

3. (a) Explain why Old Blue was so important: _____

_____

_____

(b) Explain the possible risk associated with all the robins being directly related to one female: _____

_____

_____

Related activities: Endangered Species, In-Situ Conservation

© Biozone International 2007-2011
Photocopying Prohibited

KEY TERMS: Mix and Match

INSTRUCTIONS: Test your vocabulary by matching each term to its definition, as identified by its preceding letter code.

BIODIVERSITY

CARBON CREDIT

DEFORESTATION

ENDANGERED SPECIES

EX-SITU CONSERVATION

GLOBAL WARMING

GLOBALIZATION

GREENHOUSE EFFECT

GREENHOUSE GAS

HABITAT RESTORATION

INDICATOR ORGANISM

IN-SITU CONSERVATION

NATIONAL PARK

OCEAN ACIDIFICATION

OZONE DEPLETION

SEEDBANK

STRATOSPHERIC OZONE

THREATENED SPECIES

ULTRAVIOLET RADIATION

A   Tradeable unit given to 1000 kg of carbon dioxide.

B   A term describing the variation of life at all levels of biological organization.

C   The replanting, regrowing and rebuilding of habitats that were previously damaged or destroyed.

D   Conservation method using ecosystem management and legislation to protect and preserve ecosystem function and diversity within the natural environment.

E   The process of decreasing the pH of ocean surface waters due to the addition of excess CO_2 from the atmosphere.

F   The exchanges between and merging of global markets, cultures, and ideas.

G   The removal of forested areas, e.g. for timber or agriculture.

H   Ozone found naturally occurring in a layer in the lower portion of the stratosphere.

I   Conservation that uses techniques operating away from the natural environment e.g. captive breeding and is particularly useful where species are critically endangered.

J   Species in which death rate exceeds the birth rate, population is critically small, and likely to become extinct within a very short span of time.

K   Area (usually of natural habitat) of national interest set aside for conservation and recreation purposes.

L   Species with a very small population and an equal birth and death rate which are likely to become endangered in the near future.

M   Building which is designed to store seeds from many types of economically and genetically important plants and plant groups.

N   The retention of solar energy in the Earth's atmosphere by gases that absorb heat and prevent it being released back into space.

O   The removal of stratospheric ozone, primarily by interactions with CFCs that cause ozone to be degraded into oxygen gas.

P   Any gas in the atmosphere that causes the retention of heat in the Earth's atmosphere. Examples are water vapor and carbon dioxide.

Q   The process of the Earth's surface steadily increasing in temperature (and its projected continuation). Usually attributed to the rise in gases produced by fossil fuels and industrial processes.

R   High energy radiation emitted by the Sun, most of which is blocked by the ozone layer and which is responsible for sunburn.

S   Organism whose presence, absence or abundance can be used as a determination of the health of the habitat being studied.

Appendix

THE EARTH'S SYSTEMS

▶ **How Old is...**
National Geographic, 200(3) Sept. 2001, pp. 79-101. *A discussion of dating methods and their applications.*

▶ **The Quick and the Dead**
New Scientist, 5 June 1999 pp. 44-48. *The formation of fossils: fossil types and preservation in different environments.*

▶ **Earth, Fire and Fury**
New Scientist 27 May 2006, pp. 32-36. *How global warming might affect the Earth's crust and what this might mean for volcanism and seismic activity.*

▶ **Climate and the Evolution of Mountains**
Scientific American, Aug. 2006, pp. 54-61. *Although climate can sculpt the Earth's surface, research shows that it may also play a role in deformational history of mountain systems.*

▶ **Hotspots Unplugged**
Scientific American, January 2008, pp. 72-77. *Hotspots that were once thought to fixed points in the mantle may actually be mobile.*

▶ **El Niño, La Niña**
National Geographic, 195(3) March 1999, pp. 72-95. *Causes and effects of El niño and La niña. Supported by clear and detailed graphics showing atmospheric and oceanic changes during each.*

▶ **New Eyes on the Ocean**
National Geographic, 198(4) October 2000, pp. 86-115. *Explores new technologies to map the movements of the oceans.*

▶ **Water, Water Everywhere**
New Scientist, 23 August 2008, pp 28-32. *Water use and the possible looming water crisis for many countries.*

▶ **Water: Our Thirsty World**
National Geographic: **SPECIAL ISSUE** 217(4) April 2010. *A special issue covering the use and misuse of water.*
• **Water is life** pp. 36-59. *The distribution of water and its effect on communities.*
• **The Big Melt** pp. 60-79. *Effects and consequences of climate change on the glaciers of the Central Asian plateau.*
• **Scared Water** pp. 80-94. *Waters religious and spiritual value.*
• **The Burden of Thirst** pp. 96-111. *The health and social costs of drought in Africa.*
• **Silent Streams** pp. 116-127. *The effect of water diversions, treatment and chemical dumping on stream inhabitants in the USA.*
• **California's Pipe Dream** pp. 132-145. *The extensive canal system used to move water around California and the growing problem of water shortage.*
• **The Parting of the Waters** pp. 155-171. *The environmental and political issues surrounding the river Jordan.*
• **The Last Drop** pp. 132-145. *Some of the efforts being used to conserve water in the USA.*

▶ **Water Pressure**
National Geographic, Sept. 2002, pp 2-13. *The demand for freshwater for human consumption and hygiene and the problems associated with increased pressure on supplies.*

ECOSYSTEMS

▶ **Ecosystems**
Biol. Sci. Rev., 9(4) March 1997, pp. 9-14. *Ecosystems: food chains & webs, energy flows, nutrient cycles, and ecological pyramids.*

▶ **The Other Side of Eden**
Biol. Sci. Rev., 15(3) Feb. 2003, pp 2-7. *An account of the Eden Project: the collection of artificial ecosystems in Cornwall. Its aims, future directions, and its role in the study of natural ecosystems are discussed.*

▶ **The Ecological Niche**
Biol. Sci. Rev., 12(4) March 2000, pp. 31-35. *An excellent account of the niche - an often misunderstood concept that is never-the-less central to ecological theory.*

▶ **Fuelled for Life**
New Scientist, 13 January 1996 (Inside Science). *Energy and metabolism: ATP, glycolysis, electron transport, Krebs cycle, and enzymes and cofactors.*

▶ **Photosynthesis.... Most Hated Topic?**
Biol. Sci. Rev., 20(1) Sept. 2007, pp. 13-16. *A useful account documenting key points when learning about processes in photosynthesis.*

▶ **The Lake Ecosystem**
Biol. Sci. Rev., 20(3) Feb. 2008, pp. 21-25. *An account of the components and functioning of lake ecosystems.*

▶ **All Life is Here**
New Scientist, 15 March 1997, pp. 24-26. *Small water bodies provide ideal ecosystems in which to study ecological function.*

NATURAL ECOSYSTEM CHANGE

▶ **The Carbon Cycle**
New Scientist 2 Nov. 1991 (Inside Science). *Carbon in ecosystems.*

▶ **The Nitrogen Cycle**
Biol. Sci. Rev., 13(2) Nov. 2000, pp. 25-27. *An excellent account of the nitrogen cycle: conversions, role in ecosystems, and the influence of human activity.*

▶ **Microbes and Nutrient Cycling**
Biol. Sci. Rev., 19(1) Sept. 2006, pp. 16-20. *The roles of microorganisms in nutrient cycling.*

▶ **Phosphorus: A Looming Crisis**
Scientific American 300(6), June 2009. *An account of the sate of the world's phosphorus supplies and how to conserve them. Includes aspects of the phosphorus cycle.*

▶ **Plant Succession**
Biol. Sci. Rev., 14(2) Nov. 2001, pp 2-6 *Thorough coverage of primary and secondary succession, including the causes of different types of succession.*

▶ **Biodiversity and Ecosystems**
Biol. Sci. Rev., 11(4) March 1999, pp. 18-23. *Species richness and the breadth and overlap of niches. An account of how biodiversity influences ecosystem dynamics.*

POPULATIONS

▶ **Logarithms and Life**
Biol. Sci. Rev., 13(4) March 2001, pp 13-15. *The basics of logarithmic growth and its application to real populations*

▶ **Human Population Grows Up**
Scientific American, Sept. 2005, pp 26-33. *Projections for global population change, the Earth's carrying capacity, and the effects of the growing human population on sustainability.*

▶ **Population Bombshell**
New Scientist, 11 July 1998 (Inside Science). *Current and predicted growth rates in human populations. This excellent account includes some interesting analyzes of population age distributions using pyramids.*

▶ **Time to Rethink Everything**
New Scientist, 27 April-18 May 2002 (4 issues) *Globalization, human impact, and the sustainability of our future.*

▶ **Inside Story**
New Scientist, 29 April 2000, pp. 36-39 *Interactions between fungi and plants and animals: what are the benefits?*

▶ **The Future of Red Squirrels in Britain**
Biol. Sci. Rev., 16(2) Nov. 2003, pp. 8-11 *A further account of the impact of the grey squirrel on Britain's native red squirrel populations.*

INVESTIGATING ECOSYSTEMS

▶ **Bird Ringing**
Biol. Sci. Rev., 14(3), Feb. 2002, pp. 14-19. *Techniques used in investigating populations of highly mobile organisms: mark and recapture, ringing techniques, and application of diversity indices.*

Appendix

▶ **Bowels of the Beast**
New Scientist, 22 August 1998, pp. 36-39. *Analyses of animal feces can reveal much about the make-up, size, and genetic diversity of a population.*

LAND AND WATER

▶ **Feeding the 9 Billion**
New Scientist, 21 Nov. 2009, pp. 8-9. *Assessing the four keys ways in which to boost food production.*

▶ **Sowing a Gene Revolution**
Scientific American, Sept. 2007, pp. 76-83. *Genetically modifying crops to enhance production and nutrition in developing nations.*

▶ **The Adaptations of Cereals**
Biol. Sci. Rev., 13(3) Jan. 2001, pp. 30-33. *The world's major cereal crops: production and adaptations.*

▶ **Quick and Dirty**
New Scientist, 11 August 2007, pp. 33-35. *An account of the effect of agriculture on global soil erosion. Methods of soil conservation and generating new soil are discussed.*

▶ **Our Good Earth**
National Geographic 214(3), Sept. 2008, pp. 80-111. *An account of the state of soils from around the world and the methods to try and restore them*

▶ **Back to the Future of Cereals**
Scientific American, August 2004, pp. 26-33. *Comparisons of the genomes of major cereal crops shows their close interrelationships and reveals the hand of humans in directing their evolution.*

▶ **The Rise of the Vertical Farms**
Scientific American, Nov. 2009, pp. 60-67. *Future cities will grow crops in sky scrappers rather than importing them from farms.*

▶ **Earth Audit**
New Scientist, 26 May 2007 pp 34-41. *An audit of the Earth mineral reserves. And some are looking in an uncomfortably short supply.*

▶ **Time to Rethink Everything**
New Scientist, 27 April-18 May 2002 (4 issues). *Globalization, human impact, and the sustainability of our future.*

▶ **Oceans of Nothing**
Time magazine, 13 Nov. 2006, pp. 42-43. *A study of the impact of human activity on fish populations over 50 years.*

ENERGY

▶ **Ice on Fire**
New Scientist, 27 June 2009, pp 30-33. *The possible methods to exploit methane clathrates - the methane frozen in ice - for fuel.*

▶ **The Canadian Oil Boom: Scraping Bottom**
National Geographic, 215(3) March 2009, pp. 34-59. *Excellent account of the features of the Albertan oil sands boom, including extraction methods.*

▶ **Scraping the Bottom of the Barrel**
New Scientist, 5 Dec., 2009, pp. 34-39. *Concise but never-the-less in-depth account of the viability and methods of extracting the last drops of oil.*

▶ **Can Nuclear Power Compete?**
Scientific American, Special issue, Earth 3.0, 18(5) 2008, pp 26-33. *An up-to-date and objective look at how nuclear power compares with other electricity generation technologies.*

▶ **A Path to Sustainable Energy**
Scientific American, Nov. 2009, pp. 38-45. *An account of how renewable energy could power the Earth.*

▶ **Where the Wind Blows**
New Scientist, 11 Oct. 2008 pp. 37-40. *The developing world of wind power.*

▶ **Plugging into the Sun**
National Geographic, 216(3), Sept. 2009, pp. 29-53. *The methods and future of solar electricity generation.*

▶ **Going Underground**
New Scientist, 11 October 2008 pp. 37-40. *New technology is making geothermal power a much more viable option, even in countries with little geothermal activity.*

▶ **Turning the Tide**
Scientific American, Special issue, Earth 3.0, 18(5) 2008 pp. 72-73. *Ways in which new companies are using the waves and tides to produce electricity.*

▶ **High Hopes for Hydrogen**
Scientific American, Sept. 2006, pp.70-77. *Hydrogen fuel cell cars could become commercially feasible if automakers succeed in developing safe, inexpensive, durable models that can travel long distances before refuelling.*

▶ **It Starts at Home**
National Geographic, 215(3) March 2009, pp. 60-81. *Insightful article on improving energy efficiency.*

POLLUTION

▶ **The Activated Sludge Process**
Biol. Sci. Rev., 13(4) March 2001, pp. 25-28. *The principles and processes of treating sewage by aeration.*

▶ **Making Landfill History**
New Scientist, 20 October 2007, pp. 30-31. *Plans to recycle up to 50% of waste in the UK by 2015.*

▶ **In the Wake of the Spill**
National Geographic, 195(3) March 1999, pp. 96-117. *The recovery of Prince William Sound ten years after the oil spill from the Exxon Valdez.*

▶ **The Meaning of the Mess**
Time magazine, 175(19) 17 May 2010, pp. 32-39. *The catastrophe in the Gulf of Mexico, its possible effect, and the efforts to clean it up.*

▶ **Stopping the Oil Spill**
Time magazine, 176(5) 2 Aug. 2010, pp. 26-27. *A summary of BP's efforts to stop the oil flow from the Macondo well.*

▶ **Accidental Laboratory**
New Scientist, 24 July 2010, pp. 6-7. *The various way in which the effects of oil from the Deepwater Horizon spill are being studied.*

GLOBAL CHANGE

▶ **Global Warming**
Time magazine, special issue, 2007. *A special issue on global warming: the causes, perils, solutions, and actions. Comprehensive and well illustrated, this account provides up-to-date information at a readable level.*

▶ **The Big Thaw**
National Geographic, Sept. 2004, pp. 12-75. *Part of a special issue providing an account of the state of global warming and climate change.*

▶ **Arctic Land Grab**
National Geographic, 215(5) May 2009, pp 104-121. *Accompanied by a poster-The New Arctic Ocean - this insightful article covers the search for oil below the melting ice.*

▶ **Sea Life in Peril as Oceans Turn Acid**
New Scientist, 9 July 2005, pp. 15 *The concerns and predictions of ocean acidification and some of the plans to try and stop it.*

▶ **Carbon Cowboys**
Scientific American, Special issue, Earth 3.0, 18(5) 2008 pp 52-57. *An account of how carbon credits can operate to benefit the environment.*

▶ **Cleaning up Coal**
New Scientist, 29 March, 2008, pp. 36-39. *A look at the viability and possible problems involved in trying to capture and store CO_2 from power stations.*

▶ **The Last of the Amazon**
National Geographic, 211(1) January 2007, pp. 40-71. *The current state of the Amazon rainforest, one of the words most biologically diverse regions.*

▶ **Conflicted Conservation**
Scientific American, Sept. 2009, pp. 10-11. *Measures to protect biodiversity could force indigenous peoples off their land into poverty.*

Appendix

Carrying out calculations:

When answering computational questions, it is important to show all the working associated with calculating the answer. Some examples of the calculations and conversions you may encounter are described below.

1. **Converting between multiples:**
   (a) Convert the following to kilometers:

      (i) 5 millimeters: $5 \text{ mm} = 0.000\,005 \text{ km} = 5 \times 10^{-6} \text{ km}$.

      (ii) 10 000 centimeters: $10\,000 \text{ cm} = 0.1 \text{ km}$.

      (iii) 8000 meters: $8000 \text{ m} = 8 \text{ km}$.

   (b) Convert 12 ms⁻¹ to kmhr⁻¹: $12 \times 60 \times 60 = 43\,200 \text{ mhr}^{-1}$. $43\,200/1000 = 43.2 \text{ kmhr}^{-1}$.

2. **Energy calculations:**
   (a) Calculate the amount of electricity (in joules) produced by a 5 MW generator over three hours:
      $1 \text{ W} = 1 \text{ Js}^{-1}$. $5 \text{ MW} = 5\,000\,000 \text{ Js}^{-1}$. Seconds in three hours $= 60 \times 60 \times 3 = 10\,800$.

      $10\,800 \times 5\,000\,000 = 54\,000\,000\,000 \text{ J} = 54\,000 \text{ MJ}$.

   (b) Calculate the energy (in joules) used by a 2000 W heater over two hours:
      $2000 \text{ W} = 2000 \text{ Js}^{-1}$. $2000 \times 60 \times 60 \times 2 = 14\,400\,000 \text{ J} = 14.4 \text{ MJ}$.

   (c) Calculate the amount of energy (in joules) expressed by the notation 5 kWh.
      $1 \text{ kWh} = 1000 \text{ Whr}^{-1} = 1000 \text{ Js}^{-1}\text{hr}^{-1}$. $1000 \times 60 \times 60 \times 1 = 3\,600\,000 \text{ J} = 3.6 \text{ MJ}$. $5 \times 3.6 = 18 \text{ MJ}$.

3. **Sampling:**
   (a) A study of a bear population discovers that there were 5 bears living within a 4 km² area of a forest:

      (i) Calculate the total population if the forest is 100 km².
         $5/4 = 1.25$ bears per 1 km². $1.25 \times 100 = 125$ bears.

      (ii) It is estimated that the bear population may be 20% larger than the sample suggests. Calculate the new population: $125 + (125 \times 0.20) = 150$ bears.

      (iii) It is estimated that the population has an annual growth rate of 1.3 percent. Calculate the bear population in a further five years:
         $\text{Pop}_{\text{future bears}} = \text{Pop}_{\text{present bears}} \times (1 + 0.013)^5 = 150 \times (1.013)^5 = 160$ bears in 5 years time.

   (b) A coal deposit is estimated at 2000 tonnes (t). If the coal is extracted at a rate of 30 thr⁻¹ calculate how long the deposit will last: $2000/30 = 66.67$ hours.

4. **Reading off a graph:**

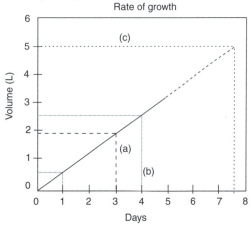

Rate of growth

   (a) State the volume after 3 days: 1.95 L
   (b) Calculate the rate of growth per day:
      Day 1 = 0.5 L Day 4 = 2.5 L Change = 2.5-0.5 = 2.0 over 3 days. 2.0/3 = 0.667 L per day.
   (c) Extrapolate the graph to determine how long it will take to reach a volume of 5 L: 7.55-7.65 days. (confirm from calculation 5/0.667 = 7.5).

INTERNATIONAL SYSTEM OF UNITS (SI)

Examples of SI derived units

DERIVED QUANTITY	NAME	SYMBOL
area	square meter	m²
volume	cubic meter	m³
speed, velocity	meter per second	ms⁻¹
acceleration	meter per second squared	ms⁻²
mass density	kilogram per cubic meter	kgm⁻³
specific volume	cubic meter per kilogram	m³kg⁻¹
amount-of-substance/ concentration	mole per cubic meter mole per liter	molm⁻³ molL⁻¹
luminance	candela per square meter	cdm⁻²

MULTIPLES

MULTIPLE	PREFIX	SYMBOL	EXAMPLE
10⁹	giga	G	gigawatt (GW)
10⁶	mega	M	megawatt (MW)
10³	kilo	k	kilogram (kg)
10²	hecto	h	hectare (ha)
10⁻¹	deci	d	decimeter (dm)
10⁻²	centi	c	centimeter (cm)
10⁻³	milli	m	milliimeter (mm)
10⁻⁶	micro	µ	microsecond (µs)
10⁻⁹	nano	n	nanometer (nm)
10⁻¹²	pico	p	picosecond (ps)

CONVERSION FACTORS FOR COMMON UNITS OF MEASURE

For all conversions multiply by the factor shown

LENGTH	
Centimeters to inches:	0.393
Meters to feet:	3.280
Kilometers to miles:	0.621

VOLUME	
Milliliters to fluid ounces:	0.034
Liters to gallons:	0.264
Cubic meters to gallons:	264.1

AREA	
Square meters to square feet:	10.76
Hectares to acres:	2.471
Square kilometers to square miles	0.386

TEMPERATURE	
°C to °F:	0 °C = 32 °F
	100 °C = 212 °F
Formula °C to °F:	°F = °C x 1.8 + 32

Index

Index